CHICAGO PUBLIC LIBRARY

D0207466

JC
71
.A7
S25
1990

Salkever, Stephen G.,
1943-

Finding the mean.

$35.00   MAY 2 8 1992

DATE			

SOCIAL SCIENCES AND HISTORY DIVISION

SOCIAL SCIENCES DIVISION
CHICAGO PUBLIC LIBRARY
400 SOUTH STATE STREET
CHICAGO, IL 60605

© THE BAKER & TAYLOR CO.

FINDING THE MEAN

STUDIES IN MORAL, POLITICAL,
AND LEGAL PHILOSOPHY

General Editor: Marshall Cohen

FINDING THE MEAN

Theory and Practice
in Aristotelian
Political Philosophy

Stephen G. Salkever

PRINCETON UNIVERSITY PRESS
PRINCETON, NEW JERSEY

Copyright © 1990 by Princeton University Press
Published by Princeton University Press,
41 William Street,
Princeton, New Jersey 08540
In the United Kingdom:
Princeton University Press, Oxford

All Rights Reserved

Library of Congress Cataloging-in-Publication Data

Salkever, Stephen G., 1943–
Finding the mean :
theory and practice in Aristotelian political philosophy /
Stephen G. Salkever.
p. cm.—(Studies in moral, political, and legal philosophy)
Includes bibliographical references.
ISBN 0-691-07803-3
1. Aristotle—Contributions in political science. 2. Aristotle—Ethics.
3. Mean (Philosophy) I. Title. II. Series.
JC71.A7S25   1990
320.1'01—dc20   89–28742

Publication of this book has been aided
by the Whitney Darrow Fund
of Princeton University Press

This book has been composed in Linotron Palatino

Princeton University Press books are printed on acid-free paper,
and meet the guidelines for permanence and durability of the
Committee on Production Guidelines for Book Longevity of the
Council on Library Resources

Printed in the United States of America
by Princeton University Press,
Princeton, New Jersey
1 3 5 7 9 10 8 6 4 2

84640573

To my parents, Edna and Louis Salkever

SOCIAL SCIENCES DIVISION
CHICAGO PUBLIC LIBRARY
400 SOUTH STATE STREET
CHICAGO, IL 60605

CONTENTS

ACKNOWLEDGMENTS

This book developed over a long period of time, and with the help of many people and several institutions. As a student at Amherst College and the University of Chicago, and as a teacher at Bryn Mawr College, I have had the privilege of working in nearly ideal settings. The first complete draft of the book was materially assisted by a National Endowment for the Humanities Summer Stipend. The encouragement received from Sanford Thatcher of Princeton University Press has been all I could wish for, and I am grateful for the intelligent and careful copyediting done by Frank Hunt and Jane Lincoln Taylor. The entire manuscript was read by William Galston and Carnes Lord and is, I hope, much the better for their searching criticism.

Earlier versions of parts of the book have appeared elsewhere. A version of Chapter 2 appeared as "Aristotle's Social Science," *Political Theory* 9 (1981); a version of Chapter 4 appeared as "Women, Soldiers, Citizens: Plato & Aristotle on the Politics of Virility," *Polity* 19 (1986); part of Chapter 5 appeared in my essay "Tragedy and the Education of the *Dēmos*: Aristotle's Response to Plato," in *Greek Tragedy and Political Theory*, edited by J. Peter Euben (Berkeley and Los Angeles: University of California Press, 1986); and parts of Chapters 5 and 6 appeared in my essay "The Crisis of Liberal Democracy: Liberality and Democratic Citizenship," in *The Crisis of Liberal Democracy: A Straussian Perspective*, edited by Kenneth L. Deutsch and Walter Soffer (Albany: State University of New York Press, 1987). Permission to reprint is gratefully acknowledged.

I have learned from a number of superb teachers, among them George Kateb, Joseph Cropsey, and the late Leo Strauss. My debts to a generation of students at Bryn Mawr and Haverford Colleges are beyond my reckoning; nearly every argument in the book first came to light, and has been many times refined, in the friendly pressure of the classrooms of the Bi-College community.

Conversations with Bryn Mawr–Haverford colleagues over the years have been a continual source of reflection and new learning. In particular, I thank Patrice DiQuinzio, Bob Dostal, Jane Hedley (who invented the title for the book), Michael Nylan, Sara Shumer, Adam Sloane, Tracy Taft, and Kathleen Wright. In the somewhat wider world, my understanding of political philosophy owes much to often renewed conversations with Peter Euben, Gerry Mara, Arlene Saxonhouse, and Bill Sullivan.

A number of people have read parts of the work or clarified my understanding of particular issues. For their help, I am grateful to Frank Balog, Larry Berns, Rosemary Desjardins, Robert Faulkner, Leslie Goldstein, Rick Hamilton, Aryeh Kosman, Roger Masters, Ros Petchesky, Meili Steele, Paul Sunstein, Bill Werpehowski, and Catherine Zuckert.

My parents, Louis and Edna Salkever, to whom I dedicate the book, have been a source of help of many kinds over the years. Thanks are due to my daughter Emily, who has taught me more than I can say. It is a pleasure to acknowledge my wife and coconspirator, Jane Hedley, whose energy and intelligence are a daily challenge and support.

FINDING THE MEAN

INTRODUCTION

This book presents and defends what I take to be a characteristically Aristotelian approach to problems of ethics and politics. This
project originated not with any abstract theoretical interest but
with the quite practical problem of how to go about teaching Aristotle's *Politics* and *Nicomachean Ethics* to college students. As a
teacher, I began with the assumption that these books, along with
others like Plato's *Republic* and Hobbes's *Leviathan*—works that
have become an accepted part of the canon of political philosophy—are an important part of what we now call liberal education.
Teaching, however, is a practice that encourages to an unusual degree reflection upon its governing presuppositions, and I was soon
confronted with the need to give a more adequate account not of
whether Aristotle should be read (this comes later) but of how he
should be read, of what there is to learn from his practical writings
from the standpoint of the goals of liberal education. Such an education does not aim (except incidentally) at providing students
with true beliefs about various aspects of the world; there are
surely more efficient ways of obtaining up-to-date information
than spending four years at a liberal arts college. Traditionally, the
goal of liberal education has been taken to be the development of
habits of mind and character that are likely to lead to better
choices, better citizenship on a variety of levels. But how can reading Aristotle—or any political philosopher—be of assistance to
someone preparing for an active life in the contemporary world?

There are two very tempting answers that are, I think, wrong in
interesting ways. The first (and rarer) response would be that of a
reverent or zealous Aristotelian, someone for whom the texts have
a kind of scriptural authority. To read Aristotle in this way would
be to bring to light true but forgotten maxims informing us how to
think, feel, and act. Such an approach establishes the value of the
Aristotelian text, but only at the impossible price of calling on us
to accept Aristotle's infallibility at the outset. The impossibility
here is not only that Aristotle is plainly wrong about a number of
observable phenomena from the position of the earth in the cosmos to the process of human reproduction; even more to the

point, such an approach does violence both to Aristotle's self-understanding and to that of liberal education. According to Aristotle, practical philosophy is necessarily imprecise and in the form of an outline (the reasons for this will be discussed in Chapter 2), and thus should be treated not as a source of definite answers to definite questions about how to act but rather as a preparation for informed deliberation in cases where no such answers are available, a goal shared by liberal education.

A more widespread but equally misleading approach to Aristotle is to read him as if he were attempting to establish some sort of Archimedean point, an absolute perspective from which the accuracy of ethical and political choices could be guaranteed by reference to some rule or system of rules. This kind of reading gets its plausibility from the way it reflects modern expectations about philosophy. We assume that Aristotle is a "philosopher," and we expect philosophers to be in the business of replacing practical doubt with theoretical certainty—an expectation that seems adequately met by, say, Hobbes, Kant, and J. S. Mill. To say that systematic philosophy is adequate philosophy is not, of course, to say that it is true or successful in providing the absolute perspective— if it were, then it would make perfect sense (as Hobbes forthrightly points out in chapter 30 of *Leviathan*) to replace liberal education with, for example, Hobbes. Since liberal education must reject the notion that any one book or system is a sufficient guide to action, it necessarily takes an ironical attitude toward the claims of philosophy understood as the genre of systematic justifications. Given this, treating Aristotle as a philosopher means explicating his system and then showing how the system fails to achieve its supposed goals of absolute certainty and justificatory power.

But however adequate such an approach may be with respect to Mill or Kant, it misses Aristotle's point by misconceiving his project. Aristotle certainly takes himself to be a philosopher, but for him practical philosophy does not consist in the establishment of systematic justifications. This much is clear from his statements in the *Nicomachean Ethics* about the necessary imprecision of such theorizing, and his claim there that he intends to retain, as far as possible, reputable opinions (*endoxa*) that guide political life, rather than replace them with theoretically derived universal rules of practice. To be sure, his aim is not to protect conventional practice against all theoretical critique; the *Ethics* and particularly the *Politics* are filled with arguments deeply critical of prevailing political ideas, arguments that follow from an elaboration of the evaluative implications of the Aristotelian conception of nature. But his oddly gingerly use of "nature" (to be considered at length in Chapter 3) in the *Politics*, and his thematic statement in Book 5 of the *Nicomachean Ethics*[1] that while nature is a standard for assessing the justice of conventions it is somehow a changeable standard, suggest that he is not engaged in developing a systematic alternative to the fluctuating opinions of ordinary political life.

I begin then with the thought that Aristotle's practical philosophy is neither outmoded prophecy nor deluded foundationalism, nor yet the conscious articulation and defense of Greek political culture. My intention is to clarify the character of that philosophy. I suggest that while it is quite different from modern theorizing, Aristotelian practical philosophy supplies a plausible and appropriate set of terms and questions for contemporary discussions of liberal democracy. Reading Aristotle is not a source of solutions to modern political problems, but it can be the starting point for discussing those problems in new ways, ways that avoid some familiar dead ends, such as the opposition between liberal individualism and republican communitarianism, between the politics of rights and the politics of the virtues. My brief for Aristotelian political philosophy is that it is more supple and inclusive than any modern alternative; reading Aristotle well helps us ask better questions about what we are doing as political actors.

Thus I want to show that Aristotle exemplifies a theoretical tone that avoids treating politics either as a perfectly soluble problem or as a tragic dilemma or paradox. Modern political theory takes the first path in a variety of forms: Hobbes's argument that deliberation or prudence can be replaced by a precise science of human nature, Smith's "invisible hand" and the harmonious play of private interests, Rousseau's conception of a perfectly public general will that excludes deliberation among citizens, and Hegel's and Marx's depiction of a compelling and providential narrative built into the course of human history. By combining the languages of modern physical science and a secularized Christianity, modern political theorizing in the West offers the possibility that the practice of deliberation, and along with it the liberal education that de-

---

[1] "With us, though probably not at all for the gods, there is somehow a 'by nature' and a 'not by nature' even though everything changes." *NE* 5, 1134b28–30. The following abbreviations will be used in referring to works by Aristotle: *Pol.* = *Politics*; *NE* = *Nicomachean Ethics*; *EE* = *Eudemian Ethics*; *Rhet.* = *Rhetoric*. Translations are mine, though greatly helped by the translations of the *NE* by Martin Ostwald and by Terence Irwin, and of the *Pol.* by H. Rackham and by Carnes Lord.

velops the habits and skills of thoughtful conversation, can be replaced by something surer and better.

Against modern theory, the belief that politics is, by absolute contrast, a tragic dilemma, is the broad teaching of the romantic reaction that has its peak in Nietzsche and Heidegger. But this reaction is equally utopian and abstract in its understanding of the possibilities of thoughtful political life, holding that politics in no way contains the seeds of its own redemption, requiring us to give it up altogether and await the arrival of a new god or *Übermensch*. Like the mainstream of modern theory, the romantic position holds that theorizing provides a perfectly sufficient alternative to ordinary political life.

Running alongside these two major modern positions is a third, which rejects the utopian claims of universal theory to supplant practice, and defends the integrity of deliberation within particular communities or traditions. But this conventionalist defense of practice, in the hands of writers such as Burke, Oakeshott, Rorty, and MacIntyre, requires an attack on theory (usually deprecated as "metaphysics") that closes off local political deliberation from theoretical critique and guidance. My motive for turning to Aristotle is to examine the possibility that political theory can be plausibly understood as something other than a sufficient foundation for practical choice or a corrosive threat to political life.

The book is divided into two parts, the first considering what Aristotelian theory is, the second discussing some ways in which that theory was (by Aristotle) and might be (by us) used to explain and evaluate political institutions and attitudes.

In Part I, Chapter 1 examines the question of Aristotle's teleology. My argument there is that Aristotle's understanding of theory brings together explanation and evaluation—activities that we tend to separate into two distinct genres or discourses, political philosophy and political science—and does so in a way that avoids both reductionist science *and* antiscientific vitalism or romantic holism, both Hobbes and Heidegger. Chapter 2 moves from the question of theory or science in general to the question of social science. I argue there that Aristotle's conception of social science rests upon a particular understanding of the human good, an understanding that draws attention to the peculiarly complex nature of human biological inheritance, and construes human actions as criticizable efforts to come to terms with that inheritance in a variety of circumstances. In order to live satisfactory lives, we must find ways of developing our sometimes conflicting capacities for rational inquiry, for living together with one another, and for living securely—such ways need to be *found* because, unlike the needs which require them, they are not inherited biologically. Human beings are neither predictable machines nor self-creating deities, and the science appropriate to the explanation and evaluation of our doings is neither social physics nor interpretive reconstruction, neither Skinner nor Geertz. The suggestion here is that Aristotelian social science is oriented toward thinking about our own action—rather than toward predicting or narrating the action of others—in a way that modern alternatives are not.

The character of that orientation forms the topic of Chapter 3, in which I take up the question of the Aristotelian understanding of the relationship of theory and practice. There I clarify and defend an Aristotelian agent morality against the claims of modern rule morality, through examining Aristotle's own theoretical interventions in Greek affairs in the *Politics*, and by offering Aristotelian readings of a modern novel and a contemporary debate in developmental psychology. The central thesis of the book is developed here. This is the argument that in Aristotle's understanding the relationship of theory to practice is not direct—not a form of natural law deductivism—but rather an indirect connection that avoids both dogmatism and relativism: the theory of the human good aids practice by serving as a basis for drawing out and criticizing presuppositions about human needs that are implicit in particular political institutions and policies. These presuppositions are open to critical evaluation because of the objectivity and commensurability of human goods (for example, the goods of rationality, community, and security). But such criticisms cannot lead to action-determining rules or principles because the way in which goods are ranked relative to human needs in the abstract will not be the same as their ranking in any particular situation. Theory can inform practical deliberation and judgment, but cannot replace it.

How theory does this is the subject of Chapters 4–6. Just as Part I argues that the Aristotelian mode of theorizing offers a third alternative to the foundationalist/corrosive metaphysics choice, Part II aims at defending a conception of liberal politics that avoids either side of the individualist contractarian/civic humanist dichotomy. In Chapter 4, I argue that both Aristotle and Plato are sharply critical of the Greek tendency implicitly to equate virility and virtue (to rank the need for courage as the greatest human need), and that this ancient critique can provide us with a way of understanding our own politics that is free of the distorting effects of both republican and abstract individualist imagery, giving us a picture of political life to place alongside the band of citizen-soldiers and the contract of equal individuals. The implication of this discussion of the virtues is that we ought to think about democracy as a regime that can take a variety of directions and support a number of different ways of life, some better and some worse, and not—as modern theory tends to do—treat it as something that must simply be either good or bad as such.

Chapters 5 and 6 speak more directly of the American political tradition and offer suggestions about the possibilities of political education in a regime deeply committed to individual liberty, using as a model the unobtrusive and indirect formation of preferences that Plato sees as the result of Socratic *elenchos*, that Aristotle calls moral education, and that we may discern as the function of our own liberal education and our participation in a variety of other modern institutions. My contention here is that Aristotelian theorizing can produce a more attractive and useful picture of modern liberal democracy—its problems and its possibilities— than those yielded by classical republican or individualist democratic theories. The principal advantage of the Aristotelian conception is that it allows us to overcome our unhappy preoccupation with the distinction between public and private realms. In place of concern with the relative superiority of public to private life or vice versa, or with issues of where to draw the line between the two spheres, attention would center on questions of how various public policies affect the development of democratic virtues and vices (in the Aristotelian sense)—of how such policies and institutions affect the manner in which individuals go about the characteristically modern democratic activity of making lives for themselves.

In arguing for the importance of attending to Aristotelian arguments, I am thus not suggesting that Aristotle should be seen as formulating a dramatic alternative to modernity or liberalism. Indeed, I think there is fundamental agreement between Aristotle, Enlightenment science, and modern liberalism, at least insofar as each is opposed to arbitrary restraints on inquiry and individual freedom. My concern is thus not to defend a "return" to Aristotle contra modernity, but to make a case for the centrality of Aristotelian practical philosophy as a source of education within the structure of modern life and the liberal polity—as an interesting point of departure for better understanding ourselves as moderns and liberals, not as a recipe for fundamental utopian revision or conservative defense.

So we turn to Aristotle's science first for the sake of thinking about the possibility of overcoming the tendency to draw hard and fast lines of separation between science and ordinary life, or metaphysics and morals, or theory and practice. The reason for reading Aristotle in this context is best expressed by Iris Murdoch, speaking against the idea that we now live in "two cultures":

> There is only one culture, of which science, so interesting and so dangerous, is now an important part. But the most essential and fundamental aspect of culture is the study of literature, since this is an education in how to picture and understand human situations. We are men and we are moral agents before we are scientists, and the place of science in human life must be discussed in *words*. That is why it is and always will be more important to know about Shakespeare than to know about any scientist: and if there is a 'Shakespeare of science' his name is Aristotle.[2]

[2] *Sovereignty of Good*, p. 34. Emphasis in text.

PART I

FROM PRACTICE TO THEORY

ONE

ARISTOTLE'S TELEOLOGY AND THE TRADITION OF EVALUATIVE EXPLANATION

The theoretical basis of Aristotelian practical philosophy is a particular understanding of the human good, a particular kind of teleology. In compact form, this understanding goes as follows: practical philosophy takes its bearings from a concept of the human good, but a very precise conception of the human good makes practical philosophy unnecessary. The Aristotelian notion of the human good, which I will try to present and defend in this and the following chapter, thus must meet two challenges. The first is the relativist or reductionist claim that there is no such thing as a human good apart from the goods or desires of particular individuals or cultures. The second is equally though less obviously anti-Aristotelian: the claim that there is indeed a human good, and that this good is clearly and precisely intelligible to those who know how to see it. For us, the Aristotelian "human good" is especially difficult to understand, since the debate about teleology in our time seems to be entirely a matter of choosing between the adherents of these two anti-Aristotelian positions, the defenders of scientific reduction and those supporting some form of prophecy, whether religious or political. The Aristotelian position is all the more obscure today because it is covered over not by dull hegemony but by a sharp controversy. In order to arrive at the Aristotelian notion of the human good, then, and to see how it might be useful to entertain it, we must consider some of the ways in which contemporary theoretical discourse quite unintentionally makes Aristotle's teleology so difficult to understand.

One of these categorical concealments is the distinction between political philosophy and empirical political science, a separation that by now has the status of a traditional institution within the academic discipline of political science. From one perspective this separation is not only commonplace but perfectly reasonable: it simply reflects a sensible division of labor within the field, since it is surely impossible for one person to become sufficiently expert both in the interpretation of those texts and problems which compose the subject matter of political philosophy and in those techniques and sets of data which define the field of empirical political studies. And yet this distinction has other, less desirable consequences and implications than the institutionalization of mutual tolerance, and perhaps even respect, between two groups of scholars approaching similar problems from different points of view. The separation between political philosophy and political science, or between normative and empirical political theory, carries with it or implies a number of important assertions about the character of things known and the way they are knowable.

Chief among these is the distinction between facts and values or goods, and the claim that facts are known empirically, while values are either not objectively knowable or knowable in some a priori way. Such commitments, all the more powerful for being deeply embedded in a reasonable and historically sanctioned division of labor, have the effect of unobtrusively shaping political discourse, although they may themselves appear highly implausible when subjected to direct scrutiny. I have in mind primarily the way in which the distinction between political philosophy and political science (as well as the more general distinction between moral philosophy or ethics and social science) works to separate the processes of evaluation and explanation, of critique and understanding, against the intentions of many within the discipline to practice a political science that is both evaluative and explanatory.

My goal in this chapter is to propose an explanation of how this separation arose and why it is so tenacious, and to suggest the conditions under which it might be overcome. The project is Aristotelian in several ways: it sets out to defend Aristotle's political science as a plausible and attractive explanatory (and evaluative) approach, and it tries to do so while retaining what is valuable in the present-day separation of political philosophy and political science. The second part of the project is Aristotelian in the sense that it aims at preserving the phenomena (in the sense of the *endoxa*, or reputable opinions)[1] of our contemporary distinction

---

[1] Owen ("Tithenai ta Phainomena") shows that Aristotle uses *phainomena* to refer

while reinterpreting it in such a way as to avoid what seem to be its unfortunate consequences.

The Tradition of Evaluative Explanation

Long before the origin of the modern distinction, political philosophy and science took shape as a particular tradition of discourse in Greece. Even before Plato, the outlines of this tradition are visible in the aphoristic thrusts of Heraclitus. The hallmark of this enterprise is the attempt to theorize, to articulate a perspective that is both more universal and more objective than those that are otherwise available. These claims to universalization and to the overcoming of subjectivity are combined in this Heraclitean injunction: "Listening not to me but to the *logos*, it is wise to agree that all things are one" (DK 50).[2] The theoretical *logos* aims at disclosing the structure that informs all the phenomena of our ordinary experience (DK 1), and doing so in a way that will be compelling quite independently of the personal identity of the philosopher. The entity which grounds Heraclitus' *logos* (and into which it vanishes) is the permanent *kosmos*, which is said to be prior to both divinity and humanity: "The *kosmos* is the same for all things, was made by no one among the gods or human beings, but always was and is and will be" (DK 30). This perspective is humanly important (or *good*) because it makes true speech and action possible, by giving us the power to grasp things according to their natures: "*Sōphrosunē*[3] is the greatest virtue and wisdom: acting and speaking truly, perceiving things according to their nature (*kata phusin*)" (DK 32).

The natural order is hard to see, both because it loves to hide (DK 123) and because it has the character of a harmony or ordering of things (DK 54), rather than a simple substance. It is also obscure because of the powerful human tendency to subjectivity: "Although the *logos* is common, the many (*hoi polloi*) live as if their wisdom were private" (DK 23). Philosophy is undertaken as a cor-

---

either to observed facts or to *endoxa*. It is the latter sense of the term which Aristotle uses to name the starting points for the kind of dialectical reasoning characteristic of both the *Physics* and the political works. See also Nussbaum, *Fragility of Goodness*, chap. 8.

[2] References to Heraclitean fragments are to Diels and Kranz, *Die Fragmente der Vorsokratiker* (abbreviated DK).

[3] For a discussion of the meaning of *sōphrosunē* (usually translated as "moderation") in Heraclitus, and of the way in which Heraclitus alters the meaning implicit in the Homeric use of the term, see Kahn, *Heraclitus*, pp. 120–123.

rective to the human tendency to think and act against our great need for theorizing, a destructive tendency reinforced by the words of both the poets and the people organized as a political unit, the *dēmos* (DK 104). Heraclitus' attitude toward the *polis* is ambivalent, however: while the order established by the city does obscure and compete with the natural order, the *polis* nevertheless reflects nature even as it distorts it, "for all human *nomoi* are nourished by the divine one" (DK 114). Our interest in a simulacrum of theoretical rationality is thus the foundation of our interest in the political life, and is the basis for the claim that "it is necessary for the *dēmos* to fight for the *nomos* as for the city wall" (DK 44).[4] Just as Heraclitus attempts to establish a perspective that reveals the uses as well as the abuses of political order, so does his theorizing in general aim at establishing a perspective on the basis of which the ordinary world of phenomena can be understood, rather than at providing an alternative dwelling place. This is nicely illustrated by the story Aristotle tells of Heraclitus' response to some strangers who hesitated to enter his house when they found the great man warming himself by the kitchen fire: "Come in, don't be afraid; for there are gods in here too" (*Parts of Animals* 645a20–21). The theoretical enterprise is thus at its inception both evaluative and explanatory: it begins with the sense that there is a human need for a universal perspective on the basis of which the local and particular things take on a new and better meaning, a meaning not supplied by the traditional accounts of the gods, by the poets, or by the city and its laws. This enterprise, whether we call it scientific or philosophic, is inseparable from the perception of a human interest in rationality as a way of life.

Plato is sharply critical of several aspects of Heraclitean science, particularly the assertion of universal flux (DK 12, 91) and the claim that all things can be explained by reference to a fiery first cause (DK 30). But in spite of this criticism, it is clear that he is extending and elaborating the central features of the Heraclitean project: the theoretical aim of universalization for the sake of explaining particular things;[5] the demand for objectivity, for listen-

[4] See also DK 33 and Kahn, *Heraclitus*, p. 181.

[5] As opposed to universalization as an end in itself. The Socratic critique of Heraclitus in the *Theaetetus* turns on the claim that if all things are in motion then there is no standard for distinguishing true from erroneous statements or arguments. In precisely the same way, Socrates tells of his rejection of Anaxagoras' *nous* in the *Phaedo*, 97b8–99d2. The concept of a universal *nous* must be abandoned, not because it is false, but because it does not lead to any further inquiries. The Eleatic Stranger in the *Sophist* (241d5–249d4) makes a similar argument against the Par-

ing to the *logos* rather than to particular persons or traditions; and the thought that scientific inquiry is inseparable from our interest in living well. This last thought involves the assertion that living according to nature, or the forms, or whatever name we give to the universal perspective theory discloses, is more desirable than a life which takes its bearings from the goods embedded in the practices of the various human cultures or cities. Being and value, explanation and evaluation, are intimately related here, but in a particular way: the forms or nature do not create or announce rules of conduct, as a god, a prophet, or a legislator might; instead they provide a perspective or center from which we can make choices among conflicting goods. Platonic and Heraclitean science are thus both teleological, in the sense that they explain the phenomena in such a way as to make a certain disposition and orientation toward those phenomena inescapable for anyone who accepts the explanation. This happens because the explanations take the form of insights into the ordering of the elements that constitute our particular world, as in the Heraclitean claim that the hidden harmony is prior to the visible elements, and the Platonic assertion of the priority of forms or natures to visible things.

Plato and Heraclitus are thus in agreement concerning the two key points which, according to Leo Strauss, define the origins of philosophic discourse in Greece: the discovery of nature as a principle of organization, and the opposition of that principle to traditional or political authority.[6] But in bringing philosophy down from the heavens and into the political controversies of human life, Socrates and Plato make two key revisions in the Heraclitean understanding, one thematic and one stylistic. The first is the extensive development of a language for understanding *human* activity, for treating humanity as a whole. The only way to give an adequate answer to the question of what justice is, the *Republic* (352d2–6) tells us, is by recasting the question of the definition of justice into a question about the best human life; this in turn can be answered only by opening the question of the nature of the human soul (435c4–d8), which turns out to involve not the discovery of some occult entity but the discovery of the proper ordering of the various desires that animate human activity (580d3–e5). What Plato does is to establish a theoretical perspective that will

---

menidean denial of nonbeing and motion. He finds both Heraclitus and Parmenides wanting when measured against the standard of possible further argument about particulars, not on grounds of metaphysical truth.

[6] Strauss, *Natural Right and History*, pp. 85, 92.

allow us to make the choices that are forced on us by the multiple and conflicting character of human needs and wants. Toward the end of Book 1 of the *Republic* (352d8–353e11), Socrates gives a compact version of an approach to this question that is later elaborated by Aristotle: the way to determine whether a proposed virtue or way of life is truly desirable is to ask whether that life corresponds to the function or work (*ergon*) that defines human beings as a specific class, different from, say, horses and knives. Part of this inquiry turns out to require an understanding of the way in which human life is related to the rest of the universe; but while an inquiry into the good as such is necessary to complete an understanding of the human good (or the appropriate human ordering of wants and needs), it cannot make the understanding of the human soul otiose. At any rate, the good as presented in *Republic* 6 (505a2–509b10) cannot be described with sufficient precision to serve as such a norm, since it can be referred to only through an image, and even then is said to be "beyond being" rather than one of the knowable beings.[7]

The other important difference between Plato and Heraclitus is the relative lack of any prophetic or revolutionary tone in the dialogues. Socrates' irony and playfulness, his unwillingness to say all that he knows, and his insistence on saying different things to different people consistently defeat the expectation that theorizing should result in a set of general rules or customs of the same order of determinateness and precision as those of the city. For whatever reason—perhaps because no particular human being can act in a perfectly human way at all times—nothing can be done as it is said,[8] and moderation and tact are the virtues controlling the philosopher's speech. Explanation and evaluation are linked within the account of the human soul, within the theory of the appropriate organization of human needs and wants, but this theorizing is not a substitute for particular choices; rather, it is a preparation for making them.[9]

[7] As Socrates says in the *Philebus* (61a4–b6), the road to the good is not a Parmenidean journey to some shining place apart; rather, "we must not seek the good in the unmixed life, but in the mixed." For an elaboration of this interpretation of the meaning of the Platonic good in the *Philebus*, see Gadamer, *Idea of the Good*, pp. 104–125. See also Wieland, "Plato and the Idea of the Good."

[8] *Republic* 5, 473a1–3, 452a7–8. In the critique of laws in the *Statesman*, the Eleatic Stranger says that since laws must always say precisely the same things, and since, "so to speak," no human thing is ever at rest, even the best theoretically justified laws must be too precise to provide an adequate response to the human situation. The Stranger generalizes this: "it is impossible for what is always simple to be a good response to the things that are never simple" (294c7–8).

[9] In Plato, the characters most eager for theory as an escape from the nontheo-

Aristotle's criticism of Platonic science is in many respects similar to the Platonic critique of Anaxagoras. His contention is that
the notion of universal and separate forms or ideas cannot serve
as an explanation for the existence of particulars; Plato's "participation" metaphor is insufficient as a causal account (*Metaphysics*
Eta, 1045b7–9). Leaving aside Plato's experiments with forms and
taking up instead his suggestions about natures, Aristotle says
that while there are no universals which exist separately from individual instances (*Metaphysics* Zeta, 1040b26–27), every natural
thing can be understood in terms of the potentiality (*dunamis*) and
function or actuality (*energeia*) which define it. More will be said
below about Aristotle's use of "potentiality" and "actuality" as the
basic terms of causal explanation, but we may note here that with
these terms Aristotle attempts to develop an approach to the study
of living things that is both explanatory and evaluative. In doing
so, he makes claims about the specific character of human needs
and capacities which are more explicit and detailed than anything
found in Plato. The content of Aristotle's psychology, his substantive account of the human good, is complex and will form the
theme of Chapter 2, but a rough summary would note his view
that human beings are unique among living things in being threatened with the danger of an episodic or disorganized life, and that
our greatest need (though generally not, as a matter of fact, our
strongest desire) is to actualize our capacity for living according to
some reasonable plan, the details of which will vary widely, just
as our capacities and situations vary.

The form (*eidos*) or end (*telos*) or actuality (*energeia*) of a thing is
the primary means of explaining what each natural thing is (*Physics* 2, 193b6–18), and this explanation is at the same time evaluative
or critical, since in giving an account of any given human being or
human culture we must characterize its goals or practices in terms
of and relative to the goals that define human being as a certain
kind of entity. The *Politics*, *Ethics*, and *Rhetoric* are filled with ex-
planations/evaluations of this kind; in all of them, human nature
understood as a hierarchy of ends serves as the perspective from
which to judge the extent to which various characteristic ways of
life and cultural institutions are just or right (*dikaios*) by nature.
Human nature provides a ground for judgments that are at once

---

retical world are mathematicians such as Theodorus (*Theaetetus* 173c1–5) and Py-
thagoreans such as Simmias and Cebes, not Socrates, who by contrast is presented
as ever avid for new argument and acquaintance. As Benardete says, the most elevated and unworldly individual, such as young Theaetetus, "is more a potential
convert of Parmenides than Socrates." *Being of the Beautiful*, vol. 1, pp. 161–162.

causal and evaluative, even though what is just or right by nature does not—for Aristotle any more than for Plato—take the form of universal laws, but varies, within limits, from place to place and person to person.[10]

The claims made by the original understanding of political philosophy or science, if my account of it is correct, may well appear surprisingly modest.[11] The central activity of this science is that of giving a causal account of particular things; such causal explanation is taken to mean placing a particular individual or practice relative to the universal which defines it as human or mammalian or whatever. In Aristotelian terms, this is known as functional explanation, or explanation by final causes. We constantly give explanations of this kind in ordinary speech. When we say that a legal system is repressive, or an employer is negligent in providing for the safety of workers, or a person suffers from amnesia, we are placing that institution or person relative to our understanding of the problems and possibilities of human beings in particular circumstances. Such explanations are implicitly evaluative: they express judgments about whether a thing is being done as well as it could be done, not only relative to our private tastes or the norms of our culture, but relative to a definitive species-specific context. These explanations all presuppose claims about invisible matters of fact (fair laws, conscientious employers, mentally healthy human beings), and these are subject to criticism on the grounds of possible mistakes about either the individual or the universal. Teleological explanations do indeed depend upon certain assumptions about the world that cannot be proven and that are always contestable; but these assumptions are not shocking or contrary to the way in which we all encounter the world, without science, through language: they amount only to the premise that our world happens to be the sort of place in which events are not loose and disconnected but occur in the context of wholes of the sort we call kinds or species and Aristotle calls natures (*Physics* 2, 193a1–4).[12]

[10] *NE* 5, 1134b8–1135a3. For discussion of this, see Gadamer, *Truth and Method*, pp. 471–472, and Strauss, *Natural Right and History*, pp. 157–162.

[11] Contrast, for instance, Walzer, "Philosophy and Democracy." Plato is keenly aware that one must guard against taking *logoi* too seriously, of assuming that philosophic speech can do too much. In the *Phaedo*, 89c11–90c6, Socrates says that *logoi* are like human beings: the surest way to end up hating either is to trust them without limit.

[12] There is nothing peculiarly archaic about this assumption. It is the belief about our universe that is sometimes called "emergence," and is described thus by Mayr: "Systems almost always have the peculiarity that the characteristics of the whole cannot (not even in theory) be deduced from the most complete knowledge of the

While this priority of wholes to individual events cannot be proven, it is an insight about the sort of world we inhabit that is contained in every human language; the goal of Aristotelian and Platonic science is not to oppose or undermine but to define and elaborate that insight.[13]

But in addition to the assumption of the priority of wholes to individuals, and the consequent teleological character of scientific explanation, classical political philosophy has a third characteristic tenet, a hypothesis which requires justification[14] precisely because it is at odds with ordinary understanding. This is the claim that rationality, defined not as the discovery of means to satisfy given ends, but as the name given in the first instance to the activity of scientific inquiry itself, that of placing particulars relative to relevant universals, is the single most desirable human acquisition or good, at least most of the time. It is at this point—and *not*, I think, at the level of metaphysics or epistemology—that the tension between classical political science and nonscientific political understanding comes into play. What is worth noting here is that with modern philosophy and science, which takes its bearings from the Enlightenment critique of classical teleology, the situation is precisely reversed: Enlightenment science subverts the ordinary way of encountering and articulating the world while endorsing the judgment of the great majority that the greatest human need is not rationality, but power or freedom.

The Enlightenment Critique of Teleology

The new understanding set forth by early modern philosophy and science can be summarized briefly. The natural world is made up of particular events, rather than wholes or structures (which are all conventional), and the causal explanation of that world consists

---

components, taken separately or in other partial combinations." *Growth of Biological Thought*, p. 63.

[13] Before beginning the discussion of forms and images in *Republic* 10, 596a5–8, Socrates asks Glaucon: "Do you wish then that we begin inquiring from this point, according to our accustomed method? For we are presumably in the habit of establishing some one particular form for each of the particular manys to which we give the same name." Names are not the last word; they are the starting point, just as Socrates describes his method of inquiry as a flight to the *logoi* in the *Phaedo* (99e4–6). Ideally, we would bypass language and go directly to the wholes language indicates, but this would be divine rather than human wisdom—and to pretend to be divine is human foolishness. Socrates' own inquiry into the causes of things follows the "second sailing" through the causal claims implicit in speech.

[14] This justification is the core argument of both the *Republic* and the *Pol.*

in the prediction of the consequences of events in terms of other events. This is the world of Cartesian *res extensa*, within which, according to Thomas Kuhn,

> most physical scientists assumed that the universe was composed of microscopic corpuscles and that all natural phenomena could be explained in terms of corpuscular shape, size, motion, and interaction. That nest of commitments proved to be both metaphysical and methodological. As metaphysical, it told scientists what sorts of entities the universe did and did not contain: there was only shaped matter in motion. As methodological, it told them what ultimate laws and fundamental explanations must be like: laws must specify corpuscular motion and interaction, and explanation must reduce any given natural phenomenon to corpuscular action under these laws.[15]

This revolution in scientific understanding has three important aspects that might lead us to raise questions about its adequacy. First, scientific reasoning thus understood explains natural phenomena by treating them as imaginary wholes in need of being reduced to the lawful motion of their smallest parts or components: real science is in part the search for the smallest elements. Scientific sophistication involves unwillingness to treat apparent wholes—such as plants and animals—as if they were real wholes, substances with properties distinct from their components or the properties of those components. Thus, by reducing wholes to parts and living to nonliving entities, modern science privileges physics over biology,[16] or rather it implies that the best biology and the best social science will resemble mathematical physics as closely as the awkwardly bulky and protean quality of their data permits.

The second aspect of the project relevant here is that, historically, it takes its bearings from a rejection of Aristotelian physics. This was in many ways a clear gain; overcoming Aristotle's mistakes about the immobility of the earth, the primacy of circular motion, and especially the distinction between sublunary and celestial matter made extraordinary scientific progress possible.[17] On the other hand, it is not so easy to justify the modern rejection of another part of the Aristotelian world-view—the idea that living

---

[15] *Structure of Scientific Revolutions*, p. 41.
[16] Mayr, *Growth of Biological Thought*, chap. 2.
[17] See Cohen, *Birth of a New Physics*.

organisms and species are in some respects wholes that cannot be reduced without loss of meaning to an interaction of their elements. Using a characteristically Aristotelian metaphor of an artifact for a natural organism, Ernst Mayr makes the following point about the distorting effects of reductionism in modern biology: "One can translate these qualitative aspects into quantitative ones, but one loses thereby the real significance of the respective biological phenomena, exactly as if one would describe a painting of Rembrandt in terms of the wave lengths of the prevailing color reflected by each square millimeter of the painting."[18] As Mayr further notes, the case for reductionism in modern biology has been immeasurably strengthened by the opinion that the only possible alternative to reductionism was some sort of irrationalist vitalism. The highly problematic claim that the very idea of science excludes *any* form of teleology[19] makes its seventeenth-century appearance in the typical caricatures of the Aristotelian understanding of natures and of final causality. Instead of examining the Aristotelian idea of species, that is, of organizations of needs and powers which regularly occur together, defenders of the new science like Hobbes and Spinoza set up a specter of occult entities or innate ideas or hidden desires and proceed to ridicule the attempt to divine the presence of these fictive particulars.[20] One may well wonder, as I shall do in my discussion of Aristotle's biology, whether the flowering of the modern physical sciences could have gotten along without these distortions, at least in principle if not as a matter of historical fact. What is at stake here is the question whether the modern understanding of science necessarily excludes an Aristotelian conception of the human good.

The result of the early modern association of Aristotle and irrationalism was the rejection of all teleological explanation as unsci-

[18] *Growth of Biological Thought*, p. 54.

[19] For a discussion of the current status of the question of the independent reality of species, see Eldredge, *Time Frames*, pp. 98–218, and Mayr, *Growth of Biological Thought*, pp. 21–82.

[20] Good examples are Hobbes, *Leviathan*, chap. 46, and Spinoza, *Ethics*, pt. 4, preface. On Hobbes's critique of Aristotle, see Cropsey, *Political Philosophy*, pp. 307–314. There is a certain symmetry of argument between the early modern rejections of Aristotle and the Platonic and Aristotelian critiques of Heraclitus and Parmenides—later writers dismissing claims about reality made by earlier writers, but not so much because of their falsehood as because of their apparent incompatibility with scientific method and practice. Aristotle says that the Heraclitean "all is in motion" and the Parmenidean "all is at rest" are equally false as matters of observed fact but that the latter is more opposed to the method of the sciences. *Physics* 8, 253b6–7.

entific, methodologically inappropriate. This rules out talk about the relationship between particular traits or behaviors and the way of life of an organism, except insofar as these teleological propositions can be restated as predictive hypotheses. Thus, for example, the teleological hypothesis that the function of politics is to make economic exchange easier would be replaced by the prediction that politics results in easier economic exchange. But the two propositions are not equivalent: the latter is only a claim about the consequences of politics, while the former, the teleological hypothesis (and note that it is a hypothesis, open to rational challenge), implies the additional evaluative claim that politics is a good thing for human beings *because* it leads to certain economic consequences—in addition to the other consequences that might follow. In other words, the teleological analysis includes the predictive but adds to it an implication about the relationship of particular phenomena to the whole (in this case, the life of the species) of which they are a part. For modern, anti-Aristotelian science, on the other hand, there are no universals save universally valid laws. As Hobbes says, there is "nothing in the world Universall but Names; for the things named, are every one of them Individuall and Singular."[21]

The third major aspect of the Enlightenment project that concerns us here—in addition to the assertion of reduction as the only legitimate explanatory mode, and the association of teleology and irrationalism—may seem surprising: in spite of the unreserved contempt they express for explanations in the mode of final causality, whenever Enlightenment writers proceed to take up the questions of political philosophy they inevitably continue to practice the sort of evaluative explanations which their understanding of science should disallow. Functional explanation in political philosophy hardly ended with the Aristotelian tradition: whenever Hobbes, Locke, and Hume want to show that a particular virtue or institution or way of life is desirable, they do so by presenting an argument that the desideratum in question satisfies or is connected with some particular human need, problem, or possibility, with just that sort of whole or structure that Plato and Aristotle refer to as the human *ergon* or function. This is the manner of argument that Mary Midgley calls an argument of specification or placing, and which she shows, even in the case of Nietzsche, to consist in connecting a proposed virtue or goal with some human

[21] *Leviathan*, chap. 4, sixth paragraph.

want, with some specific facts about human nature that make us need just these things.[22]

This is the sort of argument that Alasdair MacIntyre identifies as central to the Aristotelian perspective in moral philosophy, and which he says has three crucial elements: "untutored human nature, man-as-he-could-be-if-he-realized-his-*telos*, and the moral precepts which enable him to pass from one state to the other."[23] One must quarrel with MacIntyre's use of "precepts" in discussing this perspective,[24] but the main point here is that evaluative explanation in political philosophy seems to have survived the new understanding of causality which should have undermined it; what Robert McShea calls human nature ethical and political theory[25] persists even in writers like Hume,[26] Spinoza,[27] and Nietzsche[28] who explicitly reject the intelligibility of final causality which such theory inevitably implies.[29]

In identifying the troubled accommodation between these two forms of explanation, explanation by predictive, lawlike generalizations and explanation by linking possible virtues and practices to human needs, we have arrived at what seems to me to be the origin of the current distinction between political science and political philosophy. The accommodation is troubled because of the apparent incompatibility between predictive and functional explanation and by the claim set forth especially by the "scientific" side that the only really causal accounts are predictive rather than functional. Thus Hobbes, for instance, must be considered a "philosopher" rather than a "scientist" unless we can translate his account of the human problem into a set of testable predictive claims. Sim-

---

[22] Midgley, "Absence of a Gap," pp. 213–214.

[23] MacIntyre, *After Virtue*, p. 52.

[24] See *NE* 2, 1104a7–8. Moral philosophy cannot be transmitted by precept, according to Aristotle; the importance of this will be my theme in Chapter 3.

[25] McShea, "Human Nature Theory."

[26] Salkever, " 'Cool Reflexion.' "

[27] Mara, "Liberal Politics."

[28] Midgley, "Absence of a Gap," pp. 213–214.

[29] It is not that political theory as such entails teleology, but that the sort of theorizing in question presupposes it. One would expect that such theoretical tension would have substantive consequences for the understanding of the human good. The principal effect seems to be that Platonic-Aristotelian teleology is much more complex. Instead of presenting a variety of hypotheses about human good, modern theorists tend to pick out a single characteristic—preservation, power, profit, pleasure—and claim it as *the* good. Where rational discussion is impossible, presumably, controversy is to be avoided. One unfortunate consequence of this is the thought that *every* teleology must have a single clear good, a thought that leads to a misreading of Plato and Aristotle.

ilarly, we might be able to save functional accounts for "scientific" purposes by replacing the Platonic and Aristotelian picture of human nature as a structure of frequently conflicting needs with a picture of human action understood as organized by a single all-powerful drive, whether for the preservation of life, or for power as such, or for (hypostatized) pleasure, or profit, or inclusive fitness. Such accounts may succeed to some degree as predictions of behavior, but they effectively rule out the possibility of an account which is at once explanatory and critical or evaluative, a possibility that seems to be the motive (were I to retrodict) and is the reason (on my functional account) for political philosophy or science in the first place. Two questions arise here: what explains the tenacity of the notion that all causal accounts must be predictions, and is it necessary to assent to the belief in the absolute links between science and prediction and between teleology and unreason?

In response to the first question, I cannot give a predictive account, but I believe that a plausible functional explanation is possible: What human need or want is satisfied by this assertion of causal exclusivity? Some explanation seems called for, not only because of the persistence of functional explanation under the rubric of unscientific philosophy, but also because of the odd yet pervasive "conception of animals as machines"[30] that underlies modern social science. As I have tried to show elsewhere,[31] this identification has two possible results within social science: either humans are understood as animals (and hence as machines), and human behavior is explained by Hempelian predictions, or humans are understood as fundamentally distinct from animals and hence as beyond the reach of scientific or theoretical explanation—the alternative taken by hermeneutic or interpretive social scientists. Both alternatives fail to satisfy the desire for evaluative explanation, since they issue either in predictions only, or in the endorsement of some set of existing practices, in the mode of cultural relativism. Yet they are powerful and appealing, and so we must ask, what human good or want do they serve?

We may make an indirect beginning on this inquiry by noting the character of the functional explanations deployed against the possibility of functional explanations, arguments that work by associating the use of terms like "the human good" or "final causality" with some evidently undesirable character trait. The charac-

[30] Caton, "Domesticating Nature," p. 100.
[31] Salkever, "Beyond Interpretation."

teristic form of such accounts in the seventeenth and eighteenth centuries was the strategy, of which Hobbes was the master,[32] of saying that arguments from final causes satisfy an unattractive pride, exhibited in the unreflective elevation of one's own preferences into a standard for the rest of humanity. The twentieth-century equivalent is to place functional accounts as reflections of a neurotically obsessive desire for certainty in moral and political arguments[33] (or perhaps, in a more sinister vein, a hidden yearning for tyranny). This apparently unconsciously functionalist attack on functionalism is vividly displayed by Richard Rorty. The tradition of political philosophy or science, according to Rorty, is unified by a "common urge to escape the vocabulary and practices of one's own time and find something ahistorical and necessary to cling to."[34] The pragmatic refusal to theorize concerning the human good is then justified by Rorty on the perfectly theoretical and functionalist grounds that this refusal in fact satisfies a more important human need:

> If we give up this hope, we shall lose what Nietzsche called "metaphysical comfort," but we may gain a renewed sense of community. Our identification with our community—our society, our political tradition, our intellectual heritage—is heightened when we see this community as *ours* rather than *nature's, shaped* rather than *found*, one among many which men have made. In the end, the pragmatists tell us, what matters is our loyalty to other human beings clinging together against the dark, not our hope of getting things right.[35]

This is not an accidental slip, but a necessary move if Rorty is to justify his radical attack on "foundationalism." But since he has ruled out the intelligibility of claims about human needs and capacities, he frees himself from the responsibility of making a theoretical psychological case for the plausibility of characterizing the

[32] Speaking of the Greeks in chap. 46 of *Leviathan* ("Of Darkness from Vain Philosophy, and Fabulous Traditions"), Hobbes says that "their moral philosophy is but a description of their passions." More specifically, chap. 15 contains this wonderful sentence: "I know that Aristotle in the first book of his *Politics*, for a foundation of his doctrine, maketh men by nature, some more worthy to command, meaning the wiser sort, such as he thought himself to be for his philosophy; others to serve, meaning those that had strong bodies, but were not philosophers as he." This is, of course, part of the discussion of the natural law against pride. See also Hobbes's discussion of claims about "right reason" in chap. 5.

[33] For example, Geertz, "Anti Anti-Relativism."

[34] Rorty, "Pragmatism, Relativism, Irrationalism," p. 165.

[35] Ibid., p. 166.

27

human environment as "the dark," and thus for the primacy of the human need for community. But why should the need for community be more important than, for instance, the need for theoretical inquiry? This is not intended as a rhetorical question, but it is one which can be taken seriously only if we avoid the temptation, as Rorty (unlike Nietzsche) does not, to erect pseudological barriers to functional explanation. To say that liberals can best justify themselves if they "simply drop the distinction between rational judgment and cultural bias"[36] is to deny the possibility of evaluative explanation at the same time one is practicing it, and to give as a reason the thoroughly false claim that the tradition of such evaluation has aimed at finding "something ahistorical and necessary to cling to." It is as if there were no serious difference between Parmenides and Aristotle.

One may even suspect some hypocrisy here. Midgley raises this possibility: "The hypocrisy of past ages was usually classical and dogmatic, the hypocrisy of this age is romantic and skeptical. We pretend not to know. Instead of trying to see, we shut the curtains and revel in tragic darkness, concentrating carefully on impossible cases and taking the boring possible for granted."[37] But such suspicion is unnecessary and, to a certain extent, trivializes the significance of modern skepticism. As Hilary Putnam argues, the central doctrines of the separation of fact and value and the instrumental character of reason draw their power from "the idea that it is built into the very idea of rationality that what is rationally verifiable is verifiable to the satisfaction of the overwhelming majority" whether of individuals considered separately or of the major tendencies of any given culture. Both logical empiricism (the notion that explanation is "simply the deduction of predictions and retrodictions from laws") and relativism or contextualism of the kind set forth by Foucault, Rorty, Feyerabend, and others (the notion that to explain is to point out the coherence of a particular cultural system) can be seen as a "sophisticated expression of the broad cultural tendencies to instrumentalism and majoritarianism."[38] Putnam places both of these opponents of the possibility of theoretical functional explanations, whatever their apparent mutual antagonism, as two aspects of the pervasive Enlightenment reduction of the scope of rationality: "That rationality is defined by an ideal computer program is a scientistic theory inspired by the exact

[36] Rorty, "On Ethnocentrism."
[37] *Beast and Man*, p. 261.
[38] Putnam, *Reason, Truth, and History*, pp. 184, 186.

sciences; that it is simply defined by the local cultural norms is a scientistic theory inspired by anthropology."[39] Logical empiricism and cultural relativism can thus be seen as two stages of a process whereby the claims of reason are first elevated as against the claims of authority and tradition (as Gadamer says, "the real consequence of the enlightenment is . . . the subjection of all authority to reason"),[40] and the scope of reason is then limited to pointing out verifiable connections among events or matters of "fact" in such a way that it becomes impossible to ask the central question which constitutes the enterprise of political philosophy or science, namely, "What distinguishes legitimate prejudices from all the countless ones which it is the undeniable task of critical reason to overcome?"[41]

The suggestion here is that the research programs which dominate contemporary discussion in the social sciences, and which are united in their opposition to the possibility of theoretical functional explanation, are convincing not because of their intrinsic power but because they uncritically reflect an idea of the human good that is embodied in the idea of democracy narrowly understood as egalitarianism and majority rule. This radically democratic conception of the human good is variously expressed by Plato and Aristotle as the idea that the greatest human need is the need for power (what they call, critically, *pleonexia*), in the sense of the maximally efficient accumulation of resources for achieving whatever goals our hearts happen to desire, and as the idea that the greatest threat to humanity, the thing most of all to be feared, is slavery (an idea expressed in our time as the need for emancipation or liberation or empowerment). Without this concealed argument from a final cause, both logical empiricism and cultural relativism are unpersuasive—logical empiricism because of the failure (all "methods" courses to the contrary) of the attempt to formalize inductive logic or devise an algorithm for empirical science,[42] relativism because of the self-dissolving character of relativist arguments, a feature pointed out by Plato's response to Protagoras in the *Theaetetus* and by Aristotle in *Metaphysics* Gamma.

The democratic claim that the human good is freedom and power may of course be true, but it needs to be articulated and examined in the light of what we know about human beings—in

[39] Ibid., p. 126.
[40] Gadamer, *Truth and Method*, p. 246.
[41] Ibid., p. 246.
[42] Putnam, *Reason, Truth, and History*, p. 126.

the light, broadly speaking, of psychology and biology. The Platonic-Aristotelian critique of this belief does not result from a prejudice against the lower classes, but rather reflects a judgment that the one desire common to all humans is the desire to have things happen according to the commands of our soul (*Laws* 3, 686e4–687c7). This common desire supports the tyrannical belief that the most powerful life is the best life (*Republic* 8, 568a–b). According to Aristotle, this belief is even more dangerous when held by the wealthy than when held by the *dēmos* (*Pol.* 4, 1297a11–13); but it is uniquely dangerous to democracies because it acquires a certain respectability through the false identification of freedom with living as one pleases (*Pol.* 5, 1310a26–36; 6, 1317b10–17).[43]

The belief that freedom and power are the chief human goods is less satisfying than it seems at first glance, in part because it suggests no way of showing how (and even denies that) rationality as a way of life (the life of philosophy or science) is good. As Putnam says,[44] a major consequence of the majoritarian hegemony is that we have endless debates about whether it is rational to be good (Rawls, Gewirth, and so on), but have lost touch with the more pressing and perhaps even more answerable question of why it is good (humanly speaking) to be rational, to engage in the practice of theorizing at various levels. I think it is no exaggeration to say that this is the question to which works like the *Republic* and the *Politics* are answers, and that such works (as well as Hume's *Treatise* and Rousseau's *Social Contract*) are thoroughly distorted and trivialized if they are construed as hypothetical attempts to prove to some disbelieving Nazi that it is rational to be just. The question that needs to be asked here is that of what we must assume about our world in order to ask the question about the goodness of rationality, and to compare the desire for rationality with other human desires, such as the characteristically democratic wish to avoid slavery and achieve a measure of power against either "the dark" or other human beings.

Teleology without Nature

The need to address this question becomes even sharper if we think, as many modern critics do, that something has gone terribly wrong with the democratic aspirations implicit in the Enlighten-

---

[43] According to Aristotle, this definition is a mistaken inference drawn from the observation that slaves, unlike free persons, are unable to live as they please.

[44] Putnam, *Reason, Truth, and History*, pp. 172–174.

ment project. There is a widespread sense today that the moderation of the egalitarian impulse that Tocqueville hoped for has failed to occur, and that we are now confronted by powerful institutionalized expressions of technocratic bureaucracy on the one hand and the uncritical endorsement of dangerous prejudices on the other, the modern alternatives Weber darkly saw: "either complete spiritual emptiness or religious revival."[45] There are a variety of theoretical responses to this dilemma, among them Gadamer's proposal for a critical hermeneutic rehabilitation of the idea of tradition, and Habermas's Kantian or transcendental deduction of rationality as a necessary presupposition of human action.[46] To what extent is it possible, contra logical empiricism and cultural relativism, to discuss this problem in the language of teleological explanation that characterizes the tradition of political philosophy or science?

Alasdair MacIntyre's *After Virtue* raises the possibility of a recovery of the tradition of evaluative explanation, and even asserts its practical necessity, but only, in the end, to deny it (seduced, perhaps, by the undeniable charms of Weberian anguish). MacIntyre's central contention is that the phenomenon of morality itself is threatened in our time by the prevailing Enlightenment institutions of liberal individualism and the separation of facts and values. If we are somehow to preserve the vital distinction between moral judgments and individual preferences, we are, he says, compelled to choose between the groundless acceptance of some Nietzschean romantic fantasy (the idolatry of the *Übermensch* or some equivalent) and a recovery of the Aristotelian tradition, broadly defined:

> To call something good is also to make a factual statement. . . . Within this tradition moral and evaluative statements can be called true or false in precisely the way in which all other factual statements can be so called. But once the notion of essential human purposes or functions disappears from morality, it begins to appear implausible to treat moral judgments as factual statements.[47]

[45] Strauss, *Natural Right and History*, p. 74.

[46] Habermas, *Communication*, pp. 204–205; *Knowledge and Human Interests*, pp. 308–315.

[47] MacIntyre, *After Virtue*, p. 57 (subsequent page references appear in parentheses in the text).

31

Contrary to the account I have given in the first part of this chapter, MacIntyre asserts that the classical philosophical tradition is fundamentally a continuation or expression (rather than a critique) of the prevailing views of Greek political culture; he further asserts that all forms of ethical functionalism—whether Aristotle's view or the one embedded in traditional Greek politics—are essentially the same because of their common origin in an opposition to moral and methodological individualism:

> But the use of "man" as a functional concept is far older than Aristotle and does not initially derive from Aristotle's *metaphysical biology*. It is rooted in the forms of social life to which the theorists of the classical tradition give expression. For according to that tradition to be a man is to fill a set of roles each of which has its own point and purpose: member of the family, citizen, soldier, philosopher, servant of God. It is only when man is thought of as an individual prior to and apart from all roles that "man" ceases to be a functional concept. (P. 56; emphasis added)

There are several interesting features in this passage, one of which, the implicit (later explicit, p. 152) rejection of Aristotle's biology as "metaphysical," will be considered in the next section of this chapter. The rejection of the possibility of any natural or biological grounding for teleological explanation (p. 183), coupled with his depiction of the core of Aristotelian teleology as the proposition that human beings are individuated within social roles, without qualification—as if Aristotle had never insisted on the distinction between the good human being and the good citizen, or as if for Aristotle political activity were an end in itself, rather than a means of developing the biologically inherited potential for human rationality—renders MacIntyre's Aristotelianism highly suspect. As Richard Bernstein says, MacIntyre's defense of the virtues seems to be, against its author's intention, a defense of Nietzsche rather than Aristotle, and *After Virtue*'s "social teleology" an apologia for Nietzsche.[48]

The distance between MacIntyre and Aristotle becomes clearer as the argument unfolds. Since inquiry into the character of human needs and tendencies is barred at the outset as "metaphysical," or impossibly "universal" (since every human life is essen-

---

[48] Bernstein, *Philosophical Profiles*. See also Frankena, "MacIntyre and Modern Morality."

tially a local story or narrative, p. 201), the identification of the human *telos* which will serve as the first step in evaluative or functional explanations is to be made by an examination of "history" (since the "unitary core concept" of the virtues "in some sense embodies the history of which it is the outcome," p. 174), in particular the history of "practices," defined as those human activities which are both internally purposive and structured by impersonal standards and principles (p. 177), such as farming, physics, and football. Those qualities which all practices necessarily presuppose are likely to be *the* human virtues: "we have to accept as necessary components of any practice with internal goods and standards of excellence the virtues of justice, courage, and honesty" (p. 178). The substantial modernity of this conception of virtue is indicated by the absence of moderation and, especially, rationality from MacIntyre's list; MacIntyre's reason, like Hegel's, is in the first instance a power implicit in human history, and not a human attribute. But as MacIntyre himself says, his model for philosophizing is not Aristotle; his project attempts "what Hegel called philosophical history."[49] The result of this is that MacIntyre expects both more and less from philosophy than Aristotle does: more, because he expects philosophy to issue a specific and practically directive universal answer to the question of virtue, a full and precise conception of the human good; less, because he sets philosophy only the task of recapitulating history, rather than criticizing it in the light of an inquiry into the nature of things. MacIntyre's critique of the Enlightenment shares the thin Enlightenment conception of rationality as something that belongs to all agents who are persuaded rather than compelled to act in a certain way (p. 44), a view said, strangely, to be shared by the *Gorgias*. We are now squarely in the midst of Putnam's world of the Enlightenment, in which the key issue is the rationality (as judged by any mature human being) of virtue, rather than the goodness of rationality.

This derogation of rationality echoes, in its romantic quality, MacIntyre's chief objection to the content of the virtues as understood by Plato and Aristotle, the charge that they (along with Aquinas) share a false belief in the unity of the virtues, an illusion that derives from their commitment to a cosmic teleology: "The presupposition which all three share is that there exists a cosmic

---

[49] On the tacit Hegelianism of MacIntyre's critique of the Enlightenment, see Bernstein, *Philosophical Profiles*, pp. 138–139. MacIntyre's belief that rationality is an attribute of traditions rather than persons is made explicit in the sequel to *After Virtue*, called *Whose Justice? Which Rationality?*, especially chap. 18.

order which dictates the place of each virtue in a total harmonious scheme of human life. Truth in the moral sphere consists in the conformity of moral judgment to the order of this scheme" (p. 133). MacIntyre does not, of course, endorse some form of ethical individualism in opposition to what he sees as the fanatic rigidity of the classical view, but presents a third alternative, an insight which he says is present in Sophocles and Homer, according to which the unresolvable conflict among goods is part of the "essential human condition" (p. 148): "our situation is tragic in that we have to recognise the authority of both claims. There *is* an objective moral order, but our perceptions of it are such that we cannot bring rival moral truths into complete harmony with each other" (p. 134).

But the textual basis for attributing to Aristotle the view that conflicts among proposed human goods are always susceptible of binding theoretical resolution is surely weak. The *Politics* is filled with the presentation of puzzles or *aporiai* which involve conflicting goods and which are explicitly said to resist solution by reference to any "cosmic order"—among them the conflict between the traditional and the rational in Book 2, the conflict among different claims about justice in Book 3, and the conflict between the goods of practice and those of theory in Book 7.[50] The issue of the adequacy of MacIntyre's reading of Aristotle is even more sharply raised by his effort to play off the supposedly Sophoclean insight into the centrality of tragic conflict against the view of his Aristotle, for whom there can be no "tragedy that is not the outcome of human flaws, of sin and error" (p. 167). This requires MacIntyre to read the *hamartia* which Aristotle says defines the tragic *praxis* as if it were identical with Christian "sin" (rather than a straightforward mistake about the identity of people we encounter), a view not commonly supported today.[51] The issue, of course, goes beyond the question of interpreting the texts; MacIntyre's caricature of Aristotelian rigidity is in the service of a view of the human condition that has more in common with Goethe and Hegel[52] than with either Sophocles or Aristotle, a view that undermines the very project of evaluative explanation MacIntyre hopes to revive.

[50] These cases will be discussed in Chapter 3.

[51] For a historical summary of interpretations of *hamartia* in the *Poetics*, see Lucas, *Aristotle, Poetics*, pp. 299–307.

[52] Or with Nietzsche. See Kennington, "Strauss's *Natural Right and History*," p. 64, and Strauss, *Natural Right and History*, p. 26n., asserting a connection between historicism and the "tragic view of life."

MacIntyre wants to combine two central elements of the tradition of political philosophy or science—the logic of functional explanation and the conception of the virtues as defined by ways of life rather than by abstract rules or principles[53]—with a *rejection* of the traditional view that the human *telos* can be the subject of natural science. Not surprisingly, the book concludes with a recognition of at least temporary failure: the internal goods of historical practices cannot define the *telos*, because, MacIntyre says, some practices may be evil (p. 186), and at any rate there are "too many conflicts and too much arbitrariness" (p. 187) within and among practices to add up to a satisfactory account of the *telos* of a whole human life, one which may incorporate a variety of practices. While his assertion of the priority of life as a whole to any institution reenacts the initial thought of classical political science, his frequently repeated (though unexplained) characterizations of Aristotle's biology as "metaphysical" and untenable[54] make it clear that such a science is for MacIntyre (as distinct from, say, Hume) as impossible as it is desirable. The tone of frustration with philosophy as a whole that marks the final pages of *After Virtue* is enhanced by a strong praise of republicanism (pp. 219–220), and by the proposal that what we need most now is not rationality but "the construction of local forms of community," the virtues of the monastery rather than the study (p. 245).

This combination of admiration for the vanished glories of classical republicanism and an antirationalist inclination to hope for a religious revival of community spirit is not uncommon among modern foes of the Enlightenment (Hannah Arendt's resistance to this inclination is noteworthy).[55] The history of this association suggests that a frustration with reason motivates a good deal of post-Enlightenment republicanism and gives credence to a separation of philosophy and science. A nice account of the grounds of this frustration and longing is contained in an unfinished essay by Rousseau, published some years after his death under the title "An Allegorical Fragment or Fiction on Revelation."[56] In it, Rousseau presents a parable in the form of a dream of "the first person who attempted to philosophize." The story unfolds a horrible vi-

---

[53] *After Virtue*, pp. 140–145; for a pre-MacIntyre review of the issue of virtues vs. rules, see Flemming, "Reviving the Virtues."

[54] *After Virtue*, pp. 56, 139, 152, 166–167, 183, 220.

[55] See, for instance, the praise of messianism as the only possible antidote to individualist drift in Bellah, *Broken Covenant*, pp. 139–163. For a thoughtful diagnosis of this condition, see Berns, "Speculations on Liberal and Illiberal Politics."

[56] Rousseau, *Oeuvres Complètes*, vol. 4, pp. 1044–1054.

sion of a city governed by priests of a cult of deities of (almost) unspeakable grossness and viciousness. None of the oppressed citizens dares to expose the deformity of the idols of the city until an old man, Socrates without the name, plays a clever trick on the priests by feigning blindness, unmasks evil, and exposes the false gods. This man, seized by the priests, chooses to "die like a philosopher" in order to prove to witnesses that he had not lived as a sophist. But just before his death he, like Socrates in the *Crito*, makes a very clear homage to the same cult he had unmasked, leaving his followers in a state of aporetic bewilderment. At just that moment, a clear voice announces the appearance of "the son of man," a figure who easily and without paradox and irony destroys the cult once and for all and announces the coming of a new order.

In the *Phaedo*, Socrates says that no worse thing can happen to a person than becoming a despiser of arguments, a misologue, because such people are deprived of "science and of truth about the beings" (90d6–7). The cause of misology, Socrates says, is not ignorance or egoism but artless confidence in the truth of arguments followed by complete and artless disillusion once the trusted arguments fall to pieces. Expecting too much of *logoi*, whether ironically or not, is the opening move in the contemporary game that ends either with a wistful and admiring glance at the monastery or with a carefree wink that we "should simply drop the distinction between rational judgment and cultural bias." Still, we must recall that the pathos with which the narrative of *After Virtue* concludes (which may leave us longing for its comedic counterpart, Rorty's *Philosophy and the Mirror of Nature*) is achieved by the unexamined rejection of the possibility of establishing a plausible functionalism or teleology on the basis of a theoretical understanding of human needs or of the human good (since this constitutes "metaphysical biology" and dogmatic moralizing). Is this really an impossibility? A first step toward answering this question may be provided by an inquiry into the character of Aristotle's naturalist functionalism.

Aristotelian Teleology: The World It Explains

Making a case for the scientific character of teleological explanation is less difficult than it may at first appear to be. This is so because the case against it is not as strong as it seems, or rather because the strength of the antiteleology view derives more from its polit-

ical character and the weight of recent tradition than from its intrinsic plausibility. Showing that Aristotle's social science rests on
plausible theoretic ground does not require exegetic virtuosity;
what is needed is a removal of the obstacles, the distorting interpretive categories, that stand between us and the text and which
can lead even well-disposed readers to errors such as MacIntyre's
reading of the *Poetics* and his casual acceptance of the persistent
falsehood that Aristotle uncritically endorses the prevailing Greek
prejudices concerning barbarians, slaves, and women.[57] Teleology
appears impossible only when we accept the proposition that teleology and irrationality always go together and so begin by assuming that the only two possible forms of explanation are the
predictive and reductionist on the one hand and the holistic and
historically romantic on the other.

Moreover, in arguing for the reasonableness of Aristotelian natural right,[58] my contention is not that the logic of evaluative explanation is an esoteric ancient ceremony which calls for revival, but
rather that it is a more sensible way of understanding what modern social scientists are doing most of the time, and what the tradition of what we call political philosophy has continued to do
even after that logic was rejected. It continues to do so because an
argument from the specific character of human beings is the only
way to distinguish between arbitrary and nonarbitrary human
laws. So long as the latter question is taken seriously—and giving
it up means abandoning the critical character of social science and
history—discourse is constrained by its subject matter against its
methodological self-understanding. The modern tendency is to acknowledge the need for some teleological basis, but not to take its
implications seriously, perhaps because of the false assumption
that the species character of human beings is somehow obvious,
as in Hobbes's metaphor of the state of nature. A good example of
this is H.L.A. Hart's attempt to distinguish laws from meaningless
taboos by asking us to imagine what we might think of laws for-
bidding assault and theft if we happened to be giant, armored,
self-sufficient land crabs.[59]

What needs to be shown, then, is that there is an adequate fit
between Aristotle's naturalism and the kind of teleological reason-

---

[57] *After Virtue*, p. 149. Aristotle's attitude toward prevailing political norms will
be discussed in Chapter 4.

[58] As does Masters, in "Value—and Limits—of Sociobiology," pp. 156–159, and
"Biological Nature of the State," pp. 191–193.

[59] Hart, "Positivism," pp. 35–37.

ing that goes on every day in law courts, in doctors' offices, and in less specialized forms of practical deliberation. I do not mean to imply that all practical deliberation is self-consciously teleological, but much more of it is than we might be inclined to think from MacIntyre's assumption of the pervasiveness of the Enlightenment critique of teleology. We might consult our own experience as teachers, parents, committee members, and so on here. A lovely contrast between teleological and nonteleological reasoning (though not, unfortunately, analyzed as such) is to be found in Carol Gilligan's examples of different styles of moral deliberation.[60] She presents a contrast between two patterns of moral development, one of which (typically male) accords with Lawrence Kohlberg's antiteleological developmental theory, and the other of which (typically female) seems to me to be characterized by a reliance on teleological specification. In the course of presenting this contrast (pp. 19–21) she reports the responses of two interviewees to similar questions about moral reasoning. The first is a twenty-five-year-old man:

> [*What does the word morality mean to you?*] Nobody in the world knows the answer. I think it is recognizing the right of the individual, the rights of other individuals, not interfering with those. . . . [*How have your views on morality changed since the last interview?*] I think I am more aware of an individual's rights now. . . .

The second respondent is a twenty-five-year-old woman:

> [*Is there really some correct solution to moral problems, or is everybody's opinion equally right?*] No, I don't think everybody's opinion is equally right. . . . there are other situations in which I think there are right and wrong answers, that sort of inhere in the nature of existence, of all individuals here who need to live with each other to live. . . . [*Is there a time in the past when you would have thought about these things differently? . . . When was that?*] When I was in high school. I guess that it just sort of dawned on me that my own ideas changed, and because my own judgment changed, I felt I couldn't judge another person's judgment. But now I think even when it is only the person himself who is going to be affected, I say it is wrong to the extent it doesn't cohere with what I know about

[60] *In a Different Voice*, pp. 19–21 (subsequent page references appear in parentheses in the text).

human nature and what I know about you, and just from what I think is true about the operation of the universe, I could say I think you are making a mistake. [*What led you to change, do you think?*] Just seeing more of life, just recognizing that there are an awful lot of things that are common among people. There are certain things that you come to learn promote a better life and better relationships and more personal fulfillment than other things that in general tend to do the opposite, and the things that promote these things, you would call morally right.

It is symptomatic of the power of the Enlightenment critique of teleology over philosophers and scientists, if not over ordinary actors, that what Gilligan notices about these two people is that one speaks only of individuals and the other about relationships, rather than that one aspires to nonrational universal principles of morality while the other sees the need to connect practical choice with an increasingly theoretical understanding of the specific character of human needs and capacities, of the human good.

In order to make a case for the theoretical plausibility of Aristotelian teleology, I will have to show that Aristotle's social science is empirical and not hopelessly "metaphysical"; that it is not inextricably bound to a false cosmology; and, finally, that it does not rigidly override the problematic character of most important human choices. The first two topics will be taken up in the remainder of this chapter, the third in Chapter 3 after a closer examination of the substance of Aristotle's social science.

MacIntyre does not explain his charge of "metaphysics," but I think it can be broken down into three aspects: Aristotle posits the existence of strange entities, similar to those found in religious dogma, particularly Roman Catholic dogma; Aristotle assumes the possibility of a strange process by which these entities can be known, more like revelation than empirical science; and Aristotle posits a cosmic teleology, in which the place of all beings is fixed once and for all by something like a divine intention. All of these charges presuppose a basic identity between the teachings of Aristotle and those of the Church: the two are seen as the twin sources of that repressive authority which the Enlightenment took to be the prime enemy of reason and science.[61] Hobbes's *Leviathan* (especially chapter 46) is the *locus classicus* for this interpretation, and good evidence of the distortion it involves. As Putnam

---

[61] See Gadamer, *Truth and Method*, p. 246.

notes,[62] it is a commonplace of the kind of science which understands its work as predictive to use the term "metaphysical" to refer to all forms of religious and transcendental speculation. Such a science presupposes what may today be called the myth of metaphysical neutrality, or the view that science can begin without any presuppositions or hypotheses concerning the character of being. But this confidence in the possibility of an entirely open beginning is surely unfounded, at any rate in practice; even Hume's thorough experimentalism depends upon the initial acceptance of the belief that "all beings in the universe, consider'd in themselves, appear entirely loose and independent of each other."[63] Free as we are from the threat of Scholastic tyranny, it should be easier for us than it was for Hobbes to judge the plausibility of Aristotle's starting points as compared with those of Hume's corpuscular worldview.

My argument is that Aristotle's biology is empirical rather than metaphysical in the sense that it is not derived or deduced from his metaphysics. But this is not to deny that Aristotle's biology clearly relies on contestable presuppositions about the world. He presupposes that the world of observable change, of the generation and corruption of organisms, follows certain patterns. The work of his biology is to determine what these patterns are, to distinguish species from species. His presupposition thus works to set the problem or question for biology, rather than to establish fundamental premises from which conclusions can be dogmatically drawn.

But this dependence on a contestable problem-setting worldview is true for all empirical science. Early modern physical science is not presuppositionless, nor is it dogmatically metaphysical: its tasks are set by the presupposition that the world is composed of corpuscular bits. Both the Aristotelian and the corpuscular presuppositions are coherent and plausible accounts of some possible world—but which fits our world better? This cannot be known in advance of observations made with the aid of such presuppositions; this is what makes them contestable. Contestability of this kind does not imply that empirical science is beyond evaluation except in terms of its own presuppositions. Precisely because there

[62] *Reason, Truth, and History*, p. 185.

[63] Hume, *Treatise of Human Nature*, Bk. 3, pt. 1, sec. 1; see also Bk. 1, pt. 3, sec. 14. Hume's understanding of "nature" is more complex than I am taking it here to be. Prufer ("Hume's *A Treatise of Human Nature*") gives an account of two senses of nature in Hume, one of which corrects and informs the other.

are a variety of scientific languages, it is possible to make comparative judgments about their success at the task of explaining the world. Thus we need to look carefully at what teleology presupposes about the world, and consider the extent to which such presuppositions complement or conflict with the world as problematized by the categories of modern science.

The starting point of Aristotle's biology is the hypothesis that the whole organism is prior to its parts, not in time but in being.[64] What distinguishes Aristotle's teleology from modern physical reductionism is his presupposition that the properties of living organisms are not reducible to those of their inanimate components.[65] That is, he assumes that to be alive is to be a living something, a horse, a human being, and so on—organisms are individuated within species. Midgley characterizes the extent of what is taken for granted by this style of analysis as follows: "The only assumption made here is the general biologist's one that there is some system in an organism, some point in any widespread plant or animal habit. . . . The nature of a species, then, consists in a certain range of powers and tendencies, a repertoire, inherited and forming a fairly firm characteristic pattern."[66] To be is to be determinate, to be this rather than that; some but not all determinate beings are living things: plants and animals are, while the elements (for Aristotle, earth, air, fire, and water) are not. The difference is that living beings are to some extent self-moving, capable of self-nutrition and growth (*De Anima* 2, 412a13–15). Aristotle articulates this difference by saying that living things have souls, that is, are organized in such a way that their various parts, their organs and powers, combine to form a whole, a way of life definitive of a particular species. The soul of a living thing is not separate from its matter or body, except in analysis (as whole is not separate from parts, or actuality from potentiality), and is not simply a surface configuration; a corpse is not a human being. It is important to note that soul and matter are not themselves beings or entities; "matter" is always relative to the form it takes (*Physics* 2, 194b8–9), and soul is simply the functional state of such mat-

---

[64] "Priority" is understood as "that without which a thing cannot be," and the distinction between temporal-necessity and substance-necessity is made in a variety of places; for example, *Physics* 8, 260b16–19. The fullest discussion of the senses of priority is in *Metaphysics* Delta, 1018b9–1019a14.

[65] Gotthelf, "Aristotle's Conception of Final Causality," provides a good statement and defense of this reading.

[66] *Beast and Man*, p. 58.

ter.[67] What is primary here is the living organism, although that organism is a determinate substance because of its soul rather than its matter, so that an organism's nature is determined more by its soul than by its matter (*Physics* 2, 193b6–8), more by its species character than by its organs. Another name for the soul of an animal is thus its actuality (*energeia*), its particular mode of life (*De Anima* 2, 412a27–b1), which is also called its work and its end: "the *ergon* is the *telos*, and *energeia* is the *ergon*" (*Metaphysics* Theta, 1050a21–22). The terminology is initially complex, but the problem Aristotle is trying to solve is easily stated: How to give an account of the world that squares with the scientist's or philosopher's experience that the world is neither pure motion (as for Heraclitus) nor pure rest (as for Parmenides)?—the same problem Plato sets out to solve in the *Sophist* by redescribing not-being as "otherness." Aristotle's solution is to develop a language that points to grades of being, from purely random potentiality (matter, body, parts) to purely organized actuality (form, soul, wholes, function). Living organisms are neither purely potential nor purely actual, but these terms provide us with ways of thinking and talking about how such organisms exist.

A teleological explanation, or an account in terms of final causes, places a particular organ or behavior within the framework of the way of life which defines the organism.[68] To say that the heart exists to pump blood is to give a causal account of this kind: what is involved is not simply predicting the consequences of the motions of a heart, but picking out *one* of those consequences— and not, say, making noise or supplying weight—and proposing it as a function. This choice presupposes an opinion about the goals of the organism, and cannot be derived from an account, either chemical or evolutionary, of the antecedent conditions which are the predictive causes of the heart's motion.[69] The same is true, as we will see, for the claim that we are political and famil-

[67] Nussbaum, *De Motu Animalium*, p. 72.

[68] Sorabji, *Necessity, Cause, and Blame*, p. 153.

[69] As Boorse says, "Given a little knowledge about what happens inside mammals, it is obvious that the function of the heart is to circulate the blood. That is what the heart contributes to the organism's overall goals, rather than its weight or its noise. But it cannot be obvious in any strict sense that the heart had an etiology in which this effect rather than the others played a role." "Wright on Functions," pp. 74–75. It should be noted that in his empirical biological writings, Aristotle frequently treats functional explanations as unclear and disputable (the more we know about an animal, the better we can account for its parts and doings) and notes a number of cases where the same organ can have several functions (the tongue is for tasting and talking).

ial animals because we are rational animals. Moreover, to say that this heart is beating too rapidly or that ethnic slavery is unjust is also to speak teleologically. Such accounts are both evaluative and explanatory in that they presuppose the desirability of the way of life of the particular animal being discussed; or rather, "desirability" is defined by that life—the good for each species is the central fact about its life.

Functional explanation of this sort thus presupposes only that living things are, prior to any conventional or scientific judgment, organized around a norm or normal way of life which allows us to make judgments about whether members of a particular species are young or old, healthy or ill representatives of their class. This is what Aristotle means by saying that natures exist, and that their existence cannot be demonstrated to anyone who refuses to accept it (*Physics* 2, 193a4–6), except perhaps by the indirect proof that such refusal is inconsistent with the practices of science or, for that matter, of everyday speech (there is no point in arguing with a plant; *Metaphysics* Gamma, 1005b35–1006a15).

Final causality in this sense presupposes neither conscious intention nor a separation between the body as thing caused and the soul (or a supernatural being) as causal agent,[70] and here the metaphor of artifacts for natural objects, so useful for indicating the organized character of the natural world, breaks down; the final cause or good of a natural object is not external to it, and a new metaphor is required: nature is not like a shipbuilder building a ship but like a doctor doctoring himself (*Physics* 2, 199b30–32). There is, in other words, no assumption that such causes exist separately from or are prior in time to the events which they explain (*Metaphysics* Lambda, 1070a13–18). The Aristotelian assumption about being, then, is entirely consistent with the way in which explanations generally run in physiology or ethology, and indeed with the sort of logic by which a judge or jury determines whether reasonable care has been taken in a case involving liability or negligence. It seems fair to say that while this assumption about the existence of natures as distinct and nonintentionally goal-oriented systems cannot be proven to be true, it is in fact quite common,

[70] As Sorabji says, "the assumption that the soul has to do only with *consciousness* is a legacy from Descartes. Descartes deliberately rejected the Aristotelian conception. Aristotle made the soul coextensive not with consciousness but with life." *Necessity, Cause, and Blame*, p. 168. Wilkes contrasts Aristotle and Descartes on soul and body, and argues for the greater plausibility of the Aristotelian account. *Physicalism*, pp. 114–135.

and is in some measure justified by its success.[71] The same kind of case can be made, of course, for the plausibility of the reductionist assumptions characteristic of mathematical physics. But it is widely held that these two views are incompatible, requiring us to choose between them; perhaps, however, they are not.

Several features of Aristotle's teleology suggest a compatibility between these two kinds of science, explanation by reference to final causes and explanation by reference to antecedent and necessitating (predictive) conditions. The first is that Aristotle generally limits the scope of teleological explanation to living things: some events, such as rainfall (*Physics* 2, 198b16–21) and eclipses (*Metaphysics* Eta, 1044b10–20), have no final causes.[72] Such things are not, however, random occurrences, but can be explained by reference to antecedent conditions that allow the scientist to predict them: they "can be predicted or deduced on the basis of laws without being [teleologically] explained."[73]

More importantly, within the class of living things, teleological explanation does not replace predictive explanation, or render it otiose. This is what David Balme means by saying that Aristotle was not an "essentialist."[74] It is not simply that animal life can be explained in two ways, but that both modes of explanation are necessary for a full understanding of the organism, because of two factors that characterize living things. The first is that some attributes of animals, like eye color, serve no purpose with respect to the specific life of the animal (*Generation of Animals* 5, 778a32–34). The same is true of skin color and sex; whiteness and maleness in a particular human, for instance, cannot be explained by reference to the specific character of human life, but only by reference to antecedent conditions (*Metaphysics* Iota, 1058a29–b25). In addition, emotions like human anger can and must be explained both in terms of antecedent conditions and in relation to way of life: anger is both the boiling of the blood surrounding the heart and the desire for revenge. *Either* sort of causal explanation by itself is incomplete and scientifically unsatisfactory (*De Anima* 1, 403a29–b9).[75] To

---

[71] Midgley, *Beast and Man*, p. 58.

[72] Aristotle's discussions of the principles of explanation are scattered throughout his writings. For a good discussion focusing on the *Posterior Analytics*, see Kosman, "Understanding, Explanation, and Insight"; on *Physics* bk. 2, see Waterlow, *Nature, Change, and Agency*, chap. 2.

[73] Sorabji, *Necessity, Cause, and Blame*, p. 25.

[74] Balme, "Aristotle's Biology."

[75] See also the account of respiration in *Parts of Animals* 1, 642a, and Nussbaum, *De Motu Animalium*, p. 60.

know an animal, to explain it, is to know both its specific way of life and the *specific* matter of its parts: to say that humans are composed of fiery and earthy parts is not a sufficient antecedent causal explanation of human being (*Metaphysics* Eta, 1044b2–3).

Aristotle's political works are filled with causal accounts of both kinds. The discussions of the relationship of age, economic status, and geography to personality type, for example, are predictive; the discussion of why certain forms of rule are more just than others is teleological. Most frequently, both kinds of explanation are combined in a single account, as in the discussion of the causes of and cures for crime in *Politics* 2, 1267a2–17:

> Phaleas holds that equality of possessions, by ensuring that no one will resort to stealing because he is hungry, is a sufficient cure for crimes. But people commit crimes not only for the sake of obtaining the necessities of life. They also wish to enjoy things and not go on desiring them; and if their desire goes beyond necessities, they will seek a cure in crime. Nor is that the only motive; even those who feel no such desires wish to enjoy pleasures that bring no pain. What are the cures for [these] three different causes of crime? For the first, employment and moderate possessions; for the second, *sōphrosunē*; for the third, if someone desires pleasures which depend on himself alone, there is no cure but philosophy. . . . The greatest crimes are from extravagance, and not necessity (so people do not become tyrants in order to keep warm, and there is more honor in killing a tyrant than a thief). Thus the way (*tropos*) of Phaleas' *politeia* [regime] is a help only against small crimes.

I have quoted this passage at length because I think it epitomizes Aristotle's philosophy and science in its combination of evaluative and predictive explanation. The claims about the motives and cures for crimes are predictive, and the claims about the relative seriousness of different crimes are functional or teleologically evaluative. Neither type of causal account is dogmatic or "metaphysical," since both are open to criticism and further discussion on the basis of counterevidence: a reader of Arendt's *On Revolution* might say that tyranny follows most naturally from an obsessive concern with poverty, and perhaps there are cultures in which the killer of a thief is held in greater esteem than the killer of a tyrant.[76] At any

---

[76] There could, of course, be theoretical as well as historical counterexamples,

rate, crime cannot be adequately explained without considerations involving *both* types of causal account.

Aristotelian Teleology: Explaining the World

By this point in the argument, I hope to have responded to the first aspect of the "metaphysics" charge mentioned above—that Aristotle's science posits the existence of occult entities. This is also the appropriate place to observe that Aristotle's approach to explanation necessarily excludes the distinction between empirical political science and political philosophy noted at the beginning of this chapter, a distinction which institutionalizes a rejection of the view that both predictive and functional explanations are necessary components of any adequate theoretical (or practical) discussion of political life—that discussing the motives of crime without considering the relative importance of different crimes, or the relative importance and not the motives, involves a distorted sense of what we want from an explanation. A similar apparently benign but actually harmful distinction is found in the frequent suggestion that the word "cause" should be reserved for explanations which refer to antecedent conditions, while another word, perhaps "reason," should be used to describe functional accounts.[77] This distinction does not simply report current English usage, but enshrines the Humean view (*Treatise*, Bk. 1, pt. 3, sec. 14) that the only "real" causes are efficient, or predictive, causes. Aristotle regularly uses the same word, *aitia*, for both efficient and final causes, and this is not simply a deficiency of the Greek language; the core meaning of *aitia* is "responsibility" or "blame" in a legal or practical sense. Thus to give an explanation of something is, as Aryeh Kosman says, to point out "that which is responsible for it being the case,"[78] which means, for Aristotle, more the way in which a thing is organized than the forces that effectively brought about its organization. This organization, moreover, exists independently

since appeals to conventional definitions are always, for Aristotle, subject to theoretical criticism. (In this passage, Aristotle's restraint in bringing "nature" to bear as a criticism of practice is nicely illustrated.) The clearest theoretical controversy about the causes of crime might be arranged by comparing chap. 27 of *Leviathan* with the Aristotelian discussion. One would also bear in mind the Hobbesian discussion of pathological tyrannophobia in chap. 29.

[77] Vlastos, "Reasons and Causes in the *Phaedo*."
[78] "Understanding, Explanation, and Insight," p. 376.

of the observer as much as do the four elements or simple bodies.[79] The cause/reason distinction has the same unintended function as the political science/political philosophy distinction: each identifies objective science with accounts which are wholly predictive, and assigns philosophy and teleology together to the realm of the subjective, speculative, and unempirical.

This tendency to hold that science excludes teleology is reinforced by the second aspect of the "metaphysics" charge—that Aristotle's science requires acceptance of its first principles in some peculiarly a priori way, or as deductions from more remote cosmological conclusions. This is Habermas's way of dismissing Aristotle: "The ethics and politics of Aristotle are unthinkable without the connection to physics and metaphysics, in which the basic concepts of form, substance, act, potency, final cause, and so forth, are developed. . . . Today it is no longer easy to render the approach of this metaphysical mode of thought possible."[80] Aristotle does insist on a connection between politics and metaphysics, but that connection does not involve the claim that the central starting points of the former must be derived from the latter. Nor does he say or imply that our understanding of being is an act discontinuous with our everyday experience of beings. In *Metaphysics* Theta, 1048a35–b9, he argues that we can have no direct or a priori perception of actuality and potentiality, the most basic categories of his metaphysics: these must be understood as *indefinable* attributes of being. Our knowledge of these starting points is neither mystical nor analytic (nor transcendentally deductive), but

[79] As Gotthelf says, "*Aitiai*, like causes, are what we discover; reasons, for the most part, are what we give. . . . The resistance to the traditional translation comes from an assumption that only efficient causes, not for instance final causes, are 'causes' in our sense, but this assumption is a mistake." Review of *Aristotle's De Motu Animalium* by Martha Nussbaum, p. 368. The rejection of "teleology" in favor of "teleonomy" by modern biologists rests on a similar mistake about Aristotelian final causes: "Present day biologists still favour teleological explanations. But . . . since 1958, some have preferred to call it *'teleonomic'* rather than *'teleological'* explanation. In that year, C. S. Pittendrigh introduced the new term, in order to distinguish his own form of teleology from what he called 'Aristotelian teleology' as an efficient causal principle." Sorabji, *Necessity, Cause, and Blame*, pp. 160–161. But as Sorabji notes, Aristotle distinguishes teleological from efficient causes and holds that both are necessary for scientific explanation. Mayr discusses the Aristotelian character of teleonomic explanation in *Growth of Biological Thought*, pp. 48–49, and says that "Aristotle's *eidos* [form or formal cause] is a teleonomic principle which performed in Aristotle's thinking precisely what the genetic program of the modern biologist performs" (p. 88).

[80] Habermas, *Communication*, p. 201. The first sentence quoted is undoubtedly true; it only becomes damning in the light of the polemical deployment of "metaphysical" in the second sentence.

empirical and by analogy: "What we mean is clear by induction (*epagōgē*) from individual cases, and we should not seek a definition (*horos*) of everything, but should also perceive an object by means of an analogy." The relation between actuality and potentiality comes into view as we reflect on what is common to the relationships between waking and sleeping, seeing and having our eyes shut, and the finished product and the raw material.

A similar account of how we come to know the starting points of scientific explanation is given in *Posterior Analytics* 2, 99b15–100b17. Aristotle there takes up Meno's paradox,[81] rejecting both the view that the primary universal terms of science are innate (perhaps brought by the soul from a previous existence) and the view that we derive them from direct knowledge of metaphysical things. We can, he says, acquire such universals through the recollection and grouping of our individual perceptions (see also *Metaphysics* Alpha, 980a5–7). Having said that we achieve universals by perception—which seems here, as often in Aristotle, to be a very general class term for a kind of thinking, not a reference to sensation—he then supplies an image of the process: "It is like a rout in battle stopped by first one man making a stand and then another, until the original formation has been restored. The soul is so constituted as to be capable of the same experience."[82] Similarly, the knowledge of the defining qualities of any species presupposes the experience of individuals, mediated through habitually acquired linguistic categories, rather than vice versa. As Richard Sorabji says: "Aristotle tells us . . . that to discover the full essence of a natural kind takes empirical investigation. . . . To discover the essence of man, he would think we had to investigate

[81] In Plato's *Meno*, young Meno challenges Socrates to prove to him that we can ever learn anything. Either we know X, Meno says, or we do not; if we know it, we do not need to learn it; if we do not know it, we will never recognize it even if we happen to stumble onto it; therefore, learning or inquiry is impossible. This paradox, of course, is a central challenge to the philosophic life, as understood by both Plato and Aristotle. For them, the question "Under what circumstances is inquiry possible?" is always central; note the difference between this and the analogous Kantian question "Under what circumstances is *certain* knowledge possible?"

[82] Gadamer's discussion of this passage (*Philosophical Hermeneutics*, p. 64) is worth quoting, as it picks out two key features: that the acquisition of knowledge of universals cannot be reduced to a methodical set of operations, and that it obviously occurs: "How it [the halt of the army] begins, how it spreads, and how the army finally at some point stands again (that is, how it once again comes to obey the unity of the command) is not knowingly prescribed, controlled by planning, or known with precision by anyone. And nonetheless it has undoubtedly happened. It is precisely this way with knowledge of the universal, because this is really the same as its entrance into language."

48

human individuals."[83] The above passages from *Metaphysics* Theta and *Posterior Analytics* 2 thus suggest that, for Aristotle, universal categories or properties, whether at the level of discrete species or at the level of those attributes of being that are common to all living things, are empirically knowable. No arcane scientific method is envisaged here: as the army metaphor suggests, we grow in our knowledge of universals insofar as we live attentively.

The last aspect of the "metaphysics" charge, that Aristotle's teleology presupposes a false cosmology, is more complex and difficult than the others, but its most common version should not be extremely troubling. This is the claim that Aristotle is committed to a cosmic teleology in which the status of all beings is fixed once and for all by something like a divine artificer. The chief evidence for this reading comes from those few places, such as *Politics* 1, 1256b15–22, in which the personification of the defining power of final causes among living things—as in the formula "nature makes nothing in vain"—leads to the conclusion that plants are made for animals and animals for humans. But this statement, made in the opening section of a political work, is in clear conflict not only with what Aristotle says about the particularity of final causes in a more theoretical context (to give the final cause is to say that something "is better thus, not simply, but with reference to the being [*ousia*] of each sort of thing"; *Physics* 2, 198b8–9), but with the way he employs the logic of teleology throughout his biological and political writings, and with his criticism of what he takes to be the Platonic conception of a universal good (*NE* 1, 1096a11–1097a14).[84] Aristotle's criticisms of, for instance, the Spartan notion of virtue or the barbarian practice of treating women like slaves are not deductions from a universal or cosmic good, but specifications relative to the human *ergon* and *telos*. Analogical metaphors are constantly used by Aristotle, and disanalogies that might not have troubled his contemporaries may present greater difficulties for later readers. In this case, we should recall that the metaphor Aristotle explicitly endorses for nature is the doctor doctoring himself—not the implied demiurge of "nature makes nothing in vain": "this is especially clear whenever someone is a doctor to himself; nature seems to be like that" (*Physics* 2, 199b30–32).

But the issue of the rationality of Aristotle's teleology can be framed more sharply: Doesn't acceptance of his teleological world-

---

[83] *Necessity, Cause, and Blame*, p. 200.
[84] Nussbaum, *De Motu Animalium*, pp. 93–99. Cf. Clark, *Aristotle's Man*, pp. 59–60.

view commit us to a rejection of modern nonteleological physical science and of evolutionary biology? Such is the clear implication of Leo Strauss's remark in the opening pages of *Natural Right and History* that "the teleological view of the universe, of which the teleological view of man forms a part, would seem to have been destroyed by modern natural science." He goes on to say that the conflict between the two views of the universe "is decided by the manner in which the problem of the heavens, the heavenly bodies, and their motion is solved."[85] If this were so, Aristotle's teleology would be thoroughly unacceptable, since his account of the heavens holds, falsely, that the heavenly bodies are made out of special unearthly matter, that the only process of change they undergo is locomotion, and that they move in fixed circular orbits, with the earth at the center. But the Aristotelian passages Strauss cites as evidence for the decisiveness of this question (*Physics* 2, 196a25ff. and 199a3–5) are brief and hardly conclusive. Neither of these passages presents an independent Aristotelian theoretical statement; both aim at exposing (ad hominem) incoherences in the thought of several of his opponents who assert both necessity and chance as causes. But even in their implications, neither passage makes any claims about the final cause of the whole or about the way it is related to particular living things.[86]

In light of Aristotle's claims that the need for teleological explanation does not rule out the need for mechanical or efficient causal explanation of the same events,[87] it seems better to say that the

[85] *Natural Right and History*, pp. 7–8. As Kennington notes, however, we cannot overlook the tentative character of this book and the fact that it "consists in great part of reasonings for the necessity of investigations rarely if ever undertaken by others yet left incomplete by Strauss." "Strauss's *Natural Right and History*," pp. 58–59.

[86] The passage at 199a3–5 makes the following argument: (1) the parts of animals, such as teeth, either arise spontaneously or coincidentally, *or* for an end; (2) they cannot arise spontaneously or coincidentally, since they occur as they do either always or for the most part (198b35–36); therefore (3) they are for an end. This argument says nothing about those things that occur *neither* spontaneously *nor* for an end, such as rain, which is caused by necessity (198b16–23)—those things that are necessary consequences of the properties of simple bodies or elements, like fire and water. The argument at 196a24ff. is similarly dialectical: (1) some people (perhaps Democritus is intended) say that the heavens and all universes are caused spontaneously; (2) these same people say that plants and animals neither are nor came into being by chance, but that nature or *nous* or some such other thing is the cause of them; but (3) this is absurd since these people can in fact see nothing in the heavens coming into being spontaneously, but where (among plants and animals) they expect nothing to come into being by chance, much is seen to happen by chance. In effect, the message here seems to be "Use your eyes and don't be swept away by catchy theories."

[87] For example, "the same thing may exist for an end and be necessitated as well." *Posterior Analytics* 2, 94b27–28.

possibility of Aristotelian teleology turns on the question of whether, as Hume says, all teleological explanations are really confused or inverted mechanical explanations, or, in other words, whether the attributes of living organisms are all reducible to attributes of their nonliving components, so that all teleological explanations can be translated without loss of meaning into nonteleological explanations. If the reasonableness of teleology turns on this question, then it would appear that the modern case for an Aristotelian duality of explanation is at least as strong as that for a Humean causal monism.[88] That Aristotle is a dualist (in this sense) is surely indicated by his view that the prime mover is not an efficient cause (*Metaphysics* Lambda, 1072b1–4), or at least not an antecedent condition, and his account of the permanent things as ensuring the continuity of change or coming-into-being, but not determining its particular character (*On Generation and Corruption* 2, 336b–337a). The universe is neither a random heap nor a gigantic unitary animal; rather, it is composed of interdependent parts which are themselves wholes.

Modern evolutionary biology is no more a threat to the plausibility of the Aristotelian dual structure of explanation than is modern physics. While Aristotle was surely not an early evolutionist, there are no solid grounds for attributing to Aristotle the view that species are absolutely fixed and distinct: he seems to want to hold both that species are distinct natural kinds and that there is some kind of continuity across species.[89] Throughout his biological writings, his concern is to provide explanations that link particular physiological and behavioral traits to the particular way of life (*idios bios*) of different animals. While it is true that this concern presupposes the reality of species (as opposed to regarding species as ephemeral effects of individual behavior), which Darwin thought incompatible with the doctrine of the evolution of species, it is possible now to say that Darwin's opposition to the reality of species can be explained in the same way as Galileo's opposition to final causes: the primary need in both cases was to liberate scientific inquiry from religious constraint. Thus there no longer

---

[88] See Masters, "Politics as a Biological Phenomenon," pp. 31–34. According to Mayr, "the renewed appreciation in modern times of Aristotle's importance grew to the degree that the biological sciences emancipated themselves from the physical sciences." *Growth of Biological Thought*, p. 89.

[89] Doubt arises here because Aristotle—unlike a modern biologist—aims in his biological writings to explain particular things and not to develop systematic theory. For discussion of Aristotle on the continuity and fixity of species, see Clark, *Aristotle's Man*, pp. 34–37; Lennox, "Aristotle on Genera"; Granger, "Scala Naturae."

seems to be any reason not to recognize at least the theoretical compatibility of evolutionary theory and the reality of species: "The world of nature is, in some fundamental sense, really divided into reasonably discrete packages of creatures as a result of evolution."[90] Leaving out the predictive (or retrodictive) causal claim in the words "as a result of evolution," this view of the basic structure of the natural world is perfectly compatible with the Aristotelian notion of natures and is clearly at odds with the reductionist Humean picture of a world of corpuscular events unrelated except by statistical laws.

Thus Aristotle's possible beliefs concerning the evolution or eternal fixity of species have no bearing on the question of the compatibility of modern evolutionary theory and Aristotelian teleology, since evolutionary biology is not a form of teleological explanation at all; rather, it is a set of predictive hypotheses designed to explain the *origin* of different species, by reference either to a slow cumulation of incremental changes or to these plus a number of sudden and discontinuous environmental shifts.[91] Such explanations work by pointing to the antecedent conditions of species change, and yield only a partial account of the way of life characteristic of each species once evolved. Knowledge of how the human brain has evolved does not tell us how the brain functions with respect to human life, although it may help to rule out a number of implausible hypotheses.[92] Similarly, for Aristotle, an ac-

---

[90] Gould, *Panda's Thumb*, p. 212. The stability of species as a fact about nature is discussed extensively by Eldredge in *Time Frames*; he defends ways of seeing "species more as independent actors themselves in the evolutionary arena" (p. 122). Recent debate seems to be concerned with the sense in which species are more real than other groupings, rather than whether they are. See Ruse, *Philosophy of Biology*, pp. 126–139.

[91] Ruse, *Philosophy of Biology*, pp. 47–68.

[92] See Masters, "Value—and Limits—of Sociobiology," p. 158; Midgley, *Beast and Man*, pp. 165–166. It is interesting to note that some attempts to save teleology from the association with mysticism do so at the expense of reducing functional explanations to predictive hypotheses in the model of evolutionary theory. For example, Clark notes correctly that "final causes need not be equated with occult entities, backward causation, or the divine will." But his example dissolves a functional account into a predictive one: "The function of an organ or a behaviour pattern is that consequence without whose general occurrence the organ or behaviour would not have been selected." *Nature of the Beast*, p. 10. This is simply not the case. Ruse, in *Philosophy of Biology*, puts the point as follows:

One might just replace every functional explanation with a non-teleological explanation—for example, one might explain the udders on present cows by reference to selection on past cows, rather than by reference to what one thinks that present-cows' udders will do. In fact, I think this is the kind of move biologists might often be tempted to make. However, it does seem to me

count of the reasons for the evolution of the *polis* does not fully explain the function of the *polis* relative to the human *bios*: the *polis* comes into being for the sake of "living," but once it has come into being it exists for the sake of "living well" (*Pol.* 1, 1252b29–30). The teleological appearance of some presentations of evolutionary biology results from the romantic inclination of some biologists to convert predictive hypotheses about the emergence and death of species into the narrative of the way of life of some permanent and imaginary organism, either the universe (as for Teilhard de Chardin) or the gene (as for E. O. Wilson).[93] These fantasies reflect a failure to discriminate among different types of explanations; what is scientific in evolutionary biology is wholly compatible with, and yet clearly distinct from, a functional evaluation of particular living beings and human institutions.

Teleology and the Human Good

Does the concept of the human good, central to Aristotelian practical philosophy, derive its intelligibility from assumptions about the world that are no longer tenable? Aristotle's human good is a way of life that is definitive or normal for us as a species. The background assumption this concept demands is a view of the biological world as a place in which wholes are prior to parts and in which these wholes (organisms) are defined by belonging to species, groups that are more than random aggregates of individuals. To be a living thing is to be a member of a species, a group defined by certain norms that are really there in nature, though by no means obvious, and that are to be discovered by empirical inquiry. This biological world must be investigated on its own terms, and cannot be reduced to the nonliving elements of which its parts are entirely composed. This distinction between living and nonliving beings does not attribute any special vital stuff or matter to living

---

that in a case like this, one is not translating a teleological explanation. Rather, one is replacing one's teleological explanation with a different, non-teleological explanation. The teleology itself cannot be translated away. (p. 196)

[93] See Sorabji, *Necessity, Cause, and Blame*, pp. 161–162 n. 20. In complex animals, very few attributes are determined by a single gene, and individual genes are often predictive or necessitating causes of a variety of physiological and behavioral characteristics. The antecedent genetic conditions for an organism's way of life are thus not heaps of individual genes, but the entire ordered genetic composite, or genome, of the organism. For a good brief account of this, see Caton, "Domesticating Nature," pp. 117–118.

things,[94] but assumes that our world happens to be one in which emergence obtains, one in which certain structures (not necessarily more complex than others) develop characteristics that cannot be deduced from the characteristics of their parts. This is what it means to say that these structures have souls, and are thus moved by needs and powers proper to themselves, as well as by external forces. Because of this ontological variety, several kinds of explanation are needed to explain particular beings. Can this Aristotelian assumption contend against the corpuscular world-view that has supported science since the seventeenth century?

The most straightforward way to decide this—by discovering which set of assumptions is empirically superior—is clearly not available to us; if it were, the world could be encountered directly, without science based on assumptions. But there are ways of thinking about the choice between the Aristotelian and the Humean worlds because the two concepts are not wholly incommensurable: each gives shape in a different way to the project, initiated by Heraclitus, of interpreting a world whose surface is like the Delphic oracle, who "neither speaks nor conceals, but gives signs" (DK 93).[95] The importance of the reductionist world-view in furthering this project in modern times is undeniable; it provided inquiry with a demystified world, free for examination. Joseph Cropsey's explanation of the cause of the difference between ancient and modern science is worth noting: "The ideological characteristic of modern thought entered . . . via the need to assert the claim of nature as opposed to supernature, rather than as opposed to convention."[96] Along with opening blocked channels of inquiry, the reduction of complex wholes to simple parts made possible a level of precision and system excluded by the world of Aristotelian natural science, in which the basic terms for the analysis of living things, the norms or actualities that define each species, can be known only after long experience and can never be known with

[94] Thus it makes no sense to call Aristotle a dualist, at least with respect to the sublunary world. His distinction between living and nonliving distinguishes kinds or levels of organization and does not split, for instance, *res extensa* and *res cogitans*. Speaking of the difference between the Aristotelian and the Cartesian soul, Wilkes says that for Descartes the soul "is a distinct entity, for the influence of the Church Fathers has been at work—the soul must, *pace* Aristotle, be a separable substance capable of disembodied existence. So Descartes undoes Aristotle's monism, and returns to the pre-Aristotelian *psuchē*-body dualism." *Physicalism*, p. 128.

[95] See Kahn, *Heraclitus*, pp. 123–124.

[96] "Hobbes," pp. 312–313. The scientific project itself displays a certain continuity, but it is affected by the character of its adversary (political convention in antiquity, religion later). See also Strauss, *Studies in Platonic Political Philosophy*, p. 176.

the certainty and precision of mathematics. But here, I think, is the point at which the terms of the choice can be most clearly stated: to what extent does the elevation of precision, system, and certainty as scientific norms open the way to "an increasingly detailed and refined understanding of nature"?[97] The answer to this question must vary over time; for Galileo and Darwin, reductionism was an important opening for inquiry. But with respect to the study of living things, it can quite reasonably be doubted whether this is still the case, especially if the alternative is a teleology that does not exclude reduction and the precise sciences where they are appropriate. In this important respect, the differences between Greek philosophy and Enlightenment science are much less than they are often said to be.

The major resistance to the assumptions of Aristotelian science is, however, more likely to be political than scientific. The energy for modern science comes also from the advantage precision gives to the project of controlling nature for human ends. We want science to be precise and certain because we are interested not only in seeking truth about the beings but in gaining control over a chaotic and potentially dangerous environment. Part of the political ground for the modern democratic opposition to teleological science is that we want science to serve human freedom and power, and the way to those goals appears to lie through reduction. Science must be precise and certain in order to control nature, or else what good is it? Our quite appropriate anxiety about life in a world without traditional structures of reassurance may lead to a reluctance to regard imprecise science as anything other than a dispensable luxury.

On the other hand, the same democratic concerns can produce opposition to the scientific project as such, and acceptance of a third assumption about the world, different from those of either Hume or Aristotle—the belief that there is no world at all but only human interpretations that constitute "worlds." Although its initial Nietzschean formulation is anything but liberal, this vision converges with a serious liberal reservation about all science, and about teleological sciences in particular: if science is precise and certain, and if teleological talk about the human good is scientific, then teleology will yield a precise and certain conception of the human good; but this is unacceptable, because it conflicts with the

[97] This is Kuhn's way of defining scientific progress; see *Structure of Scientific Revolutions*, p. 170.

liberal commitment to tolerate a variety of conceptions of the human good. Thus, for the liberal who thinks along these lines, teleology must be either imprecise and hence unscientific, or scientific and hence politically unacceptable. What is needed, then, is to show that evaluative explanation of an Aristotelian kind, in which particular events are placed relative to an understanding of the human good, can be scientific and yet imprecise. This is the goal of the next chapter, which advances the claim that Aristotle's discussion of the human good is a theoretical account that explains human action by pointing to typical though not obvious human problems and possibilities, rather than by invoking deterministic laws. My eventual claim will be that this Aristotelian version of the human good is essential to our own contemporary political theorizing because it sets the stage for the discussion of contemporary political life in a way superior both to science understood in the Humean fashion and to science rejected and replaced by interpretation and romance.

T W O

THEORIZING THE HUMAN GOOD

Aristotle and Contemporary Social Science

In the first chapter, we examined the connection between Aristotle's teleological philosophy or science and the kind of world it presupposes. We now move from the world of species in general to the human world, and from science as such to Aristotle's human or social science; my aim is to show that the Aristotelian position suggests a way of being scientific without determinism or excessive and intrusive precision. I will argue that Aristotle's approach to social science is superior to the two principal approaches characteristic of our time, empiricist and interpretive social science. My defense is not of the specific results of Aristotle's analysis; my claim, in fact, is that the great merit of Aristotle's approach (I avoid "method" here for reasons that will be clear in a moment) is that when practiced well it yields results that are both interesting and open to further discussion.

The *Politics* and the *Nicomachean Ethics*, the primary texts to be considered here, are not repositories of immutable truths calling for belief or rejection—any more than they are oblique reflections of Greek popular opinion. Instead, we find a discourse made up of arguable judgments of four major kinds: (1) Descriptions of general facts or phenomena, the sort of phenomena-in-need-of-explanation we might refer to as empirical assertions. Examples are the claims that human beings are political animals (*Pol.* 1, 1253a2–3), that mothers love their children more than fathers do (*NE* 8, 1161b27), that most human beings consider any amount of virtue enough but seek without limit to amass quantities of wealth or reputation (*Pol.* 7, 1323a36–38), and that deliberation is less powerful in women's lives than in those of men (*Pol.* 1, 1260a12–13).[1]

---

[1] Or that democrats tend to identify freedom with unlimited power (*Pol.* 5, 1310a31–32), or that in barbarian cultures women are treated as slaves (*Pol.* 1, 1252b5–6).

(2) Propositions about the efficient causal (predictive) relationship of several phenomena or variables. These are hypothetical propositions such as the claim that large cities tend to be freer of internal conflict than small cities (*Pol*. 4, 1296a12–13) or the proposition discussed in the previous chapter that equalizing property will not result in a decrease in some classes of crime (*Pol*. 2, 1267a2–17). (3) Teleological propositions about the place or function of various activities and institutions in the lives of human beings, such as the claim that security and friendship are necessary but not constitutive conditions of political life (*Pol*. 3, 1280b8–1281a3) or the proposition that the activities of leisure are more determinative of the quality of a human life than are the activities of occupation and war (*Pol*. 7, 1333a30–b5). (4) Finally, there are evaluative judgments, both general and particular: for example, the political life is better than the life of war and conquest, and the Spartan culture rests on a mistaken conception of human virtue (*Pol*. 7, 1333b5–1334a10).

In summary, the Aristotelian approach to social science characteristically weaves together four separate kinds of judgments in the following logical order: in response to descriptions of observed phenomena, relational propositions of two distinct kinds—predictive hypotheses and functional or teleological placements—are set out; and on the basis of these propositions, action-orienting evaluative conclusions are drawn about institutions, policies, and ways of life. An initial contrast with modern social science would suggest that Aristotle's approach is more inclusive than either the empiricist approach, which culminates in a system of hypothetical propositions, or the interpretive approach, which culminates in teleological propositions relative to the particular context under study, more or less "from the native's point of view."[2] This much could well be granted by empiricists and interpretive social scientists, who would then go on to challenge Aristotle's procedures by pointing out—quite correctly—that his four types of discussion do not occur in a metaphysical vacuum, but presuppose a particular conception of human nature and of nature simply. In order to defend Aristotle's approach, I will need to say just what that background conception is and how it allows him to do two things I assume to be of the greatest value for any social science: to reach conclusions that can inform practical deliberation, and to do so in a nondogmatic language that invites further discussion and revi-

[2] Geertz, "From the Native's Point of View."

sion. My claim is that the background conception of human nature on which Aristotle's social science rests is more plausible in itself and more likely to result in an adequate social science—one that is both practical and open—than either of the contemporary alternatives.

Before taking this up I need to explain briefly why I choose to refer to Aristotle here as a social scientist, rather than a political philosopher or theorist. I do this mainly because Aristotle's overall project is closer to the inquiry into the nature of things we associate with the word "science" than to the anti-Enlightenment-science posture built into current use of the term "philosophy." The idea here is to broaden our conception of science to include teleology, rather than to suggest "philosophical" alternatives to science. In addition, Aristotle's own word for what he is doing is *politikē*, or the science of the *polis*. *Politikē* does seem to be the equivalent of modern social science with respect to the subject matter it embraces; Aristotle uses the term throughout the *Politics* and the *Ethics* to refer to the consideration of topics we would to-day assign to political science, anthropology, sociology, psychology, economics, and history. I will of course have to argue that Aristotle intended *politikē* in something like the modern sense of "science," and even "natural science." The surface plausibility of this reading is indicated by the way Aristotle uses the word itself: while *politikē* most frequently, in both Plato and Aristotle, stands by itself as a noun, its ordinary meaning flows from its adjectival use to modify nouns like *technē* (skill or craft; *Pol.* 4, 1288b10–1289a25), *epistēmē* (science; *NE* 1, 1094a24–29), and *philosophia* (*Pol.* 3, 1282b23). The question, for Aristotle, seems to be not whether there is a social science, but rather just what kind of science *politikē* is.

The "social" in "social science" poses a more difficult problem, since it seems to imply (anachronistically) that "society" rather than the *polis* is the fundamental human community. Aristotle does indeed regard the *polis* as the most important form of human relationship, rather than just one among many. But it is also true that his definition of politics and his account of its importance do not simply reproduce standard Greek views on the subject. Briefly, politics according to Aristotle is marked by three characteristics—two structural and one functional. It is structured by *nomoi* (laws, customs) rather than by individual choice; decisions are made according to some procedure for ruling and being ruled in turn, rather than, say, by force, chance, or wisdom; and decisions

59

are motivated by the desire to improve the lives of all the citizens. The reasons for defining politics in this way will be taken up later in the chapter; here, we should note that Aristotle is fully aware that Greeks generally apply the term *polis* to communities that do not exhibit these features, and further that genuine *poleis* (in his sense) are rare. A large part of his *politikē*, then, is devoted to explaining why politics is so unusual and how other kinds of associations (such as families, friendships, armies, and markets) approximate or distort real politics in his sense of the term. The focus is thus not on the kinds of interaction that happen to be called political (as is the case with our "political science"), but on a wide range of human associations and failures to associate, on the advantages and dangers of human relationships of many kinds.

Before we turn to the details of Aristotle's views concerning the place of politics in human life in general, more must be said about why we might want to consult Aristotle in the first place: Why, in other words, is it desirable to look for an alternative to the claims of empiricist and interpretive social science?

Empiricism and Interpretation

The genealogy and general structure of the debate between the proponents of empiricism and interpretation in contemporary social science are too well known to call for extended comment here. The central issue is one that goes back to the Enlightenment critique of teleology: the question of whether there is an essential difference between the methods appropriate to natural science and the methods of the human or social sciences. The empiricist position holds that there is no serious methodological difference and that all science aims at reducing wholes to elements and developing explanations for the consequences of events in terms of hypothetical or predictive propositions. These propositions, when sufficiently general and sufficiently tested, can be treated as general or covering laws that serve to explain particular events. As far as method and logic are concerned, there is no difference between establishing connections among force, mass, and acceleration and establishing connections among social class, ethnic identification, and political behavior. The specific work of social scientific inquiry understood in this way is the prediction and control of behavioral events; moral quandaries about the uses of its results no doubt arise, but this is at least equally true of the natural sciences. For an empiricist there is no strong connection between explanation and evaluation, between giving accurate explanations and deciding how to act in a given situation. As W. G. Runciman says:

> The difference of subject-matter imposes difference of technique, as it does between one science and another on both sides of the frontier between nature and culture. But this does not impose a requirement on social scientists either to adopt different criteria of validity or to disclaim a capacity to achieve it at all. It is true that there is a difference in the level at which theoretical grounding is to be sought. But again, it is a difference which can be paralleled within the natural sciences as well as between the natural and the social; and it is still a difference within a common mode of reasoning.[3]

It must be remembered, however, that the "common mode of reasoning" of which Runciman speaks has a very particular provenance and rests—at least historically—on a distinctly uncommon view of the world to be explained by scientific reasoning. This is Kuhn's universe of corpuscular matter in motion,[4] a world which supports the modern exclusion of teleology from science, and effectively rules out the need for reference to norms or characteristic ways of life in the explanation of living things. This association of teleology and irrationality is captured nicely in Ernest Gellner's claim that the difference between the savage and the scientific mind is most clearly marked by the absence of reference to norms in the latter: "By contrast [to the savage mind], the crucial feature of scientific thought-systems is that the notion of normality is not conspicuously present in them."[5] In the last chapter, I noted that it would be possible to contest this view of science from within, as do those modern biologists who, like Aristotle, insist on the centrality of organism and species in the life sciences, and on the reality of the difference between the living and the nonliving worlds.

Be that as it may, the first challenge to the extension of modern empiricist science into the study of human affairs came not from biologists, but from those challenging the view that human beings

---

[3] Runciman, *Methodology of Social Theory*, p. 221.

[4] Kuhn, *Structure of Scientific Revolutions*, p. 41.

[5] Gellner, *Legitimation of Belief*, pp. 158–159. Gellner's is the best defense of empiricism I know; his argument defends reduction and a mechanistic world by saying that these are necessary conditions for publicity and repeatability in science. But since he does not insist on any particular logic of reductive explanation (explanations "are certainly not bound to any crude, simple model of structures built of heavy stuff" [p. 207]), reduction appears to be little more than another name for an insistence on Kantian impartiality and universality in scientific explanation.

could be studied in the same way that natural (living *or* nonliving) phenomena can be. Sharing the empiricist view, made prominent by Descartes, that nonhuman animals are in no essential way different from machines,[6] critics of a unified natural and social science argued that there was a fundamental difference between human beings and "merely" natural beings. Rousseau was one of the first to adopt this position: "Nature commands every animal, and the beast obeys. Man feels the same impetus, but he realizes that he is free to acquiesce or resist; and it is above all in the consciousness of this freedom that the spirituality of the soul is shown."[7] This assertion of the essential uniqueness of human beings shares with empiricism—and against Aristotle—the questionable view that animals are essentially machines. It differs from empiricism in its claim that human action is so different from animal-mechanical behavior as to require an entirely different form of explanation. As elaborated in the nineteenth century, this sense of difference is expressed in concepts like subjectivity, historicity, and the historical sense, categories that draw their vitality from the belief that human beings indirectly constitute themselves, create their own significance, through social action.[8]

The twentieth-century heir to the romantic reaction against the Enlightenment ideal of a unified science is interpretive social science. Instead of "laws-and-causes social physics," in Clifford Geertz's phrase,[9] the study of human affairs should emulate the process of construing a text; societies are to be "read" rather than "predicted."[10] While it would be a caricature to say that this method requires a deep empathy or perfect identification with the culture being studied, it is surely very different from the business of providing causal explanations by reference to universal hypothetical laws. Interpretive social science equally aims, however, at

[6] For a discussion of the analogy between animals and machines in light of the *res cogitans/res extensa* distinction, see Jonas, "Philosophical Aspects of Darwinism." For Descartes on the difference between human beings and beasts, see *Discours de la Méthode*, pt. 5, next to last paragraph. A good example of the animals-are-machines thesis is found in Hume, "On the Reason of Animals," *Enquiry concerning Human Understanding*, sec. 9, last paragraph.

[7] Rousseau, *Origin of Inequality*, p. 114. On this view, of course, nonhuman animals have no souls, no internal systems of organization.

[8] On the centrality of "historicity" in the development of interpretive social science, see Gadamer, "Problem of Historical Consciousness."

[9] Geertz, *Local Knowledge*, p. 3.

[10] The link between Diltheyan historical romanticism and the more recent claims for the primacy of interpretation without any historical ground is Nietzsche. See *Beyond Good and Evil*, pt. 1, paragraph 22.

explanation, though teleological rather than predictive, insofar as it attempts both to describe particular symbolic forms and to place such forms within the context of the structure of meaning that defines them.[11] But if this is teleology, the limits of its explanatory power are strictly local: the aim is to explain the society in its own terms, given the principle that "societies, like lives, contain their own interpretations."[12]

Interpretation, however, cannot be simply passive, allowing societies or "natives" to speak for themselves. If cultures are texts, they are texts of a special kind: for Geertz, "doing ethnography is like trying to read (in the sense of 'construct a reading of') a manuscript—foreign, faded, full of ellipses, incoherencies . . . but written not in conventional graphs of sound but in transient examples of shaped behavior."[13] For the interpretive social scientist, the meaning of an action is internal to the social context, but it is assumed to be hidden from the view of the actors themselves. Geertz's interpreter does not aim at establishing universal laws, but he seems at least as sure as any physicist (or economist) that his data are not capable of supplying an adequate self-interpretation: "The ethnographer does not, and in my opinion, largely cannot, perceive what his informants perceive. What he perceives— and that uncertainly enough—is what they perceive 'with,' or 'by means of,' or 'through' or whatever word one may choose. In the country of the blind, who are not as unobservant as they appear, the one-eyed is not king but spectator."[14] Just as the Physicist ferrets out the laws of the interaction of matter, the Interpreter unmasks the hidden categories that inform perception and action: each supplies by science the coherence the data otherwise but mutely display. Indeed, for Geertz, the "study of culture [is] a positive science like any other,"[15] no matter what the metaphor of social textuality may suggest. Empiricists aim at universal laws, interpreters at "local knowledge," but both understand their activity as fundamentally disinterested: evaluations are to be avoided in the analysis, and few if any evaluative conclusions can be drawn from such analysis. Thus on either account the function of social science relative to everyday life appears to be archival rather than

[11] Geertz, *Interpretation of Cultures*, chap. 1.
[12] Geertz, "Deep Play," p. 223.
[13] Geertz, *Interpretation of Cultures*, p. 10.
[14] Geertz, "From the Native's Point of View," p. 228. What the native cannot see are the formal and final causes of native behavior.
[15] Geertz, *Interpretation of Cultures*, p. 362.

action-orienting.[16] This situation is characterized by Gadamer as a "false objectification,"[17] falsely treating the subjects of analysis as fundamentally different from the analyst. In interpretive social science, this is achieved by treating humanness—that attribute shared by analyst and subject—as a property of minimal significance.

The problem with this orientation is that it prevents social science from functioning as a guide to political self-criticism, as a way of arriving at practical conclusions concerning how to change or maintain our lives. To serve this goal, social science must try to do more than "seek and acknowledge the immanent coherence contained within the meaning-claim of the other." What is required in addition is, in Gadamer's words, "a readiness to recognize the other as potentially right and let him or it prevail against me."[18] The moral danger posed by cultural relativism is thus not that it leads its adherents into anarchy—they are a generally civilized lot—but that it leads to smugness.[19]

It is his interest in a future- or action-oriented approach to human affairs that leads Gadamer to suggest that Aristotle can supply a language for inquiry that is superior to the contemporary adversaries, whether empirical or interpretive.[20] To this it may be added that Aristotle differs from both varieties of current social science in being open to the influence of biological reflection in the study of human affairs. In this way, Aristotle's account of human action rejects both the empiricist assumption that animals are machines (or that nature as such is mechanical) and the romantic dichotomy between the human and the natural.[21]

An Aristotelian social science begins with a sense of nature, or

---

[16] Ibid., pp. 230–231.

[17] *Truth and Method*, p. 280.

[18] Gadamer's criticism of Dilthey here seems to apply fully to Geertz.

[19] Cf. Geertz, "Anti Anti-Relativism." Geertz himself approaches platitude in saying that the truth of cultural relativism is limited to the view that "we can never apprehend another people's or another period's imagination neatly, as though it were our own." *Local Knowledge*, p. 44.

[20] Gadamer, *Truth and Method*, pp. 278–279.

[21] Gadamer appears to deny this: "Aristotle sees ethos as differing from physis in that it is a sphere in which the laws of nature do not operate, yet not a sphere of lawlessness, but of human institutions and human attitudes that can be changed and have the quality of rules only to a limited degree." *Truth and Method*, p. 279. My argument is that Aristotle's natural science is *not* directed toward the presentation of natural laws, and that he is thus able to overcome the reduction/transcendence dilemma. For an excellent analysis of some difficulties in Gadamer's account of the relationship between human activity and the world in which that activity occurs, see Dostal, "World Never Lost."

biological inheritance, as neither wholly determinative of human action nor irrelevant to it, but rather as a source of problems to be solved and capacities and inclinations to be shaped. In presenting the Aristotelian possibility, I will consider first Aristotle's conception of human action and convention, and then his notion of the kind of social science that would provide the most adequate account of these actions and conventions.

Aristotle and Praxis

Both of Aristotle's major works of social science, the *Nicomachean Ethics* and the *Politics*, begin with observations concerning the intentional character of human conduct: "We see that . . . everyone does everything for the sake of some apparent good" (*Pol.* 1, 1251a1–4) and "Every art . . . and similarly every *praxis* and choice seems to aim at some good" (*NE* 1, 1094a1–2). This serves to distinguish human actions from several other classes of events in nature: those that serve a purpose in the life of the organism but are not intentional, like eye blinks and the motion of the heart (*Parts of Animals* 2, 657a31–b3; *Motion of Animals* 703b5–6), and those that serve no purpose, like eye color (*Generation of Animals* 778a32ff.; cf. 778b11ff.). Human actions are intentional in the sense that they are voluntary (*hekōn*). But a motion is not identified as voluntary by any prior events (such as internal processes of reasoning or willing) which may have led up to it: "Both 'voluntary' and 'involuntary' must be said when the action occurs. An action is voluntary when the source (*archē*) of the motion of the bodily parts is the agent" (*NE* 3, 1110a14–17). Voluntary actions are distinguished from other events or kinds of motion by the presence in the agent of the power to act or not at the moment of action. But this power is not the privileged preserve of any uniquely human or transcendent faculty. Other animals are as capable of voluntary action as human beings, because this internal source of motion is neither reason nor will, but desire (*orexis*), which is common to all animals (*De Anima* 3, 433a32–33).[22] Desires are always directed toward some object of desire (some apparent good), and this is an object of sensation or imagination (*phantasia*), a power that is common to

[22] A seemingly different account of the origin of voluntary motion is given in *Metaphysics* Lambda, 1072a29–30: "We desire [an object] because it seems [good], rather than it seems [good] because we desire [it]; for thinking (*noēsis*) is the *archē*." These passages can be reconciled if we bear in mind that "desire" and "opinion" are both abstractions; when it comes to action, they are aspects of a single process common to all animals.

all animals (*Motion of Animals* 700b15–18). Thus intentional or voluntary motion can be understood as an interaction of an apparent good, the agent's perception of that good, and the agent's desire for the good in question—all this without reference to any concept of willing. Nonetheless, it makes sense to call desire the source or efficient cause of the action, because neither the attracting object nor the perception of that object can cause motion in the absence of desire (*De Anima* 3, 433a15–b1).

Nevertheless, it is also possible for Aristotle to say, in response to Democritus' assertion of the universality of external efficient causality (a claim shared by modern science), that *all* animals move by choice (*prohairesis*) or intellection (*noēsis*) (*De Anima* 1, 406b24–25). The reason for the apparent ambiguity here is Aristotle's view that reason and desire are not separate entities but interacting "parts" or attributes of soul (*psuchē*). Soul itself, moreover, is not a thing separate from body, but "a beginning of animal life" (*De Anima* 1, 402a6–7; 408b25–27).[23] That is, to speak of soul, for Aristotle, is to consider the manner in which living organisms are self-moving and thus distinct from nonliving things: "Of natural things, some have life and some not; we say 'life' where there is nurture, growth, and decay owing to the thing itself" (*De Anima* 2, 412a13–15).[24] Body and soul are properties that exist relative to one another as aspects of the individual animal whose being they define: my body is to my soul as the potential of an individual is to its actuality or function (*De Anima* 2, 412a15–21).[25] This conception of soul as the definitive activity of an organism is nicely captured in Aristotle's analogical metaphor "If the eye were an animal, sight would be its soul" (*De Anima* 2, 412b18–19).

Just as the soul is not a unique and supernatural immaterial sub-

[23] Plants are also living things (and have souls) insofar as they are capable of taking in food from the environment. *De Anima* 2, 413a25–b8.

[24] The organism is an irreducible whole; "soul" is the term we use when we want to talk about its form, "body" when we consider matter. The notion of organisms as self-moving and hence distinct from nonliving nature is similar to the modern view of life as dependent on an internal program of development, irreducibly present in the genome. As Mayr says, "Aristotle's *eidos* (form) is a teleonomic principle which performed in Aristotle's thinking precisely what the genetic program of the modern biologist performs." *Growth of Biological Thought*, p. 88. See also Delbrück, "How Aristotle Discovered DNA."

[25] For Aristotle, "the soul is just the functional organization of the entire living body." Nussbaum, "Shame, Separateness, and Political Unity," p. 415. This is another instance of the way Aristotle avoids the Cartesian *res extensa/res cogitans* dualism. See Wilkes, *Physicalism*, pp. 114–137. Because "soul" now implies the separation of body and soul, it might be best to avoid translating Aristotle's *psuchē* altogether, though that would perhaps seem a needless mystification.

stance for Aristotle, it is also not a peculiarly human property. Even if some kinds of activities, such as deliberation, belong primarily to humans, it is important to note that Aristotle explicitly rejects the view that soul and mind (*nous*) are the same. He in fact attributes such a view to the atomist Democritus, and says that the identification of mind and soul follows from the false relativistic belief that truth (the work of mind) and opinion are one and the same (*De Anima* 1, 404a27–31).[26]

Human actions are thus not distinct from the motions of other organisms by virtue of intentionality or spirituality. To grasp the significance of Aristotle's conception of human action, we should notice how it undermines the widespread modern view of the acting human being as transcendent moral hero. Still, there is a distinction to be made between humans and other animals. In the *Nicomachean Ethics*, Aristotle says that he wants to reserve the term *praxis* as a characterization of human conduct alone: "There are three things in the soul that are decisive concerning actions and truths: perception, thought, and desire. Of these, perception is in no way the source (*archē*) of *praxis*; for beasts have perception but no share in *praxis*" (*NE* 6, 1139a17–20). This is not to say that *praxis* is *caused* (in the sense of efficient causality) by mind and not desire, since *praxis* is a kind of motion, and "thought by itself moves nothing," at least insofar as actions are concerned (*NE* 6, 1139a35–36). The problem is this: the subject of *politikē* is *ta prakta*, matters concerning practice. *Praxis* is uniquely human, but it is not attributable to the existence of any uniquely creative or volitional faculty in human beings,[27] nor can it be said to follow simply from the human capability of thinking in ways that other animals cannot. If *praxis* is peculiarly human, it must be as the result of a specific kind of desire.

There can be no desire without imagination (*De Anima* 3, 433b29), that is, an imagined object of desire, an apparent good. Objects are good or desirable not in themselves (hence Aristotle's criticism of the Platonic form of the good in the first book of the *NE*), but only in relation to the animal desiring them: an object or

[26] The problem with Democritus' view is that it cannot account for error, or for learning, or for the self-critical function of mind—all of which are fundamental experiences in philosophy understood as inquiry into invisible natures. This is fundamentally the same critique that Socrates makes of Protagoras' *anthrōpos metron* in the *Theaetetus*. The same sort of objection would also apply to understanding soul as consciousness or self-consciousness.

[27] Here Aristotle decisively parts company with any interpretive social science, as well as with Kantian or existential moral heroism.

way of life may be desirable or good for cats, but not for horses.[28] Animals are defined, or individuated, for Aristotle by the activity or way of life peculiar to their kind (*idios bios*) when functioning at their best, their *ergon* or *energeia* (*NE* 10, 1176a3–5).[29] A healthy animal is one whose attributes or elements are arranged according to the *logos* that defines the animal in question (*Parts of Animals* 693b15–16). The *ergon* of the animal is determined by its *logos* or, in other words, by its soul and is identical with the internal goal or *telos* it pursues.[30] Things that seem good to an animal, and are thereby desired by it, may or may not really be good for it; the souls of animals are frequently mistaken, so that a certain attractive food may either support or detract from its consumer's way of life (*De Anima* 3, 427b1–2; 433a26–27). In general, though, an animal's pleasures are appropriate to its *ergon*: most dogs, spiders, and mules take pleasure in the sorts of things that all members of their species appropriately desire (*NE* 10, 1176a5).[31] Human beings, however, are different: "But among humans there is no small difference in pleasures. For the same things that give enjoyment to some and pain to others, are painful and hateful to some and sweet and dear to others" (*NE* 10, 1176a10–12). With other animals, pleasures and apparent goods, the starting points of desire, vary mostly by species; with humans, they vary from individual to individual, and are the major source of human inequality.

[28] While critical of what he takes to be Plato's essentialism here, Aristotle at the same time clearly rejects a nominalist interpretation of "good." "Good" is an equivocal term whose significations may be related to one another by being derived from the same thing, by pointing to the same thing, or by analogy (*NE* 1, 1096b26–29). Burnet suggests that the last proposal (analogy) represents Aristotle's own view (*Ethics of Aristotle*, p. 29n.). But from *Metaphysics* Lambda, 1075a18–23, it appears that "good" is a *pros hen* equivocal. At any rate, Aristotle's opposition to Plato is not nominalist or conventionalist, and so cannot provide grist for the interpretive mill. Words are the signs of psychic experience, which is itself a likeness of things, of a world common to all. *On Interpretation* 16a3–8. This view is shared by Heraclitus and Plato: "to those who are awake there is one common universe, but each sleeper turns to a private one" (DK 89).

[29] Living things become irreducible organisms by having the characteristics of some species. Thus I am more myself when imitating or deliberating than when sleeping or digesting. A species is a universal property or category, but it is not an individual whole: "thus human being is a universal, Kallias an individual" (*On Interpretation* 17a40–b1). It is thus *not* the case that Kallias is to human as part is to whole; Kallias himself becomes a whole by taking on the properties of his humanity.

[30] *Metaphysics* Theta, 1050a22: "For the *ergon* is the *telos*, and the *energeia* is the *ergon*." That is, function, end, and actuality are simply three different ways of indicating the specific and irreducible wholeness of an organism.

[31] What behavioral psychology calls learning and what Aristotle calls *ethos* or habit plays a relatively small role in establishing the preference schedules of non-human animals. *Pol.* 7, 1332b3–4.

Human *praxis* thus differs in the first instance from other kinds of voluntary motion by its problematic quality and its variability. Aristotle states this difference in the following way in the *Politics*: "Other animals live primarily by nature (*phusis*), and some in a lesser way by habits (*ethos*), but human beings live also by reason (*logos*), because they alone have *logos*" (*Pol.* 7, 1332b3–5). The health (in a sense the actuality or *energeia*) of nonhuman animals is largely shaped by their inherited specific potentiality (*dunamis*), or as we might now say, their genotype. But for human beings biological inheritance is much less powerful in determining a way of life. To a greater extent than other animals, we desire things as a result of habituation (or "acculturation") rather than as an un-mediated consequence of biologically inherited potentials for re-sponse. As a result, there will be important differences between the goals and hence the lives of members of different societies or cultures.

Furthermore, mature and healthy humans can live and desire in a thoughtful way—in a way involving a deliberate (not only habit-uated) choice of goals—whereas natural slaves and other animals cannot (*Pol.* 3, 1280a35). Nor can children, although children, nat-ural slaves, and nonhuman animals are perfectly capable of *vol-untary* action (*NE* 3, 1112a15). It is at this point that the famous definition of humans as the animals who have *logos*, who have the potential to live by reasoned speech, comes into play. The word Aristotle uses to indicate this defining human attribute—*prohai-resis*—is almost impossible to translate.[32] It is a voluntary action, but there are voluntary actions that do not involve *prohairesis*. It is also not only a "choice" (*hairesis*), since again there are choices that do not display this attribute. *Prohairesis* differs from choice in that it is a choice *pro*, that is, a choice made with full awareness of al-ternative possibilities, a decision that expresses a prior deliberation (*NE* 3, 1112a15). This is a form of thought, to be sure, but a thought about acting, and so it must involve a kind of desire as well as a kind of reasoning. The wonderfully concise account of *prohairesis* as the definitive human attribute in *Nicomachean Ethics* 6

---

[32] Lord suggests "intentional choice," Irwin suggests "decision." Berns, in "Spir-itedness in Ethics and Politics," proposes "forechoice" or "pre-election" (p. 337). Sherman, in "Character, Planning, and Choice," uses "reasoned choice." As Berns notes, Aristotle is intentionally imprecise about this definition. "Reasoned choice" or "reasonable choice" or "thoughtful choice" expresses this lack of a technical tone. I think it important, however, to note that this is not the same as the notion of a rational choice of a Rawlsian "life plan"—since, as we shall see in Chapter 3, for Aristotle decision-rules cannot ever be established theoretically prior to the mo-ment of action-choice.

puts it this way: "*prohairesis* is either desiring thought (*orektikos nous*) or thinking desire (*orexis dianoētikē*), and it is thus that human beings are the starting point (*archē*) [of their actions]" (*NE* 6, 1139b4–5).

It is, I think, impossible to state the matter any more clearly in the abstract, and Aristotle certainly does not try. What *prohairesis* suggests, though, is not difficult to formulate. The heart of a specifically human life is not that it is freely willed rather than necessitated, but rather that it operates as a coherent whole rather than a series of moments. Other animals operate in this way too, but we do so only as a result of some more or less thoughtful choices about what we want and how we want to obtain it. Greater clarity than this may be suggested through metaphor (such as "charting a course") or by specific examples of thoughtfully chosen lives, and in the next chapter we will consider some examples. At this point, however, we can say that Aristotle's definition of human beings as rational animals should not bring to mind the thought that we are uniquely voluntary, or that we can overcome our desires and live according to pure calculation. Rather, we are the sort of beings whose thoughts and desires can interact to produce a characteristic way of life.

But this is in no way simply to praise human beings, since perfect, fully actualized beings—gods, say, or unmoved movers—would have no use for this capacity for thoughtful choice, and since the consequence of having such a capacity is that individuals among us can turn out to be either the best or the worst of animals (*Pol.* 1, 1253a32–34). Rather, the assertion that the capacity for thoughtful choice (*prohairesis*) is central to human life serves to identify a basic human problem or need. The shape of our lives is not set for us by our biologically inherited natures or capacities; still, since we are natural beings defined by a certain definite internal *telos* or goal, our conception of the good for us as individual human beings can be correct or mistaken: we can organize our particular attributes and problems relatively well or not (I can deliberately choose to eat as much as possible and deliberate hardly ever). Therefore, our actions and the customs and thoughts that inform them (that is, our ways of life) can be read and evaluated as a series of answers to the question "What is the human good?"

The judgment that human beings are the rational animals signifies the claim that our lives are structured by dispositions that are informed by thought as well as by desire and imagination. But the capacity for thinking well does not actualize itself; rather, it comes into being as the result of the development of certain habits over which we initially have no control. Therefore Aristotle should not be understood as claiming that human lives are spontaneously or even usually happy or flourishing. Instead, his position is that our lives are uniquely controversial answers to the question of how beings like us should live. It is this controversy that provides the central problem for, and the *raison d'être* of, the social scientist. Awareness of the problematic character of human happiness leads to the realization that individual *prohairesis* requires theorizing about the human good in general.

Living Politically and Living Well

In addition to being rational animals, human beings are also said to be the most political animals. But this latter assertion is quite ambiguous, since Aristotle also identifies us as "dualizers," beings whose way of life—unlike that of the social insects—is both political and scattered, and perhaps even solitary (*History of Animals* 487a7–14).[33] This ambiguity is expressed in Book 1 of the *Politics*: "By nature there is an impulse (*hormē*) in all humans toward such a community [the *polis*], but the first person to establish one was the cause of the greatest good things" (*Pol.* 1, 1253a29–31).[34] The problem is that our biological inheritance includes a number of impulses, not all of them compatible, and that there is no master impulse or structure of drives that controls human life. One of the central natural facts about us is that we generally care for one another, or exhibit some aspects of *philia* or friendship, the impulse "to wish for someone else what one thinks to be good, for that person's sake and not for one's own" (*Rhet.* 2, 1380b35–1381a1). In this complex of social and asocial impulses, it would appear that if humanity were to be defined by its strongest spontaneous social drives alone, then we should be called familial rather than political animals, as we are told in Book 8 of the *Nicomachean Ethics*: "Friendship between male and female seems to be especially by nature. For human beings are by nature familial [or pairing] more than political animals, inasmuch as the household (*oikos*) is earlier

[33] "Dualizers" are animals who have characteristics that cross standard typological classifications. See Lloyd, *Science, Folklore, and Ideology*, pp. 44–52, and Granger, "Scala Naturae."

[34] The term *hormē* took on the sense of nonrational appetite in Stoicism, a usage that persists in Hobbes's translation of *hormē* as "appetite" in *Leviathan*, chap. 6.

and more necessary[35] than the *polis*" (*NE* 8, 1162a16–19). We have a natural (in the sense of biologically inherited) impulse to live together, but "the purpose of politics is not to make living together (*suzēn*) possible, but to make living well (*eu zēn*) possible" (*Pol.* 3, 1280b39–1281a4). What does this mean? To answer this question, it is necessary to consider the second and more important sense in which human beings are political animals.

Aristotle's argument that human beings are uniquely political animals is stated in extremely compact form in Book 1 of the *Politics* (*Pol.* 1, 1253a7–38). This concision has led to two important misconceptions of the meaning of "political animal" for Aristotle, and it will be useful to consider them before offering my own reading of the passage. The first of these is that in saying we are political animals Aristotle is endorsing the Greek ideal of civic virtue and the intrinsic superiority of the political life to all others. This is, for example, the view of J.G.A. Pocock, who speaks of "the ancient ideal of *homo politicus* (the *zōon politikon* of Aristotle), who affirms his being and his virtue by the medium of political action."[36] This position suggests that Aristotle defends the intrinsic value of political life against those who see it as having only instrumental value (for example, against Plato or the sophists,[37] or, prospectively, Hobbes and Locke). But this reading runs afoul of Aristotle's apparent relegation of the political life to a rank below the theoretical life in the concluding books of both the *Politics* and the *Nicomachean Ethics*. As a result, the politics-as-intrinsic-good reading is forced either to ignore these quite prominent passages or to read them as a residue of a generally overcome Platonism.[38]

The other position I want to contest centers on the claim at *Politics* 1, 1253a29–30, that all humans have an impulse (*hormē*) toward political community. If this is so, some ask, then why don't

---

[35] "Necessity" for Aristotle is equivocal since "cause" is equivocal. Necessity may refer either to efficient-material causality or to final-formal causality, or it may be used as the antithesis of "natural." Four meanings of "necessity" are given in *Metaphysics* Delta, 1015a20–b6. Three types of necessity are distinguished in the first book of *Parts of Animals* (639b21–640a9; 642a32–b4): simple necessity, characteristic of eternal things; teleological or hypothetical necessity, characteristic of natural things and of the products of art; and elemental necessity, characteristic of the parts of natural things (earth, air, fire, and water).

[36] Pocock, *Machiavellian Moment*, p. 550. Pocock acknowledges that his view of the link between Aristotle and the Greek idealization of politics relies on Hannah Arendt, who is the modern founder of this reading of Aristotle. More will be said about this in Chapter 4. For a good criticism of this reading, see Zuckert, "Limits and Satisfactions of Political Life."

[37] Nussbaum, *Fragility of Goodness*, pp. 345–353.

[38] Ibid., pp. 373–377.

human beings seek political life as avidly as beavers build dams or Hobbesian individuals pursue their constant endeavor for power after power? Bernard Williams presents this view in the form it generally receives, that of a criticism of Aristotle for holding such an impossible view of politics: "In Aristotle's teleological universe, every human being (or at least every nondefective male who is not a natural slave) has a kind of inner nisus toward a life of at least civic virtue, and Aristotle does not say enough about how this is frustrated by poor upbringing, to make it clear exactly how, after that upbringing, it is still in this man's interest to be other than he is."[39] The politics-as-spontaneous-drive view leads to the conclusion that Aristotle is hopelessly caught in a contradiction between his biological claim about the human political drive and his ethical and political claims that people do not usually or spontaneously act well.

The appeal of these two views is quite clear. The politics-as-intrinsic-good view allows some modern readers to find in Aristotle a powerful ally against the liberal individualism they oppose, while the politics-as-spontaneous-drive reading permits others to identify Aristotle as a familiar sort of biological student of human affairs—perhaps the biologist of the *polis* in the sense that Freud is called the biologist of the mind. The two interpretations differ most profoundly in their view of the theoretical basis of Aristotle's social science. The intrinsic-good view sees Aristotle as making an autonomous ethical argument, and not applying to political issues concepts developed in his biology.[40] The spontaneous-drive view, generally unfriendly, holds that Aristotle is in fact a biological determinist. My contention is that Aristotle's social science is indeed biological, but that it is in no sense determinist—just as his biology is not determinist. For Aristotle, humans inherit biologically a variety of inclinations—toward politics, but also toward living as we please, toward sexual partnership, and toward imitation, among others. None of these genetic potentialities are seen simply as con-

---

[39] Williams, *Ethics and the Limits of Philosophy*, p. 44. This reading suggests Alasdair MacIntyre's criticism of Aristotle's "metaphysical biology."

[40] Nussbaum's defense of this view in *Fragility of Goodness* claims that, for Aristotle, the basic truth about ethical matters is to be sought in "shared human beliefs" (p. 349) or "deeper appearances" (p. 321) rather than in his biological conception of human nature. This would seem to have the questionable advantage of reconciling Aristotle to MacIntyre, in language recalling a similar move to embrace contextualism by Rawls in "Justice as Fairness." The same strategy is at work in Beiner's *Political Judgment*. Beiner reads Aristotle's teleology as a defense of the integrity of politics and contingency, which can be complemented by a critical Kantian autonomy.

duct-determining (or justifying) drives; instead, they are potentiating inclinations that can be reinforced or inhibited by any number of experiences and institutions as we grow and encounter the world. This is also true of animals other than ourselves. What is uniquely human is that our potentialities are many and varied and by no means always compatible or consistent with one another. This lack of strict biological definition is both a strength and a problem for us. Thus for Aristotle politics—a way of living guided by laws and customs (*nomoi*) and involving both ruling others and being ruled by them—is neither an ethical ideal nor an overwhelming biological drive, neither an end in itself nor an inevitability. It is, instead, the best reasonably possible way of organizing the variety of inclinations and needs that comprise the human biological inheritance, a way that has arisen neither spontaneously from nor in opposition to that inheritance, but as the unintended consequence of our attempts to live securely.

Politics and Logos

Before presenting the argument about political animals in *Politics* 1, 1253a7–38, I will give a translation of what I take to be the key portions of that passage, leaving as many of the important terms as possible untranslated: "The reason why human beings are political animals more than the bee or any other herding animal is clear." Note that politics is *not* taken to be the central or defining attribute of human life; rather, it is assumed to be a feature that needs to be explained teleologically by reference to some more fundamentally human attribute. Politics is thus neither an overmastering drive nor an intrinsic human good.[41] What deeper human trait can account for the central part that politics plays in the life specific to human beings?

"For nature, as we assert, does nothing in vain, and human beings alone among animals possess *logos*." Other animals have a voice, and so can make sounds indicative of pleasure and pain to one another, but *logos* is more than this:

[41] For the distinction between a fact (*to hoti*) and a reason (*to dihoti*), see *Posterior Analytics* 1, 78a. The question there is the relation of attributes of a substance to their explanatory power: Do planets not twinkle because they are near, or are they near because they do not twinkle? According to Aristotle, the former is the case (see Kosman, "Understanding, Explanation, and Insight"). Here the question is "Are we political because we have *logos* or do we have *logos* because we are political?" The terms Aristotle uses suggest that the former is the case. The political implications of this will be discussed further in Chapter 4.

Logos makes plain the *sumpheron* and the *blaberon* [interest and its opposite] and *therefore* the just and the unjust. For this is unique (*idion*) to human beings as compared with other animals, that humans alone have a perception (*aisthēsis*) of good and bad, just and unjust, and other things, and it is a community (*koinōnia*) in these things that makes an *oikos* and a *polis*. And by nature a *polis* is prior to both the *oikos* and the individual.

Human beings are unique in having the capacity to perceive what is best for them ("living well") and to order their lives according to that perception, rather than responding to each moment as if it were a new world. Justice is such an ordering, and it is like politics neither simply natural nor desirable in itself, but desirable only as a way in which "living well" or simply "our interest" can be brought into being. Conceptions of justice are not to be treated as expressing commitment to a moral or ethical realm separate from self-interest, but as embodying different judgments about our long-term interests, about how we ought to live. Polities, the organized communities that through their *nomoi* assert different views of justice, are neither good nor bad as such; rather, they are to be treated as expressing opinions about what our lives require that can be evaluated as relatively correct or mistaken.[42] Although the political life is not the paradigmatically human life, since rationality about our interests, the characteristic Aristotle calls *phronēsis* or practical wisdom in Book 6 of the *Nicomachean Ethics*, is a human attribute prior in being to civility, a life of deliberative rationality in some way requires and justifies the political order that laws and rotation in office supply.

But Aristotle's claim that it is our ability to speak reasonably that explains and justifies the political order is not easy to grasp. The difficulty is caused by the fact that his sense of the function or place of speech in human life differs radically from conceptions familiar to us. In particular, Aristotle holds neither that speech is for the sake of communicating information (else it would be the

[42] Ambler, in "Aristotle on the City," makes a strong case that the *Politics* both asserts and calls into question the naturalness of the polity. Part of his argument is the claim that the *polis* springs more from the "sense (*aisthēsis*) of the good, bad, just, and unjust, than from [the human being's] ability to explain them in speech" (p. 172). I would say that the limits of politics derive rather from the necessary association of politics and law (*nomos*); thus to the extent that law approximates rational judgment—and that varies from law to law—politics is natural for human beings.

75

same as "voice") nor that it serves the purpose of expressing or constituting an identity, building up a human world alongside the world of nature.[43] *Logos* rather makes it possible for us to discover through deliberation the kinds of goals in terms of which we can best organize our lives—those means which for us constitute human happiness (*NE* 6, 1144a6–9).[44] Errors can of course be made in the process of discovery; as a result, Aristotelian speech is criticizable in a way in which world- or identity-constituting speech is not: you can say that my plans for myself are not in my interest because you know that my interest is not constituted by my present reasoning. Our deliberative conclusions about goals are also always uncertain. Nevertheless, some such conclusions are needed if we are not to drift from moment to moment; we need to deliberate about our goals because we alone are not supplied with them—at least not in any precise and usable form—by our biological inheritance.

Now, these reasoned conclusions about our interest do not spring forth spontaneously or by necessity, even though without them we are incapable of becoming flourishing human beings. The capacity for reasonable speech is a potentiality that may or may not be developed. As a result, human beings are capable to a unique degree of living badly as well as living well: of no other animal could it be said that "it is sweet for most to live without order (*ataktōs*) rather than moderately" (*Pol.* 5, 1319b31–32). Laws and conventions of human construction are needed to help bring us to an awareness of what is best for us: "For when he has reached his *telos* the human being is the best of animals, but when apart from *nomos* and justice, the worst" (*Pol.* 1, 1253a31–33). The

[43] Thus Aristotle's teleological understanding of the place of language in human life differs from the two competing twentieth-century views identified by Taylor in "Language and Human Nature": language as an ideally unequivocal way of designating discrete objects in the world (the way of modern science) and language as a mysterious and boundless way of expressing and constituting our identity (the way of the romantic reaction against modern science).

[44] In Book 6 of the *NE*, Aristotle regularly says that we aim at the right *telos* through moral virtue, and choose the means to it (*ta pros ta telē*) through *phronēsis*. But means can constitute a goal as well as lead to it; to say that I am reading as a means to relaxation does not mean I read now and relax later. That Aristotle intends "means" constitutively here is persuasively argued by Cooper, *Reason and the Human Good*, pp. 19–24, and by Nussbaum, *De Motu Animalium*, p. 170 n. 13. It should also be noted that moral virtue and *phronēsis*, like desire and reason generally, are interlaced human attributes, separable in analysis but not in nature. See also *Pol.* 7, 1331b24–38, where the ends/means distinction is clarified by analogy with the doctor who must judge both what bodily health consists in for a patient and how to bring it about.

sense in which we are political animals can now be formulated in this way: Human beings are uniquely capable of, *and uniquely in need of,* a reasonable perception of their interest, and such a perception (and therefore a good life) is somehow dependent upon the presence of *nomoi.* (This connection between reasoning and law has a surface plausibility in Greek not immediately visible in translation, since *nomos* calls to mind not only the Homeric sense of "pasture" or place, but a common verb for believing or thinking, *nomizein.*)

Living politically means living with an eye to the laws, an order which Aristotle calls "reason without desire" (*Pol.* 3, 1287a32). But Aristotle never idealizes or romanticizes the political life, and we must be careful not to read the *Politics* as a civic humanist or republican alternative to liberal individualism. The business of politics, for Aristotle, is indeed education in virtue, but political life often appears as a necessary preliminary to fully human, fully deliberative action rather than the thing itself. In Book 10 of the *Nicomachean Ethics,* the question of how we become good is raised; living according to laws is there said to be essential throughout life because unmediated *logos* is not strong enough to overcome most people's occasional resistance to moderation and living well in general (1179b31–1180a5). *Nomos* is such a wonderful contrivance because, unlike the rule of human beings, it has the power to compel without seeming to compel: "But the *nomos* has the power to compel as a *logos,* coming from some sort of *phronēsis* and *nous.* Besides, people hate those who oppose their impulses, even if this is rightly done; but the *nomos* is not oppressive (*epachthēs*) when it orders decency" (1180a21–24). The political life thus understood appears neither as the peak of human excellence nor as a strategy for protecting individual rights or powers. Perhaps the best way to characterize it in modern terms would be to say that it answers to the human need for authority, for a structure of reasonable prejudice to support and sustain good ways of life.[45]

---

[45] I am thinking of authority in Arendt's sense, as "an obedience in which men retain their freedom." "What Is Authority?" p. 106. Arendt, to be sure, denies that Greek political philosophy entertained any such concept, and says that the word is of Roman origin; I will take issue with her very influential reading of Aristotle in Chapter 4. The problem of authority in the modern world is lucidly discussed by Sennett in *Authority.* The Gadamerian rehabilitation of tradition is also relevant here, as is Bruce James Smith, *Politics and Remembrance,* chap. 5. Cf. Rousseau's discussion in *Emile* (Bk. 2, *Oeuvres Complètes,* vol. 2, pp. 361–362) of the need for the education by humans to be concealed as education by things. The point in all these cases is that there is a human need for unobtrusive ordering.

The complex relationship of politics and human virtue is also indicated by the fact that the *Politics* and the *Nicomachean Ethics* both conclude with comments that rank the political life below a "theoretical" life, on the grounds that politics cannot be, as the best life must, an end in itself; even though it is an indispensable support for virtue, political activity does not constitute virtue (*NE* 10, 1177b2–1178a8), at least not of the highest order. What does? Aristotle argues, though not conclusively, that theoretical or philosophic activity is better, but is not at all precise as to what such activities would be. In particular, he does not limit theorizing to the kind of philosophic inquiry he himself is undertaking, and even suggests some very accessible activities that can approximate the theoretical character of philosophy in supporting a virtue more continuous and intrinsic than the political kind. These are the activities of musical culture, discussed in *Politics* 8, and of friendship, discussed in Books 8–9 of the *Nicomachean Ethics* and Book 7 of the *Eudemian Ethics*.[46]

Understanding the complex relationship between politics and virtue is the central task of social science: how are living well, the rational perception of our interest, and the political life connected? Clarification is required at three major points: What does "living well" mean? What does it mean to say that this is an object of rational perception? And in what way is political life a condition for living well, however understood?

The first of these questions is taken up in Book 1 of the *Nicomachean Ethics*, where Aristotle suggests that we live well (or are virtuous, that is, display human *aretē*) insofar as our lives are ordered by the specifically human *telos*, or goal. But strangely enough to our ears, this goal is expressed not in terms of some transcendent ideal or rule of obligation, but as a mean,[47] which in turn is defined

[46] "Music" is said to be of several kinds and to have several functions: mere relaxation from labors, habituation in proper desiring, but also the development of a way of life (*diagōgē*) and of *phronēsis* (*Pol.* 8, 1339a19–26), just as drawing should be taught for the sake of developing a theoretical eye for physical beauty (1338b1–2). In reading *diagōgē* as "way of life" rather than the more trivial "pastime," I follow Newman, *Politics*, vol. 3, pp. 449, 488; Warren D. Anderson, *Ethos and Education*, p. 270, and Lord, *Education and Culture*, pp. 56–57. Friendship (*philia*) also is of three kinds and aims at three things: pleasures, utility, and virtue. The last of the three is again the best, and it is so because having a good friend allows the supremely happy person "to theorize actions that are decent and one's own" (*theōrein . . . praxeis epieikeis kai oikeias*) (*NE* 9, 1170a2–3). For this reading of the place of music, see Lord, "Politics and Philosophy," and *Education and Culture*, chaps. 2 and 3; on friendship, see Cooper, "Aristotle on Friendship," and Sherman, "Friendship and the Shared Life."

[47] See Clark, *Aristotle's Man*, pp. 84–97. The human good is similarly depicted in

as an appropriate *logos* or proportion of opposing tendencies. This metaphoric human-good-as-mean is said by Aristotle to refer to a *hexis*, a word that turns out to be quite difficult to render into English. *Hexis* is a key term in Aristotle's social science, and that science is made inaccessible to us when it is translated by words like "characteristic" or "habit" or "trained ability." Perhaps the best way to get at its sense is by example. If I say, "Mary is courageous," or "Mary is a coward," I am describing Mary's *hexis*, making a statement about those relatively stable and continuous qualities—desires, feelings, thoughts—that define Mary as an individual. Relative to her biological inheritance (or genotype), Mary's *hexis* is an actuality or actualization of a particular potentiality (and reflects the discarding or nondevelopment of other potentialities); relative to her actions, it is a sort of potentiality—bad luck or other pressures may prevent a courageous person from actually doing courageous deeds.[48] One's *hexis* is of course subject to change over time, but the term designates those qualities in an individual that are relatively firm and definite at any given moment, the qualities that identify individuals as more, or at any rate other, than a bundle of unrealized potentials. The closest English word to *hexis* in this context might be "personality," if we understand by that the qualities that define a person and distinguish him or her from others. To live well for Aristotle is thus to have (or "be") a good personality, and the primary task of the social scientist is to determine as far as possible what such a personality looks like, or what sorts of personalities are better than others, in the sense of being better blends or mixtures of the drives and capacities out of which all human beings are constituted.

But interpreting *hexis* as personality involves real distortion, insofar as "personality" ordinarily refers only to human beings, and so conceals the way in which reference to *hexis* introduces Aristotle's technical language of potentiality and actuality into the discussion of human action.[49] For this reason, Terence Irwin's "state"

---

terms of this mathematical-medical metaphor in several of the later Platonic dialogues: *Statesman* 283e3–284c3; *Philebus* 66a4–8.

[48] *Hexis* is thus called a "first actuality" in *De Anima* 2, 417a21–b16. *Dunamis* (potentiality), *hexis*, and *energeia* (actuality) are not three different substances, but rather three different points along a continuum marking the degree to which a particular organism is less or more strongly individuated or defined, beginning with (as a limiting case) limitless potentiality or "matter" and concluding with (again as a limiting case, not something occurring in nature) continuous determinate activity or function.

[49] Prior to Aristotle, the term was used in something like this sense by Plato and

might be the single best translation.[50] At any rate, in the *Categories* (8b25–9a13), *hexis* is defined generally as a certain quality (*poion*) "by virtue of which things are what they are." Thus all organisms, insofar as they are substances composed of elements organized or ordered in a certain way, can be said to exhibit a *hexis* (or at any rate a *diathesis*, which is simply a less stable *hexis*). The term plays the key role of bringing into social scientific discourse the Aristotelian picture of the natural world as one in which individuals are ordered wholes rather than heaps of elements, and thus raises for us the comparison with the Enlightenment world of loose and separate (in Hume's words) events. Thus, health and sickness are *hexeis* of bodies, and stating the *hexis* of a substance is even said to be another way of describing its actuality (*energeia*) (*Metaphysics* Delta, 1022b4–14).[51]

But while the introduction of the potentiality/actuality continuum into Aristotle's social science suggests a difference from the empiricist's world-view, it is more important to note that for Aristotle the key terms of social science are not distinct from the categories of the other natural sciences, as modern interpretive social science would suggest. Our *psuchē* is analogous to our body in that it can be either well or badly ordered. More precisely, we need to recall here that soul and body are not things or objects but complementary attributes of individuals: each individual has a certain actuality (soul) and potentiality (body) proper to it, and the soul is simply a higher level of organization than body for that individual, where "higher" refers to nearness to those activities that specifically define the individual as who or what it is. One way to speak of illness in all animals, human beings included, is to say that it is the unnatural condition in which our body rules our soul, when the battle to stay alive—to remain an irreducible organism—effaces the possibility of living well (*Pol.* 1, 1254a39–b4).

Just as the healthy involuntary motions of the body can be identified by reference to a healthy (or normal) physical condition,[52] so

by the medical writers. Some Platonic instances are *Theaetetus* 153b9 and 197b1, and *Sophist* 247a5.

[50] Irwin, *Nicomachean Ethics*, pp. 426–427. *Hexis* is used less frequently in the *Pol.*, but at 1265a35 he speaks of *hexeis hairetai* ("choiceworthy dispositions," in Lord's translation) while at 1334b19 he uses the word to refer to actualizations of different parts of the soul.

[51] But compare *NE* 1, 1095b30–1096a1, in which moral virtue is said to be a *hexis* and happiness (*eudaimonia*) an *energeia*. There is no real contradiction: how we describe the position of an organism on the potentiality/actuality continuum depends on our point of comparison.

[52] See Boorse, "Health as a Theoretical Concept."

healthy voluntary actions are defined by reference to a good or healthy personality. Of course, Aristotle is aware that both the elements and the correct blend or proportion are more difficult to grasp in the realm of action than in that of bodily health (*NE* 5, 1137a13–14), but he can at least begin by asserting that if virtue or excellence is a *hexis*, then good actions are those performed by good (*spoudaios* or *phronimos*) human beings. Actions cannot be called good or bad by reference to some universally applicable moral rule, like the categorical imperative or the principle that one should seek the greatest happiness of the greatest number. Aristotle and the various schools of modern psychiatry might disagree radically concerning the specific character of a healthy personality, but they are in fundamental agreement that the basis for any understanding of human affairs must be a perception of what constitutes a well-ordered person, just as the practice of medicine must begin with a perception of what constitutes a healthy somatic condition.

Political Resolutions and Human Problems

We live well insofar as we perceive what living well is, and act according to that perception. This is also true of physical well-being, but with one important difference: we are much less likely spontaneously to perceive our interest in becoming good persons than we are to perceive our interest in becoming healthy. Our actions and motivating desires come to be informed by a perception of the good human life as a result, in the first instance, of the process of education or socialization implicit in the laws and customs of our culture.[53] Good human beings act on the basis of rational choice, but to achieve the possibility of rational conduct we require a long period of habituation, a sort of aesthetic education demanded by the thinness of our biological inheritance as compared with our specific virtue: "For all art (*technē*) and education wish to supply what is lacking in nature" (*Pol.* 7, 1337a1–3). Every culture can thus be seen as implying an answer to the question of the best

[53] I am using "culture" here as an equivalent of Aristotle's *politeia*. The *politeia* is the form or order (*taxis*) of a given *polis* (*Pol.* 3, 1274b38, 1276b5–10). A *polis* is its particular *politeia* (as a particular game is baseball), and when the *politeia* changes the *polis* changes, even if people, buildings, and so on remain the same. The best discussion of the meaning of *politeia* is in Strauss, *Natural Right and History*, pp. 135–138. Given present English usage, I think "culture" approximates *politeia* more closely than "regime," but since neither term evokes *politeia* with perfect accuracy, I will use them interchangeably in the text.

life, or at any rate the best under the circumstances. This implicit solution is the significance or *function* of cultural and political organization, even though the most powerful *motive* for the establishment and maintenance of the political order is not the desire to live well, but the desire to live or to live together: "The *polis* comes into being for the sake of living, but it *is* for the sake of living well" (*Pol.* 1, 1253b29–30). The curious and decisive fact about human life is that we have a profound biological need for an institution that will shape our desires into healthy patterns, but a relatively weak natural impulse (*hormē*) toward institutions of that sort (as opposed to our powerful natural impulse to form families or clans). Such political inclinations as we do inherit need to be supplemented by our much stronger social inclinations toward institutions that provide security or company rather than *paideia*. Thus it is not surprising that most existing cultures are not well designed for the purpose that justifies them, but are instead promiscuous or random heaps of *ad hoc* custom and legislation (*Pol.* 7, 1324b5–6). Such cities are *poleis* in name only (as a corpse is a human body in name only) and may in fact be nothing more than concealed forms of despotism, the rule of the master over slaves.

Still, we cannot do without political life, without the process of habituation through customs and the practice in ruling and being ruled that are the necessary supports for human rationality. Since we cannot become virtuous solely by individual effort, the shaping or habituating influence of law and custom is a necessary condition for the development of virtuous or flourishing personalities: it is biologically absurd of us to hope to skip over culture, or to replace it with a set of rational principles. Thus music education, which trains us to be pleased by and, whenever we can, to emulate exemplary characters or personalities, is the most significant though not the most pressing part of political life (*Pol.* 8, 1337a11–12).

But this process of socialization is sufficient only to the extent that the conventions which inform it are in turn informed by a true conception of the human good *and* by a solid grasp of local circumstances. Just as a personality or a way of life may be based on a mistaken perception of what it means to live well, so may a *polis* or culture. Thus, there will almost always be a difference between a good human being without qualification and a good citizen of a particular city, and this in two ways: the conception of the human good implicit in the city's laws may be mistaken; and even if it is not, the good citizen must accept the interpretations of the laws made by others even if they seem less than fully rational, except when that citizen in turn holds political office (*Pol.* 3, 1276b16ff.). In spite of these problems, we need politics and *nomoi*, and thus the social scientist's task is not that of fashioning a utopian alternative institution. On the other hand, because of the intrinsic limits of political life, it is equally insufficient simply to interpret the internal significance of the conventions of existing cities; rather, the business of the social scientist is to criticize and offer guidance to these cities in the light of an adequate conception of the human good or psychic health, a notion that is surely opposed to the goals of interpretive social science.

But this task of criticizing and reforming cultures is not so easy. It is a difficult and problematic project partly because politics is an unintended consequence of activity with other ends in view (that is, because the motives for political life are not the same as the reasons for it),[54] and partly because of the unique importance of individuality and circumstance in human affairs. The essential variability of solutions to the human problem, which itself causes the peculiar difficulty and imprecision of social science as Aristotle understands it, has in turn two causes: human diversity and the multifunctional character of political organization. The fact of diversity does not simply mean that some human beings are in various ways better or worse than others (which is also true for many other species), but refers to the way human individuals differ with respect to biologically inherited potentiality much more than individuals of any other species. Humans, unlike other kinds of beings, can be beasts or gods and much else in between. Individuals are at their best when their elements are ordered in accordance with a mean, but since psychic capacity for action varies at least as much as somatic aptitudes for health, a good personality must be

---

[54] It is important to distinguish Aristotle's view here from the interpretive conception of human beings as "incomplete animals." As can be seen in Geertz, *Interpretation of Cultures*, such a position derives largely though perhaps unconsciously from nineteenth-century German philosophy:

> The tool-making, laughing, or lying animal, man, is also the incomplete—or, more accurately, self-completing—animal. The agent of his own realization, he creates out of his own general capacity for the construction of symbolic models the specific capabilities that define him. Or—to return at last to our subject—it is through the construction of ideologies, schematic images of social order, that man makes himself for better or worse a political animal. (p. 218)

For Aristotle—as opposed to Geertz and Hegel—all animals are the agents of their own realization, and human beings are political animals prior to any human activity. Politics is one of our specific potentials, not the doorway out of nature.

a mean relative to each individual's capacities and circumstances (*NE* 2, 1106b36–1107a1).

The problems caused by the multifunctionality of political life are even more complex, and more interesting for social science. The essential or definitive purpose of politics—its reason for being—is the development of flourishing or virtuous persons. But this defining activity—living well—depends upon the simultaneous presence of two other activities: before we can live well, we must both live and live together; *eu zēn* is the goal, but this presupposes the achievement of some tolerable level of *zēn* (security) and *suzēn* (integration) (*Pol.* 3, 1280b30–35). Survival or stability and political integration (a minimum of *stasis*, or civil disorder) are only necessary conditions for good politics, but they are very necessary. Moreover, the relationship between the necessary and the constitutive conditions of good politics cannot be viewed as a temporal sequence: we can't take care of them one at a time. So long as we remain the kind of animals that we are, we will not live forever, and we will continue to inherit both sociable and unsociable impulses.[55]

Political organization and authority are not fully justified unless the *nomoi* of that organization are reasonable means toward the development of healthy personalities, but that organization cannot continue to exist unless those same *nomoi* are also reasonable ways of providing for the security of the *polis* and maintaining a good level of integration or civil friendship. Individuals lead a single life within a single *polis*, but this life is inevitably an ordering of different and sometimes conflicting needs. Now, if the *nomoi* best suited to achieving the constitutive aim of politics (educating virtuous

[55] There is no standard Aristotelian formula for expressing this distinction between necessary and constitutive causes, although the distinction is crucial for *politikē*. One clear formulation of the distinction is that between a *sunaition* (co-cause or accessory) and an *aition* (cause as such) in *De Anima* 2, 416a12–15: heat is the *sunaition* of growth while soul is the *aition*. Plato uses the same terms for the same distinction in *Statesman* 281d8–e10. Two important Platonic discussions of causality make something like this distinction without using the same terms. In *Phaedo* 99a4–b6, Socrates distinguishes between genuine causes of his own actions (purposes) and things without which such causes cannot operate (bones and sinews, bodies), saying that people commonly and wrongly give the name cause to necessary conditions. In *Phaedrus* 268a8–269a3, Socrates uses the medical metaphor of the difference between knowing the effects of drugs and knowing how to cure patients to distinguish between preliminary conditions for writing good tragedies (knowing how to produce different dramatic effects) and knowing how to write tragedies simply (knowledge of "harmony"). In all these cases, two aspects of causality recur: one of the two kinds of causes is more truly a cause, and yet causality is irreducibly dual.

persons) were also in every case those most appropriate for achieving its simultaneous necessary conditions (peace and integration), then social science could in principle provide precise answers to questions concerning the sorts of *nomoi* that could best serve the ends of the *polis*. But the requirements of virtue and those of peace and integration seldom coincide; at the heart of the problem of human affairs lies a tension among conflicting needs that does not admit of precise theoretical resolution.[56]

This tension emerges in Book 3 of the *Politics* in the discussion of who should be admitted to citizenship. Citizens, for Aristotle, are those who actively engage in the deliberations of public life, not simply those whose rights are to be protected by public authority.[57] Given this, the question of the appropriate requirements for citizenship seems at first to pose no serious problem for the theorist: since the constitutive purpose of politics is moral education as understood by the laws, only those who are most capable of becoming virtuous should be admitted to citizenship, and so those who spend their lives in labor or commerce cannot be admitted without distorting the purposes of the political order. This is so even though labor and commerce (as well as military pursuits) are necessary for the existence of the *polis*: "For this is true, that not all those without whom the *polis* would not be must be made citizens" (*Pol.* 3, 1278a2–3).

The argument here seems to be less a matter of antidemocratic bias (Aristotle, as we shall see, clearly prefers democracies to oligarchies)[58] than a theoretical reflection on the link between our manner of earning a living and our attitude toward the laws and the *polis*. The argument may be stated as follows: *Poleis* will be well governed only to the extent that citizen-governors have or are virtuous *hexeis*; otherwise, the resources of the *polis* are likely to be

[56] Strauss presents this tension in these terms: "The political problem consists in reconciling the requirement for wisdom with the requirement for consent." *Natural Right and History*, p. 141. Ignatieff sees a similar tension emerging from the interplay of the needs for freedom, for solidarity, and for ultimate meaning. *Needs of Strangers*, pp. 17–18.

[57] Citizenship means participating or sharing (*metechein*) in public offices and decisions (*Pol.* 3, 1275a23–24) and not simply being entitled to protection against unjust acts (1280b11–13).

[58] He prefers aristocracy, or rule of the best, to both, but is quite explicit that democracy is, as a rule, much closer to aristocracy than oligarchy is (*Pol.* 3, 1289b2–5): "So that tyranny is the worst [of the deviant regimes—those aiming at the rulers' benefit only] and the furthest from being a real *politeia*; oligarchy is second worst (for aristocracy stands far away from this *politeia*), while democracy is the most appropriate (*metriotatē*) of them."

used for the wrong purposes. Leisure is needed for the development of a virtuous *hexis* and hence for the development of the capacity to act politically. Leisure certainly does not *constitute* virtue—people raised in luxury tend to arrogance and cannot learn to be ruled (*Pol.* 4, 1295b17–18)—but someone whose life by chance or choice is consumed by work or commerce cannot be a good citizen. Nevertheless, these unleisurely ways of life are absolutely necessary for the survival of the *polis*—even as they tend to distort political justice in favor of the economic claims of essentially economic people. Therefore, some whose ways of life are necessary for *poleis* must as far as possible be excluded from active citizenship if the *polis* is not to be twisted by the pressing claims of private or economic interest.[59]

The need for excluding such people seems clearly established at *Politics* 3, 1278a; but only a few pages further on we are told that the problem of citizenship has not in fact been resolved: "There is an *aporia* [perplexity or puzzle] concerning who must be sovereign (*to kurion*) in the city" (1281a11). But why? If the sole business of politics were education in virtue, there would be no *aporia* concerning who should rule; only those who are most virtuous themselves and most capable of recognizing and encouraging excellence in others would have a reasonable claim to citizenship. But since the *polis* must provide stability as well (not to mention civil harmony or friendship), propertyholders and, indeed, all free persons also have a teleologically reasonable claim to the honor of citizenship, "for free people and possessors of taxable property are necessary, since there could be no *polis* composed entirely of the poor, just as there could be none composed of slaves" (1283a17–19).

There is thus no unequivocal theoretical solution to the central question of who should govern—barring the extremely unlikely limiting case of the appearance of a thoroughly godlike human being (*Pol.* 7, 1332b24). If such a person were to appear, it would seem that politics—*nomoi* and rotation in office—would no longer be necessary for moral education: who wants a medical textbook when a doctor is at hand? But Aristotle argues that in this case the medical analogy is false, since doctors earn their pay by curing the sick and aren't likely to favor friends (*Pol.* 3, 1287a32–37). Thus

[59] As with the argument about the causes and cures of crime discussed in Chapter 1, this one is a combination of contestable predictive and functional propositions: one could argue that workers or merchants tend to care about their city, or that the reason for politics is the protection of economic interest.

even in this case Aristotle suggests that it would be safer to allow the laws of the *polis* to rule, since "passion perverts even the best when they are ruling" (*Pol.* 3, 1287a31–32).[60]

A determination will thus have to be made in each case concerning how far to modify the claims of excellence in view of the subordinate, though indispensable, requirements of stability and integration. This variety of political requirements mirrors the distinct character of separate human needs *and* the overarching need to deal with those needs simultaneously and in a coordinated way. Each political choice has some impact, in Aristotle's terms, on the provision of material benefits (matters of economy and defense), political benefits (answering our need for a strong political community based on friendship and consent), and moral benefits (reflecting the human need for the encouragement of thoughtful and moderate characters). The final judgment in each case as to how the balance must be struck will be the work of the wise citizen (the *phronimos*) who has a solid grasp of the possibilities and dangers of local conditions, and not the social scientist (although there is no reason why a social scientist might not also happen to be a *phronimos* in a given case). General theory based on considerations of human nature and the human good or goods is not dangerous or irrelevant to political life, as interpretive social science characteristically claims, since only through such theorizing can we gain a clear sense of the problems that politics must solve; but an adequate social scientific theory reveals its own limitations in showing that the problems it brings to light do not admit of precise theoretical solutions.

The tension produced by the multifunctionality of political order becomes even more evident in Books 4–6 of the *Politics*, as the discussion shifts from the question of what constitutes the simply best political order to the question of the sources of stability and internal tranquility in *poleis*. In outline, the problem is this: leisure is a necessary condition for moral education and for political *praxis* generally, but a low level of leisure appears to be an equally necessary condition for the development of the internal stability without which a *polis* cannot exist. Thus in Book 4, Aristotle develops the argument that the most stable (and least unjust) political cultures are those in which leisure and hence genuinely deliberative political activity are at a relatively low level, such as those *poleis* in

---

[60] But the possibility is so unlikely as to be negligible; even ordinarily virtuous people are a small minority (*Pol.* 3, 1302a1–2).

which farmers and small propertyholders are the preponderant power (*Pol.* 4, 1292b25–29 and 1295a25–31). In an argument that bears an interesting resemblance to Madison's praise of the extended commercial republic in *Federalist* 10, Aristotle contends that people who have to work for a living will be the least ambitious, the least likely to oppress one another, and—an important and peculiarly Aristotelian element—the most likely to live together in friendship (*Pol.* 4, 1295aff.; 6, 1318b6–17). But as soon as we recall that the constitutive goal of politics is not civic friendship (or integration) but virtue, we are forced to conclude that the hard-working heroes of Book 4 must be excluded from citizenship in the best-ordered city. Aristotle draws this conclusion himself in Book 7: "It is clear from these things that in the most finely ordered *polis* . . . it is necessary that the citizens live neither a worker's nor a merchant's life . . . nor should they be farmers, since leisure is necessary both for the development of *aretē* and for political *praxis*" (*Pol.* 7, 1328b37–1329a2).

The conclusions of Books 3 and 7 do not contradict those of Book 4; rather, they point to the tension characteristic of the subject matter of social science, the political order within which human excellence can be formed. The definitive or constitutive purpose of that order is the business of shaping our perception of our interest—of what is humanly good for us—so that we may, as the Aristotelian formula expresses it, live well (*eu zēn*). But this cannot occur unless several important conditions are satisfied simultaneously, conditions summarized in the formulaic terms "living" (*zēn*) and "living together" (*suzēn*). The *nomoi* best suited to achieving the necessary conditions of political life—to providing real material and political benefits—are often not the *nomoi* best suited to developing virtue in those who live and die within their light.

This does not mean that politics is an inherently absurd or paradoxical or tragic activity. Political life can be improved in a variety of ways, and the *Politics* is filled with detailed advice as to how this might be done in different situations. But while this life is both improvable and irreplaceable, Aristotle's political reflection leads to the conclusion that the political community is in some way insufficient, or at least in need of supplementation by other kinds of relationships and activities that may serve more directly the human interest in living reasonably. Thus, both the *Politics* and the *Nicomachean Ethics* conclude with reference to the possible superiority of philosophic inquiry to good citizenship. But more is involved here than a confrontation between philosophy and politics, which Aristotle takes up as a standard and already well developed controversy among people serious about virtue; in addition, we are asked to reflect on ways in which other activities, like music (*Pol.* 8), can constitute rationality, as well as on the importance of certain nonpolitical relationships—especially the family (*oikos*) and different kinds of friendship (*philia*)—for education in virtue. Some of these matters, especially music and friendship, are also to be considered from a political point of view; but it is quite clear that the best kind of music and the best kind of friendships cannot be seen as subordinate parts of the political community.[61] Just as there can be no simple theoretical answer to political questions, there can be no such solution to the general question of whether politics as such is an intrinsic human good. This is in no way to reject politics, but rather to suggest that solutions to political problems—or to problems about human lives as such—will always (so long as our nature is what it is) be somehow perplexed and imprecise. What will be the character and limits of the theoretical inquiry that addresses these questions, if indeed such inquiry is possible?

First of all, it will not be an easy inquiry. Social science would not be difficult if it were simply a matter of interpreting the *nomoi* of a particular *polis*, "because it is not hard to have understanding concerning those things which the *nomoi* say." The purpose of political inquiry, however, is not merely interpretive understanding—adding to the archives of human political narratives—but evaluation and criticism of cultures in light of the possibility of better *nomoi* as conceived from a more universal perspective than that of the *polis. Nomoi* always seem just to those who love them as their own, but in reality (that is, from a theoretical perspective) they may or may not be just: "these things [the things the laws say] are not just things (*ta dikaia*), except contingently (*kata sumbebēkos*)" (*NE* 5, 1137a9–12). Moreover, hard as it is to determine whether an ordering is just, it is even more difficult to persuade people to be just when they have the power to act unjustly; social science must always contend with a rhetorical problem (*Pol.* 6, 1318b1–5).

Nevertheless, difficult and imprecise as the conclusions of social

---

[61] Just as political music aims to develop moral virtue, while the best music aims at *phronēsis* (*Pol.* 8, 1339b5), political friendship is based on mutual advantage rather than on mutual concern with another's virtue (which is perfect or definitive friendship). Thus it is impossible to have many "real" friends, but we can have many political friendships (*NE* 9, 1171a15–19)—indeed, political *philia* seems to be the greatest of goods for cities because it reduces *stasis* (*Pol.* 2, 1262b7–9). I will discuss the different forms of friendship at greater length in Chapter 6.

science must be, they are not for that reason indeterminate or arbitrary; although it is not possible to say what the best *nomoi* are in abstraction from the particular circumstances of each *polis*, there is still one way of ordering human affairs that will be best at any given time for each (as opposed to every) *polis*.[62] This element of determinacy and universality arises from the possibility of understanding teleologically the natural functions of political activity in human life, and of evaluating existing polities in terms of their success or failure in performing these functions: "Human beings combine for the sake of some interest (*sumpheron*), to provide some of the things necessary for life. And the political community seems to be for the sake of interest . . . and this is what lawgivers aim at, and they say that the just is the common [or universal] interest (*to koinēi sumpheron*) . . . not with respect to present interest, but with respect to life as a whole" (*NE* 8, 1160a9–23). Political activity is neither a self-generating end in itself nor an association for the protection of individual rights; its constitutive and justifying function is the development of virtuous personalities and ways of life (*Pol.* 3, 1280b6–12)—that is, moral education—an activity that social science can criticize and guide but can never replace.

In a sense one can say that social science is continuous with political activity in that it addresses the same basic question, "How should we order our lives?" But as *epistēmē*[63] it addresses this question from the more universal perspective of the human good or goods as such, rather than from the necessarily parochial and culturally specific perspective of what is currently good for ourselves and our polity. Thus, from an Aristotelian point of view social science cannot simply be an orderly reconstruction of the perspective of the citizen (as it is for Geertz), nor can it replace that perspective with a perfectly adequate general theory (as in the Hobbesian dream of empiricist social science). Aristotle's social science aims to improve local discussion about politics—or education[64]—not to

[62] *NE* 5, 1135a5. This passage has received several readings. I follow Mulhern, "Mia Monon Pantachou kata Physin hē aretē." As Strauss argues (*Natural Right and History*, p. 159), for Aristotle, natural right or law resides ultimately in particular decisions, and not in universal laws or principles. Gadamer states the implications of this view: "The idea of natural law has, for Aristotle, only a critical function. No dogmatic use can be made of it, i.e., we cannot invest particular laws with the dignity and inviolability of natural law." *Truth and Method*, p. 285.

[63] "For the sciences are said to be and indeed are about the universal" (*NE* 10, 1180b15–16).

[64] "For perhaps anyone who wants to make others better through care, whether many people or few, must become versed in legislative science (*nomothetikē*), if through laws we become good" (*NE* 10, 1180b23–25).

replace that discussion with universal laws, or step back from it to spin coherent narratives out of what the natives say.

The Tasks and Limits of Social Science

What then are the appropriate questions for the social scientist? At the beginning of Book 4 of the *Politics*, Aristotle lists the four problems that an adequate social science must address. First, there must be a theoretical understanding (*theōrēsai*) of the best regime, if we assume the most favorable necessary conditions of stability, integration, and individual potentiality. The discussion of the theorists of the best regime in Book 2 falls in this category, as do Aristotle's own institutional suggestions about the best possible city in Book 7. Aristotle characteristically prefaces such discussions by saying that he is about to consider how politics should be organized under conditions that are "according to a prayer" (*kat' euchēn*).[65] Such conditions, those in which material security and civic friendship can be taken for granted, are objects of prayer not because they are impossible, but rather because their highly unlikely occurrence would be a matter of chance rather than conscious planning (*Pol.* 7, 1331b22). Aristotle's best regime in Book 7 is not an unfounded dream, since it makes no extravagant assumptions about changes in human psychology (*Pol.* 7, 1323a13–15). But the institutions of *Politics* 7 cannot be an agenda or blueprint for legislators or reformers, since the conditions they presuppose can come about only by the remotest of chances.

The second task described in Book 4 is knowing what regime will be best under less than optimal, providential conditions, when we cannot take stability and integration for granted. Aristotle's answer for his Greek world is provided in the discussion of the middle-class polity and of farming democracy in Book 4. Third, the social scientist must be able to say how any political culture, no matter how imperfect, can be made more stable and coherent—how, in other words, to bring about the necessary (as opposed to constitutive) conditions of political activity. This forms the subject matter of *Politics* 5, with its lengthy and painstaking discussion of how democracies, oligarchies, and even tyrannies can reduce internal conflict. This section of the *Politics* contains the greatest density of predictive explanations of the kind familiar to empiricist social science, but even here the discussion is informed by the

[65] *Pol.* 2, 1260a29; 4, 1288b23, 1295a29; 7, 1325b36.

evaluative hypothesis that any regime can be made less unjust by being made more stable, even though a stable regime is not necessarily a good or just political ordering. Finally, the social scientist must know the techniques of bringing existing regimes closer to the best, and so must understand the ways and uses of reform and persuasion. Aristotle is particularly insistent that while these four questions cannot be collapsed into one, they are nonetheless part of a single science, rather than different ways of considering human affairs. This insistence is repeated at the end of the *Nicomachean Ethics*, where it is argued that the social scientist must understand both the purpose or function of political life—*eu zēn*—and the ways different cultures implicitly carry out that function, and that knowledge of this science is required not only by potential legislators but by "anyone who wants to make others better through care, whether many people or few" (*NE* 10, 1180b23–24).

But what kind of science is this? Are there any other sciences that can serve as paradigms or metaphors for social scientific inquiry? Clearly mathematical physics cannot, since cultures vary too much to be subsumed under a set of precise general laws (although many lawlike generalizations about political life are both possible and highly informative). Nor can we look to literary analysis for guidance; social science must indeed "read" the meaning of regimes or cultures, but it cannot take the coherence of their *nomoi* for granted, nor can it assume that every relatively coherent *polis* (such as Sparta) is for that reason, or simply because it understands itself as such, a good *polis*. Yet social science is not sui generis; Aristotle has continual recourse to one other science in his discussions of social scientific adequacy and the relation of social science to other kinds of thought, and this is the science of medicine.[66]

In the first place, the physician, like the social scientist, must have experience of particular individuals as well as general causal knowledge of both kinds (*Metaphysics* Alpha, 981a12–29). Like medicine (or physical training), an adequate social science requires both an experience of cases and general theory; neither element can satisfactorily replace or be reduced to the other. But why is this true of social science? And if it is true, why is Aristotle compelled to rely so heavily on medical analogies—and risk misleading through disanalogy—to illustrate correct social scientific proce-

[66] Lloyd, "Role of Medical and Biological Analogies," and Jaeger, "Aristotle's Use of Medicine," collect and discuss the relevant citations. Clark's analysis is especially provocative. *Aristotle's Man*, pp. 84–97.

dure? We may approach these questions by considering the four characteristics that according to the first two books of the *Nicomachean Ethics* distinguish social science from other sciences: its relative imprecision; its dependence on the proper habituation or upbringing of the scientist; its dependence on the maturity of the scientist; and its instrumental character. The truth or falsehood of these contentions depends on the subject matter of social science—human conventions and cultures construed as criticizable attempts at solving the uniquely human problem of how to live well under a particular set of circumstances. Aristotle's claim is that given the nature of its subject, the scope of social science is limited by certain restrictions (imprecision and instrumentality), and its successful pursuit is dependent upon certain external conditions (the good upbringing and maturity of the scientist).

In Book 1 of the *Nicomachean Ethics*, Aristotle states that the precision of any art or science depends on its underlying subject matter, and that social science is particularly imprecise: "The noble and just things, which *politikē* studies, have so much variation and irregularity that they seem to be by *nomos* alone and not by *phusis*" (*NE* 1, 1094b14–16). He amplifies this point, comparing social science to medicine, in Book 2: "In matters concerning *praxis* and the things that are in our interest (*ta sumpheronta*), just as in matters of health, there is nothing fixed" (*NE* 2, 1104a3–5). The good social scientist must know two kinds of things, neither of which can be known precisely. The first is the human good, the *telos* or function of both individual and *polis* (*NE* 1, 1094b6–7). This is expressed in different places as flourishing or happiness (*eudaimonia*), or that which is in our interest (*to sumpheron*), or excellence or virtue (*aretē*). The human good can be known in general[67]—it is a deliberative way of life, the kind of *hexis* or personality analogically compared to a mean—but it cannot be known precisely for each individual, given the diversity of biologically and culturally inherited problems each of us must simultaneously solve.

The second kind of thing the social scientist must know (logically dependent on the first) is the just things, that is, those laws and customs that tend to promote the human good. Imprecision enters here because the *nomoi* that are just in one place will not

---

[67] Social science is imprecise compared to some other sciences but is nonetheless determinate. While its subject matter cannot be precisely defined, it does admit of definition in outline; although it is impossible to know with certainty which ways of life are better than others, the human good has limits or boundaries and is hence definable. *NE* 2, 1106b30.

necessarily be just in another. Nevertheless, for each place there will be one set of *nomoi* that are most just relative to the human good and to the particular circumstances of that place and time, even though it is impossible to know with certainty what they are. In the discussion of justice in Book 5 of the *Nicomachean Ethics*, Aristotle responds to the doubt he had earlier raised about whether justice can be said to be by nature (whether *nomoi* can be evaluated and criticized in terms of some determinate natural standard) in the following way: "among us, some things are by nature even though they are changeable" (*NE* 5, 1134b29–30). Social *science*—explaining the human things through theorizing universal aspects of human life—is possible, but its most important findings cannot be presented and transmitted as a set of fixed and precise rules or precepts (*NE* 2, 1104a7–9), as can those of sciences like mathematics and, to some degree, medicine (*Pol.* 3, 1287a33–35).

The assertion that a good upbringing is a necessary (though not sufficient) condition for the development of a competent social scientist is likely to strike us as hopelessly prescientific. But Aristotle is not claiming that only members of the upper classes can be good social scientists. His argument is that in order to get a preliminary grasp of the central concept of social science, the variety of human needs (or the human good, for short), it is necessary to have been habituated or socialized in such a way that we are inclined to perceive that there *is* a human good that is somehow different from our own spontaneous desires. This is simply another way of saying that we are biologically or genotypically unique in not spontaneously perceiving our own good, our interest in a well-organized life. So in *Nicomachean Ethics* 1 Aristotle says: "It is necessary to have been brought up nobly in order to understand sufficiently the noble things, the just things, and the political things as a whole."[68] The indispensable starting point of social science is a relatively inarticulate sense that there is a difference between a life (*bios*) or personality (*hexis*) that is flourishing and one that is not.

As we have seen, the human good is so composite and varied that knowledge of it cannot be transmitted in a set of precise theoretical precepts; it cannot be perceived at all except by an observer whose experience and *hexis* are relatively healthy. If poorly brought up, the observer will either have no coherent sense of the human good or be led to misperceive the good by a certain un-

---

[68] *NE* 1, 1104a7–9. Irwin's translation is a good commentary: "This is why we need to have been brought up in fine habits, if we are to be adequate students of what is fine and just, and of political questions generally."

soundness of *hexis* (*NE* 10, 1181b9–11). This is not a problem for sciences such as arithmetic and geometry that consider objects sufficiently simple to allow teaching by precept. The secondary element of social science, predictive knowledge of what sort of *nomoi* are likely to produce what sorts of consequences, can to a certain extent be transmitted in precepts or textbooks.[69] But such textbooks (or empirical studies) cannot be adequately employed by those who study them unless they have (or are) a good *hexis*, since without this basis they are incapable of making the relevant critical determinations: "those who go through such things without [the appropriate] *hexis* cannot judge them nobly" (*NE* 10, 1181b9–11). Such a person would be quite helpful in determining the effect of different tax proposals on income distribution, but would not be able to form a reasonable judgment about which were more just than others.

In Book 1 of the *Nicomachean Ethics* (1095a2–13), Aristotle presents two related reasons for thinking that youths (*hoi neoi*) are not prepared to study social science—lack of experience, and the tendency to be guided by passive emotion (*pathos*) rather than active *logos*: "a youth is not a suitable student of social science, for he is inexperienced in the actions (*apeiros praxeōn*) of life, and the arguments are drawn from and concern actions. . . . And it makes no difference whether he is young in age or in habits, for his defect is not a matter of time but comes from living according to emotion (*to kata pathos zēn*) and pursuing everything in this way." A preliminary teleological understanding of *praxis* as an attempt to solve the human problem of how to live well or according to our complex interests under particular circumstances—as opposed, say, to *praxis* understood in terms of some abstractly simple goal, such as maximizing pleasure or perpetuating genetic influence—requires experience. This experience cannot be replaced by textbook discussions of the nature of *praxis*, such as those provided by Book 1 of the *Nicomachean Ethics* and Book 7 of the *Politics*.[70] Moreover, it is a complex experience that cannot be had by those who interpret their own or others' doings through the lenses of passion or emotion. This experience of the human good or human interest, and the consequent recognition of the distinction between living and

[69] This was the purpose of the Aristotelian collection of regimes or "constitutions," of which the *Constitutions of the Athenians*, delineating the movement from moderate to extreme democracy in Athens, survives.

[70] For a critical discussion of the attempt by modern empirical social science to escape the maturity requirement, see Bellah, "Ethical Aims of Social Inquiry."

living well, comes about only through the generalizing operations of *logos*[71] rather than the senses. If we are incapable of seeing our actions and those of others as subject to criticism and justification, and view them instead through the lenses of our passionate likes and dislikes, we will be constitutionally incapable of forming an idea of human interest based on our experience of humans as humans, rather than as friends or enemies, good guys or bad guys, which from an Aristotelian point of view is the typically immature way of interpreting the human world. The distinction between youthful passion and mature reason, then, is not here a difference between heated commitment and indifferent reflection, but rather the difference between an observer who is a loosely knit collection of psychic parts and one who is closer to having become a distinct and irreducible organism.

Our initial experience of the human good thus involves grasping a thing or a name (*anthrōpos*, human being), rather than a relationship or a proposition (for example, that humans are the animals that have *logos*).[72] This relatively inarticulate experience is the starting point or *archē* of social science, and as an experience it is not something that can be demonstrated or derived from prior principles of that science or from any other science. Aristotle's psychology can never *prove* either that there is a human interest (or a final cause that marks human being as a real universal) or that the substance of this interest is a deliberative life supported by a variety of moral virtues. What it can do is seek to make our experience of this interest more precise and secure by setting forth the human capacities and problems that might render intelligible the conception of the human good revealed in it.

The human good is thus a phenomenon, yet one that is not immediately evident to the senses—a universal that cannot be im-

[71] Recall *Pol.* 1, 1253a14–15, on *logos* as the uniquely human ability to move beyond signifying pleasure and pain to being able to make plain or explain interest, and hence justice.

[72] In *Metaphysics* Theta, 1051b22ff., Aristotle distinguishes between taking hold of a substance or entity and asserting a relationship to be the case. The same point is made more from the point of view of the structure of discourse than of reality in *On Interpretation* 16a9–16. According to Aristotle, experience (*empeiria*) is a more specifically human attribute than is sensation (*aisthēsis*). All animals are capable of sensation, but humans are more capable of experience, of connecting sensations by memory and holding them together in the experience of a single universal (for example, human being) that arises from the sensation of individuals like Kallias. *Metaphysics* Alpha 980b28–981a3; *On Interpretation* 17a38–17b1. In terms of this distinction, we could say that for Aristotle the work of science is articulating experience, while for the mainstream of modern science it is connecting sensations.

mediately sensed but can be conceived in a preliminary way through experience prior to any scientific reasoning. But it is important to note that it is not the only such fact in the Aristotelian universe. The organization of the world of sensible substance into natural kinds or species (*Physics* 2, 193a1–6), the principle that the same thing cannot both be and not be at the same time (*Metaphysics* Gamma, 1011a8–13), and the fundamental qualities of actuality and potentiality (*Metaphysics* Theta, 1048a–b) discussed in Chapter 1 are facts of this kind. As a result, maturity and experience are *not* unique requirements of social scientists.

No single statement of Aristotle's marks the difference between his conception of science and the modern one more clearly than his claim in Book 6 of the *Nicomachean Ethics* that since the *archai* of first philosophy and natural science, like those of social science, come from experience, the young cannot become philosophers or natural scientists, although they can be first-class mathematicians or geometers "because the principles of mathematics come from abstraction, but the principles (*archai*) of the others [natural science, social science, and first philosophy or metaphysics] come from experience."[73] Aristotle's general term for this experience of grouping sensations into a universal prior to scientific explanation is *epagōgē*; this term is frequently translated as "induction," but induction implies the conscious rational activity of grouping sensations under general laws, a process that bypasses Aristotle's "experience" altogether and is central to the modern replacement of teleological by reductive explanation. Initial *epagōgē* for Aristotle cannot be described as a precise method; it can only be elucidated through metaphors like that of the regrouping army in *Posterior Analytics* 2. What is essential here is the claim that the process of theorizing our sensations into *archai* is something that happens in ordinary life and, as Gadamer would say, in language. The *archai* of social science are initially conceived through habit (*NE* 1, 1098b3–4), as a result of how we are brought up, rather than by science itself.

Maturity, like a good upbringing, is thus a necessary condition for social science, but it is of course not sufficient, else social *science*, the project of articulating the human good and of explaining particulars by reference to universals, would be otiose. Nor is the

---

[73] *NE* 6, 1142a12–19. "Starting point" might be better than "principle" as a rendering of *archē* because it is important to keep in mind that an *archē* is a term or phenomenon, rather than a relationship of phenomena, which the word "principle" seems to imply.

experience of the human good in any way mystical or ineffable; the point, however, is that before this good can be expressed in theoretical terms (such as Aristotle's theory of the *psuchē* and his account of *praxis* in terms of *orexis* and *prohairesis*) it must be known in some pretheoretical and relatively inarticulate way. Theory presupposes this understanding, and so cannot establish its starting point in precise theoretical terms. This gives rise to a second aspect of the rhetorical problem intrinsic to Aristotelian social science (the first being the problem of political rhetoric, of how to intervene in political debate): in order to persuade or remind us of the existence of human interest as a fact, Aristotle has continual recourse to medical analogies, suggesting that just as we all acknowledge the health of the body to be a fact, so we should acknowledge the existence of something like the "health" of a human life as a whole.[74] Of course, such analogies prove or demonstrate nothing to anyone not already disposed to grant the contention that human flourishing or interest exists independently of subjective preferences, but then no such proof is possible—any more than one can prove the law of the excluded middle or the existence of natures. Rather, such analogies are metaphoric attempts to render the project of social science plausible by suggesting that it is to the invisible health of the person as a whole what medicine is to the relatively visible strength and health of our relatively visible bodies. If the subject matter of social science were clearer and less disputed, we might be able to dispense with such analogies; but as Aristotle says after one such comparison, "it is necessary to use visible witnesses for invisible things" (*NE* 2, 1104a13–14). Metaphor would thus appear central to Aristotle's science, and it would be difficult to imagine him without such devices: the eye for the soul in *De Anima*, the self-doctoring doctor for nature in the *Physics*, the regrouping army for the formation of the experience of universals in the *Posterior Analytics*, and many others, including the doctor for the social scientist. Aristotle is indeed aware of the dangers of metaphoric speech, as appears from his discussion of the Platonic notion of participation, and at critical points runs up against disanalogies when his own metaphors (nature as Demiurge, the social scientist as doctor) seem to turn on him. But he is also aware of the significance of metaphor for education: "For learning easily is by nature pleasant to all, and words

[74] This is much like Socrates' analogical argument for the existence of human *aretē* at the end of *Republic* 1.

846470573

signify something, so that words that make us learn something are the most pleasant . . . and metaphor does this especially" (*Rhet.* 3, 1410b10–13). By connecting something unknown to something better known, Aristotle models the basic movement of his science—not from absolute doubt to absolute certainty but from what is better known to us to what is most knowable as such (*Posterior Analytics* 1, 72b25).[75]

The medical analogy also serves to indicate a secondary sense in which experience is a necessary component of social science. Just as the point of medical science is to cure particular individuals (*Metaphysics* Alpha, 981a12–29), so the point of social science is to offer criticism and guidance of particular regimes and cultures or, perhaps more directly, to improve the quality of our conversation about local political life. Some general theoretical grasp of what constitutes health or what constitutes a good *polis* may well be one of the necessary conditions for an adequate pursuit of these goals; but experience of the particular patient or culture is still required in addition to theory, since human beings vary too greatly to be treated as instances of general laws, in the manner required by the empiricist model. But this notion of human variability does not, as we have seen, rest on any romantic conception of individual or cultural creativity; rather, it is explicable in terms of human diversity, the complexity of human need, and the consequent multi-functionality of the political order.

Perhaps the best known of Aristotle's statements about social science, and the one most frequently cited as evidence of his affinity with the interpretive approach, is his claim that the purpose of studying *politikē* is not the acquisition of scientific theory, but the development of virtue or excellence: "The present study is not for the sake of theory, as are the others (for we are inquiring not in order to see what virtue is, but in order to become good individuals, since otherwise there would be no profit in it)" (*NE* 2, 1103b26–29). But why would there be no profit in a theory of the human good apart from the consequences of that theory for vir-

[75] A good discussion of Aristotle's position on the place of metaphor in reasoning is found in Arnhart, *Aristotle on Practical Reasoning*, pp. 172–176. See also Gadamer, *Truth and Method*, pp. 388–389. By contrast, empiricist social science aims at being perfectly nonmetaphorical, perhaps in the Hobbesian way: "Metaphors and senseless and ambiguous words are like *ignes fatui*; and reasoning upon them is wandering amongst innumerable absurdities" (*Leviathan*, chap. 5). At the other extreme, a fully interpretive social science might view metaphor as a way of building a human world separate from natural actuality, without any reference to connections between knowable parts of an independent reality.

SOCIAL SCIENCES DIVISION
CHICAGO PUBLIC LIBRARY
400 SOUTH STATE STREET
CHICAGO, IL 60605

tuous *praxis*? This surely cannot be because of any supposed priority of *praxis* to *theōria*; that much is clear from the surprisingly strong defense of the theoretical life presented in Book 10 of the *Nicomachean Ethics* itself and in Book 7 of the *Politics*. Why then is the science of human affairs, unlike other sciences, not an end in itself? And if this is not science for its own sake, then for whom are these books intended? What is the implied audience of the *Nicomachean Ethics* and the *Politics*?

The first Aristotelian thought that supports this conclusion about the unique instrumentality of social science is the judgment, very much at odds with the interpretivist identification of humanity and transcendence, that human beings are not the best things in the cosmos; consequently, social science is not the appropriate field for reflection concerning the primary instance of being: "For it would be strange if someone thought that social science (*politikē*) or practical wisdom (*phronēsis*) were the most serious (*spoudaiō-tatē*)[76] [forms of knowledge], since human beings are not the best of the things in the cosmos" (*NE* 6, 1141a20–22). It thus appears that the serious theorist or scientist will not be concerned with human affairs but will look instead to the unchanging entities that in some sense inform all the rest. But strangely enough, it appears that the study of beasts, who are more remote from the divine things than humans are, *is* an end in itself: Aristotle does not say that we should study the parts and lives of animals for the sake of improving agriculture or pharmacology. In the introduction to the *Parts of Animals*, he concedes that animals are indeed very far from the unchanging things, but adds this in defense of natural philosophy: "Nevertheless, for theory, the nature that fashions animals provides immeasurable pleasures for those who are able to distinguish causes and are philosophers by nature" (*Parts of Animals* 1, 645a7–11).

Theoretical activity is the constitutive cause of its own being, a self-justifying *telos*, insofar as it provides access to the structure of things, to the articulation of final-formal and efficient-material causality. But human affairs are not a good site for such theoretical activity because of their natural variability and complexity and the

[76] The word *spoudaios* is a difficult and interesting one, and can mean "eager" or simply "excellent" as well as "serious." As Irwin notes (*Nicomachean Ethics*, p. 400): "Aristotle regularly uses the term as the adjective corresponding to 'virtue,' and hence as equivalent to 'good.' " But that sense of the term is clearly different from its meaning in the famous definition of tragedy as the imitation of a *spoudaia praxis* in *Poetics* 1449b24.

SOCIAL SCIENCE DIVISION
Library

resulting problematic character of the actualization of human potentiality. Human affairs are thus peculiarly resistant to the theoretical project and to the desire for understanding that the first sentence of the *Metaphysics* tells us is ours by nature (that is, by biological inheritance), though not on the romantic ground of a profound separation between humanity and nature.

Social science is thus set apart from the other sciences by not being a self-sufficient theoretical activity. It is rather an instrumental condition of practical wisdom (*phronēsis*), the excellence of deliberating about particular choices that Aristotle sees as the way to the best of goods among the practical things (*NE* 6, 1141b13–14). The practical things (*ta prakta*) here may or may not include theory; theorizing is universal in orientation and practice is not, but for human beings theorizing is surely a *praxis* (*Pol.* 7, 1325b21). At any rate, *politikē*, theorizing about the human things, is perhaps best understood as an aspect of practical wisdom, as an inclination toward the universal that can clarify deliberation about our particular lives both by enriching our political vocabulary and by suggesting possible alternatives to political life as such. This suggests that the intended audience for *politikē* is not only future lawgivers and political people, but as Aristotle says in *Nicomachean Ethics* 10, anyone concerned with making others better, whether through laws and customs or by other, less public means. Just as Socrates in the *Gorgias* says that he is the true practitioner of *politikē* even without holding office, Aristotle's social science stresses the goal of moral education as the definitive feature of politics, thus opening the question of the ways in which politics proper (laws and rotation in office) can and should be supplemented. This nuanced evaluation of politics follows from Aristotle's recognition of the multifunctionality of political life: it is only if we assign to politics a single function—politics as a way of gaining power, say, or politics as a means of conflict resolution—that we can come to a simple conclusion about the desirability of political life.

Aristotle himself provides only one very compressed statement about the relationship between *phronēsis* and *politikē*; he says that they are the same *hexis*, but that their essence or being (*to einai autais*) is not the same (*NE* 6, 1141b23–24). This is mysterious stuff: how can two things both be and not be the same? I think this statement about the relation between *phronēsis* and *politikē* can be clarified by comparison with a similar discussion of the relation between teaching and learning in Book 3 of the *Physics*. Aristotle says that teaching and learning have the same actualization, but are not the same "in the *logos* of their essence." To clarify this kind of identity-yet-difference he then employs one of his most effective metaphors: the two are the same not as the synonyms "raiment" and "dress" are the same, "but as the road from Athens to Thebes is the same as the road from Thebes to Athens" (*Physics* 3, 202b12–14).[77] From particular good to the human good and back again—not as a single completed motion but as a continuous back and forth: the deliberative *hexis*, like nearly everything human, is composite; its primary and constitutive element, *phronēsis*, looks squarely at the particular context at hand, while social science, its complement, looks beyond for the sake of a more adequate particular choice.

Social Science and the Human Good

The other scientific activity that is similar to social science in this respect is, of course, medicine (*NE* 2, 1140a9; *Metaphysics* Alpha, 981a18–20). The critical judgments of the social scientist vary from case to case just as the judgments of the physician vary from patient to patient, in a way in which the judgments of the natural scientist do not vary from frog to frog, or those of the metaphysician from unmoved mover to unmoved mover. And yet while *politikē* is in this way analogous to medicine, there are some important disanalogies as well. Two in particular center on the special place of laws in politics as opposed to medicine: in *Politics* 3, as we have seen, one of the arguments for the importance of the rule of law is that unlike doctors, political people can be swayed by friendship; and in a passage in Book 2 (1268b22–1269a28) to be discussed in the next chapter, Aristotle argues that laws should sometimes be maintained even if they are less reasonable than conceivable alternatives, because politics, unlike medicine, must be sustained by a certain degree of habitual allegiance or, as we might say, authority.

Still, there is an important analogy between the social scientist's concern with the best *hexis* under the circumstances and the physician's concern with the best somatic *diathesis* and consequent medical treatment. What they share is an orientation toward future action and a reliance on a procedure that can be figured by

---

[77] For this passage, I am following the translation and commentary of Charles, *Aristotle's Philosophy of Action*, p. 10. This metaphor of the Thebes-Athens road becomes more interesting in the light of Zeitlin's argument in "Thebes" about the use of Thebes in tragedy as a kind of anti-Athens.

the metaphor of the mean, a certain optimal ordering of the elements of the thing being ordered, whether that thing is a person as such or simply a body. But the mean that social science has in view is much more difficult to discern than the medical mean (which is why Aristotle wants the metaphor), and is even more subject to case-by-case variation. While we may say that social science as Aristotle understands it is a sort of psychiatry, it by no means follows that psychiatry understood in this way—as the science of moral education—is simply a specialized branch of medicine.

Aristotelian social science, as an idea rather than a practice, cannot be identified with either of the two major contemporary approaches to understanding human affairs. But the reconstruction of the outlines of that social science introduces no exotic new program of social inquiry. Rather, what is most valuable about the Aristotelian approach is that it can give us a new way of thinking about human affairs, a way that permits a conversation among various forms of inquiry by freeing social science from its present pervasive concern with the supposed dichotomy between nature and uniqueness, and between science and practical discourse. From a teleological point of view human beings are both natural and unique, and only the broadest social science, one that is profoundly uneasy about the current academic divisions between moral philosophy, political theory, and the particular social sciences, can grasp the way in which this is so.

While Aristotelian social science yields no comprehensive rules of method, it is just as surely not a blanket endorsement of everything that claims to be social science. An Aristotelian approach would be seriously intolerant of attempts to achieve precision at the expense of evaluation—attempts which make the fundamental error of treating material, political, and moral issues in abstraction from one another. The Aristotelian approach is structured not by a method but by a set of questions that define the task of the social scientist—questions about how, given our specific nature and the various environmental circumstances we confront, particular communities can best solve the three great problems which, as simultaneous *problems*, are unique to the experience of human being: living, living together, and living well. Such a social science may improve political activity, but not by redescribing or formalizing it. The questions it poses are indeed the same as those raised by prescientific political life, but it may well suggest very different answers to those questions, or perhaps a different attitude about their significance. Bearing in mind the Thebes-Athens road, and Aristotle's remarks about the rank of human beings in the overall scheme of things, we might conclude that the best work of social science would be the development of more clearheaded and less vehemently serious citizens.

THREE

HOW THEORY INFORMS PRACTICE: VIRTUES AND RULES IN ARISTOTELIAN PRACTICAL PHILOSOPHY

Rationality in Moral and Political Choice

The Aristotelian account of the human good is undertaken with an eye to action—but how are the two to be related? The business of this chapter is to complete the defense of Aristotelian teleology, and the discourse of evaluative explanation it establishes, against the charge that it irrationally seeks to establish a dogmatic foundation for scientific and practical reason. In Chapter 1, I suggested that there are three principal grounds for regarding this style of thought as irrational and unscientific: the claim that Aristotelian teleology is "metaphysically" unempirical in positing strange entities, assuming special mysterious ways of knowing, and asserting an unchanging cosmic order; the claim that Aristotelian teleology as a whole is invalidated by Aristotle's false conclusions about physics and cosmology; and the claim that teleology, as applied to action, results in dogmatic pronouncements that ignore particular contexts. The discussion of the Aristotelian conception of the human good presented in the preceding chapters attempts to respond to the first two charges. It is now time to attend to the last, the charge of dogmatism that raises the issue of theory and practice.

As we have seen, there is a sense in which the term "rationality" summarizes Aristotle's understanding of the best human life or human virtue, and for him political and all other relationships must be considered in the context of their bearing on human rationality. But "rationality" has several meanings: how does Aristotle mean it when he says in *Politics* 1 that the best human life is one in which our *logos* makes plain what is in our interest and what not? Several quite different possibilities suggest themselves:

a rational life might be one lived most according to the rules of deductive validity; or one as free as possible from the influence of prejudice and custom; or one that reflects an internally coherent form of life; or one untroubled by contingency and particularity.

None of these, I think, captures the sense in which rationality is for Aristotle a virtue, although there are important overlaps. My position is that the central sense of rationality for Aristotle is captured by his use of the term "theorizing," which for him refers not to abstract speculation alone but to the activity of seeing the universal in the particulars before us, of teleologically placing persons and events relative to the goods that define them. But having said this, we must also recall that Aristotle insists on the relative independence of practical reasoning (*phronēsis*)—the ability to deliberate well not about our immediate interest but about "living well as a whole" (*NE* 6, 1140a25–28)—from the most general theory, saying that people of much experience and little theory sometimes make excellent decisions (*NE* 6, 1143b11–14). Yet at the same time he says that social science or political philosophy (*politikē*)—the ability to deliberate not about the good as such but about the human good (*NE* 6, 1141a20–25)—is the same as *phronēsis*, in the peculiar way in which the road from Athens to Thebes is the same as the road from Thebes to Athens.

Clearly there is something perplexing about the relationship between these two kinds of rationality. If *phronēsis*—rationality about my life and the lives of people I know—is not simply a matter of applied *politikē*—rationality about the lives of human beings as a species—then how are the two connected? It is important to resist giving too quick an answer to this question; one of the most useful features of Aristotelian thought for us is precisely its way of problematizing the relationship between theory and practice, and urging, as it were, a reconsideration of what a rational life might mean in the context of political reflection. Clarification of the Aristotelian position on theory and practice must therefore await some showing of how such clarification is in our interest.

Moral Rules: For and Against

For the past hundred years, English-speaking moral and political philosophy has been dominated by the debate between Kantian and utilitarian theories of good practice. In recent decades there have been two important changes in the nature of this debate, changes that appear, at least for the time being, to have altered the terms of theoretical discourse and removed what once must have seemed a compelling need to choose between some version of either the categorical imperative or the greatest happiness principle. The first, and less radical, of these changes has been the development of what Iris Murdoch calls "a more sophisticated neo-Kantianism with a utilitarian atmosphere."[1] This synthesis of old rivals—a so-called deontological liberalism, of which John Rawls's *Theory of Justice* is perhaps the best example—attempts to justify a moral rule protecting individual human rights that is absolutely binding insofar as it cannot be challenged by utilitarian considerations of efficiency, but to do so without reference to dubious Kantian conceptions of transcendental rationality or noumenal reality. Instead, heeding the Millian fiat that "the sole evidence it is possible to produce that anything is desirable is that people do actually desire it,"[2] Rawls derives his conception of rights and the principles designed to protect them from a low but solid ground confirmed by universal desire, from "primary goods, that is, things that every rational man is presumed to want . . . rights and liberties, powers and opportunities, income and wealth."[3]

The second recent revision in the language of moral and political philosophy, with which this chapter is concerned, is more difficult to identify and to name, perhaps because its contemporary origin is in opposition rather than synthesis; however, since MacIntyre's *After Virtue* it is commonly referred to as a morality of virtues—as opposed to a morality of rules.[4] According to this view too—first

[1] Murdoch, *Sovereignty of Good*, p. 29.

[2] Mill, *Utilitarianism*, p. 34.

[3] In part 3 of *Theory of Justice*, Rawls adds "self-respect" to his list of primary goods, and says that this is in fact the most important of them all. This good has two aspects: a sense of our own self-worth, and a confidence in our ability to carry out our intentions (p. 440). This good, combined with Rawls's "Aristotelian Principle"—the proposition that "human beings enjoy the exercise of their realized capacities" (p. 426)—forms part of Rawls's attempt to confirm his two principles of justice by reference to an idea of the good life as desirable in itself, and not simply a pile of the other primary goods. But Rawls trivializes the problem of the best life by assuming that by and large people want what they need (that pleasures correspond to realized capacities) and that everyone already knows just what human needs are (p. 425). The only argument or explanation for these large and questionable assumptions about the human condition is a gesture toward evolution (pp. 431–432).

[4] For a good review of several examples of virtue or agent morality before MacIntyre, see Flemming, "Reviving the Virtues." A note on names is in order here. In general, I will use the term "agent morality" rather than "morality of the virtues" because the latter sounds needlessly polemical and may give the impression that virtues are clearly knowable things about which no dispute is possible: the phrase "morality of the virtues" is thus a little too clear. "Agent morality" suffers from the

articulated within the analytic community by G.E.M. Anscombe[5]—
the similarities between Kant and the British tradition are much
more important than their differences, but in this case the similarities are said to call for rejection rather than systematic restate-
ment. This rejection of modern moral philosophy (or the "Enlightenment Project") has two stages: first, it is argued that morality,
for the moderns, is defined in terms of the obligation to obey a
binding moral rule, rather than by reference to individual virtues
and vices; second, it is said that these rules, whether Kantian or
utilitarian, cannot be successfully derived from the grounds (abstract reason or abstract pleasure) normally brought forth in their
defense, and that they owe whatever rhetorical power they possess to our fading memories of the Judeo-Christian Lawgiver. "It
is," Anscombe says concerning the modern notion of morality as
obligation, "as if the notion 'criminal' were to remain when criminal law and criminal courts had been abolished and forgotten."[6]
Once word about the emperor's clothes gets around, the logical
consequence is likely to be some sort of emotivism (as for Mac-
Intyre), or radical historicism (as for Leo Strauss),[7] or Tocquevillean individualism.[8]

A second and related criticism of modern rule or law morality is
that by focusing on the morality of particular acts or motives it
ignores or abstracts from a central feature of human life—that we
become what we are through our ways of life, our projects, phenomena that cannot be reduced without loss of meaning to the

---

opposite defect, but I prefer it because it suggests an important contrast between
rules and persons as the central starting points of the two moralities. Agent morality begins by asking about the good life, or happiness, and about the good person
or agent. Rule or law morality (which can also be called *act* morality) begins by
asking about the good action or the good will. The center of the dispute is a question of priority: which is *first*, good actions or good agents (persons, lives)? The
term "agent morality" seems to me to capture the essence of this whole-and-part
issue better than does "morality of the virtues."

[5] Anscombe, "Modern Moral Philosophy."

[6] "Modern Moral Philosophy," p. 30. See also MacIntyre, *After Virtue*, pp. 49–59.

[7] For Strauss (in "What Is Political Philosophy?"), the theoretical consequence of
the denial of a hierarchy of values is "radical historicism," the position associated
with Nietzsche and Heidegger. Its practical consequence is a tendency to admire
extremism and moral vehemence (*Natural Right and History*, pp. 66–67), to treat
"commitment" as a good in itself.

[8] For the authors of *Habits of the Heart* (Bellah et al.), doubts about the intelligibility of public goods lead to an individualistic retreat into the language of private
satisfaction, even on the part of individuals whose lives appear to be shaped by
clear public commitments. Strauss's "extremism" and Bellah's "individualism"
may be less opposed than at first they seem to be: when institutionalized public
projects (towns, religions, nations) appear senseless, spirited and hopeless feats of
antiinstitutional daring may well come to seem uniquely honest as well as attrac-
tively grand.

actions and volitions of which they are composed.[9] The question that centrally concerns us is not "What constitutes a good action?" but the Socratic "What sort of life is worth living?" This question requires a different moral language, one which tries to distinguish between more and less virtuous characters and ways of life, one whose emphasis is on persons or agents, rather than rules and actions. Since Plato and Aristotle clearly speak a language of this kind—one in which virtues are primary, and rules and obligations have but a second place—contemporary arguments for agent morality are almost always to some extent arguments for a revival of classical moral and political philosophy; this is most explicit in the work of Leo Strauss,[10] but the intention to recover at least some aspects of Greek philosophy is clearly present in the work of Anscombe, MacIntyre, and Murdoch as well. In effect, then, to assert that the central theoretical choice is that between agent and rule morality, and not between deontology and utilitarianism, is to affirm the centrality for us of the difference between ancient and modern philosophy.

To some extent, identifying the clash between agent and act morality with the difference between ancients and moderns is surely an exaggeration. The Thomistic tradition of natural law is neither modern nor compatible with Aristotelian agent morality.[11] Moreover, Nietzsche is no less a critic of the morality of rules than Plato and Aristotle,[12] and the same might be said for Machiavelli[13] and

[9] As McDowell puts it in his excellent "Virtue and Reason," "the philosophical tradition which flowers in Aristotle's ethics" holds that the question of how one should live "is necessarily approached via the notion of a virtuous person," rather than through "the concept of right conduct, and the nature and justification of principles of behaviour" (p. 331).

[10] In "Virtue, Obligation, and Politics," I present a Straussian interpretation of agent and rule morality, stressing the degree to which this distinction captures the essence of the difference between antiquity and modernity.

[11] Jaffa, *Thomism and Aristotelianism*. Jaffa's argument is that Thomas's reading of Aristotle was informed by Christian beliefs that Aristotle did not share, among them belief in a divine particular providence, in the special creation of individual souls, and in "a divinely implanted 'natural' habit of the moral principles" (p. 187). The principal objection to Jaffa's thesis is developed in two articles by Goerner, "On Thomistic Natural Law" and "Thomistic Natural Right." Goerner argues that Thomas is truly an Aristotelian but must for political reasons conceal this behind strict natural law teaching. At any rate, there is no disagreement between Jaffa and Goerner over the difference between Aristotelian agent morality and Thomistic natural law—the issue there is the extent to which Thomas was in fact an orthodox Thomist.

[12] MacIntyre recognizes this (*After Virtue*, p. 107) and is thereby led to say that our only possible exemplars for moral theorizing—rule morality having been rejected—are Nietzsche and Aristotle.

[13] "So in all human affairs one notices, if one examines them closely, that it is impossible to remove one inconvenience without another emerging" (*Discourses*,

Rousseau.[14] Yet it might be noted that Machiavelli, Rousseau, and Nietzsche all see themselves as restoring some elements of antiquity, something that is in no way true of those moderns who understand the task of practical philosophy to be the establishment of general rules or laws that can serve as adequate guides to good or just conduct, authors such as Hobbes, Hume, Mill, Kant, and Rawls. Moreover, the difference between law and agent morality may be said to be epitomized by the difference between Hobbes's derivation of the nineteen "immutable and eternal" laws of nature in *Leviathan* and Aristotle's claim in the *Nicomachean Ethics* that actions are good insofar as they are *meta logou* (with reason, or "reasonable") and not only insofar as they are *kata logon* (according to reason or rule) (*NE* 6, 1144b26–27), or the way in which Plato's Socrates confounds the rule-oriented Euthyphro by insisting that he attend to the contextual particulars of an event, rather than abstractly apply the rule that it is always just to prosecute injustice.[15] The most explicit statement of the difference is to be found in Aristotle's claim that theorizing about practical choice must always be imprecise and in outline, since our choices cannot be brought under the heading of any art (*technē*) or any command or rule (*NE* 2, 1104a7–10).[16] Given this, Aristotle concludes that decisions about what to do in any situation calling for action must always be

---

Bk. 1, chap. 5). This expresses the position that universal rules of conduct cannot be formulated precisely because there are at least several genuinely human desiderata, and because almost all interesting cases of practical choice involve reconciling, as best one can, demands that are both plausible and incompatible. For Machiavelli, this situation arises from the power of fortune, rather than the complexity of nature or human needs, and therefore seems to call for vehement action rather than thoughtful response.

[14] In "Rousseau and the Concept of Happiness," I argue that Rousseau's works present a picture of four desirable ways of life (the solitary dreamer, the bourgeois householder, the natural human being, and the virtuous citizen) and a conception of happiness in terms of which the desirability and incompatibility of these lives can be understood.

[15] The *Euthyphro* is a particularly useful example of the Platonic deployment of an agent morality (see Flanagan and Adler, "Impartiality and Particularity," pp. 595–596), but there are many other examples in the dialogues, including the refutations of Cephalus and Polemarchus in Book 1 of the *Republic*. In general, the dialogues are marked less by a quest for essential definitions of the virtues than by the use of such a quest to induce *aporia* in the interlocutors, an *aporia* that follows from the failure of universal rules to solve practical problems.

[16] Much turns here on the meaning of Aristotle's *parangelian* (1104a7), which I translate as "command or rule." Irwin translates this as "profession," Burnet as "professional tradition," Ostwald as "art which can be transmitted by precept," Ross as "precept." The choices made by Ross and Ostwald are preferable to those of Burnet and Irwin, but their rendering does not convey the military, self-enforcing overtones of Aristotle's word.

matters of perception, rather than direct applications of scientific principle (*NE* 6, 1142a25–30, 1143a32–b5). Thus a central feature distinguishing his agent morality from rule morality is, in John McDowell's words, "Aristotle's belief that a view of how one should live is not codifiable."[17]

My concern here, however, is not primarily with historical questions, but rather with the question of whether agent morality is in fact a better way to think about practical deliberation than rule or act morality. In this regard, it seems to me that the modern revival of the virtues faces two separate problems. The first is the issue discussed in the preceding chapters, the question of the intelligibility of the human good or *telos*. Doubts about this issue have plagued modern defenders of the virtues—witness MacIntyre's summary rejection of Aristotle's "metaphysical biology," Murdoch's attempt to defend moral realism or naturalism in the absence of any natural *telos* or definable human good,[18] and McDowell's grafting of Aristotelian agent morality onto Wittgenstein's forms of life.[19] Recognition of the plausibility of Aristotelian teleology may make it less compulsory for defenders of agent morality to insist upon a very un-Aristotelian dichotomy between the world as seen by natural science and the world as seen by moral and political philosophy.

But even if the doubt about the theoretical ground of a morality of the virtues can be resolved in its favor, agent morality still faces a serious and potentially fatal challenge—the charge that it is either too dogmatic (if based on the assertion that one and only one way of life must always be desired) or simply too imprecise and indeterminate (if it manages to avoid dogmatism) to be a helpful guide to action, particularly when that action concerns the great issues of politics rather than our dealings with family and friends. If political philosophy cannot supply actors with rules possessing the generality and power of the greatest happiness principle or the

17 "Virtue and Reason," p. 342. As McDowell says, to consider the plausibility of Aristotle's account of practical rationality, we need to question a prejudice about rationality and consistency: "The prejudice is the idea that acting in the light of a specific conception of rationality must be explicable in terms of being guided by a formulable universal principle" (p. 337).

18 *Sovereignty of Good*, pp. 77–78.

19 "Virtue and Reason," pp. 336–345. Dworkin's insistence, in *Law's Empire*, that his account of the judicial decision involves "moral" considerations as distinct from "metaphysical" ones is another instance of the unnecessary and debilitating abstraction from the natural world characteristic of much of contemporary agent morality. The same is true of Dworkin's distinction between principles and policies in *Taking Rights Seriously*, chap. 4.

categorical imperative or Rawls's two principles of justice, then can it be of any use to practice at all? The remainder of the present chapter addresses this issue.

Rules and Contexts

The modern revival of the virtues takes its bearings from a critique of rule morality; to understand this critique it is necessary to grasp the central character of a morality of rules, and to do this one must identify its sense of purpose, the perceived human problem it sets out to remedy. Simply stated, this problem is the radical uncertainty of practical choice, the belief that in the absence of a clearly stated rule of conduct we are left with nothing more than our guesses, intuitions, or prejudices. J. S. Mill puts the matter as follows:

> But though in science the particular truths precede the general theory, the contrary might be expected to be the case with a practical art, such as morals or legislation. All action is for the sake of some end, and rules of action, it seems natural to suppose, must take their whole character and color from the end to which they are subservient. When we engage in a pursuit, a clear and precise conception of what we are pursuing would seem to be the first thing we need, instead of the last we are to look forward to. A test of right and wrong must be the means, one would think, of ascertaining what is right and wrong, and not a consequence of already having ascertained it.[20]

This need for certainty reflects, to a degree, the general concern of modern science to establish laws that will enable us to gain control over external nature. But it has its more immediate source in a picture of human life that identifies the greatest human need, the need that gives rise to practical philosophy or social science, as the need to find some way of arbitrating the conflict over relatively scarce resources that places us in permanent jeopardy of Hobbes's war of all against all. Rawls's account of what he calls the "circumstances of justice" expresses such a view. We need to cooperate in order to obtain a decent share of the goods we all desire, and yet in the absence of any agreement about moral rules and the struc-

[20] *Utilitarianism*, p. 2.

ture of a just society, we are inclined to competition, not out of any moral fault or original sin, but because "anxiety, bias, and a preoccupation with their own affairs . . . are simply part of men's natural situation."[21] Rules of justice are needed for the peaceful distribution of primary goods, and the aim of philosophy should be to derive a set of rules that have the certainty of a kind of "moral geometry."[22]

The certainty requirement, then, derives its meaning and persuasive power from a particular conception of the purpose of society and of the deepest human need: that purpose is the distribution of goods, and that need, peace without slavery. We may note that these claims are controversial. If, for example, we hold that the principal function of society is the formation of preferences or characters rather than (or as well as) the distribution of resources, then we may begin to entertain doubts about the overriding need for certainty as a feature of action-guiding rules. If moral education is a need to be met by practical choice, then the need for certainty may have to be compromised in favor of a need for a contextual sensitivity to the requirements of particular individuals in particular circumstances, a situation familiar enough in the Platonic dialogues and, I will argue, in Aristotle's *Politics* as well.

After certainty, the second essential feature of any law morality is an insistence on impartiality or impersonality. The subjects of moral rules are not particular individuals, but abstractions—wills, or bearers of utilities, or representative individuals in the original position. Impersonality is closely linked to the certainty condition insofar as it allows a moral theory to overcome the sort of personal bias or prejudice that inevitably leads to moral and political conflict.[23] Such abstraction from particular characters may be either of the utilitarian sort that ignores individual differences, or of the Kantian kind that tends to ignore common interests. In either of these forms, rule morality treats social life as fundamentally unproblematic, and hence eliminates from practical discourse questions of love and friendship, subjects that form the matter for discussion of two books of the *Nicomachean Ethics*. It should be noted in passing here that the charge that rule morality has a necessarily

---

[21] *Theory of Justice*, p. 127.
[22] Ibid., p. 121.
[23] Rawls, *Theory of Justice*, p. 190.

"individualistic" bias—perhaps reflective of its supposed capitalist sources—is fundamentally mistaken. The key abstraction reflected in the impartiality or impersonality criterion is *not* an abstraction from society—Mill's perfectly sympathetic utilitarian observer can hardly be called asocial—but an abstraction from *character*, from the fact that individual human lives are shaped by certain desires or goals that mark us as whole persons. Such impersonality is as strong an element of Marx's conception of the ideal community (in which perfectly universal species-beings develop their gifts in *all* directions) as it is of Mill's.

It is this feature of rule morality that has recently come under the heaviest attack, particularly in Bernard Williams's essay "Persons, Character, and Morality."[24] According to Williams, Kantian abstract individualism is in its way an honorable attempt to overcome the "agglomerative indifference" of utilitarianism. But its value is strictly limited by the "impoverished and abstract character of persons as moral agents which the Kantian view seems to impose" (p. 4). The problem with the Kantian view is that it purchases impartiality at the price of neglecting those attachments to particular projects, persons, institutions, and places that motivate and give meaning to our lives and make them worth living: "Once one thinks about what is involved in having a character, one can see that the Kantian omission of character is a condition of [the Kantians'] ultimate insistence on the demands of impartial morality, just as it is a reason for finding inadequate their account of the individual" (p. 14). The abstraction fundamental to rule morality, then, is not simply a legitimate device for clarifying practical choice and moral thought, but a "misrepresentation, since it leaves out what both limits and helps to define that aspect of thought" (p. 19). If, in other words, the question of character, of the need to clarify the difference between virtuous and vicious projects and personalities, is what calls moral philosophy into being, abstraction from character is an unacceptable feature of any such philosophy.

It may be helpful at this point to remind ourselves that there is no Latin or Greek equivalent for our current sense of "moral," a word practically synonymous with "rules of conduct." The corresponding Greek and Latin terms refer rather to "character" or "habit," and what we speak of as Aristotle's moral philosophy (he calls it *ēthikē*) is more closely rendered as the science or theory of

---

[24] In his *Moral Luck*. Page references in this paragraph are to this work.

character. Thus to call the propriety of rule morality into question is not only to raise a philosophical issue, but to reflect on the limits and implications of our language.[25] Without such reflection, we risk missing entirely the sense of Aristotle's "moral philosophy" by trying to understand it in the light of contemporary usage, philosophic even more than popular, which insists on a strong distinction between "moral" and "natural." The simplest way of putting this is to note that for Aristotle "moral science" is, like "social science," a special part of biological or natural science. For him, the most important distinction within the sciences is not between *Natur-* and *Geisteswissenschaften* but between mathematics and natural science: "For the precise *logoi* of mathematics must not be demanded except for those things that have no matter; thus this is not the way to proceed in natural science, for perhaps matter is a property of nature" (*Metaphysics* alpha, 995a14–17). The key distinction is thus between sciences whose objects are always what they are and those that study beings whose potentiality (or matter) can be actualized in a variety of ways: teleological biology is neither as precise nor as deterministic as mathematics, and ethics and politics are in a way biological sciences. This way of understanding ethics and politics makes evaluative explanation possible, allowing us to consider the ways in which lives and cultures are accurate or mistaken in their understanding and pursuit of their human interests.

Opening lives and cultures to this kind of critical discourse is central to Platonic as well as Aristotelian practical philosophy, but there is no reason to assume that this form of inquiry was characteristic of nonphilosophic Greek thought, or that the assignment of morality to a sphere separate from the world to be explained through scientific rationality is uniquely modern. A nice moment suggestive of a profound Greek conflict over this issue occurs in Plato's *Philebus* (40e9–41a4). Socrates, developing a version of the virtue-is-knowledge thesis, asks young Protarchus whether opinions can be bad in any way except by being false. Protarchus readily agrees that they cannot. Then trouble starts:

SOCRATES: Nor do we understand that pleasures are bad (*ponērai*) in any other way except insofar as they are false.
PROTARCHUS: But certainly it's just the opposite of what

---

[25] "In Latin, as in ancient Greek, there is *no* word correctly translated by our word 'moral'; or rather there is no such word until our word 'moral' is translated back into Latin." MacIntyre, *After Virtue*, p. 37, emphasis MacIntyre's.

you've said, Socrates! For surely no one would be likely to call pains and pleasures bad insofar as they were false, but insofar as they were involved in some other great and manifold badness (*ponēria*).

Socrates does not try to meet Protarchus' objection directly, but instead points out some bad pleasures that rest noncontroversially on mistakes. But this is enough to suggest that the quarrel over a separate sphere of morality may have more to do with the tension between inquiry and popular morality, between philosophy and the city, than with any difference between antiquity and modernity as such.

Still, this difference between Aristotelian agent morality and modern rule morality suggests a third feature of the latter: the assertion of a special and autonomous moral point of view, a perspective quite different from the world in which we ordinarily live, one which defines a separate and autonomous moral sphere governed by special moral motives. Such a perspective may be that of the purified will, or the perfectly sympathetic observer, or the Hobbesian state of nature, or the representative individual in Rawls's original position.[26] As with the criteria of certainty and impersonality, this separation of morality from ordinary life may appear simply to be a necessary step toward theoretical clarification, a movement away from the messiness and conflicting demands of an ordinary choice among differing opinions. But as with the other criteria, this too carries with it an important, and highly dubious, claim about human needs—the claim that particular and local relationships, ties of family, friends, and country, are in general obstacles rather than aids to living well or justly. To criticize this view is not, of course, to say that local ties are inevitably good or that universalization is always a bad thing—although vulgar sentimentality does seem to be the easiest and most common response to the excesses of rule morality. Local ties and affections may be either better or worse things, and deciding about them requires careful thought and attention to available alternatives, rather than the application of a universal rule. To be sure, the kind of Aristotelian agent morality I want to defend does indeed make reference to a perspective that is distanced from the local context. But reference to this perspective—that of the *phronimos*, the person of prac-

[26] Or the Marxian posthistorical being for whom, in "Private Property and Communism," the senses have become theoreticians in practice, or the true citizens of the *Social Contract*.

tical wisdom or prudence—results not in the statement of a rule, but in the creation of a metaphor—the metaphor of the mean—whose function is to clarify problems of practical choice, and not to resolve them. As we saw in the previous chapter, this metaphor calls attention to a similarity between moral choice and medical judgment. More broadly, the metaphor of "finding the mean" is used by both Plato (especially in the *Statesman*) and Aristotle to bring to mind a kind of *technē* that is yet imprecise and involves looking at some situation to determine what response is appropriate (*to metrion* is *to prepon*), knowing in advance that the problem cannot be solved by any precise measurement.[27]

A fourth and final feature of rule morality is perhaps less often noticed than the other three. This is the background assumption that motives of authority are always unreasonable from the moral point of view. By motives of authority I mean a sense that there are certain particular and local standards or structures (which may or may not be represented by identifiable persons or traditions) that have decisive and attractive claims on our allegiance, even though we are not quite clear about the reasons why.[28] The central point at issue here is not any factual claim—such as the claim that local authorities or traditions or practices (in Wittgenstein's and MacIntyre's sense) are always justified—but rather a question, the question of whether such structures are necessary for human well-being. The charge against rule morality is that it avoids and obscures this question by assuming at the outset an antithesis between reason and tradition, between rational and authoritative motives.[29] This hides from view both the general question of a hu-

[27] This refers to the distinction between the two arts of measurement described by the Eleatic Stranger in *Statesman* 283c11–284e9, measurement relative to the dimension being measured (height, weight, etc.) and measurement relative to a mean. There is a similar use of the mean in reference to two kinds of disagreements in *Euthyphro* 7c4. In the *Philebus*, Socrates makes the mean the most desirable human possession. On the central role of metaphor in moral philosophy, see Murdoch, *Sovereignty of Good*, pp. 77–78.

[28] As I noted in Chapter 2, Aristotle seems to think of the power of *nomos* in something like these terms (*NE* 10, 1179b31–1180a24). In addition to Arendt's "What Is Authority?", a clear presentation of this conception of authority is to be found in Gadamer, "Hermeneutical Reflection," pp. 33–34.

[29] MacIntyre (*After Virtue*, pp. 204–206) argues that the antithesis between tradition and reason blinds us to the way in which culturally inherited roles and concepts are a part of moral individuality—either by dismissing tradition or (as with, in MacIntyre's view, conservatives like Burke) exaggerating its importance. This position is developed further in *Whose Justice?*, chap. 18. Gadamer, who is equally critical of both the Enlightenment critique and the Romantic rehabilitation of traditional authority, says that both miss the point that "tradition is constantly an element of freedom." *Truth and Method*, p. 250. The important difference between

man need for authority and the more pressing practical question of whether some particular authority is making a reasonable claim on our allegiance. The complexity of these problems emerges once we consider the possibility that a need for authority is not simply the same as a need for some tolerable social order, or for peace; if this were all that were at stake, the matter might be assimilable to the kinds of questions that can be brought under a rule, particularly one of the utilitarian kind. But as can perhaps best be seen in examples drawn from the arts,[30] what is in question is the need for authoritative structures and motives as a means to forming moral virtues, to eliciting those excellences of character that can make life desirable. Is the belief that certain forms of life and action (a family, a college, a poem) are independent of and superior to us a constitutive feature of moral education? As with the abstraction from the difficulties surrounding love and character, the theoretical abstraction from the problem of authority seems to leave too much of life outside the realm of moral philosophy, and hence suggests the superiority of a way of thought that focuses on the goodness or virtue of particular agents or persons rather than on the construction of universally applicable rules.

And yet this defense of agent morality may not be altogether convincing. Even if one were to accept, as I think reasonable, the thought that the problem of the human good—the possibility of giving a teleological account of human life—is sufficiently knowable to serve as the basis for a discussion of the virtues, a strong doubt remains about whether agent morality can ever be clear and certain enough to serve as a language appropriate for public choice. Hume raises this doubt very nicely in defense of his three

---

MacIntyre and Gadamer is that the former thinks, with Nietzsche, that our political tradition is effectively dead (*After Virtue*, p. 244). Gadamer is less romantic on this score.

[30] See Sennett's nice discussion in *Authority* of Pierre Monteux's exemplification of musical authority (pp. 17–18). Sennett's discussion of the fear of authority as a specifically modern pathology provides an interesting explanation of the strong appeal of rule morality. Murdoch takes a similar line, and also uses the arts as key examples of the motive of authority. A good illustration of this is the following: "An understanding of any art involves a recognition of hierarchy and authority. There are very evident degrees of merit, there are heights and distances; even Shakespeare is not perfect." *Sovereignty of Good*, p. 88. Or, as Eliot says, what is required of the poet "is a continual surrender of himself as he is at the moment to something which is more valuable." "Tradition and the Individual Talent," pp. 6–7. It should be noted that the self-surrender that is part of Murdoch's and Eliot's accounts of authoritative motivation seems not to be present in Plato and Aristotle, who were not Christians; but perhaps this is a manageable difference in tone— neither Murdoch nor Eliot is thinking of a form of slavery.

rules of justice—stability of possessions, transfer by consent, and the performance of promises—against the claim that distributions are just only insofar as they are determined by merit or desert or need. He does *not* say that merit and need are impossible to determine; Hume is not in any simple way a relativist concerning the human good.[31] What he does claim, however, is that distribution according to need or merit, no matter how reasonable it may appear, would inevitably lead to unbearable controversy and disorder *in practice*: "But 'tis easy to observe, that this wou'd produce an infinite confusion in human society, and that the avidity and partiality of men wou'd quickly bring disorder into the world, if not restrain'd by some general and inflexible principles."[32] Hume is quite correct in noting that distribution according to need or merit is not an impartial or impersonal rule in the same way that his principles of justice are; is he also correct in saying that precise rules are necessary for guiding political action even though they may run counter to accurate perceptions of what is good in a particular case or context?

A recent argument in a similar vein is presented in section 50 of Rawls's *Theory of Justice*, entitled "The Principle of Perfection." In this section, Rawls contrasts his two principles of justice with what he calls "intuitionistic perfectionism"—a position no doubt prejudicially named, but, as he describes it, one that accurately characterizes the kind of Aristotelian agent morality I want to defend here. Such a position holds that some "forms of life" or characters are better or more virtuous than others, but also that the claims of the virtues must be balanced in each case against the need to provide basic services to everyone, virtuous or not—to provide, in Aristotelian language, for the requirements of life as well as for those of living well. Such a position, Rawls acknowledges, is "not easy to argue against." But the "intuitive" balance to be achieved in each particular case or context cannot be determined by the application of any rule, nor can we conclude *with deductive certainty* what constitutes virtue or excellence in a given case. As a result of its indefiniteness, Rawls concludes, agent morality must fail as a

---

[31] Hume's apparent relativism stems from his awkwardness in using the language of final causality, a language he rejects in theory but, as does Hobbes, employs very well in practice. Salkever, " 'Cool Reflexion,' " pp. 75–76. On Hume's virtues, see Ignatieff, *Needs of Strangers*, chap. 3.

[32] *Treatise of Human Nature*, Bk. 3, pt. 2, sec. 6; see also, generally, Bk. 3, pt. 2, sec. 2–4.

theory of practice because its style of discourse would threaten both political order and individual liberty:

> Criteria of excellence are imprecise *as political principles*, and their application to *public questions* is bound to be unsettled and idiosyncratic, however reasonably they may be invoked and accepted *within narrower traditions and communities of thought.* . . . Since these uncertainties plague perfectionist criteria and jeopardize individual liberty, it seems best to rely entirely on the principles of justice which have a more definite structure.[33]

A morality of the virtues may indeed be appropriate in certain "private" settings; but in "public" or "political" life, where the bonds of community are relatively impersonal, it will not do.

Similar reservations of a practical or political, rather than a theoretical kind are expressed by other modern writers more sympathetic to agent morality. Hilary Putnam urges that moral rules "are important because they are the main mechanism we have for challenging (and, if we are successful, shaping) one another's consciences."[34] Iris Murdoch, in the course of a sustained attack on Kantian rule morality, feels compelled to acknowledge that the Kantian moral hero "is the ideal citizen of the liberal state, a warning held up to tyrants. . . . It must be said in its favour that this image of human nature has been the inspiration of political liberalism. However, as Hume once wisely observed, good political philosophy is not necessarily good moral philosophy."[35] This insistence on the need to employ different languages in private and public contexts, and hence to sharply distinguish moral from political philosophy, is stated with particular acuteness by Bernard Williams:

> In particular, in a modern complex society functions which are ethically significant are performed by public agencies and, if the society is relatively open, this requires that they be governed by an explicable order which allows those agencies to be answerable. In a public, large and impersonal forum "intuition" will not serve, though it will serve (and nothing else could serve) in personal life and in a more closely shared existence.[36]

[33] *Theory of Justice*, pp. 330–331, emphasis added.
[34] Putnam, "Taking Rules Seriously," p. 195.
[35] *Sovereignty of Good*, pp. 80–81.
[36] *Moral Luck*, p. 81.

A complex and impersonal political world demands a simple and impersonal evaluative language; while the language of the virtues may be appropriate for articulating and choosing courses of conduct involving family and friends, such a language cannot be extended to the political world without seriously endangering social cohesion, individual liberty, and political responsibility.

Now, as we saw in Chapter 2, Aristotle is certainly alive to the need for impersonal *nomoi* to organize human life (as is Plato),[37] and yet is unwilling to conclude that practical philosophy should be expressed in commands or laws: is it necessary to conclude, as Rawls, Murdoch, and Williams do, that we need two moral languages, one for private and the other for public situations? Must political evaluation and choice abstract from those considerations of character that seem inseparable from our interest in human life itself? One simple, and as far as it goes quite adequate, response to these doubts concerning the political appropriateness of agent morality would be to say that these worries are in fact empirical questions—or rather that they are assertions about efficient causality ("the practice of agent morality threatens order and liberty") that need to be considered empirically. What is required here is a careful social scientific consideration of a variety of modern polities, an inquiry informed (teleologically) by a complex sense of what constitutes virtuous characters or ways of life, a sense that necessarily requires acquaintance with the language and style of agent morality. Before we can be sure about the extent to which judgments concerning virtue need to be mediated, and to some extent distorted, by impersonal rules, we must weigh carefully the extent to which, *in each particular case*, the demands of excellence or character need to be qualified by the demands of secure political order or individual liberty. The decision in each case cannot be reached by the application of a universal rule, and therefore the theory that such decisions require must take the form of an agent rather than a rule morality.

But this solution is too simple, and calls for a further elaboration of the way in which the relationship between moral and political theory on the one hand and practical moral and political choice on

[37] See especially the defense and criticism of the rule of law toward the end of the *Statesman*, which makes much the same case as Aristotle does in *Pol.* 3, 1282b1–1288a32, and *NE* 10, 1180a34–1181b12, concerning the strengths and weaknesses of living according to the laws. As in the parallel critique of writing in the *Phaedrus*, the purpose of the Platonic critique of laws is legal improvement rather than a proposal for a government without laws.

the other is to be characterized. Before attempting such an elaboration via a consideration of Aristotle's *Politics*, it will be helpful to
rethink the problem of the two moralities in two twentieth-century
settings apparently far removed from the controversies of moral
and political philosophy.

Contextual Discernment and "Unweeded Kindness"
 Gendered Voices and Howards End

Agent morality must be grounded in a conception of human happiness or flourishing—an understanding of the range of lives and
characters that are to be called good or bad by reference to the
appropriate actualization or suppression of human potentialities.
Such conceptions can, of course, be quite wrong—nothing is easier
than to point to examples of such errors, some trivial and some
horribly dangerous, from master races or castes to the maximization of inclusive fitness. But it is equally the case that some such
conception does in fact inform most serious reflection about human action,[38] accounting for the persistence of the tradition of
evaluative explanation in spite of the modern rejection of teleology. Neutrality about the human good, inspired by a reasonable
fear of going wrong or by disgust at past efforts, can have the
same paralyzing effect as a fear of authority;[39] the consequences of
indifference about the human good, whether feigned or genuine,
are not necessarily benign.[40] At best, as in the case of cultural relativism, the result will be a blanket endorsement of prevailing
views.[41] The undoubted dangers of the practice of agent morality
would seem to call for thought and care, both about the human

[38] I argue in "Freedom, Participation, and Happiness" that both liberal rights theorists and defenders of communitarian politics rely, implicitly, on some view of
human needs or human flourishing. These views are sometimes not acknowledged
and sometimes treated as being obvious and hence not worth justifying (for example, Rawls, *Theory of Justice*, p. 425).

[39] Sennett details the way in which the flight from authority, as opposed to the
quest for better authority, can lead to tyranny. His principal text is Hegel's "Lord-
ship and Bondage," but the movement he describes is reminiscent of Plato's discussion of the transition from democracy to tyranny. Sennett, *Authority*, pp. 125–
164.

[40] This is the theme explored in chap. 2 of Strauss's *Natural Right and History*.

[41] For a recent discussion of the incoherence and undesirability of cultural relativism from an anthropological point of view, see Hatch, *Culture and Morality*. Geertz
(in "Anti Anti-Relativism") provides an amusing though perhaps not responsive
rejoinder to this critique from within, resting his case on the diagnostic claim that
rampant hysteria is at the root of all criticisms of cultural relativism.

good in general and about its relationship to particular contexts, rather than resignation to things as they are.

Such considerations have led proponents of a revival of the virtues to conclude that agent morality depends upon an adequate philosophical psychology.[42] While some writers have tried to turn Freud to such purposes,[43] a more promising candidate for an adequately philosophical psychology would appear to be the theory of stages of moral development presented in a series of books and papers by Lawrence Kohlberg,[44] particularly since Kohlberg himself is so evidently interested in linking his theory to contemporary discussions in moral and political philosophy. According to Kohlberg, human moral development proceeds through an invariant and progressive sequence of levels, from preconventional (or childishly egotistical) through conventional to postconventional styles of solving moral dilemmas. Following Piaget's model of cognitive development, Kohlberg defines moral progress in terms of an ever-increasing universalization and "reversibility" (or impartiality)[45] on the part of the agent; at the highest level ("post-conventional, autonomous, or principled"), "there is a clear effort to define moral values and principles that have validity and application apart from the authority of the groups or persons holding these principles and apart from the individual's own identification with these groups."[46] At the less advanced conventional level, by contrast, "maintaining the expectations of the individual's family, group, or nation is perceived as valuable in its own right. . . . The attitude is not only one of *conformity* . . . but of actively *maintaining*, supporting, and justifying the social order, and of identifying with the persons or groups involved in it."[47] In line with the common tendency of modern rule moralities, Kohlberg's model defines moral progress in terms of overcoming the claims of any local authority whatsoever; one interesting consequence of this would be to obscure the differences in character between, say, Adolf Eichmann and Abraham Lincoln: practical intelligence and devo-

---

[42] Anscombe, "Modern Moral Philosophy," p. 29; Murdoch, *Sovereignty of Good*, p. 46. In "Losing Your Concepts," Diamond develops a complementary argument to the effect that the source of the poverty of modern moral philosophy is analytic philosophy's failure to grasp the function of language in human life.

[43] Wollheim, *Thread of Life*.

[44] Kohlberg discusses the philosophic implications of his project in "From Is to Ought," and in "Claim to Moral Adequacy." For a good critical discussion, see Sullivan, *Reconstructing Public Philosophy*, chap. 4.

[45] "Claim to Moral Adequacy," p. 641.

[46] Ibid., pp. 631–632.

[47] Ibid., p. 631, emphasis Kohlberg's.

tion to a particular institution are by definition incompatible. Kohlberg initially distinguished two stages within the highest, postconventional level, which he identified with the two major versions of modern rule morality—a utilitarian orientation and a higher stage said to be "naturally allied to the formalistic tradition in philosophic ethics from Kant to Rawls"[48]—although he has more recently indicated that it may be empirically impossible to distinguish between these two stages.[49]

Kohlberg's model has been the subject of vigorous criticism (and equally vigorous defense) on a variety of issues, including the internal necessity of the developmental sequence (no stage-skipping, no stage-regression under normal circumstances) and the cross-cultural empirical applicability of the model. But interest in the model persists, largely, I think, because of the need to supply any morality—that is, even rule morality—with a psychological grounding, with a conception of human excellence or virtue, of what a good character is and how such characters resolve practical problems, if the rules of morality are not to be seen as merely arbitrary prescriptions or relics of a decaying religious culture. Kohlberg himself tends to take for granted the adequacy of his highest (postconventional) stage as a characterization of human virtue, or to view its agreement with the major voices in modern moral philosophy as a sufficient defense:[50] if utilitarians and neo-Kantians agree on the desirability of impartiality, the rejection of local authority, and the need to distinguish the moral perspective from that of ordinary life, who is to say no?

Much of the nay-saying has come from those who object to Kohlberg's moral ideal on the ground that it reflects an undesirable liberalism or individualism.[51] But perhaps the most interesting, and surely the best-known, critique has been that of Carol Gilligan. Gilligan[52] begins by noting that, as an empirical matter, Kohlberg's model seems to fit the moral development of males better than that of females,[53] and that one must therefore conclude

---

[48] Ibid., p. 633.

[49] Kohlberg, "Reply to Owen Flanagan."

[50] Ibid., p. 524; Flanagan, "Virtue, Sex, and Gender," p. 507.

[51] See Habermas, *Communication*, pp. 73–90, for such an account that suggests supplementing Kohlberg's model by adding a seventh stage—the moral and political freedom of fictive members of a world society. This supplement may be less than meets the eye: abstract individuality transformed into abstract communality.

[52] Gilligan, *In a Different Voice*.

[53] The claim about the empirical difference between scores of male and female respondents to Kohlberg dilemmas is a matter of dispute. See Haan, "Two Moralities," p. 287; Kohlberg, "Reply to Owen Flanagan," pp. 517–519; and Broughton,

either that women are morally inferior to men or that women tend to exhibit a different pattern of moral development and a different moral ideal from the one described by Kohlberg. In particular, Gilligan argues that for morally mature women "the moral problem arises from conflicting responsibilities rather than competing rights and requires for its resolution a mode of thinking that is contextual and narrative rather than formal and abstract."[54] This initial stress on the importance of contextual discernment and balancing of the needs of particular people, rather than principled judgment from a special and universal moral perspective, has led several commentators to suggest that Gilligan's moral ideal embodies a metaethical challenge to rule morality from a perspective of something like an Aristotelian morality of the virtues.[55]

As Gilligan's discussion proceeds, however, via an analysis of the way women respond to both hypothetical (Kohlbergian) and real life (abortion decision) dilemmas, the distinction between her conception of the ideal character and that of Kohlberg becomes more and more obscure. Viewed from the perspective of ethical theory, Gilligan's "ethic of responsibility" may simply show that both Kohlberg's and her own models depend upon largely unexamined and undefended assumptions about ideal (or normal) characters or virtues—in other words, that they are both agent moralists in spite of themselves. At any rate, Gilligan soon leaves behind her initial emphasis on thoughtful sensitivity to contextual particularity and ambivalence about universal rules. Screening out ways in which her respondents refer to individual and contextually specific needs as elements of their approach to practical decisions,[56] she ends by proposing that the highest level of moral development (her third stage) involves the application of a universal rule to moral dilemmas.

Gilligan's rule requires an abstract commitment to a universal

---

"Women's Rationality and Men's Virtues," pp. 616–622. It does seem probable that Gilligan tends to exaggerate the male bias of the Kohlberg model.

[54] *In a Different Voice*, p. 19.

[55] Flanagan and Adler, "Impartiality and Particularity," pp. 585–586; Broughton, "Women's Rationality and Men's Virtues," p. 623. For an Aristotelian discussion of the theoretical implications of Gilligan's position, highlighting the contrast between Kantian rules and Aristotelian judgments, see Tronto, "Beyond Gender Difference."

[56] For examples, consider Gilligan's construals of subjects' comments on pp. 20–21 (discussed here in Chapter 1) and pp. 101–102 of *In a Different Voice*. For a discussion of various ways in which Gilligan's conclusions would appear to involve important distortions (or at least highly selective readings) of her own interview data, see Broughton, "Women's Rationality and Men's Virtues," pp. 603–609.

principle of "caring" or "nonviolence," rather than the Kohlbergian abstract commitment to respect for individual human rights,
but an abstraction from context and from the need for contextual
discernment is equally a feature of both models. Referring to the
moral stance of her favorite subject, Gilligan describes her conception of the moral norm or ideal as follows:

> Sarah, a twenty-five-year-old who also faces disappointment,
> finds a way to reconcile the initially disparate concepts of self-
> ishness and responsibility through a transformed understand-
> ing of relationships. Examining the assumptions underlying
> the conventions of female self-abnegation and moral self-sac-
> rifice, she rejects these conventions as immoral in their power
> to hurt. By elevating nonviolence, the injunction against hurt-
> ing, to a principle governing all moral judgment and action,
> she is able to assert a moral equality between self and other
> and to include both in the compass of care. Care then becomes
> a universal injunction, a self-chosen ethic which, freed from
> its conventional interpretation, leads to a recasting of the di-
> lemma in a way that allows the assumption of responsibility
> for choice.[57]

Gilligan is in perfect agreement with Kohlberg (and the rule morality of modern moral philosophy) in asserting that moral maturity means bringing particular problems under the control of self-
chosen universal rules,[58] and in her rejection (as "conventional")
of the moral significance of local structures of authority. Many of
her differences with Kohlberg appear in this light to be largely ver-
bal (especially the distinction between "responsibilities" and
"rights" as different ways of characterizing moral obligation),[59]
and even the initially striking gender dimorphism of her different
voices is muted by her concluding claim that the "ethic of care"
and the "ethic of justice" can and should coexist in the fully developed moral character.[60] Seen in this light, Gilligan appears no
less devoted to the norm of autonomy than Kohlberg—she wants

---

[57] *In a Different Voice*, p. 90.

[58] This is Kantian *Mündigkeit* indeed. O'Laughlin has reason to say that Gilligan
exhibits a methodical "blindness to the circumstance in which [her respondents]
live." "Responsibility and Moral Maturity," p. 572.

[59] O'Laughlin, "Responsibility and Moral Maturity," pp. 558–565; Broughton,
"Women's Rationality and Men's Virtues," pp. 604–605.

[60] *In a Different Voice*, p. 174.

only to say that autonomy is compatible with interdependence, something Kohlberg would be unlikely to deny.[61]

Both Gilligan and Kohlberg follow the modern practice of gaining critical purchase by sharply separating the abstract and universal moral perspective from the rules and practices of ordinary life. This idealistic and, in some hands, sentimental formalism methodically neglects the way practical intelligence can operate within particular contexts without any explicit reference to or concern with universal views or principles. One psychologist who resists this powerful tendency is Norma Haan, whose challenge to Kohlberg is much more radical, though less well known, than Gilligan's. Haan begins by considering two discrepancies in the scoring of Kohlberg's hypothetical dilemmas: the gender difference noted by Gilligan, and the fact that people often tend to explain their real life decisions in language that falls under a different Kohlberg stage from the language they use in solving hypothetical dilemmas.[62] In response to these findings, she presents an alternative model of moral development whose highest stage involves contextual discernment rather than principled universality and which, in a quite Aristotelian way,[63] describes moral judgments as discoveries of specific mutual interests.[64]

Haan's model is made up of five ascending levels of which the fourth captures the impartiality and certainty of rule morality. Of

---

[61] Her position sounds much like the one characterized by the authors of *Habits of the Heart* (Bellah et al., pp. 333–334) as "expressive individualism" (as opposed to "utilitarian individualism"). According to *Habits*, American political culture reflects the tension between two moral languages: that of individualism and that of the American republican tradition, with its particular mix of biblical and classical resonances. The authors argue convincingly that the second language differs from the first in lacking abstraction and in requiring contextual discernment rather than rule application. But they do not recognize a need to defend and qualify this second language by reference to any general perspective that might permit its speakers to be self-critical as well as committed. It is worth noting here that they worry about "managers" and "therapists"—the avatars of utilitarian and expressive individualism—but not about fanatics or terrorists. See Sennett, *Authority*, pp. 157–158.

[62] Haan, "Hypothetical and Actual Moral Reasoning."

[63] Although this is not noted by Haan, who thinks (wrongly) that her conception of the moral norm is identical with that of Rawls and Habermas: "Rawls and Habermas have recently advanced the conceptualization that moral truth is achieved through dialogue and that it is ultimately based on people's agreements." "Two Moralities," p. 289. This is clearly false: there is no "dialogue" in Rawls's original position, and Habermas's conception of a knowledge-constitutive interest in autonomy and responsibility (the Kantian alternative to the Aristotelian *phronimos*) is founded on a transcendental deduction that abstracts from all particular conversations, not "people's agreements." See Habermas, *Knowledge and Human Interests*, pp. 311–315.

[64] Haan, "Two Moralities," p. 287.

127

the person at this level, Haan says that "he recognizes aspects of others' individuality, but his central idea that rule following should regulate moral exchange means that individualities only confuse moral discussions"[65]—a feature that seems to hold for both Kohlberg's and Gilligan's moral ideals. The fifth stage is defined by reference to contextually specific needs and interests: the purpose of practical choice is that of "achieving new or maintaining old moral balances, which may represent compromises or identifications of mutual interests. . . . Both the content and structure of moral dialogue reflect the specific characteristics of the actors" (p. 287). Decisions are reached not by ascending to a separate or self-constructed moral sphere and then applying principles therein discovered, but through deliberation about interests: "moral truth is based on agreements moral agents achieve about their common interests and is not predetermined by rules or principles, that is, truth is to be achieved, not revealed" (p. 289).[66] The virtues characteristic of Haan's moral norm are neither Kohlberg's principled autonomy nor Gilligan's heroic responsibility, but qualities of perspicacity and tact that may recall Socrates or Elizabeth Bennett; of the person at the fifth stage, Haan says that "he has a sense of detachment and humor about himself. In so doing, he recognizes the delicacy and complexity of the moral balance and, most importantly, he recognizes that he as well as others frequently contributes to imbalances" (pp. 288–289). In an experimental situation comparing the incidence of her moral language and Kohlberg's, Haan found that her adolescent subjects tended to use the language of rules in solving hypothetical dilemmas and the language of mutual interests in solving a series of interpersonal game situations, situations more like ordinary life problems (p. 294)—a finding that led her to conclude that the two moralities "represent distinctively different phenomena" (p. 295).[67]

Haan's achievement lies in expressing, within the limits of a strictly modern social scientific vocabulary, two propositions central to agent morality. The first is that, contrary to Kant, Mill, Piaget, Rawls, Kohlberg, et al., practical rationality is not identical

[65] Ibid., pp. 288–289. Other page references in this paragraph refer to this work.

[66] Aristotle says much the same thing in his claim in *Pol.* 1 (1253a14–15) that the function of our rationality is to discover what is in our interest and *therefore* what is just. This thesis is a central element in the Aristotelian rejection of the requirement to assume the existence of a separate moral sphere.

[67] She found no significant male-female differences in the use of the different languages (p. 295), and no socioeconomic differences, though blacks were more likely than whites to employ the "interpersonal" model.

with ever-increasing formal universality.[68] The second is that morality or good conduct need not be defined in opposition to, or as the overcoming of, local conventions. But these objections to abstraction are largely negative in force; they leave the reader wondering about the *way* in which the good person is both attached to and good-humoredly detached from particular relationships, and about the relative merits of agent and rule morality as modes of approaching large-scale political problems, problems involving relationships that are not directly "interpersonal" but mediated through relatively impersonal customs and rules.[69] What is lacking here is a clarifying theoretical ground for agent morality, a ground whose outline can, I will argue, be found in the Aristotelian understanding of the relationship between psychological theory and political practice.

The single modern text that most clearly presents this problem is not a work of academic moral philosophy or psychology, but E. M. Forster's novel *Howards End*.[70] Although the book contains

[68] Flanagan and Adler, "Impartiality and Particularity," p. 579. Within academic philosophy, this point is well expressed by Ruddick in her account of "maternal thinking." Like Haan, Ruddick attributes her basic conception of focused thinking to Habermas ("Maternal Thinking," p. 347 and n. 17), although she refers to Murdoch (and so, without apparently noticing it, to Plato). She gestures toward a possible theoretical basis for her position by saying of the thoughtful mother, who attempts to balance conflicting demands in preserving her small world, that "her conceptual scheme, in terms of which she makes sense of herself, her child, and the common world will be more the Aristotelian biologist's than the Platonic mathematician's" (p. 352). Moreover, the sort of contextual discernment she defends is at home only in a domestic setting, and politics seems possible only as a generalization of the household: "All feminists must join in articulating a theory of justice shaped by and incorporating maternal thinking. Moreover, the generalization of attentive love to *all* children requires politics" (p. 361, emphasis Ruddick's). Ruddick's thesis has given rise to an interesting debate that exemplifies the contrast between agent and rule morality. For a critique from a Kantian perspective, see Grimshaw, *Philosophy and Feminist Thinking*, chap. 8; from an Arendtian perspective, see Dietz, "Citizenship with a Feminist Face."

[69] Haan does offer a speculative comment on the relationship of these two moralities, suggesting that rule morality is a special case of agent morality: "formal morality . . . is one particular late-developing branch of interpersonal morality, preferred by specialized problem-solvers and used in special kinds of rule-governed, impersonal situations." "Two Moralities," p. 304. Are all modern political problems of this kind?

[70] Nussbaum makes a strong case from an Aristotelian point of view for considering novels as integral parts of moral philosophy: "Aristotle makes it very clear that his own writing provides at most a 'sketch' or 'outline' of the good life, whose content must be given by experience, and whose central claims can be clarified only by appeal to life and to works of literature" ("Flawed Crystals," p. 43). Furbank makes a lively argument for the thesis that the modern novel as such (including Forster) has as a central mission the attempt to overthrow the paralyzing rhetoric of class analysis. See *Unholy Pleasure*, especially chap. 10.

no explicit reference to Aristotle, it is, I think, strikingly Aristotelian both in its embodiment of "the very simple Aristotelian idea that ethics is the search for a specification of the good life for a human being"[71] and in its substantive account of the virtues and of the character and difficulties of practical choice. The novel's central character is Margaret Schlegel, daughter of an English mother and a German émigré father—an English woman, but decidedly not "English to the backbone."[72] Forster's narrative is the story of Margaret's unlikely marriage, an event elaborately prepared by the author's comparison of her character—taste is perhaps a better word here—with those of the other persons in her drama. In brief, Margaret sees things as they are, and not only specifically "moral" things. Attending a performance of Beethoven's Fifth Symphony, Margaret "can only see the music"; her precocious schoolboy brother Tibby follows the counterpoint; her romantic sister Helen "can see heroes and shipwrecks in the music's flood"; her lovable and limited Aunt Juley will wait to "tap surreptitiously when the tunes come"; and her German-to-the-backbone cousin Frieda "remembers all the time that Beethoven is 'echt Deutsch' " (p. 31). Margaret sees and discriminates—thinks Beethoven is fine, doesn't like Brahms and Mendelssohn, despises Elgar, and hates Wagner (the great "muddler" of arts, p. 39)—and finely rebukes attempts to inflate or reduce musical meaning. But she cannot articulate a convincing defense of her taste; her more or less playful anger at Helen and Tibby leads to quarrels and silences rather than persuasion (p. 39).

Margaret's moral intuitions are as sharp as her musical ones; but here too she experiences difficulty in moving from complex perception to general rule. Smilingly reproached by her older friend Ruth Wilcox for her inexperience in life, she tries to defend herself by ascending into theory:

> Life's very difficult and full of surprises. At all events, I've got as far as that. To be humble and kind, to go straight ahead, to love people rather than pity them, to remember the submerged—well, one can't do all these things at once, worse luck, because they're so contradictory. It's then that proportion comes in—to live by proportion. Don't *begin* with proportion. Only prigs do that. Let proportion come in as a last re-

[71] "Flawed Crystals," p. 40.
[72] Forster, *Howards End*, p. 28. Subsequent page references will be to the Random House edition.

source, when the better things have failed, and a deadlock—
Gracious me, I've started preaching! (P. 73)

Virtues conflict, and one must follow a mean, though not in the
sense of some abstract a priori rule—but saying all this, theorizing
it, seems to undermine the delicacy that makes it attractive to begin with. Margaret knows and cares about particular people and
their lives; she resists abstract obligatory appeals to justice (p. 179)
and duty: "Nor am I concerned with duty. I'm concerned with the
characters of various people whom we know, and how, things being as they are, things may be made a little better" (p. 228). But
she seems reluctant or unable to capture her vision in general
speech—even to a kindred spirit.[73]

Margaret's *aporia* at articulating her sense of proportion, her
phronēsis, places her at an extreme disadvantage in matters of
larger political debate. In the only explicit discussion of a political
issue in *Howards End*—in a scene that might have come out of Aristotle's *Politics*, as we shall see—Margaret attempts, without the
least success, to defend a position on private philanthropy consistent with her character before a gathering of abstractly theoretical
opponents:

> Others had attacked the fabric of Society—Property, Interest,
> etc.; she only fixed her eyes on a few human beings, to see
> how, under present conditions, they could be made happier.
> Doing good to humanity was useless. . . . To do good to one,
> or, as in this case, to a few, was the utmost she dare hope for.
>   Between the idealists and the political economists, Margaret
> had a bad time. Disagreeing elsewhere, they agreed in dis-
> owning her. (p. 128)

In the modern political arena, proportion and contextual discernment seem to be without resource when confronted by the voices
of abstract theory, no matter how obtuse the latter may be.

Small wonder that Margaret admires, from a distance, an easi-
ness with universals that she associates with being German (pp.
28, 75). In Margaret's absence, the narrator remarks of her undis-
tinguished cousin Frieda that her unphilosophic mind "betrayed
that interest in the universal which the average Teuton possesses
and the average Englishman does not" (pp. 170–171). Still more

---

[73] Mrs. Wilcox is even less articulate than Margaret, but exhibits even more fully
the character of the *hexis* to choose the mean. Of her way of dying, we are told that
she "had taken the middle course, which only rarer natures can pursue. She had
kept proportion" (p. 102).

dangerous is the self-forgetting admiration Margaret feels toward Henry Wilcox, husband of her friend Ruth, master of the Imperial and West African Rubber Company, a man whose manipulative public power is suggested by his own feeling that "his hands were on all the ropes of life, and that what he did not know could not be worth knowing" (p. 131). After Ruth's death, Henry courts Margaret Schlegel, who comes quite genuinely to love and eventually to marry him. What is not clear, however, is the extent to which Margaret's love stems from frustration at her own *aporia* and public insignificance. Certainly, her defense of Henry and his family (his adult children are his lieutenants at the I&WA) takes the form of an admonition to bear in mind who, after all, makes the world go round. To her sister Helen, appalled at her coming marriage to one so grossly unlike her, Margaret contends, "If Wilcoxes hadn't worked and died in England for thousands of years, you and I couldn't sit here without having our throats cut" (p. 175). Wilcoxes, with their hands on the ropes, systematically and easily avoid that attention to the personal (pp. 92, 192) that is the source of Margaret's virtue and her frustration. Keeping her sensibility to herself, playing the helpless female, she doggedly sets out to use "the methods of the harem" (p. 230) to make Henry a better man (p. 243). Dissembling, holding her tongue (p. 221), she sees her marriage as a potentially powerful union of complementary strengths and weaknesses, one that can "connect the prose in us with the passion" (p. 186).

Margaret's project fails owing to the depth of Henry's vices; but it is important to be clear about just what those vices are. Henry is by no means a perfect villain—he possesses "such virtues as neatness, decision, and obedience, virtues of the second rank, no doubt, but they have formed our civilization" (p. 103). He is, moreover, hard-working, honest, self-confident, and cheerful (pp. 111, 161–162). His virtues are not simply the ones we might expect of a stereotypical Weberian capitalist: he does not reduce everything to profit and loss, is inherently hospitable (p. 229), and is unfailingly generous and kind (p. 209). His vices are in fact entirely *intellectual*, failings of mind and vision rather than sympathy and feeling. Margaret's project of reform fails because of Henry's intractable obtuseness: "He simply did not notice things" (p. 187). Full of generosity and utterly lacking in contextual discernment, in practical wisdom, Henry and his son Charles become the cause of misery and violent death, the unwitting agents of great harm to others and of the destruction of their own way of life: "The Wilcoxes were not lacking in affection; they had it royally, but they did not know how to use it" (p. 329). Finally realizing the uselessness of her efforts at redemption, Margaret turns on Henry and says, "I've had enough of your unweeded kindness" (p. 308).

What sort of vice is unweeded kindness? Henry Wilcox's character provides a modern dramatic specification of a moral type outlined by Aristotle in Book 6 of the *Nicomachean Ethics* (1144b1–25). Aristotle describes this figure as one who possesses "natural virtue" (*phusikē aretē*) but not effective or controlling virtue (*aretē pros tēn kurian*), that is, someone whose virtue or excellence is only potential, relatively indefinite and unfocused, as opposed to someone whose good inclinations are fully actualized as part of a characteristic structure of motives.[74] What such a person lacks is *phronēsis*, practical wisdom, the capacity for discerning one's own good or interest and the good of others one cares about in particular contexts calling for action. Such people are like well-intended children; without mind, their potentially good inclinations lack focus and may indeed be harmful to themselves and those around them. Once again, Aristotle explains this flaw by means of an analogy: "just as a mighty body moving around without sight chances to be mightily overthrown on account of not having sight, so it is with these matters." What is lacking in such a person is not the ability to desire or will some universal goal, but an ability to understand the problems and possibilities that belong to a particular context. This failure cannot be corrected by, and indeed may be quite compatible with, the special moral perspective assumed by rule moralities: neither Gilligan's universal injunction to care and nonviolence[75] nor Kohlberg's principled commitment to respect universal rights suggests a remedy for unweeded kindness.

After Henry's mighty overthrow, Margaret gathers him up and, along with her sister Helen and Helen's child, establishes a self-sufficient household at Howards End, the small farm that was Ruth Wilcox's family home. Margaret does indeed achieve a kind of victory, partly by accident—Henry is not reformed but reduced, and becomes a quiet, docile, tired, and kindly figure, sitting in his chair, playing with the children, and following Margaret's instructions. As Helen says, she has become a kind of hero (p. 339), rescuing the others from the shipwreck of their lives and establishing an order in which they can live and be happy. She has acquired a

[74] For a good discussion of the use of *pros tēn kurian* and *kuriōs* in the *NE*, see Irwin, *Nicomachean Ethics*, p. 391.

[75] See Broughton, "Women's Rationality and Men's Virtues," p. 615.

new power over the course of the novel, partly through recognition of her own limits, but in part also by gaining a sense of a way of life that permits her to connect aspiration and personal circumstance. This mediating vision is particularly (as opposed to universally) political—a revelation of a peculiarly English life and virtue that comes to her as she reflects, toward the middle of the novel, on her fondness for Howards End: "an unexpected love of the island awoke in her, connecting on this side with the joys of the flesh, on that with the inconceivable" (p. 204). The action-orienting vision becomes specifically moral as she looks at a giant wych-elm growing by the side of the house:

> No report had prepared her for its peculiar glory. It was neither warrior, nor lover, nor god; in none of these roles do the English excel. It was a comrade, bending over the house, strength and adventure in its roots, but in its utmost fingers tenderness, and the girth, that a dozen men could not have spanned, became in the end evanescent, till pale bud clusters seemed to float in the air. It was a comrade. House and tree transcended any similes of sex. (P. 206)

Margaret's England is not England as it is; imperialism, cosmopolitanism, and the ropes of life have nothing to do with Howards End. But neither is it simply fond nostalgia. It represents a hope for a future civilization, for a polity that embodies certain local virtues, and does so in a way that enables Margaret to plan and direct the life of the farm and the disposition of her own and Henry's income. Margaret's discovery of England is the discovery of an authoritative ground that specifies and invigorates her formerly indeterminate and passive practical wisdom. This ground is supplied not by the acceptance of any universal moral rule, but through an image of a national way of life within which Margaret's sense of the appropriate finds the depth and clarity it formerly lacked.

Forster's solution to the problem of extending agent morality to the public realm, however, seems fragile in two ways. The first is practical and historical: is the resistance of the world really so great that the only reasonable response to the difficulties of modern society is a withdrawal into "a new life, obscure, yet gilded with tranquillity" (p. 336)? We will return to this question in the final section of this chapter. The other fragility is theoretical: is formulation of an authority-bestowing national or cultural vision the best that practical philosophy can do in support of a morality of the virtues? If so, we may be forced to conclude that the rejection of the possibility of universal rules of conduct requires the rejection of abstraction and theory altogether—thus depriving us of the possibility of either justifying or gaining critical distance from the political cultures in which we live. It is this question I want to address to Aristotle's *Politics*: To what extent can theorizing suggest a way of approaching issues of action and practical choice that allows both devotion to and critical distance from the local political context in a manner clear enough to be politically useful?[76]

Aristotle on Theory and Practice

Aristotle's practical philosophy combines two premises that appear, from the standpoint of modern moral philosophy, to contradict one another. The first is the view elaborated in the previous chapter that there is an intelligible human good, one accessible to ordinary experience and to scientific inquiry or theory, a good that holds universally for all human beings and does not vary from context to context. The character of this good is outlined in the first books of the *Nicomachean Ethics* and the *Politics*; it is expressed not as a separate thing or substance to be achieved, but as a specific kind of work or activity—the human *ergon*, which is further elaborated (though still, it must be stressed, only in outline) as a particular way of life, a way of life that is reasonable (with *logos*) or deliberative (*not* "freely chosen") rather than episodically emotional. A virtuous or good person is one who is characteristically inclined and able to respond to the various circumstances and emotions of life (whether fear or love or money or honor) in a reasonable way.

The second key Aristotelian premise responds to the question of how, assuming we accept the Aristotelian conception of the human good, we go about deciding how to act virtuously or reasonably, and here is where the problem arises. Aristotle's answer to this question is that the appropriate response to problems arising from our emotions and circumstances will vary from context to context and that the only standard or criterion for distinguishing appropriate from inappropriate responses is the formal image of what a person of practical wisdom would be likely to do in a given case. That is, for Aristotle there are no natural laws comparable to

[76] Or: how would Margaret Schlegel read Aristotle's *Politics*?

those we find in Hobbes or, for that matter, in Thomas Aquinas.[77] The clearest statement of this position and the reason for it is found in Book 5 of the *Nicomachean Ethics*, in Aristotle's response to the *aporia* about the difference between justice and "decency" (*to epieikes*) (1137b2). Aristotle says that justice and decency are really the same—that is, they both aim at the human good in situations calling for the distribution of goods or the righting of wrongs—but that decency is in a way better, because justice is bound to and limited by the idea of *nomos*:

> What sets up this *aporia* is that while decency is justice, yet it is not according to law, but instead corrects legal justice. And the cause (*aition*) of this is that law is always universal, but it is not possible to speak correctly about some things in a universal way. Therefore in those things where it is necessary to speak universally, yet impossible to do so correctly, the law takes the line of speaking in terms of what is usually the case, and is not ignorant of the fact that it is making a mistake. And the law is no less right, for the error is neither in the law nor in the legislator but in the nature of the thing itself; for the matter of practical things is like this from the start. (1137b11–19)

As a result of this variability of human events, there will be times when even the best laws need to be supplemented by particular political decisions (or "decrees" [*psēphismata*]) (1137b27–29) which cannot be deduced from any higher laws,[78] even though we are indeed beings whose interest is served by living according to laws.

But how can this be? There is something troubling about saying both (a) that there is a rationally discoverable human good and (b) that there are no rationally discoverable or justifiable rules of conduct. Responses to this puzzle tend to go in one of two directions, asserting either that (b) is Aristotle's real view, and that therefore his account of the human good is hopelessly inadequate (this is

[77] On Thomas's transformation of Aristotle's "just (or right) by nature" into "natural law," see Jaffa, *Thomism and Aristotelianism*, pp. 167–188. It is as if one were to transform the statement "20/20 vision is generally good for human beings" into "Humans must have 20/20 vision."

[78] For an excellent discussion of these passages, see Nussbaum, *De Motu Animalium*, pp. 211–219, and *Fragility of Goodness*, pp. 294–306. I am much indebted to these analyses, although I disagree with Nussbaum's claim that the Platonic view of the possibility of eternal laws is significantly different from the Aristotelian one. Speaking of the laws and the human things, the Eleatic Stranger asks: "Isn't it impossible for that which is always simple to hold good for things that are never simple?" (*Statesman* 294c7–8).

Kohlberg's way of dismissing Aristotle as a "bag of virtues" theorist, of no help in constructing an ideal personality type),[79] or that (a) is his real view, and that therefore he must really be committed to a natural law doctrine.[80] It thus commonly appears that Aristotle's position on theory and practice, that good actions are those that a person of practical wisdom would likely perform in similar circumstances, is either uninformatively circular or in clear contradiction with his teleological account of the human good. The position I want to defend here is that Aristotle's conception of theory and practice differs both from deductivism—the thesis that a conception of the good dictates a certain action-choice (that "is" implies "ought")—*and* from noncognitivism—the thesis that conceptions of the human good cannot provide theoretical grounding or justification for action-choice. In brief, Aristotle's position is that while particular action-choices can never be deduced from conceptions of the human good, each particular action-choice presupposes a criticizable conception of this good, and the work of practical philosophy is precisely to open such presuppositions to criticism in the light of a teleological understanding of human being.

Before looking at some examples of this kind of criticism in the *Politics* and the *Nicomachean Ethics*, it will be helpful to review Aristotle's conception of the human good in order to see how that conception leads to Aristotle's distinctive sense of the relationship of theory and practice. His initial claim is that human needs, like those of all other living things, are biologically inherited—and are thus constituted for us by nature, rather than created by our wants, desires, or actions. Reasonable people are those who have a correct perception of these needs. But unlike the needs of other living things, our needs are complex and may frequently conflict with one another. Thus, in Aristotle's shorthand, political choices must take into account our interest in *zēn*, *eu zēn*, and *suzēn*. In order to develop well we need, among other things, material security, family, a political order, friends, and time and room to

[79] See Flanagan and Jackson, "Justice, Care, and Gender," pp. 622–623.

[80] "If you start from within the Thomistic web of belief, and proceed to undermine its Aristotelian confidence in the use of human reason as an instrument for discovering the value-laden facts of natural law . . . you will have greatly diminished the network of 'conceptual connections' that donate meaning to moral terms and propositions." Stout, *Flight from Authority*, p. 249. It is perhaps because MacIntyre misconstrues Aristotelian natural right in this way that he ends up seeking a rational foundation for morality in a thoroughly un-Aristotelian way. See Kateb, "Looking for Mr. Good Life," p. 434.

think; and, in any given circumstance, actions that help obtain some of the things we need will tend to hinder the pursuit of others. Being reasonable about our interest is no simple matter of applying a rule (maximize food, say, or maximize thought), but rather involves arriving at an intelligent balance of competing needs or interests, an action-choice informed by our sense of which needs are most closely connected with human virtue, of the contextual urgency of satisfying certain needs, and of our own and others' limits, since human beings in fact differ from one another more than do animals of other species.[81]

Because of this multidimensionality of the problem of human needs, questions of practical choice cannot be resolved either by a single universal rule or by a series of rules ("metapreference schedules") that assign priority weights in advance to possibly competing goods. The human good happens to be such that practical wisdom cannot be codified. John McDowell puts Aristotle's point in the following way: "If the conception of how to live involved a ranking of concerns, or perhaps a set of rankings each relativized to some type of situation, the explanation of why one concern was operative rather than another would be straightforward. But uncodifiability rules out laying down such general rankings in advance of all the predicaments with which life may confront one."[82] The empirical complexity of human needs and interests—and not any misty ineffability or godlike autonomy of the human condition—is what gives moral and political problems their indefiniteness. This picture of human life supplies the ground for the Aristotelian conclusion that good or reasonable action-choices are not deductively valid and necessary applications of universal rules, but more like well-informed guesses, resting on complex perceptions of that balance of importance and urgency that is likely to be best for us.

A good illustration on the nonpolitical level of the extent to which theorizing about these matters is possible and helpful is the discussion (*NE* 9, 1164b22–1165a35) of the *aporia* or perplexity involved in trying to decide what sort of regard is owed to different persons. For Aristotle, this way of beginning a theoretical reflec-

---

[81] We must ask, for example, whether in a particular case we can achieve genuine friendship with another, or whether it would be better not to risk the advantages we get from our legally mediated political relationship. Friendship is for Aristotle the best human relationship, the one that corresponds to and satisfies the best needs we have for one another. Even justice is only an approximation of friendship. *NE* 7, 1155a22–28.

[82] "Virtue and Reason," p. 344.

tion is characteristic: practical theorizing has the aspect of an intervention into a current dispute (*amphisbētēma*) or perplexity, an *aporia*—the situation that arises when people are unable to decide
between contradictory and equally attractive lines of reasoning
(*Topics* 6, 145b16–20). Inducing this sort of condition is just what
Plato's Socrates characteristically does; for both Plato and Aristotle, *aporia* (such as the one about decency and justice in *NE* 5) is
the necessary motive or occasion for philosophizing or theorizing
about actions.

The *aporia* about conflicting duties in *Nicomachean Ethics* 9 is
stated as follows: Should one always obey and respect one's father, or should one obey experts, depending on the situation?
Should one help friends or help virtuous people, when these are
not the same and it is impossible to do both? Is it better to repay a
debt or to do a favor for a friend, if you cannot do both? Aristotle's
response is that although theory cannot provide a precise rule or
decision procedure for solving such practical dilemmas, it can be
helpful in several ways. It can explain that the reason precise universal solutions are not possible is the *variety* of differences among
the people involved: in deciding to whom we should accord primary regard, we need to consider both the relative importance of
the claims of different individuals and the extent to which these
claims reflect either fineness or necessity (*to kalon kai anangkaion*),
comparable here to our simultaneous yet diverse interests in living
and living well. In addition, theory can suggest rules of thumb
that hold true usually or for the most part (*epi to polu*), such as the
rule that one should repay debts in preference to doing favors.

Aristotle frequently refers to such rules; they seem to reflect empirical generalizations about the kinds of mistakes people are most
likely to make in practical choice. In *Nicomachean Ethics* 2, for example, at the conclusion of the discussion of the mean as the controlling metaphor for virtuous character or choice, he suggests two
such rules: avoid the extreme more opposed to the mean (1109a30–
31),[83] and avoid the extreme toward which you are most attracted—something that will surely vary greatly from person to
person. Such rules are, of course, not always consistent with one
another and represent a "second sailing" (*deuteros plous*) (1109a34–
35), a metaphoric idiom that refers to the sailors' need to have recourse to oars when the wind fails—we need rules when our per-

[83] For example, in aiming at liberality, avoid stinginess rather than extravagance
(*NE* 3, 1121a27–30).

ceptions are not likely to be accurate.[84] Rules of thumb can help us avoid the more usual errors, but they cannot adequately determine action-choices, which require a perception (*aisthēsis*) in each case (1109b21–23).

In the passage in *Nicomachean Ethics* 9, Aristotle goes on to reiterate that rules do not always hold true, and then says why: we must always consider the people involved, and ask how we should treat this parent, this neighbor, this fellow citizen, and so on. The problem of interpersonal comparison cannot be avoided either by the creation of an impersonal rule (such as "treat everyone in the same way") *or* by following a rule that requires us to give all respect to one sort of person—presumably the most virtuous ("just as we do not offer every sacrifice to Zeus," 1165a15). We must treat each person "appropriately" (1165a17), but appropriateness cannot be expressed as a rule. Individuals are heterogeneous, and they reflect heterogeneous interests and needs—needs for family, polity, friendship, virtue. In hard cases such needs conflict, and their relative importance for us will vary from occasion to occasion. Aristotle concludes this discussion of the uses and limits of theory by saying that interpersonal comparison is difficult "with people of different kinds. But one must not on this account give up the comparison; rather, it is necessary to make discriminations as well as we can" (1165a33–35).

Theory is too abstract and impersonal to supply practice with determinate rules of action, but it can inform and improve situational judgment in three ways: by explaining why such judgment must attend to persons, by pointing out the way in which different persons or relationships correspond to different needs, and by calling attention to the commonest sorts of errors. Aristotelian agent morality takes its bearings from an articulation of the richness and complexity of the natural world of human needs and interests, in contrast with modern moral philosophy, which would reduce all interests to a single "genuine" need—a least common denominator—or escape that world altogether by describing a special and separate "moral" domain.

[84] The second sailing metaphor is used in several key places by Plato, in ways that suggest an important similarity between Plato and Aristotle in theory and practice. Perhaps the best known is in Socrates' characterization of his own "flight to the *logoi*" and away from trying to explain particulars by unmediated reference to an Anaxagorean universal *nous* as a second sailing (*Phaedo* 99c9–d1). Another is the Eleatic Stranger's reference to the rule of laws rather than of the wise as a second sailing (*Statesman* 300c2); and Protarchus' similar reference to Socratic knowledge of ignorance in contrast with divine knowledge (*Philebus* 19c2–3).

The discussion in *Nicomachean Ethics* 9 refers to situations we might call "personal" or "private," situations in which we know the people involved and their relation to our interests. Can this approach to moral reasoning be extended to political or public matters as well? For Aristotle it can (hence the celebrated continuity between the *Nicomachean Ethics* and the *Politics*), for a reason that is a part of his theory of human needs. If human beings are to flourish, to live well or virtuously according to their specific potentialities, they require a variety of more or less extended institutional affiliations: the greatest human good, happiness or flourishing (*eudaimonia*), is a kind of self-sufficiency, "but we say 'self-sufficiency' not with respect to a solitary self, one living a solitary life, but with respect to a life with parents and children and a wife and friends and fellow citizens generally, since human being (*anthrōpos*) is by nature political" (1097b8–11). We have a quite natural interest in the well-being of our family, our friendships, our political order, and as a result our political judgments should not differ *in kind* from the complex balancing of heterogeneous interests that characterizes the operation of practical wisdom in private life. In *Nicomachean Ethics* 6, Aristotle explicitly denies any qualitative difference between *phronēsis* and political wisdom in part by noting that "we cannot live well without a familial order (*oikonomia*), nor without a political order (*politeia*)" (1142a9–10). Personal and political judgments are continuous rather than dichotomous because each involves a consideration of individual interests; there is no separate political sphere (as, say, for Hannah Arendt) that defines a separate political interest. Moreover, as can be seen from the discussion of conflicting duties in *Nicomachean Ethics* 9, private judgments are hardly as simple as they may seem; complexity and difficult choices are not unique to political deliberation.

Still, political judgments are more difficult insofar as they typically involve *classes* of persons, rather than known individuals. In addition, the consequences of political decisions may well be greater (and less subject to subsequent control) than those of nonpolitical life. These considerations might incline us to seek the safety of a "second sailing" guided by universal rules—or to acknowledge the wisdom of adhering to time-honored customary norms. But in the *Politics* as in the *Nicomachean Ethics*, Aristotle holds that good practical judgments are the work of *phronēsis* rather than theory *or* adherence to traditional authority. And yet, in politics as elsewhere, good action-choice can be aided by some theoretical grasp of human needs. Both those who ignore theory and those who think it can be applied directly are dangerous to good politics, and the latter much more so than the former. Leo Strauss expresses this view of the relevance of theory to political practice in the following terms in his discussion of classical natural right: "There is a universally valid hierarchy of ends, but there are no universally valid rules of action. . . . one has to consider not only which of the various competing objectives is higher in rank but also which is most urgent in the circumstances."[85] In what follows, we will see how Aristotle attempts to achieve this difficult balance in the *Politics*.

Theoretical Interventions in the Politics

Inferring Aristotle's intention from the words of the *Politics* is no easy matter. On the one hand, that intention seems to be strictly theoretical: we are presented with a deductive movement from statements about universal human needs (in Book 1) to conclusions about what sorts of polities can best satisfy those needs (in Book 3). On the other hand, Aristotle's intention seems quite local and practical: starting with contemporary political debates that seem stalemated in *aporia* or *amphisbētēma*, he suggests how these perplexities or disputes should be construed and resolved. The striking thing here is that Aristotle does *not* claim that such practical problems can be settled by applying theoretical principles in a deductive manner: he offers no "practical syllogisms." Where his intention—his understanding of the purpose of a theoretical approach to practical questions—lies can be seen by considering examples of his theoretical interventions in the political disputes of his time: the question of slavery, the question of whether legal reform should be encouraged, the question of who or what should be sovereign in the city, and the question of the most desirable human life. In all these cases a single understanding of the relationship of theory and practice emerges: theory is useful to practice in clarifying the real issues involved and in exposing false solutions (that is, solutions that presuppose false propositions), but not in providing answers. Theory cannot resolve such debates— no theoretical "is" can entail a practical "ought"—but it can improve their quality by decreasing the extent and power of false

[85] *Natural Right and History*, p. 162. This is the same point made by McDowell in his discussion of the "uncodifiability" of practical wisdom, and by Nussbaum in her characterization of Aristotelian universal law as "a summary of wise decisions" (*Fragility of Goodness*, p. 301).

claims about human interests within them, and as a result increase the chances for the kind of well-informed guessing that constitutes practical wisdom.

The beginning of the *Politics* is highly abstract and theoretical, using language derived from Aristotle's biology to support the claim that the *polis* properly understood is prior by nature to the individual. This short course in theory breaks off at 1253b14 with the introduction of the question of slavery. Aristotle's introduction to the question bespeaks the duality of intention noted above: "Let us speak first of the master and the slave, in order to see things relative to practical necessity and in order that we may get a better grasp of these things relative to knowledge (*pros to eidenai*) than people have nowadays." The two dominant contemporary views are that mastery is like politics, a science and a good thing, and that mastery is contrary to nature because people belong to others only by convention (*nomos*) and force (on the assumption that all conventions are, like force, contrary to nature). Aristotle's strategy is to show that both sides are wrong because each is too simple and should be informed by a more adequate knowledge of the needs universally predicable of human beings. In opposition to both slavemasters and abolitionists, Aristotle concludes that slavery is justified only insofar as (a) it is necessary for the leisure without which virtue cannot be developed, (b) it does not threaten the *philia* or friendship without which politics is impossible (1255b12–16), and (c) the slaves differ from the masters as much as the body from the soul or other animals from human beings generally. He is absolutely silent about whether this or that system or instance of slavery is a good thing (though he does criticize some systems later on, such as the helot-slavery of Sparta [*Pol.* 2, 1269a34–b12]); his theoretical contribution to practice lies in showing that the absolute solutions offered by slavemasters and abolitionists are wrong insofar as they rest on false theoretical presuppositions, and in indicating the kinds of considerations a good action-choice would require. But the nature of that choice will vary from circumstance to circumstance, depending on the dangers and possibilities of the moment: it may, for instance, be necessary to defer the hopes of leisure in order to secure *philia*, or it may not.[86]

[86] The conditions Aristotle sets for legitimate or natural slavery seem prohibitively high, and yet in the highly simplified and abstract polity in speech in which everything exists "according to wish" (*kat' euchēn*) rather than in the complex manner of the natural world of human interests, farming would be done exclusively by slaves—since farming, like commercial and laboring activity (*Pol.* 7, 1328b33–

The question of legal reform emerges in *Politics* 2 from the consideration of a proposal made by the very theoretical Hippodamus[87] that citizens ought to be rewarded for recommending changes in the laws or customs (*nomoi*) of the *polis*. Hippodamus' specific proposal is soon left behind as Aristotle shifts the discussion to the level of theoretical presupposition by posing the question of whether laws should be subject to change as a debate between two groups of politicians, the conservatives and the progressives. The conservatives say that the ancestral is the good and that the *nomoi* should always be allowed to stand. The progressives counter that this is as silly as saying that old surgical techniques should be allowed to remain in spite of new discoveries. As with the slavery debate, Aristotle's technique here is to show that the claims of both sides rest on presuppositions involving serious theoretical errors. The conservatives are wrong in identifying the old and the good, and the progressives are wrong in ignoring the differences between *nomoi* and medical techniques. Both sides fail to understand something about human nature and human needs, and so defend positions that are unreasonable and inappropriate. An appropriate judgment will be informed by the recognition that *nomoi* should be understood as criticizable proposals for satisfying human needs under the circumstances. Thus, unquestioning acceptance of traditional authority simply represents a mistake about the true character of *nomoi*. The progressives, however, also err— by failing to recognize that no *nomos*, good or bad, can work if it is not accepted, more or less without question, by the people whose lives it orders. In this way, Aristotle suggests the importance of balancing the human need for authority against other needs— those for security, or civil friendship, or moral education, for example. In both cases the error is theoretical, and can be corrected

1329a2), makes leisure hard to come by, and leisure is a necessary condition for education in virtue (though not a sufficient one—the very rich have plenty of leisure, but tend to be ineducable for other reasons [*Pol.* 3, 1295b13–18]). This solution is abstract—not useful as a rule to be followed in the real world—because it assumes that other conditions for education in virtue (such as *philia*) have already been satisfied once and for all. Nussbaum suggests here that "his application of his own criteria may be marred by prejudice and xenophobia" (*Fragility of Goodness*, p. 348n.). Ambler, in his excellent "Aristotle on Nature and Politics," sees this discrepancy as showing that for Aristotle the standard of nature is primarily a reminder of our limitations rather than a substantive guide to political choice. This seems to me unduly to limit the scope of theoretical reflection on politics. See Nichols, "Good Life, Slavery, and Acquisition."

[87] Hippodamus is mentioned again in *Pol.* 7, 1330b24, where his proposal for a regular street plan is praised for its beauty but criticized for its neglect of wartime requirements.

by a more accurate understanding of the complexity and diversity of universally predicable human interests, that is, of the human good. But this is as far as theory can properly go. The question of whether specific laws should be changed here and now is a question theory cannot answer. Aristotle poses this question, observes that it is terribly important, and concludes by saying, "let us leave this inquiry aside now, for it belongs to other occasions (*kairoi*)" (1269a28–29). This conclusion illustrates the general point (*NE* 2, 1104a3–10) that practical choice is always relative to the occasion (*pros ton kairon*) and cannot be understood as a specific application of a universally valid command or rule.

The practical dispute over who or what should govern in the *polis*—discussed in Chapter 2 with an eye to the distinction between the necessary and constitutive conditions of political life—is more serious and more complex than the two discussed so far, but the form of Aristotle's theoretical intervention in the politics of his time is much the same. The issue is more complex because there are three competing positions rather than two: those who say that the well-off should rule, those who say that the people (*dēmos*) should rule, and those who say that neutral laws, and not any group of persons, should rule. All three—oligarchs, democrats, and legalists—approach the question in the style of rule morality, and all are mistaken in their understanding of the human good. Aristotle isolates the theoretical issue by showing that all sides base their political positions upon empirically mistaken assumptions about equality, presupposing either that equal wealth deserves equal power, or that all humans are equal, or that all should be equal before the law. Aristotle says that they are all right in assuming that justice involves some sort of equality, but wrong in their teleological understanding of what equality means for human beings—that is, about the way relationships of equality can play a part in political solutions to the problem of human needs and interests. Settling the issue requires clarity about what equality is for, and this requires theory: "It is necessary to grasp 'Equality in what things?' and 'Inequality in what things?' and this *aporia* calls for political philosophy (*philosophia politikē*)" (1282b22–24).

The ensuing discussion of equality does not result in a once-and-for-all solution to the problem of who should govern, but it does clarify the problem by showing that distribution of power in a *polis* should correspond to contribution to, or effect on, the ends of the *polis*, the purposes or functions of political life established by universal human needs. As we saw in Chapter 2, there are sev-

145

eral such ends—protecting life and security, ensuring a sort of *phi-lia* or political community, and educating in virtue or the capacity for acting reasonably. This last is the highest, constitutive purpose of political life, but electoral policies (perhaps literacy or other tests for eligibility to vote) that support this definitive end will almost always threaten the security and internal harmony of the *polis*, since inequality is the main necessitating cause of *stasis* or civil disorder.[88] As with slavery and legal change, the conclusion is that any reasonable decision about the appropriate distribution of political power will avoid blind adherence to unreasonable rules—rules that abstractly favor only one of the purposes of political life (education, integration, security), and neglect the rest. Since urgency and nobility must each be taken into account, and since necessary and constitutive conditions often make conflicting demands simultaneously, theorizing about equality further demonstrates that rational principles (or rationally justified principles) are simply not to be had and that a good political choice will therefore be one that weighs the possibilities of the present situation in light of those natural goals that theory can help to clarify.

If the different purposes or goods the city requires could somehow be reduced to a common measure (in the way that the value of economic goods—houses and shoes—*can* be translated into money [*NE* 5, 1132b31–1133b28]), then we could in principle calculate precisely how much material security could be exchanged for how much political friendship or moral virtue, just as five beds are worth one house. But political goods are not commensurable (*sumblēton*, an Aristotelian coinage) in the way that economic goods are (*Pol.* 3, 1283a3–11). They can be ranked, but not converted into units of exchange.

The last practical issue to be considered here is the debate over whether the political life as such is better than a life apart from politics—with some anachronism, this might be called the debate between civic republicans and philosophic idealists. This controversy, taken up at the beginning of *Politics* 7, is essentially the same as the well-known Aristotelian puzzle set out in *Nicomachean Ethics* 10, about whether the theoretical life is better than the political life. The answer given to this question is the same in both places: in theory—that is, on the basis of an abstract and universal consideration of the constitutive potentiality or first actuality of

---

[88] Note here that Aristotle's explanation blends teleological claims with predictive ones—and that, as in the case of the hypothesis that *stasis* always follows from inequality, his hypotheses are themselves criticizable empirically.

human nature—the theoretical life is best; but this theoretical conclusion cannot be translated without considerable distortion into a practical rule, like "Be as theoretical as you can." Just as we should not offer all sacrifices to Zeus, and just as it would be a disastrous error to claim abstractly that the most virtuous people should always have sole political power, so it would be wrong to transform the definitive end or possibility of human nature into a developmental stage or a practical rule, equally applicable in all particular cases.

Aristotle is clear about the need to avoid converting teleological explanations directly into action-choices. For example, as regards what determines the identity of a *polis*—is it the land, the inhabitants, or the *politeia*?—there is no doubt that from a teleological point of view a city's character and identity are determined by its form or end, not its geographical or biological matter, as it were (*Pol.* 3, 1276b1–13). But this does not settle the issue of whether a new regime should honor agreements contracted by the one it has replaced: "But whether it is just to fulfill [such agreements] or not whenever a *polis* is changed into another *politeia*, that is another *logos*" (1276b13–15). Similarly, the fact that in theory decrees (*psēphismata*) are more accurate than laws (*nomoi*) does not prevent democracies where laws generally rule from being better than those in which rule by decree is more common (*Pol.* 4, 1292a1–38)—after a point, a city ruled by decree ceases to be a politically organized community at all, since "wherever the laws do not rule, there is no *politeia*" (1292a32).[89]

Aristotle's discussion, here as elsewhere, is intended to inform rather than control or replace practical choice, as well as to warn against misleading principles that abstract one human interest or possibility—even the highest or most definitive—from the complex range of human needs. The question of what sort of life should be chosen in a particular case is a question theory *must* not answer, although every answer will presuppose some theoretically criticizable conclusions. Aristotle makes this quite clear in *Politics* 7, 1324a14–23:

---

[89] A similar issue arises in the *aporia* concerning whether the best human being will want friends. If the best human is godlike, and if gods (being independently self-sufficient) have no friends, then friendship will be a bother for the best humans. Aristotle rejects this in both *NE* 9, 1169b3–1170b19, and the *EE*. In the latter, Aristotle says that the view that the best people do not need friends is only plausible to those who are misled by the analogy with gods (*EE* 7, 1244b). Whoever knows only the constitutive *ergon* of a being will not be able to say much about how that being should act.

147

These two things need inquiry: first, which is the more desirable way of life, the life of politics and the community of the *polis*, or the life of the outsider (*xenikos*) who is cut loose from the political community; second, what is the regime (*politeia*) and disposition (*diathesis*) of the best *polis*, if sharing in the *polis* is desirable either for all or for most though not for some. And since the business of political thought and theory is this second question *and not* [the question of] *what is desirable for the individual* . . . it is the second question that is the business of this inquiry (*methodos*).

The theoretical conclusion that the philosophic life is humanly better than the political can help protect me against the charms of civic republicanism, something especially important to Aristotle because of his belief that those who are single-mindedly committed to the political easily make the kind of mistakes proper to slavemasters and lovers of war—in their treatment of foreigners if not of fellow citizens (1324a38–b3). But this theoretical conclusion does not provide sufficient ground for deciding either how I can best live my life or how public education ought to be organized in any given polity. To assume otherwise, in the spirit of philosophical idealism, would be to act according to wish or prayer (*kat' euchēn*)[90] rather than with appropriate contextual discernment. After several pages discussing the institutional arrangements of the best regime according to prayer, Aristotle breaks off abruptly with this comment: "But it is fruitless to spend time now giving precise discussions and speaking about such things; for it is not hard to think of them, but rather to produce them; for speaking about them, on the one hand, is a work of prayer, but their being brought about, on the other, is the work of chance" (*Pol.* 7, 1331b18–22). Theorizing can inform and improve the quality of my deliberate guesses about what measures will bring about well-being in a particular case, but it cannot cleanse those guesses of their humanly necessary uncertainty. To imagine otherwise is to subscribe to the delusions built into rule morality, modern or ancient—to forget, as it were, that the road from Athens to Thebes is not precisely the same as the road from Thebes to Athens.

As we have seen, Aristotle characteristically begins his theoretical interventions with a statement of contradictory claims that turn

[90] See Chapter 2, p. 91, and note 86 in this chapter. For a fine account of the subtle way the praise of the philosophic life informs Aristotle's sense of the possibilities of politics, see Mara, "Philosophy in Aristotle's Political Science."

out, upon reflection, to be false; but it would be a mistake to read such interventions as simply attempts to find a middle way or compromise between extremes. This sort of mistake is very precisely described by the narrator of *Howards End*:

> Perhaps Margaret grew too old for metaphysics, perhaps Henry was weaning her from them, but she felt that there was something a little unbalanced in the mind that so readily shreds the visible. The business man who assumes that this life is everything, and the mystic who asserts that it is nothing, fail, on this side and on that, to hit the truth. "Yes, I see, dear; it's about halfway between," Aunt Juley had hazarded in earlier years. No; truth, being alive, was not halfway between anything. It was only to be found by continuous excursions into either realm, and though proportion is the final secret, to espouse it at the outset is to insure sterility. (PP. 194–195)

Aristotle's theoretical solutions to practical controversies are always different in kind as well as in content from the alternatives they are meant to replace. That difference defines Aristotelian agent morality and suggests its primary intellectual virtue, a certain *tact*, a knowing when to speak and when to be silent, a virtue systematically absent from all forms of rule morality.[91] Theoretical tact is a virtue insofar as we acknowledge the essential complexity of human interests[92]—a complexity that is avoided rather than denied by the procedures of modern moral philosophy. The superiority of agent morality—quite apart from the truth or falsehood of any of Aristotle's substantive claims about human needs or their ranking—rests upon the thought that political complexity calls for

[91] Another way of stating that distinct difference is Strauss's comment that "the only universally valid standard is the hierarchy of ends. This standard is sufficient for passing judgment on the level of nobility of individuals and groups and of actions and institutions. But it is insufficient for guiding our actions." *Natural Right and History*, p. 163.

[92] Ambler's close reading of the discussion of the art of acquisition in Bk. 1 of the *Pol.* provides a fine example of this characteristic of Aristotle's theoretical style, by showing how Aristotle at first offers and then subverts the possibility of simple applications of nature ("Acquisition is by nature good" or "Acquisition is by nature bad") as an evaluative standard to politics. Ambler's conclusion is that "if nature emerges as a standard whose bearing on politics is less direct than we had hoped, it may also be that its foundation is more secure than others have claimed." "Aristotle on Acquisition," p. 502. Ignatieff's conclusion about the relationship of a theory of needs to practical choice exemplifies the Aristotelian position: "A language of needs cannot reconcile our contradictory goods; it can only help us to say what they are." *Needs of Strangers*, p. 137.

understanding rather than dissolution. From this perspective, the function of political philosophy, as the link between theory and practice, is not to furnish rules but to show why theoretically derived principles are mistaken if understood in an unqualified fashion—and to perform the delicate task of thinking about what aspects of our knowledge of human needs and possibilities are most relevant to political choice, in the hope of informing such choice in ways that rules never can.

Agent Morality and the Analysis of Modern Politics

The central feature of the Aristotelian understanding of the relation between theory and practice is the thought that theorizing should inform practice by opening the presuppositions of action to critical discussion, rather than by producing binding rules of conduct. This is, I think, the task of the tradition of evaluative explanation as a whole. Such theorizing provides a language—the language of nature understood teleologically—for thinking about the appropriateness of commitments to authoritative traditions, like Forster's version of England, without determining the outcome of such thought—the eventual action-choice—in advance. This theorizing functions as a part of contextual discernment, rather than an independent alternative to it. By informing local perceptions or "intuitions," and by pointing out the meretricious attractiveness of universal rules, a complex theory of the virtues (of human needs and interests) serves to clarify action-choice to a much greater degree than Rawls's critique of "intuitionistic perfectionism" supposes. But even if we accept the attractiveness of Aristotelian agent morality, a question must still remain as to whether the circumstances of modernity—either political or philosophical—are not so remote from Aristotelian theorizing as to render this perspective untranslatable into our context. This question is parallel to the one about teleology and modern science discussed in Chapter 1, though not reducible to it: the plausibility and value of teleological science is a question independent of the issue of whether Aristotle's practical philosophizing (which rests on a version of teleological science) is intelligible to modern readers. We may divide this question into two parts. First, in what way and to what extent does Aristotelian theory differ from modern political philosophy? And second, to what extent does modern Western

150

politics itself demand a mode of theorizing different from that demanded by the politics of the ancient Greek world?

The core of Aristotelian practical philosophy can be expressed in two propositions: first, the human good is knowable but complex, since we inherit biologically not a single overriding need or impulse, but a set of competing needs that can be ranked, though only abstractly; and second, as a result, theorizing about the human good can evaluate the presuppositions of conduct but not generate rules of conduct that will bind all rational persons. While I have stressed Aristotle's exposition of this position, I do not think it is peculiar to Aristotle or dependent on any particularly Aristotelian understanding of the substance of the human good.[93] Plato's view of the relationship between theory and practice, for example, is strikingly similar.[94] Socrates does, of course, propose the establishment of a "science of measurement" (*metrētikē technē*) in the *Protagoras* (356d4), a proposal which led J. S. Mill to hail him as the first utilitarian. But it is hard not to regard this endorsement of the program of rule morality as ironic, resting as it does on the highly eccentric (for Socrates and Plato) equation of the good and the pleasant.[95] Most of the early and middle dialogues show Socrates practicing agent morality by replacing confidence in rules

[93] There are a number of present-day examples of Aristotelian theoretical intervention in political debate, most without any specific reference to or reliance on either Aristotle's views concerning theory and practice or his substantive conception of the human good. One very good one is Elkin's consideration of the public policy debate between the partisans of equality and those of efficiency in *City and Regime*. Elkin argues that both sides assume wrongly that the purpose of politics is the distribution of goods, and thus abstract from the question of how different policies affect character formation. Another is Dworkin's argument that contemporary political debate between legal conservatives (who hold that judges should never be political) and legal progressives (who hold that judges should be political) conceals a shared agreement on the false premise that law is a matter of historical fact rather than something requiring moral interpretation (*Law's Empire*, pp. 6–11). Like Aristotle in Athens, Elkin and Dworkin both aim at improving the quality of political debate rather than resolving it once and for all.

[94] This is the position generally defended by Gadamer's *Idea of the Good* and vigorously attacked by Nussbaum's *Fragility of Goodness*.

[95] Nussbaum recognizes the problem, but argues that Socrates is wholly committed to rule morality and is simply trying out pleasure as a candidate for the basic unit of his felicific calculus, only to reject it at the end of the dialogue. *Fragility of Goodness*, pp. 89–117. I think that too much in her argument depends on what seems to me the doubtful premise that Plato considers the elimination of conflict and contingency the primary human need. Much here turns on the question of irony as an aspect of Platonic style. While simple answers to this question are of little value, it seems to me necessary to be alive to the possibilities of irony everywhere in Plato. For excellent discussions of this question, see Berger, "Levels of Discourse," and Klein, *Commentary on Plato's Meno*, pp. 3–31.

with aporetic bewilderment, and exhorting his interlocutors to care about their souls and ways of life. This Socratic practice receives its most complete Platonic justification not from Socrates, but from the Eleatic Stranger in the *Statesman*, subsequent to his distinction between two kinds of *metrētikē*, one like that of the *Protagoras* involving measuring units of a single variable (like pleasure), and the other requiring judgments that are not quantitative but relative to a mean or to what is appropriate (283e11). The Stranger goes on to evaluate the rule of *nomoi* in terms of the art of political measurement understood in the second way (293c5–303c5). He argues that the best regime must be lawless to a degree, on the basis of the premise that *nomoi* can never issue a precise command binding for all which is at the same time in the best interest of each.[96] Human things are said never to go "calmly," calmness having been identified in a myth presented earlier in the dialogue (269d5–e4) as a property of divine things only, and not an attribute of human affairs. Thus, those who promote a rule morality foolishly mistake, as it were, the Age of Zeus for the Age of Cronos. As we have seen, this is easily translated into Aristotelian language: those who try to establish a morality of rules are making a foolish attempt to be as precise in natural and moral philosophy as it is possible to be only in mathematics or first philosophy (*Metaphysics* alpha, 994b32–995a20; *NE* 1, 1094b11–27). Still, laws are necessary as *imitations* of the real science of politics (which must attend to each person as well as to all in general); at any rate, laws are, as a second sailing, better imitations than greedy lawlessness (*Statesman* 301a10–c4). The key metaphor operating throughout this Platonic discussion (one also employed in a similar context in the *Gorgias*) is the metaphor of orderliness. The science of politics—or the best sort of moral philosophy—is the orderly person's attempt to establish some degree of order in a necessarily disorderly world, not an attempt to provide an abstract and universally binding rational justification for morality.

Several modern political philosophers, moreover, maintain what I have called the Aristotelian core by devoting more energy to articulating the way in which political problems are caused (both efficiently and teleologically) by conflicts of genuine interest than to

---

[96] Nussbaum recognizes the presence of this "proto-Aristotelian point" in the *Statesman* and elsewhere, but does not discuss the difficulty it might pose for her reading of the *Protagoras*, beyond asserting that the position of the *Statesman* on theory and practice is fundamentally at odds with that of the *Republic*. *Fragility of Goodness*, p. 218n.

establishing precise decision rules for resolving such conflicts. Indeed, it might be argued that prior to the self-conscious elaboration of rule morality in the nineteenth and twentieth centuries, the Christian natural law tradition originating with Aquinas was as powerful an alternative to agent morality as any more modern system.[97] A good example of early modern analysis of this kind is Rousseau's presentation of a series of mutually incompatible images of human virtue; even in his most "modern" rule-oriented work, the *Social Contract*, Rousseau refuses to dissolve what he sees as an inherent tension between our need for security and our need for autonomy—a refusal that, on the Aristotelian view, marks the superiority of Rousseau's thought to its later narrowing into universal principles at the hands of Kant. A similar theoretical style marks Tocqueville's articulation of the tension between the need for order or authority and the need for equality and liberty—a tension that for him must be resolved in different ways relative to different local customs and practices, and not by deductions from a universal rule assigning priorities to the competing values.

In general, modern philosophy as well as ancient tends to begin considerations of morals and politics with a discussion of human needs and interests; the difference is that the moderns tend to assign one particular interest (such as the need for peace, or for prosperity, or for autonomy) the role of the only one worth considering, and then to deduce rules of justice and morality generally from that single dominant interest. In contrast with Aristotle, they tend to assert without argument a highly simplified psychology or theory of human nature as the basis for practical philosophy, and to deny the intelligibility of such assertions insofar as they involve claims of final causality. The Aristotelian conception of the human good is sufficiently complex to resist the tyrannical inferences that can be drawn from more single-minded "genuine needs" theories,[98] and Aristotelian theory can recognize its own activity without blushing. Rethinking Aristotelian agent morality is thus not as radical a project as it first might seem, and certainly does not require a wholesale rejection of modern philosophy. The idea that

---

[97] See Jaffa, *Thomism and Aristotelianism*, and Nussbaum, *De Motu Animalium*, pp. 168–170, on attempts to link Aristotle with natural law deductivism.

[98] Speaking of Marxism, Sadurski argues cogently for the conclusion that "such a philosophy of needs . . . leads inevitably to paternalistic and authoritarian consequences." "To Each According to His (Genuine?) Needs," p. 430. On the other side, Ignatieff makes a strong case for the necessity of speaking a language of needs and against the sufficiency of a moral language of human rights. *Needs of Strangers*, especially chap. 1–2.

the human good is made up of different and imperfectly commensurable needs and interests is, to be sure, an empirical claim, and
it may be a misreading of humanness. But I suspect that the idea
of a good of this kind is quite widespread and is rejected *in philosophy* not because of its inherent implausibility but because of the
Enlightenment notion that any valid science must be a precise and
certain one. As I have tried to show, however, the exclusion of
agent morality from philosophy has simply pushed it into a variety
of nonphilosophic contexts, including psychology and literature.
Modern philosophy's rejection of agent morality might be said to
combine two doubtful moments: the separation of philosophy
from scientific inquiry, and the conception of practical philosophy
as a problem-solving procedure separate from practical wisdom.
In this light, rethinking the Aristotelian model can be seen as an
attempt to restore philosophic perspicuity, rather than an articulation of nostalgia or disaffection with modernity.

The second issue raised at the beginning of this section—the relationship between the political world addressed by Aristotle and
our own—is more complex, and will be considered again in Chapter 5. But the problem can be identified now as stemming from the
view that the Greek polity was small, traditional in culture and
organization, and unfamiliar with the concepts of individual rights
and of neutrality with respect to ways of life, whereas ours are
large, deeply suspicious of traditional authority, and centrally
committed to rights and neutrality. As for size, it is clear that the
Greek *polis* was tiny by comparison with the modern nation-state,
and Aristotle himself says that in order for citizens to make accurate political judgments, the city must be small enough for them
to be familiar with one another's qualities (*Pol.* 7, 1326b14–17).[99]
Can an agent morality be appropriate to a polity that for Aristotle
would be an *ethnos* (like Persia) rather than a *polis*? The *Politics* 7
passage appears less decisive when we recall that at the beginning
of that discussion Aristotle says that he is considering the qualities
of a *polis* according to wish or prayer (*kat' euchēn*) and not actually
existing polities. In addition, Aristotle is aware that large cities
may be less prone to conflict, and is especially careful to note that
political friendships are quite superficial as compared with other
kinds (*NE* 9, 1171a14–20). He does not envision the best *polis* as an
intimate community of friends.

[99] Aristotle does not give an upper population limit in the *Pol.*; in *NE* 9, 1170b30–
32, he says a hundred thousand would be too large.

In addition, most of Aristotle's discussions of political issues refer to characteristics of *classes* of people (the rich, farmers, merchants, wage-earners, those of middling wealth), characteristics that may be found in polities of any size. Moreover, most of Aristotle's theoretical interventions are discussions of the *indirect* effects that various institutions (like slavery, or the distribution of power, or limits on private property, or the rule of law) have on education in virtue. Again, these sorts of considerations apply independently of the size of the political unit, and speak against the claim that a politics that aims at *zēn*, *suzēn*, and *eu zēn* is conceivable only in a small-scale society.

But is it conceivable in any but a "traditional" society, one in which structural differentiation is minimal, conduct is governed by religiously sanctioned norms, and independent rational choice is kept in close check by inherited status? The view that our world is uniquely "modern," that it represents a sharp break with the past rather than a more or less continuous development from it, is shared by Marx, Weber, Freud, and Nietzsche, and so is almost second nature with us. But however accurate this Enlightenment picture of a watershed between medieval and modern Europe may be, we cannot apply the concept of traditional society without further qualification to fifth- and fourth-century Greece. The political world confronted by Plato and Aristotle was by no means a stable, religiously saturated society, but a self-consciously young culture, one with a complex sense of its own past. The Athenians in particular, as Thucydides describes them, seem as inimical to everything old and solid as the most vehement Marxian bourgeois or Weberian entrepreneur. In particular, the Greeks of this time were quite aware of their social rules as humanly constituted and subject to human control. The word *nomos* itself is in the fifth century a novelty, a substitution for terms like *themis* and *thesmos*, which suggest divine sanctions in a way that *nomos* does not.[100] Aristotle's theoretical response is to a world whose attitude toward authority and political order is less different from our own than the conventional categories of modernization theory might suggest. In particular, it

---

[100] Ostwald puts the distinction in the following way: "*Thesmos* envisages [a rule or statute] as being imposed upon a people by a lawgiver legislating for it, while *nomos* looks upon a statute as the expression of what the people as a whole regard as a valid and binding norm." *Nomos*, p. 55. Vernant, in *Origins of Greek Thought*, draws an even sharper distinction between the Mycenaean culture and the disenchanted world of the *polis*.

would be wrong to assume that his world was less in need of or more resistant to theoretical intervention than our own.

Another challenge to the appropriateness of Aristotelian agent morality is raised by the claim that our political world differs *conceptually* from Aristotle's—in particular because the central evaluative term of our political discourse, the concept of a *right*, cannot be adequately translated by any term in Aristotle's Greek.[101] The importance of this consideration can be seen by noting the way in which Rawls's claim for the priority of "right" over "good" derives much of its force from his argument that it matches "our considered convictions of justice" better than the teleological agent moralist's privileging of good over right,[102] since Rawls's notion of the content of these "considered convictions" seems to derive very much from common-law conceptions of individual rights. Still, even though this notion is indeed historically and culturally specific, one must note that it presupposes and in a sense contains a concept of freedom (*eleutheria*) that seems specifically Greek in origin.[103] To be sure, the Greek conception of freedom refers to a status rather than a claim against the community, but Aristotle was not unaware of a related notion, the idea that the function of the *polis* is to "protect [people's] just claims against one another," a view he attributes to the sophist Lukophron (*Pol.* 3, 1280b10–11). Aristotle rejects the view that protecting rights is the constitutive condition of politics not because of its strangeness, but on the basis of a teleological argument supporting his view that the protection of "just claims" may conflict with other, more important political goals. Indeed, approaching the issue of rights from the standpoint of agent morality could give us a certain critical distance that might help demystify the notion of rights as utterly incommensurable with other kinds of political goals.[104] In particular, the language of agent morality can help us think about how the concern with rights is related to, and may need to be compromised for the sake of, other politically desirable goals, like widespread political participation, the application of technical knowledge, and economic efficiency.[105]

[101] MacIntyre, *After Virtue*, p. 67.

[102] *Theory of Justice*, p. 7.

[103] "It is almost enough to point out that it is impossible to translate the word 'freedom,' *eleutheria* in Greek, *libertas* in Latin, or 'free man,' into any ancient Near Eastern language, including Hebrew, or into any Far Eastern language either, for that matter." Finley, *Ancient Economy*, p. 28.

[104] As for Dworkin, *Taking Rights Seriously*, pp. 90–94.

[105] For an excellent discussion of liberalism in these terms, see Zuckert, "Theory of Political Economy."

Another difference between our polity and Aristotle's is the apparent impersonality of modern social arrangements. Modern liberal polities, it may be urged, are absolutely neutral as regards claims about virtues—regarding these as private matters—and so cannot be grasped through the categories of agent morality. Neutrality about the human good is indeed often asserted to be a central feature of modern politics, in political philosophy (Rawls and Nozick) as well as in American constitutional theory. This view is not without authoritative support (as in *Federalist* 10), but it is by no means an uncontroversial characterization of the liberal regime, as can be seen from recent efforts to identify the virtues central to liberalism and to articulate a liberal theory of the good life as informing the American Constitution.[106] At any rate, it would be difficult to dispute Tocqueville's claim that the modern liberal regime, in fact and in aspiration, exhibits a strong preference for certain virtues and ways of life—even though modern political philosophy is in general not comfortable with such preferences. One might even claim that these traditional preferences are being undermined by the spread of self-consciously value-neutral languages of public and individual choice.[107] Neutrality as regards the virtues is perhaps best seen as one component of modern culture rather than the whole story, a component that can be discussed in the language of agent morality under the heading of the virtue of toleration.

A last major difference between our world and the world of the *polis* is the importance of history to us. To say that modern political culture is deeply historical is not necessarily to accept Nietzsche's claim that moderns are unique possessors of a historical sense, a special insight into the relativity of all actions and evaluations. Nor need we say with Hegel and Marx that we have a special insight into the substantive or providential character of human history. But our political history and our traditions are much older and deeper than those of any *politeia* that Aristotle discussed. We appear to depend more than any premodern people on interpretations of our history as a motive or source for action. Aristotle has little to say about the importance of historical interpretation for action, beyond the few remarks about the law's dependence on *ethos* for its power in the discussion of Hippodamus in *Politics* 2.

[106] Good examples are Galston, "Defending Liberalism" and "Liberalism and Public Morality," Barber, *What the Constitution Means*, Kateb, "Moral Distinctiveness," Gutmann, *Democratic Education*, chap. 1, and Elkin, *City and Regime*.

[107] This is the argument made against therapists and managers by the authors of *Habits of the Heart* (Bellah et al.).

For us, reconstructions of the past are important sources for action, both good and bad—Nietzsche's *Advantage and Disadvantage of History for Life* is the classic text for the discussion of this problem.

Does the self-conscious historicity of our *politeia* render it resistant to the questions and categories of Aristotelian theorizing? I think not: our attitude toward our history is a part of the way in which we are political animals, in which we rule and are ruled within the context of a set of laws and customs, one of which is the custom of basing our political self-understanding on a history that is continually open to a variety of interpretations. (Perhaps the theater played something like this role of a context for political self-definition in Aristotle's Athens.)[108] These interpretations of a shared past—in the American case, the practice of judicial review is the most important example—are subject to evaluation not only in terms of their historical accuracy, but in terms of what they presuppose about human virtue and how they promote or exclude various ways of life. To realize this is to begin an Aristotelian inquiry into the advantages and disadvantages of historical interpretation for human virtue.

My purpose in briefly noting the ways in which modern politics seems to resist the core of Aristotelian agent morality is to bring to light the following charge against this mode of practical philosophy: In a large, frequently anomic, and impersonal society, one in which legal rights are the chief security an individual has, much *more*—perhaps something closer to prophecy or the act of founding a nation—is required of philosophy today than theorizing in the Aristotelian style can offer. I have suggested reasons for doubting the reasonableness of this charge, but I think it is nevertheless a much more serious challenge to agent morality than the various theoretical critiques of teleology or foundationalism. I think, however, that we have much to gain by reading and discussing Plato and Aristotle with this challenge in mind, and encouraging such discussion is, after all, my only intention here.

Thus the most important risk in using the language of Aristotelian agent morality may well be practical rather than theoretical. By refusing to accord the concept of rights or the practice of toleration a privileged position at the outset, agent moralists may fail to appreciate adequately the fragility as well as the importance of

---

[108] Consider Euben's discussion of tragedy as both conservative and radically questioning, in his introductory essay to *Greek Tragedy and Political Theory*, especially pp. 23–30.

some of the best aspects of the modern political tradition. But to say this is to warn against the possibility of a tactless Aristotelianism, rather than to question the value of the project itself. To be sure, if the primary use of political philosophy is to inspire us to persevere courageously against great odds and endure much hardship for the sake of a principle, then Kant is a more valuable philosopher than Aristotle. But we need other kinds of help from theorizing as well, both politically and in other settings, and unless we want to reconceive our *praxis* as a form of military activity calling for the unquestionable rules we associate with a lost religious past, the hopes for the future of both the liberal tradition and the still older tradition of evaluative explanation would seem to rest most securely with an approach to theoretical intervention that values tact more highly than precision and certainty.

Rationality as a Goal

Aristotle's practical philosophy, like his science, seems to be fundamentally at odds both with modernity and with the reaction against the Enlightenment. He is indeed opposed both to reductionism and to irrational prophecy, to conventionalism/relativism and to deductivism. And yet his position does not seem to be that the truth lies somewhere in between—managing, as it were, to avoid error by taking no position at all concerning theory or practice. From an Aristotelian perspective modernity appears not as an error, but as a successful cultural movement that has unnecessarily excluded certain possibilities which are in fact compatible with its central commitments, commitments shared by Plato and Aristotle. The shared commitments are persistent causal inquiry in science and freedom from repressive control in morals and politics; the unnecessarily excluded possibilities are teleological explanation in science and agent morality in practical matters.

In saying that these have been *unnecessarily* excluded, I do not mean to suggest that the antiteleological and antivirtue orientation of modern theory has been an accident; the critique of teleology opened the way for great progress in the physical sciences by removing obstacles to inquiry, and modern rule morality has been a central element in the attack on privilege and in general the emancipation of the West. All of us who read and teach and think are its beneficiaries. My thought is rather that these orientations are no longer necessary to sustain the projects in question, and that the modern animus against teleology and agent morality was

159

never essentially required by the goals of free inquiry and liberal citizenship.

In the case of agent morality, the treatment of rationality as a virtue rather than an instrument for acquiring goods has a clear oligarchic ring; nothing is more common, in Aristotle's time or ours, than the sight of rich and well-born people claiming superior rationality as their birthright. Thus it surely appeared to Hobbes, to Rousseau, to Kant, for whom agent morality must always be a mask for privilege. At the beginning of the *Second Discourse*, Rousseau says that he will investigate the origins of political inequality rather than ask the agent moralist's question (posed by the Academy of Dijon) of whether political inequality corresponds to natural inequality. The latter, he says, is "perhaps a good question to air among slaves being overheard by their master, but not one that is appropriate for reasonable and free people who are looking for the truth."[109] We need to consider whether the exclusion of this question, appropriate enough in the eighteenth-century setting, is so any longer. To do that, we need to be clear about what might be meant by saying, as Aristotle does, that rationality is a virtue, and that the life of the *phronimos* can serve as the evaluative goal and standard for explaining human actions.

I have argued that rationality for Aristotle does not mean the habit of deducing practical conclusions from eternal natural laws. But it seems equally clear that Aristotle is not a noncognitivist as regards action-choice. That is, while it is true that his conception of the human good is a complex one which takes account of a variety of separate interests, it is not, I think, the case that Aristotle "argues that the values that are constitutive of a good human life are plural and incommensurable," or that he has "denied the commensurability of values."[110] The fact is that Aristotle frequently compares and ranks human interests—friendship and honor are both human interests, but friendship is higher than honor, as thinking is higher than political action and moderation higher than courage.[111] The key question here is one of "commensurability": how can Aristotle hold that values are commensurable and yet not be a deductivist, not codify such "measurements" into action-guiding rules?

[109] *Oeuvres Complètes*, vol. 3, p. 132.
[110] Nussbaum, *Fragility of Goodness*, pp. 294, 309.
[111] Nussbaum argues that these rankings are either claims about the "deeper appearances" of the Greek community, or, where they clearly clash with conventional values, evidence that "ethical Platonism of some sort exercised a hold over Aristotle's imagination in one or more periods of his career." *Fragility of Goodness*, p. 377.

He does this, in effect, by saying that goods are commensurable—not quantitatively, but relative to a mean (as in the Eleatic Stranger's second art of measurement or Aristotle's own example of economic justice in *NE* 5)—in two different ways: in relation to the *ousia* or specific nature of human beings, and in relation to the *kairos*, to the particular moment at which an action-choice arises and the particular individuals involved. These two perspectives describe two different kinds of rationality, *politikē* and *phronēsis*. As we have seen in this chapter, *politikē* can assist *phronēsis* by drawing attention to the theoretical presuppositions of various possible courses of action and subjecting these to criticism in light of the human *ousia*, of the rankings appropriate at the level of nature. But theorizing cannot replace practical wisdom.

Finally, we must be careful not to reify theoretical and practical wisdom; they are not separate entities, but human attributes, and furthermore attributes that must, apparently, belong to the same human being if either is to be present at all. That is, it will not do to identify Margaret Schlegel, say, with practical wisdom only and Aristotle with practical theorizing. As we saw in Chapter 2, *politikē* and *phronēsis* are aspects of the same personality or disposition: "*Politikē* and *phronēsis* are the same *hexis*, but not the same essence (*to mentoi einai ou tauton autais*)" (*NE* 6, 1141b23–24). That is, these two "arts of measurement" are different actualizations of the same human rational potentiality, just as, for the traveler, the Athens-Thebes road runs both ways, only one of which can be taken at a time. Human rationality as a virtue is the ability to move between the two perspectives, though always bearing in mind the greater seriousness of *phronēsis*.

The ways of life toward which this virtue inclines, the manner in which these may be approximated or supported through a variety of human relationships—political and nonpolitical—and the dangers to rationality posed by other attractive activities and relationships are the major problems addressed by Aristotle's political philosophy. They form the subject of the three chapters to follow. The first deals with Aristotle's discussion of a threat to political rationality that directly concerned him: the Greek tendency to identify virtue and virility. The last two chapters move away from the problems of Aristotle's time to our own by suggesting ways in which a concept of the virtue of rationality would enrich our theoretical justification of the modern liberal regime and indicating how such a justification might inform thinking about liberal public policy.

PART II

BACK AGAIN

F O U R

GENDERED VIRTUE:
PLATO AND ARISTOTLE ON THE
POLITICS OF VIRILITY

Theory, Practice, and Feminist Critique

Aristotelian practical philosophy aims at bringing to light the presuppositions about human virtue that tacitly underlie political deliberation, and subjecting those presuppositions to criticism in the light of a theoretical understanding of human needs. Socrates describes his role in Athenian political life in much the same way when he tells the jury that his project has been to jolt decent Athenians into caring about the character, or virtue, of their lives (*Apology* 30e1–31b5). Neither Aristotle nor Plato takes the task of practical philosophy to be the formulation of entirely new rules or systems to replace the norms and practices governing existing moral and political life; their aim is to enrich political deliberation by pushing the conversation, as it were, to take an evaluative step outside itself for a moment. The goal of evaluative explanation understood in this way is thus not to describe a separate dwelling place or a newly structured world, but to spark a theoretical movement within the context of a definite, this-worldly political culture. This movement calls neither for a withdrawal from politics nor for a wholesale revision of one's approach to it; rather it encourages political actors to reflect on the adequacy of their ways of posing political problems and their sense of the range of political options. Given this intention, the appropriate theoretical tone is one that avoids both prophetic certainty and self-abnegating neutrality. What practice needs from theory is a discourse that calls to mind simultaneously the human good, the ways in which different passions and moral types tend toward or away from that good, and the tendency of particular institutions or norms to further or frustrate that good.

Modern political philosophy as a whole understands the relationship between theory and practice in an entirely different way, searching instead for the terms in which philosophy can provide precise answers to fundamental political questions.[1] This can be done cheerfully and optimistically, as with Hobbes and Locke, or with dreadful anxiety, in the manner of Nietzsche or Sartre, or with unshakable Marxian certainty. But whatever its tone, modern practical philosophy appears to have passed through a Rousseauian moment—recall the dream of the first philosopher presented in Rousseau's "Allegorical Fragment on Revelation," in which frustration with the inconclusiveness of Socratic critique gives way to a longing for the appearance of the perfect Lawgiver. Practical philosophy in the West has long since exchanged the role of gadfly for that of prophet, whether Moses or Jeremiah or Jesus.

But although the Platonic-Aristotelian style of evaluative explanation gradually loses its place in modern philosophy, it by no means disappears from other kinds of writing. Excluded from philosophy, the kind of theorizing about practice that encourages us to deliberate again about what exists, rather than providing us with new rules and principles, finds a home in a variety of literary settings, in books like *Howards End* and Iris Murdoch's novels of contemporary English life. As presently understood, practical philosophy must try to derive precise rules or refute the derivations of others. By contrast, a writer of fiction can say what James Joyce says of *Dubliners*: "My intention was to write a chapter of the moral history of my country"[2]—and produce not a mirror reflection but a characterization from a certain distance, one that perplexes the reader and demands an evaluative response. My point is not that novels and stories are inappropriate places for this kind of theoretical account, but that there is something troubling about the decline of evaluative explanation within philosophy, a genre explicitly committed to self-conscious argumentation.

There has, however, been a strong movement in recent years to restore the place of provocative critique in philosophic discourse. This has been the work of feminist theorizing—perhaps because

[1] Or defending existing cultural practice against abstract theoretical challenge, as in the work of Edmund Burke and Richard Rorty. But both modern philosophical alternatives—resignation and revolution—exclude the Platonic-Aristotelian style of culture critique.

[2] "Letter to Grant Richards," May 5, 1906. In Joyce, *Letters*, vol. 2, pp. 132–135, at p. 134. In "Flawed Crystals," Nussbaum develops an Aristotelian argument for the importance of literature to moral philosophy as a corrective for the tendency to reduce complex moral situations to simple matters of principle. For an interesting argument that the modern novel corrects a specific error of modern social theory—the tendency to treat the analytic term "class" as if it were a physical reality—see Furbank, *Unholy Pleasure*, chap. 10.

such theorizing begins with a specific practical issue, rather than with an abstract and universal theoretical question. Its special emphasis has been on bringing to light the ways in which political and philosophic programs are shaped by the categories and concepts people use when viewing the world and one another. In particular, the feminist critique of philosophy has stressed ways in which philosophical discourse is shaped by dichotomies that reflect and reinforce stereotypes of gender differences: the pair woman/man is used to persuade us of the fundamental character of oppositions like private/public, feeling/thought, chaos/order, body/mind, wordless expression/language, and so on. These dichotomies, according to a recent commentator, indicate a widespread assumption that the fundamental metaphysical problem consists in deciding whether our world is a trackless wilderness or a perfectly intelligible sunlit whole.[3] I would add that this kind of dichotomizing discourse flows easily from the Enlightenment presupposition that animals are simply machines, and that to be human is to be either a merely passive animal or a godlike transcendent being.[4]

To see how the gender distinction functions as the epitome of a bipolar view of the world, consider the way in which certain modern theorists have employed the distinction to establish a sharp dichotomy between two modes of existence, one (the feminine) somehow earlier or less formed than the other. In each case, the theorist's voice comes from within the masculine mode, even when (as with Nietzsche and Engels) that way of being is called into question:

THEORIST[5]	MASCULINE MODE	FEMININE MODE
Rousseau	Modern Nature (Emile)	Appearance (Sophie)
Kant	Sublime	Beautiful
Hegel	Public, Universal	Private, Particular
Engels	Patriarchy; Historical Class Domination	Matriarchy; Prehistorical Primitive Domination
Nietzsche	Logic, Language	Body, Expression, Feeling

[3] Nye, "Woman Clothed with the Sun," p. 681.

[4] As Nye says (ibid., p. 684), human speech can have no real existence in this vision of human possibilities. I discuss the significance of the widespread modern tendency to regard animals as machines in "Beyond Interpretation."

[5] The reference to Kant is to his *Observations on the Sense of the Beautiful and the Sublime*, sec. 3, reprinted in Mahowald's *Philosophy of Woman*, pp. 193–203. For Hegel, see the section on the "Ethical World" in *Phenomenology of Mind*. Mahowald's arrangement of text and commentary provides a clear history of the use of gender distinction as a way of summing up fundamental alternatives, and making them seem fixed and exclusive of all other possibilities.

These dichotomies clarify certain alternatives for political and moral choice, but at the same time exclude other possibilities. How can we respond to these exclusions?

There are several possible responses. The first, characteristic of Nietzsche and of feminists who follow the paths of Nietzsche and Derrida, is simply to reverse the value-signs of the categories, and celebrate what was formerly despised. Aside from self-referential problems (as in the case of arguing against argument), however, this approach retains the same dichotomies, and thus fails to address the problem of excluding other, as yet unarticulated possibilities. One way to answer this difficulty would be to argue against dichotomous categorization or against categorization as such, and to claim that all practical judgments must be open to every possibility the context allows. But this requires too much of each separate choice, and overlooks the way language points us toward real interests, even though any given human language must obscure some ways of understanding the world in order to make others possible. It is here that the Aristotelian understanding of the function of theoretical intervention in practical disputes seems most helpful. As we have seen, such an approach allows criticism of the categories and presuppositions of a particular culture or regime in the light of human needs, without denying that the words and concepts for understanding and changing institutions and attitudes must always emerge from the cultures themselves, and not from theoretical pronouncements. Aristotelian practical philosophy proposes to remind us of human needs and human virtue as standards for evaluating the categories without which we cannot live. The aim is neither the perfect set of categories, nor thought utterly free from established categories, nor yet despair at the tragic imperfection of human access to the world. What theory can give to practice is a certain reflective attitude toward our evaluative language, a sense that the language is always provisional and open to revision, and that it calls for thoughtful deployment rather than mindless attachment.

To illustrate this process, the present chapter looks at the complex manner in which Aristotle and Plato responded to the gender dichotomies that informed the political life of ancient Greece. My intention here is to show how both Plato and Aristotle make use of the gender distinction as a point of entry for theoretical intervention in political life. My thesis is that both philosophers employ the gender distinction for the sake of calling into question the implicit and pervasive tendency in Greek culture to conceive of virility as the highest virtue. This will serve as preparation for the discussion in the final chapter of the way in which Aristotelian theorizing can help overcome the contemporary tendency to view our political alternatives in terms of an unattractive choice between abstract individualism and contextual communitarianism.

Virility and Virtue in Greek Politics

Interpretations of Platonic and Aristotelian texts play an increasingly important role in several debates concerning central issues in contemporary political life. Particularly since the publication of Hannah Arendt's book *The Human Condition*, the study of Plato and especially of Aristotle has been seen as a key element in the critique of liberal individualism, or of the modern tendency to confuse technical rationality and practical reason. For Arendt, Gadamer, and MacIntyre, Aristotle is a guide to understanding politics as a way of life rather than as a mere instrument for the protection of prepolitical rights. Plato's role in this contemporary debate is less clear; while surely no liberal individualist, he appears to some modern writers to present an unattractively antipolitical or deductivist counterpart to Aristotle, who is seen as the defender of the "deep beliefs"[6] that constitute the political order against the dissolving critique of a rule-oriented theoretical wisdom.

Plato and Aristotle have also received attention in discussions of the sources of the tendency to identify masculinity and humanness (or human virtue) in the tradition of Western political thought and practice. Here, however, their relationship to the tradition being criticized is generally reversed: Plato is sometimes cited as an early opponent of a prevailing misogyny, while Aristotle is almost invariably identified as the champion of male domination.[7]

These two ways of reexamining Aristotle—from the perspective of the meaning of citizenship and from the perspective of gender valuation—have proceeded independently of each other. This separation of the questions of citizenship and gender is unfortunate,

[6] Nussbaum, *Fragility of Goodness*, p. 320.

[7] See Elshtain, *Public Man, Private Woman*, and especially Okin, *Women in Western Political Thought*, who relies heavily on Lloyd's *Aristotle*. Lloyd there asserts without much text argument (the book is intended for the beginning student) that Aristotle tends to support the majority view in politics and ethics. Lloyd's later and more thorough *Science, Folklore, and Ideology* explains flaws in Aristotle's biology by reference to Aristotle's acceptance of "the ideological presuppositions of contemporaries concerning the differences between men and women" (p. 105). This assertion is made without discussing any of Aristotle's remarks about gender and gender attributes in political and ethical contexts.

since in the views of both Plato and Aristotle, as I will try to show, the two issues are inextricably mingled. Moreover, I think that Plato and Aristotle are very much in agreement concerning both citizenship and gender. My argument is that there is an essential connection between participatory politics and male domination, at least insofar as such politics is shaped by our recollection of the Periclean political culture that formed the point of departure for the philosophizing of Plato and Aristotle. Both philosophers identify this connection and are similarly critical of the way of life it supports. As a result, while neither Plato nor Aristotle can be called a feminist, both urge a significant improvement in the status of women. The source of their opposition to Greek misogyny is not to be found in any theory of the rights of individuals, or in reference to fundamental Greek customs, but in the significant reservations each has concerning the view that the best human life is that of the committed citizen, the life that cares most for the things of the city or the political community. Properly understood, the Platonic-Aristotelian project is in part an attempt to call attention to a deep psychological connection between republican virtue and misogyny, a connection simply ignored by later writers in the tradition, whether liberal or republican.

It is difficult to speak with assurance concerning the actual practices of Greek political life in the fourth and fifth centuries, but it is by no means hard to see that the language in which that political life was articulated placed a high value on both political activity and maleness. So much is clear from Pericles' funeral speech: women should be quiet and remain at home, and "we [Athenians] alone think of one who does not participate in public affairs not as a quiet man, but as a useless one."[8] For Pericles, human happiness is impossible outside an autonomous *polis*, and the existence of such a polity depends on the courage or stoutheartedness of its citizens: "happiness depends on freedom, and freedom depends on being courageous (*eupsuchos*)."[9] Arendt's recollection of this tradition stresses the special status of courage among the Greek political virtues: "Courage therefore became the political virtue par excellence, and only those men who possessed it could be admitted to a fellowship that was political in content and purpose."[10] The Greek word most frequently used to express this quality is

---

[8] Thucydides, *Peloponnesian War* 2.40. For a valuable discussion of Athenian groups that stood outside this moral consensus, see Carter, *Quiet Athenian*.

[9] Thucydides, *Peloponnesian War* 2.43.

[10] *Human Condition*, p. 36.

andreia—the virtue of *andres*, or real males—a word ordinarily translated as "courage," but perhaps more tellingly rendered by "virility" or "manliness." In a world dominated by war and the threat of war, it is perhaps not surprising that an aptitude for battle was a chief requisite for free citizenship. As Michael Shaw puts it, speaking of the Greek political understanding, "the first necessity of society is that it be autonomous; to gain this autonomy, society's members must put hatred above love, in order that enemies may be repelled."[11]

The equation of virility and virtue in prephilosophic Greek political thought is further reinforced by the habit of drawing a sharp distinction between the world of the household or family and that of the *polis*, by the association of the *oikia* with women and the *polis* with men, and by the designation of the *polis* as clearly superior to and even threatened by the household or family—Sophocles' Creon in the *Antigone* exhibits such a view pushed to an extreme. As Arendt says, "according to Greek thought, the human capacity for political organization is not only different from but stands in direct opposition to that natural association whose center is the home (*oikia*) and the family."[12] Moreover, "the public realm stands in the sharpest possible contrast to our private domain, where, in the protection of family and home, everything serves and must serve the security of the life process. . . . Courage liberates men from their worry about life."[13] This tendency to polarize *oikia* and

[11] Shaw, "Female Intruder," p. 266. Both Shaw and especially Euben, "Justice and the *Oresteia*," pp. 22–33, make a convincing case for the view that the Greek tragedians were more aware of the fragility of human virtue and the insufficiency of heroic virility than my remarks here may suggest. Euben's argument that tragedy is at once critical and conservative is persuasively set out in his introduction to *Greek Tragedy and Political Theory*. See also Nussbaum's discussion of the conflict of duties and the resistance to simple solutions in the *Agamemnon* and the *Antigone* in *Fragility of Goodness*, pp. 25–82. A similar point with regard to Homer is made by Flaumenhaft in "Undercover Hero." These works suggest the limited utility of asserting any monolithic "Greek" identification of virility with virtue by calling attention to the probable differences between Greek popular morality (which does identify the two) and the rich and critical reflections of Greek literary culture. Perhaps the most attractive feature of Greek culture was that it managed to give rise to so many interesting people who were a little uncomfortable with their Greekness.

[12] *Human Condition*, p. 24.

[13] Arendt, "What Is Freedom?" p. 156. In *Human Condition*, pp. 72–73, Arendt also notes that women and slaves had the same status among the Greeks since both were kept within the *oikia*, hidden from public view. It is difficult to know precisely what the relative positions of women and slaves were; see Pomeroy, *Goddesses, Whores, Wives, and Slaves*, pp. 58–60. Aristotle, craftily, attributes the view that women and slaves should be treated in the same way to barbarians, not to Greeks. *Pol.* 1, 1252b5–6.

polis and to articulate their relationship in terms of the imagery of conflict is associated in speech—whatever may have been the case in political practice—with the tendency similarly to oppose female and male, and to define human virtue in terms of the hard-won triumph of the second member of each of these pairs. Thus Froma Zeitlin characterizes "the misogynistic tradition which pervades Greek thought" as "a bias which both projects a combative dialogue in male-female interactions and which relates the mastery of the female to higher social goals."[14]

The Greek political imagination, then, revolves around a norm of manly valor, according to which courageous citizens display their patriotism by the spirit of anger (*thumos*) with which they pursue not peace or justice but honor (*timē*) and fame (*kleos*), a norm that takes its substance from a contrast with the idealized life of women, who toil in silence and seclusion, like slaves.[15] Finally, the passionate love of honor marks not only manliness but the principal difference between human being and beast. Simonides in Xenophon's *Hiero* (7.3) puts it this way: "Love of honor arises naturally neither in irrational animals nor in all human beings; but those in whom an *erōs* for honor and praise arises naturally are the ones who differ most from the beasts of the field, and it is they who are considered real men (*andres*) and not just mere human beings (*anthrōpoi*)." Genuine humanity requires a love of honor that belongs only to the male of the species.

The republican political imagination of Periclean Athens turns on a polarized opposition of male, war, and *polis* on the one hand and female, peace, and family on the other. Both the tone and the content of the brief advice to the ladies at the close of Pericles' funeral oration make this clear: "If it is necessary for me to recall anything of feminine virtue for those of you now widowed, I shall signify all by this brief exhortation: great will be your repute if you do not become worse than your proper nature, and especially she of whom the least is said, whether of her virtue or her flaws, in the reports of the men."[16] This association of politics, publicity, and virility has not been ignored by latter-day admirers of the vir-

---

[14] Zeitlin, "Dynamics of Misogyny," p. 150.

[15] Shaw, "Female Intruder," pp. 256–257.

[16] *Peloponnesian War* 2.45. That Thucydides is not inclined to admire exaggerated maleness is indicated in his discussion of *stasis* at 3.82. Arendt cites Pericles for the "Greek" thought that, from the perspective of the *polis*, immoderate philosophy is effeminate. "Crisis in Culture," pp. 213–215.

tues of ancient republics, such as Machiavelli (whose *virtù* is a wholly adequate translation of *andreia*) and Arendt.

But what of the first political philosophers—Socrates, Plato, and Aristotle? How is their thought related to the political context from which it arose? According to Arendt, the first philosophical understanding of politics is essentially a reflection of prephilosophic opinion: "The true character of this *polis* is still quite manifest in Plato's and Aristotle's political philosophies, even if the borderline between household and *polis* is occasionally blurred, especially in Plato."[17] It is part of Arendt's rhetorical strategy to suggest that her own preferred notion of politics as sharply antithetical to the household is present in Aristotle, if not in Plato, and that the esteem for republican virtue that she finds in the Greek experience of the public realm is preserved in Aristotle's theoretical reflections:

> According to Greek thought, the human capacity for political organization is not only different from but stands in direct opposition to that natural association whose center is the home (*oikia*) and the family. The rise of the city-state meant that man received "besides his private life a sort of second life, his *bios politikos*. Now every citizen belongs to two orders of existence; and there is a sharp distinction in his life between what is his own (*idion*) and what is communal (*koinon*)."[18]

One must consult Arendt's footnote to discover that she is quoting Werner Jaeger rather than Aristotle. Arendt's insistence on attributing a non-Aristotelian view of politics to Aristotle[19] has led to understandable misreadings of both Arendt and Aristotle. Jürgen Habermas, for example, displays excusable and edifying confusion in saying that Arendt's "emphatic concept of praxis is more Marxist than Aristotelian," but then, two pages later, that Arendt's con-

---

[17] *Human Condition*, p. 37.

[18] Ibid., p. 24. Arendt's claim that Aristotle's view of the relationship between *polis* and *oikia* is close to that of the prevailing Greek culture is effectively challenged by Zuckert, "Limits and Satisfactions of Political Life," and by Pitkin, "Justice."

[19] Arendt is a wonderfully intelligent reader of Aristotle, though she is not always a scrupulous one. In *Human Condition*, she attributes to him the view that the central function of politics is conversation among citizens (p. 27), the view that politics is the route to immortality (p. 56), and strangest of all, the view—again, a view she herself holds—that "being" is simply a name for common appearance (p. 199). A mixture of sharp perception and odd formulation is shown in her critical comment that Aristotle is the first "materialist" for holding that *to sumpheron* (interest) "does and should reign supreme in political matters." Arendt, *On Revolution*, p. 14.

cept becomes useful "only if we extricate it from the clamps of an Aristotelian theory of action."[20] Arendt's reading of Aristotle is like that of Aquinas, not of course in content, but insofar as it is a careful and thoughtful reading from a perspective seriously incompatible with a central element of Aristotle's thought. In Arendt's case, the incompatibility arises from her Heideggerian commitment to situating human being in opposition to nature—as in her fundamental reliance on the distinction between the human *world* and the meaninglessly repetitive *earth*. In a sense, Arendt's antinaturalism is the antithesis of Thomas's cosmic teleology, just as her conventionalist defense of the autonomous *polis* is the antithesis of Thomistic natural law. What they have in common is that each attributes one of these antithetical positions to Aristotle; my proposal here is to show that Aristotle is no more a civic republican than he is a natural lawyer.

At any rate, Aristotle, like Plato, is much less inclined to celebrate Periclean Athens than either Arendt or Marx, and he surely views Sparta in a much less favorable light than either Machiavelli or Rousseau. The critical disposition of Plato and Aristotle toward Greek political culture is especially noticeable in their according women and womanly activities a greater dignity than does their tradition (or its modern adherents)—a revaluation that stems from a deep opposition to the view that the virtues of the best human life are most clearly displayed in the practice of war and the pursuit of undying glory. Their objection to this tradition is based on their shared view that it presupposes a mistaken assessment of the relative importance of different human needs, and thus a mistaken understanding of the best human life.

The Platonic Revaluation of Women

The elevation of women via the "first wave" of *Republic* 5 is well known. Women guardians are said there to be the equal of men, *but* weaker in every respect, including the practice of traditionally feminine arts (*Republic* 5, 455c4–e2). This, however, is only the most explicit, and I think not the most interesting, of the various instances in which we can discern a Platonic intention to elevate

---

[20] Habermas, "Hannah Arendt's Communications Concept of Power," pp. 13 and 15. On the basis of a doubtful reference to *Pol.* 1, 1257a8, Arendt herself suggests that Aristotle may have been almost as decisive an influence on Marx as Hegel. *Human Condition*, p. 254 n. 4. As Kateb says, "It is no sin to revise Aristotle, but Arendt's flat assertion [that politics is an end in itself] makes her sound more Homeric or Nietzschean than she centrally means to be." *Hannah Arendt*, p. 31.

the status of women and feminine things within the discourse-world of the dialogues. Socrates is consistently, and sometimes violently, critical of the common Greek notion that the best teachers of virtue are either Athenian gentlemen, like Pericles and Themistocles (in the *Meno* and the *Gorgias*), or poets like Homer (in the *Republic*), or philosophers like Anaxagoras. When speaking of teachers from whom he himself learned something, he almost invariably refers to women: Diotima in the *Symposium* (who is also a foreigner);[21] his mother, Phaenarete, in the *Theaetetus*; and Aspasia, Pericles' mistress, in the *Menexenus*—in which Socrates recites a funeral oration of a very different sort from Pericles', one he says he learned from Aspasia.[22] Similarly, in the *Meno* and the *Protagoras*, dialogues specifically concerned with human excellence or virtue, he pointedly includes priestesses as well as priests among his sources for the recollection *logos* (*Meno* 81a10), and claims, contrary to obvious fact, that in Sparta and Crete there are many women as well as men who can be proud of their education (*Protagoras* 342d2–4). His own particular technical expertise—the one thing that the man who only knows he knows nothing can truly know—is in erotics, the science of love, as he tells us in the *Theages* (128b2–6) as well as the *Symposium* (177d7–8), a subject he learned from Diotima.[23] Furthermore, Plato continually uses traditionally female arts as images or metaphors for Socratic activity: midwifery in the *Theaetetus* and weaving in the Eleatic Stranger's account of the political art in the *Statesman*.[24]

One very interesting instance of the indirect style of Socrates' critical response to the presuppositions of his culture is the way his *elenchos* works, in dialogue after dialogue, by substituting without comment the evaluative terms "good" and "bad" (*agathon* and *kakon*) for the terms "noble" and "base" (*kalon* and *aischron*). A nice example of this is his refutation of Polus in the *Gorgias* (476e2–477a9). Plato calls our attention to the substitution here by having

[21] *Symposium* 201d2; see also *Phaedo*, 78a1–9.

[22] For discussion of the *Menexenus* in this context, see Saxonhouse, *Women in the History of Political Thought*, pp. 55–57. There is, in addition, a similar reference to Xerxes' wife Amestris as an expert on virtue in *Alcibiades* 1, 123c3–124a7.

[23] Socrates refers to Kallikrate as a potential teacher in the *Theages* (125d13–e3), and to Sappho in the *Phaedrus* (235b6–c4). The only major exception to this rule of female teachers is the dour grammarian Prodicus of Ceos, but he is not someone likely to be mistaken for an Athenian gentleman. See also the illuminating conversation between Socrates and Theodote in Xenephon's *Memorabilia*, 3.11. For references to Xenophon's Socrates on women, see Clark, "Aristotle's Woman."

[24] Socrates also swears frequently by a foreign god, the Egyptian dog, a device which serves to cast further doubt on his virility and his Greekness.

the manly Callicles recognize it as a subliminal attack on Greek convention (482e–483a),[25] but the same pattern recurs in the *Laches* (192c5–d5), the *Lovers* (133d2–3), the *Charmides* (163b3–e2), *Alcibiades* 1 (115a1–116c2), and the *Hippias Major* (295b7–c6). Conventionally, many things may be called good which cannot be called noble (notably womanly activities), but Socrates goes out of his way to insist that all truly noble actions must be good (*Protagoras* 358b5–6), or even useful (*Hippias Major* 295c2–3). In doing this, he is in effect insisting not on the nobility of housework, say, but on the need to show that battle-courage or philosophy is good. This insistence is a critical component of the claim that no one willingly does evil, something Socrates learned from Diotima (*Symposium* 201c1–9 and 205e5–206a1). "Good" things are knowable in a way "noble" things are not—the latter perhaps being a matter of taste—and so to insist on the goodness of presumably noble things is to insist on their criticizability. Similarly, the argument for the unity and hence the commensurability of the virtues in the *Protagoras* seems motivated less by an obsessive need to develop a deductivist ethics than by the need to oppose the ordinary Greek sentiment, expressed by Protagoras, that *andreia* is somehow on a different plane from the other virtues (349d4–5), and hence beyond the reach of evaluative explanation.

In all these instances, we can see a consistent project of critique and revaluation at work. By means of unobtrusive insinuation, rather than manly didactic confrontation, Socrates subverts his noble interlocutors' instinctive disposition to see manliness and the virile arts of politics and war as making up a coherent ideal of human excellence. Plato, however, is surely not consistently profemale. Even in the *Republic* (aside from Book 5), women are not regarded as equals but relegated to the household, presented as frivolous or as temptresses. Frequent instances of the negative depiction of women occur throughout the dialogues: how can we account for this apparent inconsistency?

According to Arlene Saxonhouse,[26] the inconsistency is only apparent, and it appears because we are asking Plato the wrong question, namely, "Do you think women are the equals of men or not?" There is no good reason to think that this question formed any part of Plato's agenda. Rather, as Saxonhouse says, Socrates

[25] Callicles objects to its hiddenness, not to the fact that it is an attack on convention. See Archie, "Callicles' Redoubtable Critique."

[26] Saxonhouse, "Philosopher and the Female." My thinking on the matters discussed in this chapter derives largely from Saxonhouse's work on the meaning of gender distinctions in Plato.

intimates the need to elevate the status of women in order to attack the ordinary Greek attachment to maleness, the tendency to identify virtue or excellence with virility or courage.[27] Other examples of the tension Plato establishes between Socrates and the norm of *andreia* can be seen in the way Meno (*Meno* 71e1–5) and Callicles in the *Gorgias* express their difference from Socrates by defining virtue as virile participation in public affairs. Socrates' friends as well as his enemies, Crito as well as Callicles, suspect the philosopher of unmanliness or cowardice (*anandria*).[28] It is hardly surprising that any Greek, no matter how well disposed, would have doubts about Socrates' virility, given the deep cultural association of *andreia* with active political life and Socrates' statements that his own life is of necessity private rather than political (*Apology* 31c4–32a3), that a first-rate philosopher does not even know the way to the *agora* or other centers of political activity (*Theaetetus* 173c6–174a2), and that (paradoxically, in the Greek context) the real political art, of which he is the only true practitioner, is practiced not in the assembly or the courts, but in private, behind closed doors (*Gorgias* 521d6–8). Even Socrates' friends must have been troubled by his proud assertions that he has no honor (*timē*) in the city and is thus no gentleman (*Theages* 127e1–5).[29] Most shocking of all is the claim that the love of honor has approximately the same rank as vulgar money-grubbing,[30] a claim repeated by Aristotle in his critique of Sparta.[31]

For Saxonhouse, Socrates' women in Books 5 and 6 of the *Republic* are images of the philosopher and emblems of the claims of the private life against those of the *polis*, which is here identified with war, battle, and death.[32] She develops an elaborate set of correspondences: female, philosopher, private life (the *oikia* or household for women, the beautiful city in speech for the philosophers), peace, play, and life versus male, citizen, public life (the *polis* in action and deed as opposed to speech), war, seriousness, spiritedness, and death. This opposition is not to be understood as simply antagonistic—as in the prephilosophic Greek view of the rela-

[27] Ibid., p. 210.

[28] *Crito* 45d6–46a2; *Gorgias* 485d4.

[29] See Pangle, "Socrates." The ungentlemanly Socrates is also on prominent display in the *Hippias Major*.

[30] *Republic* 1, 347b1–4. Socrates makes this remark in passing to Glaucon, who accepts it without comment, although he later is identified as one whose life exhibits the spirited love of victory and honor, tempered in his case by his skill in music. *Republic* 8, 548c5–549a1.

[31] *Pol.* 2, 1269b23–24, connects the love of money and of honor in Sparta.

[32] "Philosopher and the Female," pp. 205–211.

tions between private and public, male and female—but as expressing both tension and mutual need or interdependence.[33] The core of the relationship between female and male is not, for Plato, the needs and capacities of the two genders relative to one another; these serve rather as metaphors for the definitive interdependent opposites that are the ground for the Platonic critique of Greek civic culture—philosophy and politics.

Plato's theorizing concerning the meaning of gender in Greek life does not produce a set of rules or criteria for the organization of gender relations. Instead, he sets his Socrates to work at changing his world indirectly by changing—or trying to change—its language, or rather the rankings and preferences embedded in that language. Thus Socrates calls into question the previously clear dichotomies between private and public, female and male, play and seriousness,[34] and philosophy and politics, often by claiming to embody both at once and thus joining things presumed to be necessarily separate. And yet of course Socrates can no more be both than he can somehow be "in between" the poles of the moral dichotomies that inform the regime, although he is precisely "in between" (*metaxu*) knowledge and ignorance, which is where he, following Diotima, locates the science of erotics (*Symposium* 201e8–202b5). Where is Socrates? or more simply, what is the Socratic way of life? is the question continually raised by the dialogues, a question that appears much more central to Platonic political philosophy than any doctrine or theory. In Socrates, Plato forces his reader to confront the strangeness of a way of life that is neither "male" nor "female" in that it is spent neither in the public space nor in the *oikia*, but in schools of various kinds and in private homes, spreading perplexity and self-concern among those it touches by calling into question the language in which they have their being.

Aristotle's Biology and the Critique of Virility

I believe that Aristotle's position is very much like Plato's. This means first of all that Aristotle, as much as Plato, must be read as a critic rather than a mirror or glorifier of Greek opinion in general

[33] See Saxonhouse, "Men, Women, War, and Politics," p. 65, and Shaw, "Female Intruder," pp. 256–257.

[34] In the *Sixth Letter*, written to support a friendship between a tyrant and two philosophy students, Plato urges them to treat his letter as the binding *nomos* of their friendship, and to swear by it "with a not unmusical seriousness, and with that playfulness that is sister to seriousness" (323c6–d6).

and the politics of virility in particular. This is contrary to the wide-spread view that "the philosophy of Aristotle, unlike that of Plato, is a codification of general social practice, a systematization of social values."[35] It is surely contrary to Arendt's claim that Aristotle's definition of humans as political animals "only formulated the current opinion of the *polis* about man and the political way of life" by insisting on a profound separation of the *polis* (and men's affairs) from the *oikia* (and womanly business).[36] Some critics, like Susan Moller Okin,[37] go even further and say that Aristotle does not merely reflect the Greek view of politics but attempts to transform Greek prejudices against women into transcendent truths by arguing that the differences between the sexes are due to nature (biologically inherited) rather than to convention or culture. I agree with Okin in holding that Aristotle's biology is absolutely essential to his political thought, but as the preceding chapters have indicated, we must be careful not to attribute to Aristotle the view that practical principles are to be directly deduced from theoretical truths. In this case, I submit that Aristotle's biology does *not* result in a theory of orthogenesis, or a kind of theodicy which bestows the blessings of the gods on a particular group of humans; rather, Aristotle's biology lays the ground for a style of political theorizing that is explicitly *critical* of some of the most important Greek political institutions and opinions, among them the notion that virtue and slavishness are biologically inherited,[38] the idea that virility or courage is the foremost human virtue (*Pol.* 7, 1334a11–34), and the Periclean opinion that all quiet people and cities are useless.[39]

In particular, as we have seen in Chapter 2, Aristotle does *not* say that our being political animals is the most important thing about us, the characteristic that essentially distinguishes us from

[35] Arthur, "Review Essay: Classics," p. 394.

[36] *Human Condition*, p. 27.

[37] *Women in Western Political Thought*, pp. 73–74. A cogent challenge to such views in terms of Aristotle's orientation to prevailing opinions in general is provided by Nussbaum, *Fragility of Goodness*, chap. 8; with regard to the status of women in particular, by Saxonhouse, *Women in the History of Political Thought*, chap. 4.

[38] *Pol.* 1, 1255a28–b4; see also *Rhet.* 2, 1390b14–31.

[39] *Pol.* 7, 1325b16–21. Other important views criticized by Aristotle are the opinions that public education in virtue is unnecessary (*Pol.* 5, 1310a12–36) and that statesmanship and mastery are one and the same (*Pol.* 1, 1252a7–9; *Pol.* 7, 1324b32–33). In general, it is an error too commonly held by readers of Aristotle that his practice of beginning his inquiries with "reputable opinions" (*endoxa*) prevents him from transcending or criticizing these opinions. For a defense of Aristotle against this charge, see Barnes, "Aristotle and the Methods of Ethics." Perhaps the motive for this misreading is the assumption that Aristotle must either be a natural law deductivist or a straightforward contextual relativist.

other animals; thus he is in no way committed to the view that political activity, ruling in turn according to *nomoi*, is an uncriticizable end in itself fixed by our nature. Arendt's claim about the Aristotelian definition of human being may accurately depict the underlying sense of Periclean political culture, but it seriously distorts Aristotle: "The twofold Aristotelian definition of man as a *zōon politikon* and a *zōon logon echon*, a being attaining his highest possibility in the faculty of speech and the life of the *polis*, was designed to distinguish the Greek from the barbarian and the free man from the slave."[40] This view, that Aristotle defines humans as equally political and rational, is frequently repeated by writers much less adept than Arendt, but it is not supported by a look at the relevant text. Rather, Aristotle's position is that we are political animals *because* we are rational animals; our political character is less fundamental than our potential rationality: "The *reason why* the human being is more a political animal than any bee or herding animal is clear; for nature, as we always say, makes nothing in vain, and humans alone among the animals have *logos*."[41] Our rationality explains us (not predictively or in terms of motives for conduct, but teleologically), whereas our political character does not, at least not to the same degree. We need to live in cities, not as an end in itself or as a perfect expression of our humanness, but because it is generally the case that by living according to reasonable laws and customs we can develop and support our biologically inherited potentiality for living rationally.

Polities that do not adequately support the goal of rational development are not, strictly speaking (that is, from the biological or natural rather than the political standpoint), *real* polities at all.[42]

---

[40] Arendt, "Tradition and the Modern Age," pp. 22–23; in *On Revolution*, p. 9, she adds that the two "definitions" supplement each other. But the attributes—"political" and "rational"—are not equally definitive or constitutive and hence, in Aristotle's teleological understanding, not of equal rank with regard to humanness.

[41] *Pol.* 1, 1253a7–9. For the distinction employed here between a mere fact, such as our being political animals (*to hoti*, a "that"), and a fact which explains (*to dihoti*, a "because that") such as our being rational or deliberative animals, see *NE* 1, 1095b2–8. The point here is that rationality is prior (in substance) to civility for human beings, in the same way that civility is prior to the family in *Pol.* 1, 1253a18–19. Moreover, in *History of Animals* 1, 488a8–b25, Aristotle notes that several animals as well as humans are political (he lists bees, wasps, ants, and cranes), but that we alone are deliberative (*bouleutikon*) since we alone can recollect. See Berns, "Spiritedness in Ethics and Politics," pp. 340–341.

[42] *Pol.* 3, 1280a31–b8. The frequency of Aristotle's use of the word *phusis* and related terms at the beginning of the *Politics* is striking. According to Ambler, "Words based on the root 'nature' are used 86 times in Book 1; no other section of

According to Aristotle, most of the so-called cities have no definite goal whatsoever, while the most coherent of them (especially Sparta) make the typically Greek error of thinking that the purpose of political life is ruling over outsiders, or war, rather than rational development. Strictly speaking, therefore, there are no real polities, either in Greece or elsewhere. This is hardly theodicy, or ideological mirroring of Greek opinion. The work of teleological or functionalist biology is thus not to endorse but to criticize the political life of Aristotle's time—a political life which Arendt and many others among us find so attractive—and to criticize it on grounds quite similar to those we find operating in the Platonic critique of the politics of virility. As in the case of the critique of slavery, we may be surprised that an apparently radical theoretical critique yields no direct practical plans for reform, and conclude that the standard of nature has been established only to be neglected. There is, however, an alternative: theoretical critique relates to the species character of human being as such, and can be applied to any particular *kairos* only through the mediation of practical wisdom.

Nevertheless, Aristotle's biology seems to give women a rank even lower than that which they held in classical Greek society.[43] This appears most strongly in his account of reproduction in the *Generation of Animals*. In the bisexual production of embryos, Aristotle says, the male semen supplies the form of the potential offspring, while the female semen (which he identifies with menstrual blood) supplies the matter. Menstrual blood is defined as semen which is lacking in form or *ergon* (it is *ou katharon alla deomenon ergasias*) (*Gen. An.* 728a26–27). Female children are produced when form cannot fully master or rule (*kratein*) matter (*Gen. An.* 767b10–13)—for example, when the parents are either too young or too cold (heat being required for the imposition of form). Females thus, to an extent, lack form, and hence can be described as imperfect (*ateleia*—lacking the *telos*, unfinished) human beings. Furthermore, sex differences are especially marked in humans: human females are much colder, weaker, and shorter-lived than males (*Gen. An.* 775a4–16). A sign of this is said to be the great pain childbearing causes human females. However, Aristotle says, this fact may be at least partly explained by the unnecessarily sed-

the *Politics* or the *Nicomachean Ethics* is similarly focussed on nature." "Aristotle on Acquisition," p. 487 n.1.

[43] Or, perhaps, in the majority of Greek medical writings dealing with the contributions of each sex to reproduction. Lloyd, *Science, Folklore, and Ideology,* p. 107.

entary way of life of Greek women; in tribes where women are more active, birth is easier.[44] Thus, Aristotle is at least open to the possibility that certain gender-linked characteristics are caused by culture rather than nature, and in general it does not make sense to say that his biology is "metaphysical" rather than empirical.[45] Still, it must be noted that for Aristotle the inferior status of women is to some degree a matter of biological rather than cultural inheritance.[46]

Now, if we follow G.E.R. Lloyd[47] in holding that the biological writings about gender difference are intended to support rather than question prevailing Greek ideological presuppositions about male superiority, we should expect to find Aristotle's political writings claiming that women are to be treated as mere matter needing to be ruled entirely by male form. And yet this is not the case. Nor does Aristotle treat the male-female relationship within the household or family as being solely for the purpose of generation. It is here that the difference between Aristotle and Arendt (or the Arendtian reading of Aristotle) becomes most important;

[44] *Gen. An.*, 775a30–35; see also *Pol.* 7, 1335b11–16.

[45] Perhaps the most thorough of the recent studies to argue the point that Aristotle's biology is not a prioristic is Gotthelf's "Aristotle's Conception of Final Causality." Mayr's *Growth of Biological Thought* is also helpful here, especially pp. 149–154. Even Lloyd, who holds that Aristotle's sexual biology is distorted by the ideological assumptions he brings to the study, finds that in general Aristotle reworks traditional assumptions in the light of his independent empirical theorizing: "While he adopts many of the classes embedded in his own natural language, he does not do so uncritically, but modifies existing usages and introduces substantial new coinages where he sees a need." *Science, Folklore, and Ideology*, p. 54. Further evidence of the empirical (if frequently mistaken) character of Aristotle's views concerning sexual differentiation is supplied by *History of Animals* 9, 680a21–b18. There he claims that the females of each species of longer-lived animal tend to differ in character (*ēthos*) from males. Females tend, for instance, to be better at learning, males simpler and more savage. Males tend to possess more spirit (*thumos*) than females, but with some exceptions: female bears and leopards are more virile (*andreiōtera*) than their male counterparts.

[46] *Metaphysics* Iota, 1058a29–b5, sets an interesting *aporia* concerning the *degree* to which sexuality defines an animal. It is less than a species difference (her rationality is a more important part of the definition of a human female than her sex): is it any more important than a difference in skin color? The conclusion is that sexuality is an "attribute proper to the animal [to its *idios bios*], but in its matter and body, and not relative to its substance (*ousia*)" (1058b21–23). The logic of contraries, rather than sexuality, is the central concern of this section of text, but it does suggest that Aristotle is not convinced that there is a radical biological difference—relative to the possibilities of human nature—between male and female. Clark, in "Aristotle's Woman," notes this passage but ends with the judgment that the weight of passages from the biological works forces one to conclude that Aristotle shared the typical prejudices of the Greek male.

[47] *Science, Folklore, and Ideology*, pp. 104–105.

the sharp functional distinction between *polis* and *oikia* understood in terms of a contrast between meaningful *praxis* and mere generation is an Arendtian (and arguably a Greek) but in no way an Aristotelian crux. For Aristotle, the *polis* is indeed prior to the *oikia* with regard to the needs and capacities which define the human form or function (just as, for example, rationality is prior to civility), but both *polis* and *oikia*, when truly rather than nominally such, aim at that virtue or excellence which is distinctly human: "Humans also have a perception of good and bad, just and unjust, and other things, and it is a community of this that makes an *oikia* and a *polis*" (*Pol.* 1, 1253a15–18). The most significant or final cause of *oikia* and *polis* alike is the development of human rationality or "living well" (*eu zēn*), even though both arise through lesser concerns[48]—procreation in the case of the family, and material security or "living" (*zēn*) in the case of the *polis*.[49]

The similarity or functional continuity of family and city is further stressed in *Politics* 1 in the way the political relationship (one of equality under *nomoi*) is defined—*not* in opposition or contrast to the household or the male-female relationship, but rather in contrast to the unequal relationship of natural master and natural slave. Particular humans are said to be fit for slavery *to the extent that* their biologically inherited difference from other humans is as great as the difference between human and beast or between form and matter. So, form is to matter as natural master is to natural slave, *not* (in Aristotle's political theorizing) as male is to female. Men and women are not as different from one another as humans and beasts.

Aristotle's biology would appear to suggest the contrary, however, and the language of the *Politics* (especially the consistent deployment of the distinction between nature and convention) makes it abundantly clear that this book must be understood through the categories developed in the biological works. But the analogy between woman and beast is treated in the *Politics* as a

[48] Lesser, that is, in relation to specifically human characteristics. It is also quite possible that Aristotle's discussion of reproduction itself invests procreation with a dignity much greater than that accorded it by those who see life, with Arendt, as "mere life"—whose notion of the human depends on treating all that is animal as mechanical and dull. Lennox, "Aristotle and the Functions of Reproduction," presents an interesting argument that, for Aristotle, the function of reproduction is to guarantee organisms "that they will share or participate as far as possible in something everlasting and divine" (pp. 10–11).

[49] *Pol.* 1, 1252a26–30, and 1252b29–30. For discussion of this point, see Nichols, "Women in Western Political Thought," p. 251.

mistake characteristically made by barbarians, who are said to treat women and slaves in the same way (*Pol.* 1, 1252b5–6).[50] Among barbarians, we are told, women and slaves have a similar order (*taxis*), and are subordinated to their rulers *in the same way*. Aristotle says that this is an error—but then how should the subordination of women be explained? Aristotle's solution to this problem does not ignore his biology; rather, he places the issue squarely in a biological context by considering which traits (needs and capacities) involved in the relationship are decisively human, and comparing the purposes of the male-female relationship to the goals (*teleis*) which distinguish a human life from that of other species. The most decisive of these traits is (not courage but) the capacity for living according to a rational perception of one's overall interest as a particular human being, rather than living according to whim or temporary passion or preference. Aristotle says that both males and females have this deliberative capacity (*bouleutikon*), but that females possess it *akuron*, without force or authority (1260a13).[51] Thus, since the male is (as a rule) in some way stronger with respect to the capacity that is decisively human, males should rule over females. But how—that is, with what kind of rule (since there are, contrary to ordinary opinion, different kinds of rule appropriate to different relationships [*Pol.* 1, 1252a7–9])?

Aristotle's answer is that the rule should be *political* rather than *despotic* (like the rule of citizens over other citizens rather than the rule of masters over slaves), and that the appropriate biological metaphor for the rule of males over females is thus *not* the rule of

[50] A similarly rhetorical evocation of "barbarians" as a device for loosing the Greeks from their prejudices is found in Antiphon's *On the Truth*, where it is said that humans are different only by convention, not by nature, and that anyone who does not think so is a barbarian, not a Greek.

[51] The meaning of *akuron* is interestingly ambiguous, perhaps intentionally so. Saxonhouse, in "Family, Polity, and Unity," p. 208 and n. 12, suggests this: "Whether this want of 'authority' in the woman's deliberative capacity inheres in the soul itself or becomes manifest in groups of men who would scorn it coming from a woman is unclear in the text"; see also Saxonhouse, *Women in the History of Political Thought*, pp. 72–76. There is a similar ambiguity in one of the first propositions of the *Pol.*, the claim that the *polis* is the "most authoritative (*kuriōtatē*) of all human associations" (*Pol.* 1, 1252a5)—it is surely not simply the best or most natural association, not compared with a certain kind of friendship. The whole issue of who or what must be the authoritative element (*to kurion*) in the *polis* is, as we have seen, treated as an *aporia* that can never be adequately resolved in theory (*Pol.* 3, 1281a11–39). That *to kurion* can mean simply powerful or effective control without any suggestion of legitimacy is surely implied by the way the term is used at *Pol.* 7, 1325a35. Cf. Clark, "Aristotle's Woman," pp. 179–180.

the soul (form) over the body (matter), but the rule of one aspect of soul or form over another (*Pol.* 1, 1260a3–7), the way *nous* (reason) rules over desire (*orexis*). It should be recalled here that *nous* and *orexis* are interdependent with respect to good *praxis* or action.[52] *Nous* is said to govern *orexis* by giving advice rather than issuing orders, by persuasion rather than command (*NE* 1, 1102b29–1103a1), a kind of rule that Aristotle calls political or monarchical, rather than despotic (*Pol.* 1, 1254b5–6). Males, he concludes, are generally fitter to rule, but only as permanent political rulers. The rotation in office that ordinarily characterizes political rule is absent here, but other key elements of political rule are not: rule is to be in the interest of both rulers and ruled (which is only incidentally so in the case of slaves), there is rough equality of ruler and ruled, and an impersonal legal authority limits and informs the action-choices of the rulers (*Pol.* 1, 1259b1–5). Women should not rule, but they should be ruled as fellow citizens—that is, they should get the same benefits from the political relationship as males—and *not* as children or slaves, whose needs, and hence whose status, are entirely different (temporarily or permanently) from the needs of their rulers.

The Moral Education of Women and the Importance of the Private Realm

But what do women need that is to be supplied by the political relationship? For Aristotle, mature human beings need politics because they need a stable and reasonable order within which they can become rational animals—can develop and sustain the habits of mind associated with contextual discernment, the kind of back-and-forth, universal-particular, thoughtful life that for Aristotle is the human way of being, the human good.[53] That is, we need politics not only to protect our rights against the community or for security generally, but to provide a context for the development of the virtues or excellences whose potential expression we inherit biologically. In general, as we have seen, Aristotle's understand-

---

[52] *NE* 6, 1139b4–5, 1144b29–30. For discussion, see Berns, "Spiritedness in Ethics and Politics," pp. 337–338. As Berns says, text evidence indicates "that Aristotle did not have high expectations for an unambiguous division of the soul into parts."

[53] " 'Rational' includes reference to aims as well as means; it is not far from 'sane.' . . . Rationality, like all our practical concepts, belongs to the vocabulary of a particular species with particular needs." Midgley, *Beast and Man*, p. 71. I discuss a similar concept of rationality in "Who Knows Whether It's Rational to Vote?" pp. 203–217.

ing of the purpose of politics is as different from the Arendtian or civic republican as it is from the liberal individualist position. Women need politics (as slaves and children do not) because they require education in virtue as much as men do—even though the virtues or potential excellences of women are not the same as the virtues of men. Socrates denies this differentiation of virtues in the *Meno*, and Aristotle explicitly disagrees with Socrates on this score (*Pol.* 1, 1260a22). But *how* different, for Aristotle, are the virtues that characterize the well-developed or rational male and the rational female? The important thing here, it seems to me, is that they are much less different than the virtues of the two sexes as defined by Pericles—males as articulate fighters, females as silent home-bodies.[54] Aristotle speaks directly to the extent of the differentiation of the virtues in *Rhetoric* 1 (1361a1–11), where the virtues of males are said to be *sōphrosunē* (moderation) and virility (*andreia*), while the virtues of females are said to be *sōphrosunē* and *philergia* (industry) without slavishness (*aneleutheria*). *Sōphrosunē* is thus *the* common virtue, although a woman's moderation (mixed with not-illiberal industry) will be different from a man's (mixed with virility). On the whole, the Aristotelian position is that *sōphrosunē*, like justice, is a human good or virtue of a higher rank than courage or virility to the same extent that leisure is of greater worth than business, and peace than war—worth here measured by the extent to which these occasions allow for the exercise of human rationality (*Pol.* 7, 1334a13–16). The virtue whose potential expression the two sexes share is of much greater importance than the one that divides them.

Plato's several discussions of the proper ordering of moderation and virility have much the same countercultural bearing as Aristotle's revaluations. This can be seen in the last third of the *Gorgias*, in which Socrates defends *sōphrosunē* by elevating it above the claims for *andreia* put forth by the manly Callicles, Socrates' chief rival in commitment to excellence and erotics (*Gorgias* 481c–482d, 486e–488b). The conventional Greek notion of courage, the ideal of the citizen soldier who stands fast at his station in battle and faces

[54] In his objection to Socrates' answer to Meno, Aristotle cites Sophocles' "silence adorns a woman" with seeming approbation. But as Nichols points out, the context of this remark in the drama—self-destructively mad Ajax addressing eminently sane Tecmessa—suggests at least the possibility of some irony at work here, especially given a plethora of other possible citations for the same sentiment. "Women in Western Political Thought," pp. 252–253. Saxonhouse suggests that Aristotle by this citation "brings home the ambiguity of the ascription of power according to sex or birth." *Women in the History of Political Thought*, p. 72.

his enemies unafraid (*Laches* 190e4–6), is criticized by the Athenian Stranger in the first book of the *Laws* (630a–631d), in the context of a critique of the views of the poet Turtaios (identified there as Athenian as well as Spartan) which anticipates Aristotle's nonstandard ranking of Greek values in *Politics* 7 by demoting this conception of courage from first to fourth (and last) place among the virtues. In Book 7 of the same dialogue, the Stranger distinguishes between two kinds of music "according to the distinguishing feature of the nature of each sex": male music is "magnificent (*megaloprepes*) and tends toward virility, while the female inclines rather to the orderly and the moderate (*to kosmion kai sōphron*)" (*Laws* 7, 802e8–11). The two gender-typical virtues are not only different, but in a way incompatible; the Eleatic Stranger in the *Statesman*, speaking of the need to blend moderation and manliness, says that the ways of life marked by the two virtues, if untempered, are not only different but deeply and extensively hostile to one another (*Statesman* 306a12–308b8).

The Eleatic Stranger says that the political art consists in strengthening the moderate and moderating the virile; Socrates, who says in the *Gorgias* that he is perhaps the only artful politician in Athens, seems to practice the latter form of the art exclusively, not only by causing spirited young men to stop and think about what they are doing, but by trying to change the ordinary meaning of the word *andreia*. He does this in the *Republic* by saying that the virtue of the spirited defender of the city is courage only in a qualified, "political" sense (*Republic* 4, 430b2–c6); true courage, amazingly, apparently has nothing to do with soldiering or citizenship and is instead described as persistence in following abstract arguments wherever they lead (*Republic* 6, 503e1–504a1). The same claim is advanced in the *Phaedo* (68c) and in the *Meno* (86b7–c2), where Socrates makes the clearly non-Greek assertion that "we will be better and manlier if we believe that one must search for the things one does not know." It should be noted that virility seems to be the only virtue for which there is any such clear Socratic definition, perhaps precisely because Socrates' intention here is to alter moral sensibility directly rather than through perplexing it. At any rate, a very similar operation on the meaning of *andreia* is carried out by Aristotle in his discussion of that virtue in *Nicomachean Ethics* 3, 1116a15–29. In that discussion, the willingness to endure danger for the sake of the laws and of honor is said to be political courage or the courage of citizens, is associated with Homeric usage, and is said only to resemble real courage rather than being the thing itself.[55] All of this is a long way from Pericles' funeral speech and from Arendt's Heraclitean maxim that the people "should fight for the *nomos* as for the city wall."[56]

After Aristotle distinguishes male and female virtue in *Rhetoric* 1, he goes on immediately to stress the common human need for both private and public education in virtue: "it is necessary for both the common *and the private* alike to seek to establish such qualities in men and women—for places where women are base, as Sparta, are half unhappy" (*Rhet.* 1, 1361a7–11). Here Aristotle joins together, as subjects for criticism, the Greek tendency to link virtue exclusively with maleness and the tendency to consider what occurs in private as beneath notice and irrelevant to the achievement of virtue or excellence. He makes the very same points about Sparta in Books 2 and 7 of the *Politics*, where he argues both that the Spartan laws and customs are deficient insofar as they neglect the education of women, and that the deficiency of these *nomoi* is the result of a false presupposition about what virtue is: the Spartans presuppose that *andreia* and *aretē* are one and the same. When we recall that for Aristotle Sparta stands out as one of the very few *poleis* even to attempt moral education (the rest being mostly heaps of laws and customs developed *ad hoc*, without any overall goal or way of life in view), and when we note that the Spartan love of victory in war is not an accidental or contingently Spartan problem but seems to follow necessarily from the proposition that political *philia* (friendship) and patriotism are based on *thumos* (spiritedness or anger) and the love of honor (*Pol.* 7, 1327b40–1328a1),[57] we can see that the neglect of women's education by the Spartan *nomoi* is no local accident but follows from the good Greek citizen's view that there are in fact no womanly virtues so elevated or difficult as to require political development. Aristotle disagrees.

But why should women require this moral development if they are not normally fit to be full participants in political life (which

[55] See Berns, "Spiritedness in Ethics and Politics," pp. 343–345, for an excellent discussion of this section.

[56] *Human Condition*, p. 63 n. 2.

[57] Lord explicates Aristotle's position here as follows: "The same impulse which interests men in the defense of their own or of the city also encourages more aggressive tendencies. The desire to subdue others and to rule over them is no less natural than the desire to remain free from alien rule and the two desires are inextricably connected. Both are inseparable from a certain harshness, from a certain kind of anger or self-assertiveness which is by its very nature unreasonable or immoderate." *Education and Culture*, p. 192. My debt to Lord's analysis should be apparent.

requires the exercise of the status of ruling as well as being ruled)? If women's lives are best lived in the sphere of the *oikia* rather than in the "public space," then why can they not simply be ordered about and controlled like slaves (for their masters' good) or like children (for their own good), rather than being educated and habituated by laws like free males? Now *if* the purpose of the *oikia* were simply that of serving as a procreative unit, then there would be absolutely no reason why women—mere procreators, or perhaps only necessary instruments of procreation—should be educated rather than mastered. But human beings, as distinguished from other animals, "live together not only for the sake of procreation but also for the sake of those things that contribute to their way of life" (*NE* 8, 1162a20–22). Furthermore, the purpose of the family is, as we have seen in the *Politics*, continuous with that of the *polis*. Aristotle makes the case for this continuity of function most clearly in the *Eudemian Ethics*: "Therefore the source and springs of friendship, political order, and justice are in the *oikia*" (*EE* 7, 1242a22–23). It is for this reason that Aristotle insists on drawing attention to the difference between the status of women on the one hand and that of slaves and children on the other.

The *Eudemian Ethics* stresses the similarity of *oikia* and *polis* as forms of living together which distinguish humans from other animals: "The human being is not only a political animal but also a familial [or economic] animal (*zōon politikon kai oikonomikon*), and does not, like other animals, couple occasionally with any chance male or female,[58] but is uniquely not solitary but communal (*koinōnikon*) toward those who are its natural kin; and thus there would be *koinōnia* and a kind of justice even if there were no *polis*" (*EE* 7, 1242a22–27). A similar passage in the *Nicomachean Ethics* is prefaced by a remark that friendship between male and female seems to be especially according to nature among humans, and by the comment that friendship between husband and wife—though generally a matter of utility or mutual advantage—can be based on

[58] The clear difference between Aristotle's comparative ethology, as it were, and Rousseau's in the *Second Discourse* is important. For Rousseau, there is absolutely no connection between family life and the virtues of civil men, largely because there is nothing humanizing about the life of the family (at least not so far as the *Discourses* and the *Social Contract* are concerned; *Emile* and *Julie* tell a different and much more Aristotelian story). It is interesting to note the modern republican tendency to accept Rousseau's central political claim (that good citizens must be entirely public-spirited) as true while ignoring or forgetting its dependence on the false biological presupposition that the human family is merely a procreative unit. This is perhaps one of the costs of the decline of teleological explanation.

virtue (as the best friendships are) rather than on utility (as is political *philia*: *EE* 7, 1242a; *NE* 9, 1171a) or episodic pleasure (*NE* 8, 1162a16–17). A consequence of this is that marital relations can be either just or unjust: when the husband's rule encompasses all the affairs of the *oikia* the rule is said to be unjust or oligarchic (*NE* 8, 1160b35–1161a1). More importantly, the *oikia* as such can be evaluated, like the *polis*, in terms of its justice. Schematically, one might say that Aristotle's intention here is to demythologize political life by making—in the language of his biology—a case for the subordination of "political animal" to "rational animal" on one side, and for the functional similarity of the attributes "political" and "economic" on the other.

When Aristotle speaks of justice, he is not referring to some abstract or transcendent principle or rule; he is characterizing a kind of order which makes the development of human virtue, or the rational or deliberative life broadly understood, possible—justice could not apply to an order whose only purpose was the preservation of merely any sort of life.[59] Thus while the *polis* is indeed prior to the *oikia* from the perspective of the needs and potentialities which define humanity, it is equally clear that the thoughtful choice (*prohairesis*) of a human good relative to us as individual humans—the presence of which distinguishes a rational from a disorderly life—is a perception developed both within the *oikia* and within the *polis*. Aristotle's claim here is not a description of the usual practices of societies, but follows from his functionalist biology; he is making an argument about a particular relationship (the family) and a particular need or potentiality that we inherit biologically and that is the cause (teleologically) of our being a recognizably separate species. Thus, just as we can say that the need and capacity for living rationally or according to thoughtful choice (*kata prohairesin*)[60] is distinctly human (*Pol.* 3, 1280a32–34)—since non-human animals can live neither according to such choice nor in a disorderly (*ataktōs*) way[61]—so we must say that the relationships

[59] No specifically human virtues could be expressed in such human relationships: we may eat or sleep well, but not justly (*NE* 1, 1102b2–12). A very clear difference between Aristotelian and Arendtian politics is exhibited by this notion of the just family; for Arendt, familial life is as far from human activity as sleeping, and justice is not a political virtue in the way that courage is. A similar criticism of Arendt is made by Pitkin, "Justice," pp. 338–339.

[60] The concept of *prohairesis* is discussed above in Chapter 2.

[61] As we saw in Chapter 2, Aristotle is not at all glorifying humanity, but presenting the problem that characterizes us as a biological species: we need to form or accept a conventional order if we are to live well (since we do not inherit one

through which we realize the needs that define us are also distinctly human. For Aristotle, the list of humanizing, and therefore human, relationships includes the family along with the *polis*, as well as other kinds of friendships that are strictly speaking neither familial nor political.

The Aristotelian Revaluation of Friendship and the Family

Aristotle's ranking of women and womanly activities above the rank normally accorded by his culture, while less pronounced than that of Plato, stems from a similar concern: the defense of the importance of nonpolitical activities for the development of human virtue. In Aristotle's case, this is reflected in an argument that the family is needed not simply for procreation or bare living, but for the development of rationality and happiness as well. There are two different evaluative judgments behind Aristotle's elevation of the family, one negative and one positive. The negative judgment reflects his sense of the unavoidable dangers built into political life; the positive judgment involves an assessment of the possible contribution of the family to moral education. Aristotle's worry about politics stems from his belief that excessive commitment to the *polis* will always be accompanied by a love of victory and rule which is dangerous to rationality and the other virtues more human than courage or virility, such as moderation and justice. The positive defense of the *oikia*, the argument about the *telos* of the family which I will take up first, is not explicitly made by Aristotle—although as we have seen, he explicitly says that the family is a source of the capacity to take part in political life and in friendships. But in what way? My proposal is that a strong Aristotelian case can be made for saying that the special work of the family is neither procreation nor security but the development in children of the sense of shame that is an indispensable precondition for deliberative or thoughtful living. Family life, then, has crucial political importance in two ways: it prepares us for public life by establishing a rationalizing sense of shame, and at the same time it provides a separate focus of attention and care—a real job to do—which can check the danger of excessive civic-mindedness that seems always to threaten to turn the most tightly knit cities into armed camps. It is thus desirable that a certain tension be maintained between public and private, and especially necessary for

---

biologically), and yet some of our strongest inherited impulses are for a disorderly life (*Pol.* 6, 1319b31–32).

political philosophy (as the theorizing moment of practical wisdom) to defend the claims of the private against the louder voices
coming from the public sphere. In all of this, there is substantial
agreement between Plato and Aristotle.[62]

My conjecture that the development of shame is a good candidate for the *telos* of the family is based on the Aristotelian view
that people who are not capable of being ashamed are not open to
persuasion and deliberation—the only motive such people have
for not living childishly or according to momentary or episodic
passionate attraction is the fear of punishment. The sense of
shame, the habitual disposition to worry that one's initial response
to a situation might be wrong, or the fear of disgrace (*NE* 4,
1128b10–13), is a necessary prelude to mature deliberation and *paideia*. The sense of carefulness or hesitancy that belongs to the modest person is nicely expressed in the definition of shame in the
Magna Moralia: a person capable of shame "will not, like the
shameless person, say and do anything in any way; nor, like the
shy person, hold back in everything in every way; but will do and
say what is appropriate" (*Magna Moralia* 1193a7–10). A related definition is given in Book 2 of the *Rhetoric*, where shame (here *ais-
chunē*) is described as "a certain pain or uneasiness about past,
present, and future bad things that bring disgrace (*adoxia*)" (*Rhet.*
2, 1383b12–14).[63] Such pain or fear, as long as it is not hopeless
dread, has the effect of making us think about what we are doing,

---

[62] Aristotle's stress on the value of the family is much more emphatic and explicit
than Plato's. However, Socrates is usually shown as well acquainted with and
much interested in the family connections of his interlocutors. A nice small instance
of this concern occurs at the beginning of the *Theaetetus*, at 144b8–c8, where Socrates is well aware of young Theaetetus' parentage, in marked contrast to the indifference of the boy's teacher, the very theoretical Theodorus. More direct evidence
is supplied by the exchange between Euthyphro and Socrates in *Euthyphro* 4b3–5a1,
in which Socrates opposes the "Platonic" position (for those who misread *Republic*
5 as Platonic "doctrine") that family ties are irrelevant where justice is concerned.
See also Xenophon, *Memorabilia* 3.6, where Socrates is shown dissuading young
Glaucon from even thinking of a political career until he is capable of managing the
affairs of his household. Still, the major components of the Platonic-Socratic defense of privacy are Socrates' own irony—his habitual self-concealment—and his
preference for enclosed spaces like private homes and wrestling schools, in contrast
to the public man's love of the market and the assembly. He also frequently calls
attention to the way in which public virtue depends on private support, something
especially noticeable in those cases where such support is entirely a Socratic fiction,
as in his claim that the Spartans would be nothing without the secret tutelage of
their hidden sophists (*Protagoras* 342a6–343c5).

[63] Arnhart puts the matter well: "Shame might be of central importance because
it is the prime example of how passion can support moral restraint." *Aristotle on
Practical Reasoning*, p. 130.

and thus of humanizing us, for Aristotle as for Hobbes: "fear makes people deliberate (*phobos bouleutikous poiei*)" (*Rhet.* 2, 1383a6–7). It is for this reason that rule by the middle class, and especially by the rural middle class, is said to be preferable to rule by the very rich or the very poor (*Pol.* 4, 1295a25–1296a21): those of moderate means are subject neither to *hubris* nor to envy or hopelessness, and so, unlike the overly wealthy, the overly manly (*Rhet.* 2, 1389a25–26), and the fearlessly immature in general (*NE* 1, 1095a2–11), they are open to actualizing their *logos*, and not likely to be swept away. Such people, then, are in a humanly appropriate middle position with respect to their confidence in their ability to rule.

But the development of a decent sense of shame is neither automatic nor easy, as can be seen (for Aristotle) by the fact that most people tend to respond only to a fear of punishment rather than to disgrace, are thus not open to argument, and so can be guided or restrained only by legal threat rather than by shame (*NE* 10, 1095a2–11). Shame is very much like a virtue (such as moderation) in being an intermediary between two extremes—in this case shamelessness and shyness. In both versions of the *Ethics*, it is described as "like a virtue" but not quite the same thing, since virtues (and vices) are relatively stable personality or character traits (*hexeis*) in mature people, while shame or modesty (like righteous indignation—*nemesis*) is better conceived as a feeling (*pathos*) (*NE* 2, 1108a30–b2; *EE* 3, 1233b17–1234a27). As with the virtues, however, shame (or modesty) is a tendency to respond to certain situations in certain ways, and can be represented as a mean that indicates a norm rather than a quantitative average: "Shame is a mean between shamelessness and shyness: one who cares about no one's opinion is shameless, one who cares about everyone's opinion is shy, while the modest person (*aidēmōn*) cares about the opinion of those who seem decent" (*EE* 3, 1233b27–29).[64] An inclination to this sort of feeling involves a certain immaturity and lack of reflection,[65] and so is more properly praised in young people than in adults, who might be expected to respond more thoughtfully and with less regard for the approval of others to the

[64] "Seem" decent, since modesty, like the moral virtues, never guarantees practical wisdom, though they are all needed to support it. Recall the discussion of Henry Wilcox and the concept of natural as opposed to full virtue in Chapter 3 above.

[65] According to the *EE*, it is said to be "without deliberate choice (*prohairesis*)" (*EE* 3, 1325a25).

kind of situations in which shame is worth praising as a motive to genuinely virtuous actions (*NE* 4, 1128b15–21). As an anticipation of practical wisdom, shame—though still a *pathos*—is much more reasonable than *thumos* or spiritedness.[66]

The family and the polity are both places where a sense of shame might be developed, but the family seems more suited to this than the *polis*, since parents are likely to be better at this kind of moral education than public officials because of the bonds of affection that operate in the *oikia*: "Just as laws and customs prevail in cities, so do ancestral *logoi* and habits prevail in families, and even more, because of kinship and benefits; and *there* loving (*stergontes*) and willingness to obey are by nature" (*NE* 10, 1180b3–7).[67] The emphasis is, of course, mine; it is intended to call attention to the difference between the ties of family affection and those of political *philia*, which are founded on spiritedness (*thumos*). The natural love that causes the family to be the most important site of moral *paideia* flows not simply from children's dependence on their parents as the source of the greatest benefits, but even more from the love parents feel for their children as emblems of parental activity—of the *energeia* that defines the actors as whatever they are. Thus, animals are said to care for their children not out of altruism

[66] Lord notes that in Aristotle's discussion of the virtues and vices connected with the passion of anger (*orgē*), he says that ordinary language lacks a name for the mean and tends to call its excess manliness (*NE* 4, 1126a36–b2), so that he chooses to apply the name of the deficiency in anger, "gentleness," to the mean. Lord comments that "it would seem that the human soul provides no real support for moderate spiritedness—for the reasonable assertion of one's rights and interests." *Education and Culture*, pp. 192–193 n. 16. By contrast, Aristotle says that full virility differs from the quality of being a good soldier because it follows from a desire for the noble, rather than from anger. This modest virility, based on shame, is much more to be praised than spirited virility (*NE* 3, 1116a27–30, 1116b23–31).

[67] A complementary way of stating the case for the teleological importance of the family in Aristotle is to see it as the site for the formation of a sense of separate personal identity (as opposed to thinking of oneself as being merely a fractional part of the whole), a sense necessary for fully deliberative animals. For this interpretation, see Nussbaum, "Shame, Separateness, and Political Unity," and also Saxonhouse, "Family, Polity, and Unity," who says that Aristotle insists on the importance of the family "from concern for affectionate ties of care and love between human beings. He insists that the sense of oneself as an individual, as different in form, must be prior to a sense of oneself as a political equal" (p. 218). This is a strong and perhaps surprising claim, but it is fully consistent with the Aristotelian proposition that we are deliberative animals *before* we are political animals, priority understood here not, of course, in time, but as a way of ranking our attributes in relation to our essential or defining humanness. It also indicates the way Karl Marx's conception of the importance of politics differs from Aristotle's when, in the introduction to the *Grundrisse*, Marx says that "human being is in the most literal sense a *zōon politikon*, not merely a gregarious animal, but an animal which can individuate itself only in the midst of society." *Marx-Engels Reader*, p. 223.

but because actors love their own activity most of all, and children are tangible expressions of that activity (*EE* 7, 1241a40–b7). For this reason, parents love children immediately, but children love their parents only as they come to develop perception and understanding (*NE* 8, 1161b24–26). Moreover, just because the basis of natural (though not of political) *philia* is the love we feel for our own activity, mothers are said to love their children more than fathers do, "because they think children are more their work (*ergon*); for people define work by its difficulty, and the mother suffers more pain in the genesis of the child" (*EE* 7, 1241b7–9).[68] The fact that, from the standpoint of the biology of reproduction, Aristotle regards mothers as being wrong about whose *ergon* the child chiefly is seems wholly irrelevant here; at any rate, Aristotle mentions it not at all in either the *Eudemian Ethics* or the *Nicomachean Ethics*. The style of these discourses, as of the ethical and political works generally, is governed not by the norm of theoretical precision, but by the attempt to persuade listeners to act well. The notion of acting well operative here is, to be sure, strictly biological, at least with regard to the species; but in a scheme of final causes, reproductive biology is not biology's most fundamental part: a woman's contribution to the "life" of the child (supplying the matter) does not determine her contribution to the child's "living well," since the latter cannot be reduced to the former.[69] Given the intention of practical theorizing, the lesson here seems plain: since women love their children more than anyone else does, their role as educators is crucial; hence the moral development of women must be accorded a higher priority and status than it is given by the barbarians, by the Spartans, by Pericles, or by anyone who asserts that the political life is the only truly human activity.

The one type of relationship that seems unquestionably human—in the sense of being essential to the thoughtful life that defines us—is neither the family nor the polity but *philia* (friendship), since living with friends makes us "more able to think and to act" (*NE* 8, 1155a15–16). But the reach of the term *philia* is quite broad, broader than that of our "friendship," for example, since it is regularly used to refer to the connections among family members, to political ties, and to economic activities, as well as to less institu-

---

[68] In *History of Animals* 9, 608a35–b2, Aristotle notes that women tend to be more interested than men in the rearing (*trophē*) of children.

[69] This is, incidentally, the clear and important difference between Aristotle's biological politics and modern sociobiology, the latter being a case of reductionism masquerading as evaluative teleology.

tionally determined personal friendships. Aristotle spends a great deal of time discussing *philia* in the *Nicomachean Ethics* and the *Eudemian Ethics*, much more than any modern writer would in a work on ethics or politics. His analysis of the term, as usual, does more than simply report contemporary usage; it presents a functional analysis of the place of different kinds of *philia*, including family and polity, in human life. Aristotle distinguishes three kinds of *philia* that vary in terms of what motivates the parties to care about each other: mutual utility (business partnerships), mutual pleasure (friendships among witty people), and a mutual sense of human virtue or goodness of character. The first two kinds are in a sense reflections or parts of the third: *philia* is a *pros hen* equivocal (like "good"), and virtue- or character-friendships come first because they, more than the others, involve *prohairesis*, and so are part of the specific way of life of human beings (*EE* 7, 1236a15–b27), although all three kinds are part of a good human life and satisfy important human needs. (Once again, we must bear in mind the distinction between necessary and constitutive conditions in order to see Aristotle's point here.)

But *philia* is more than a cognitive agreement or shared perception about pleasure or utility or goodness, quite as we would expect from Aristotle's understanding of *prohairesis* as an interlacing of thought and desire. John Cooper describes Aristotle's conception of the emotional bond operative in the definitive kind of friendship as follows: "Such friendships exist when two persons, having spent enough time together to know one another's character and to trust one another (*NE* 8, 1156b25–29), come to love one another because of their good human qualities: Aristotle's word for 'love' here is *stergein*, a word which is used most often to apply to a mother's love for her children and other such close family attachments."[70] As Cooper notes,[71] *stergein* and its noun, *sterxis*, are the terms (in addition to *philein*, of course) Aristotle generally uses to pick out the friendship bond. Thus, friendship resembles a family connection more than, for instance, an erotic relationship, although personal friendships and family friendships are dissimilar in certain respects. We will return to the question of friendship in the final chapter in discussing liberalism, a political vision in which I think some concept of the essential importance of personal or character-friendship has a central place. At this point I want

[70] Cooper, "Aristotle on Friendship," p. 308.
[71] Ibid., pp. 335–336 n. 9.

only to note that personal friendship differs from both familial and political friendship: while political *philia* is undoubtedly important, even the greatest of goods for cities, since it reduces *stasis* or internal conflict (*Pol.* 2, 1262b7–9), it is also, unlike virtue- or character-friendship, based primarily on utility (*EE* 7, 1242a; *NE* 9, 1167a26–30), or a like-mindedness about justice—a virtue not needed among the best kind of friends, whose concern for one another is based on an affection resembling in its immediacy and power the bond between family members, an affection not mediated through common acceptance of a particular set of laws. This is emphatically not to deny that we are all political animals—we need laws, and for more than mere protection, just as we need families for more than procreation. But just as the family is not by itself sufficient to constitute a fully human life, the *polis* too seems to require a supplement. Fellow citizens can of course be friends in other ways as well, as can marriage partners; personal friendship is not a separate alternative to family or politics. But what is there about the political life, so highly praised in the opening of the *Politics*, that makes it a less than fully satisfactory solution to the problem of virtue, and leads Aristotle to look beyond the political in the final books of the *Politics* and the *Nicomachean Ethics*? Why, in other words, does Aristotle so sharply question the political in his treatment of friendship and the family?

I suggest that this negative element in Aristotle's generally affirmative account of politics is based on his sense of an important empirical connection between political commitment and an exaggerated love of victory (*thumos*), a connection drawn very clearly in Book 7 of the *Politics*[72] and evident as well from the linking of military and political activities in Book 10 of the *Nicomachean Ethics* (*NE* 10, 1177b6–15). Political, as opposed to familial or personal, friendship is said to rest on *thumos* and to demand *andreia*, and good political people will treat honor (*timē*) as the goal of political life (*NE* 1, 1095b22–23). But if moderation is a more human virtue than virility, as it is for both Plato and Aristotle, then some counterweight is required to oppose our wrongheaded and unnatural (in one sense) attraction to fully committed citizenship. This connection between politics and war is an empirical and contingent

[72] In the political context "*thumos* makes friendliness; for this is the potentiality of the soul through which we are friends" (*Pol.* 7, 1327b40–1328a1). The preceding lines make the context clear; the kind of friendship we are discussing here is that which makes spirited people (like the guardians in Bks. 2–4 of Plato's *Republic*) friendly toward those they know and savage (*agrios*) toward outsiders.

matter, even though it is widespread and its roots can be predictively understood. It is because, and not simply in spite of, the *polis* that we live always in the precincts of battle; still, it is not humanly impossible to imagine a quiet and moderate *polis* (*Pol.* 7, 1324b41–1325a7), and so it is theoretically reasonable to attempt to identify resources that might oppose the politics of virility. The praise of the theoretical or philosophic life in *Politics* 7 and *Nicomachean Ethics* 10, in conjunction with the extensive discussion of the role of musical culture in the development and support of human rationality in our incomplete version of *Politics* 8, may be seen as just such a counterweight,[73] although this praise, typically, never turns tactlessly into a rule for the establishment of a new, nonpolitical way of being.

The life of the *oikia*, like that of philosophy or music, can provide an attachment to a rationalizing order different from the *polis*. This appears especially clearly in Aristotle's discussion in Book 2 of the *Politics* of the proposal in Plato's *Republic* that the guardians in the city of the armed camp have neither families nor private possessions. Aristotle's objections to the abolition of the family are two: trying to extend intimate relations from close family to all the citizens makes these connections "watery" and thin (*Pol.* 2, 1262b14–17); and eliminating the family and private property in favor of a wholly unified city eliminates support for certain virtues, particularly (sexual) moderation and liberality concerning possessions (*Pol.* 2, 1263b9–11). A good Aristotelian case can be made for saying that the moral virtues supported by the family (moderation and liberality) are more human—more supportive of the constitutive human excellence of thoughtful choice—than courage, the prime virtue of the city. The lesson to be derived from the criticism of the exclusively political life in Book 2 of the *Politics* seems to be that the greatest danger to a decent political life stems not from a reluctance to get involved in political affairs, but from an untempered love of the city. This, and not Tocqueville's individualism or a Machiavellian or Arendtian identification of the private life as a source of corruption and idleness, is the danger Aristotle addresses. His appreciation of the human desirability of a degree of tension between private and public affections is thus profoundly anti-Periclean in its appreciation of the dignity of the family and

[73] This is argued persuasively in Lord's *Education and Culture*, especially chaps. 2 and 3.

the private sphere, in its refusal to equate virility and virtue, and its appreciation of the dangers endemic to political life.

These dangers are clearest in Aristotle's account of the regime he calls polity (*politeia*, the generic name for all regimes). Polity is a regime in which the people (the *dēmos* or the *plēthos*) rule in the common interest. Such a regime is said to be closer to democracy than to oligarchy, and so provides Aristotle with some reason for hope concerning the possibilities of democratic political life. But it is especially here, because of the *way* the citizens of a polity perceive their common interest in virtue, that the line between politics and war becomes blurred:

> This is the name common to all regimes, and it is reasonable to call it this, because while it is possible for one or a few to be virtuous, it is difficult for a large number to reach a high standard in all forms of virtue—with the conspicuous exception of military virtue, which is found in a great many people. That is why in this regime the warriors are the most authoritative element (*kuriōtaton*), and those who bear arms (*ta hopla*) share in the regime. (*Pol.* 3, 1279a38–b3)

The fact that Greek democracies are hoplite democracies is surely no accident, in Aristotle's view,[74] precisely because virility (or at least a semblance of it) is the easiest of the virtues, both to conceptualize and to practice. It is also a virtue that serves us very badly when the order imposed by war ceases: "manliness possessing power is boldness (*thrasos*)" (*Pol.* 5, 1312a19), and "boldness is a quality of use in none of the affairs of daily life, but only, if at all, in war" (*Pol.* 2, 1269b34–36). Both the ease and the low rank of courage are easily explained: it is the virtue that requires the least deliberation and thought, and is, in fact, a virtue whose expression is clearest when there is the least possibility of deliberation (*NE* 3, 1117a19–22).

Reconceiving the Political
A Defense of Moderate Alienation

The significance of the diametrical opposition between the Arendtian and the Aristotelian positions concerning the rank of courage or virility among the virtues should now be plain. Arendt, of

[74] See also *Pol.* 4, 1297b1–2. Modern historians support Aristotle's judgment here. See Vernant, *Origins of Greek Thought*, pp. 60–68; Austin and Vidal-Naquet, *Economic and Social History of Ancient Greece*, p. 52.

course, is by no means alone in thinking about the hope for a truly political life in terms of an imagery of warfare sans bloodshed. Among us, the political problem is often conceived as the problem of discovering some "moral" equivalent of war, a project which presupposes that the best and most truly human qualities are likely to shine forth only under extreme pressure. This is Machiavelli's view: if a republic is always prepared for war, "there will always be a demand for citizens of repute, as there was at Rome in the early days" (*Discourses* 3.16). It is also Nietzsche's: "war and courage have accomplished more great things than love of the neighbor," and "it is the good war that hallows any cause" (*Zarathustra*, pt. 1, sec. 10). Neither Arendt nor Machiavelli nor Nietzsche, nor Hegel in his account of the struggle between Lord and Bondsman as the primary political interaction,[75] is a blood-thirsty lover of war. But they are agreed in holding that a certain tense spiritedness, characteristic of the virile warrior, is the hallmark of truly human, truly political activity. So common and powerful has this view been in recent centuries that the most irenic among us may easily think of the peak of the virtues in terms of what we call "moral courage," the ability to stand up for one's beliefs under heavy pressure.

Aristotle's imagery is very different. The figure who represents the peak of moral virtue, the great-souled person (*megalopsuchos*), does strangely little and is quite slow to do that. The *megalopsuchos* is above all not tense or tightly strung, owing to a sense that nothing much in the realm of action is very great (*oude suntonos ho mēden mega oiomenos*) (*NE* 4, 1125a15).[76] Just as Plato attempts, against the lexicon of his culture, to transfer the laurel of *andreia* from the citizen-soldier to the philosopher intent upon her or his researches into the nature of the beings, so Aristotle seeks to replace the inspiring vision of the bold warrior with that of a beast who combines magnitude and a certain gentleness. The Spartans,

---

[75] Berns's summary suggests that we see Hegel's parable in this context: "It is, in non-Hegelian language, superior spiritedness that most characterizes the political man, the natural ruler." "Spiritedness in Ethics and Politics," p. 336.

[76] For a good recent discussion of the *megalopsuchos*, see Steven B. Smith, "Goodness, Nobility, and Virtue." Aristotle, in a different context, makes some intriguing comments about who might count as a *megalopsuchos* in terms of different possible definitions: if hatred of dishonor, then Achilles, Ajax, and Alcibiades; if indifference to good or bad fortune, then Socrates and Lysander (*Posterior Analytics* 97b). In the *NE* 4 account, the *megalopsuchos* is said indeed to care about honor, as Socrates surely does not. This leaves Alcibiades, Ajax, and Achilles, along with some room for thinking Aristotle's discussion of the *megalopsuchos* a little ironic. See Mara, "Philosophy in Aristotle's Political Science," p. 398 and n. 31.

he tells us toward the end of the *Politics*, aim only at virility and as a result fail to produce even that. Real courage has nothing of savagery about it, but goes "rather with the gentler and more lionlike characters" (*Pol.* 8, 1338b17–19).

Those who think Aristotle's biology provides a pseudoscientific apology for male supremacy are as mistaken as those who read his social science as a stirring call for a participatory politics of communal identity. The error in both instances comes from failing to see how Aristotle, like Plato, strives to undermine rather than support the evaluative dichotomy between the public and the private things. For Aristotle, our human identity—as beings who can come into our own through living thoughtfully—requires both polity and family, and the latter even more (in one sense) than the former. This argument, itself thoroughly biological in character (in that it is a teleological explanation of human relationships in terms of the specific life and needs of human beings), serves as the ground for the Aristotelian derogation of the Greek attachment to virility and the love of honor, and to the hierarchy and differentiation of gender roles which is its consequence. Aristotle's biology is in fact the basis for his insistence on evaluating the dignity and importance of women more highly than did the culture in which he lived.

None of this requires that we either forget or endorse Aristotle's statements asserting women's inferiority, any more than a defense of Aristotelian teleology entails agreement with Aristotle's false beliefs about celestial matter or the position of the earth in the universe. My contention is not that all of Aristotle's conclusions are correct, but that the logic of Aristotelian social science is sufficiently powerful and flexible to permit critical examination of these conclusions.[77] My central claim is that the Platonic and Aristotelian discussions of women bring to the fore two important issues which are otherwise inaccessible. The first is that the prephilosophic or Periclean attachment to the public world is in large measure a commitment to the identification of virtue with masculinity or virility. The second is that the first people in our tradition to philosophize about politics, Plato and Aristotle, reject this attach-

---

[77] Keller puts the issue very nicely in her justification of the use of psychoanalytic theory in feminist critique: "My use of psychoanalytic theory is premised on the belief that, even with its deficiencies, it has the potentiality for self-correction. The mode of analysis it provides is sufficiently penetrating to enable us to examine developmental failures not only in the human psyche but in the theory itself." *Reflections on Gender and Science*, p. 73.

ment on the ground that it reflects and conceals a false (or only partially true) conception of human *aretē*. The various ways in which Plato and Aristotle suggest an elevation or revaluation of the status of women are thus not based on any answer, affirmative or negative, to the question whether the rights of women should equal those of men. For Aristotle, at any rate, such an answer cannot follow directly from a theoretical consideration, whatever his prudential judgment may have been concerning the best policy for his own time. Instead, the goal is to extract and criticize the prevailing conception of the best life—a conception revived for us, against classical political philosophy, by Machiavelli, by Nietzsche, and by Arendt—and to replace it by a novel, more complex, and surely less masculine vision. This reading of Plato and Aristotle enriches our political vocabulary by suggesting that there are other and better resources against a republican communitarianism saturated by the imagery of war than the anachronistic charm of the early commercial republic.

One of the difficulties posed by the political alternative implicit in the Platonic and Aristotelian critique of Periclean Athens is that the philosophers' solution to the human problem is, necessarily, much less definite and vivid than the one celebrated by the politicians. At any rate, we can at least say that their view of the best generally accessible life is surely not that of the citizen-soldier whose horizons are those of the city and whose life is a quest for *timē* and *kleos* regardless of the cost that must be borne in private. Rather, the best life open to most of us might be that of a moderately detached householder or philosopher, who is sometimes a citizen and sometimes not. The philosophizing involved in such a life need not be limited to theoretical causal inquiry; this is the primary sense, but it can be approximated in other ways. As Aristotle notes in discussing the origin of philosophy in wonder at the way things are, "someone who is perplexed (*aporōn*) and wondering is aware of not knowing (and for this reason the lover of myths or stories [*philomuthos*] is somehow a philosopher; for a *muthos* is composed of wonders)" (*Metaphysics* Alpha, 982b17–19).[78]

---

[78] Similarly broad uses of philosophy are found in the *Pol.*, for instance in the section on the causes of crime (*Pol.* 2, 1263b) discussed in Chapter 1, and again in Bk. 7. See also *Rhet.* 2, 1394a4–5. There is in addition the reference to poetry as philosophic in the *Poetics* (1451b5–7). An excellent discussion of this broader sense and its political possibilities is that of Lord in "Politics and Philosophy," who describes it as follows: "Philosophy in the broad sense does not necessarily exclude theoretical speculation, but its core is traditional culture; and traditional culture above all means literary culture. The core of that philosophy which is politically

Keeping this picture of a life rich in the enjoyment of literary and musical experience in mind may help us avoid the illusion of easy virtue that the imagined flash of battle stimulates, and encourage us to strengthen those places (like families and other schools) within which human *paideia* can occur.

Ranking Virtues and Relationships

Aristotle is not antipolitical, and he is fully alive to the important ways in which the political life contributes to human virtue by insisting on attention to justice and the interests of others. But he is also concerned that we keep in mind that one can be a very good citizen without being a good human being. The point here is that he refuses to take sides in an internal debate between the claims of the public and the private. Instead, his theorizing tries to show how the terms of this debate limit Greek moral vision by obscuring certain aspects of the problem of the human good, in particular the way in which family life, character-friendships, and "music" bring about and sustain human virtue. Aristotle's rhetorical strategy for showing this is to criticize the way his society classifies and ranks human virtues, calling particular attention to its excessive focus on political eminence and virility in contrast to the *metron* of the thoughtfully chosen life.

The issue of the preeminence of virility is one worth considering further. To what extent is it still the case that in talk about virtues and vices, reference to courage is trumps? Certainly when we want to praise Socrates highly we often refer to his courage in standing up to the city, and not to the virtue of human wisdom he claimed for himself. (Our situation is perhaps more complex than the Greek one, in that courage and compassion [or "love of the neighbor"] may stand for us as twin peaks among the virtues.) Is this reasonable, or should we be persuaded by the Platonic and Aristotelian suggestions to the contrary?

Whatever the answers to these questions, they are worth raising, as is the related matter of the importance of personal friendships. Are these simply something extra, not worth taking seriously—at least not compared with other associations that may seem more central to the human experience: lovers, families, pol-

relevant is, in the language of Aristotle and his contemporaries, music" (p. 355). Aristotle proposes to emphasize traditional literary culture more than is usually done but, as Lord says, "only in order to support more effectively a way of life that is the antithesis of tradition" (p. 357).

ities, religions, tribes, economic classes? Perhaps there is a connection between elevating the rank of certain virtues (like courage and compassion) and devaluing those relationships that give no scope to the expression of these virtues. In any event, it is worth noting that friendship is rarely at the center either of practical philosophizing or of literary work—although there are of course exceptions, such as Forster's image of the wych-elm in *Howards End*.[79]

Presuppositions about virtues and relationships form the grammar of our practical discourse, lending structure and authority to such conversation. The theorizing found in Plato and Aristotle calls attention both to the indispensability of such conventional authority and to the problematic quality of any particular conventional structure, which will always embody a particular, and hence inherently questionable, conception of the human good.

In the next two chapters we move from a consideration of ancient Greek politics to the current debate about the meaning and value of liberal democracy. My initial argument there will be that the terms in which this debate is conducted have the unfortunate effect of simplifying or excluding altogether the issue of character, of the virtues appropriate to a liberal polity, and that as a result the debate systematically underestimates the significance of institutions and practices (such as "character-friendships") that should be at the center of our concern.

[79] A brilliant exception in philosophy is Arendt's essay on the humanizing importance of nonpolitical friendship, "On Humanity in Dark Times."

FIVE

RECONCEIVING LIBERAL DEMOCRACY, PART I: DEMOCRACY AS A RANGE OF POSSIBILITIES

Learning from Aristotle's Theory

In discussing ways in which Aristotelian theorizing can give direction to the contemporary theory of liberal democracy, I make two assumptions at the outset. The first is that liberal politics, a political order aiming at the elimination of arbitrary restraints on the power of individuals to make lives for themselves, is a good thing; the second is that modern liberal democratic theory does not successfully defend liberalism, because such theory tends incoherently to depend on a conception of liberal culture or character that it cannot defend. I want to distinguish my position from the more widespread critique of liberal theory which holds that liberalism and democracy are necessarily incompatible, on the ground that authentic liberal individuals can never be authentic democratic citizens. The notion that liberalism and democracy are necessarily at odds is, I think, based on a misleading account of liberalism.[1] A more plausible statement of the dilemma of liberal theory is that it is too abstractly political, concerned too much with just distributions and not enough with the question of appropriately virtuous character, both in the works of its great seventeenth-century founders such as Hobbes and Locke and in those of modern defenders such as Rawls and Nozick.[2] In what follows I suggest

---

[1] This is the kind of objection produced in one version by rational choice theorists in the form of the free-rider paradox, and in another by those who share Marx's view that "political emancipation is a reduction of man, on the one hand, to a member of civil society, an *independent* and *egoistic* individual, and on the other hand, to a *citizen*, to a moral person." *On the Jewish Question, Marx-Engels Reader*, p. 46.

[2] For an excellent statement of this objection, see Spragens, "Reconstructing Liberal Theory." A longer exposition of this theme is found in Spragens's *Irony of Lib-*

some responses to this liberal dilemma, guided by Aristotle's theory of the virtues and by Tocqueville's theoretical reflections on American politics.

But first we must ask what precisely we have to learn from Aristotle, and in what way, under present circumstances, such learning is possible at all. We do *not* learn how to construct a more Aristotelian society, precisely because there is no such thing. The function of theory is not to construct or imagine social blueprints or foundations. What might look like an Aristotelian plan, the dream *polis* of *Politics* 7, the city according to Aristotle's wish or prayer, is intended strictly for theoretical clarification (especially of the distinction between instrumental or necessary and constitutive political activities), and not for practical emulation. The practical work of Aristotle's theory is not social engineering, but the exposure and criticism of the presuppositions that shape political institutions and practices in light of a certain teleological understanding of the human good. The Greek society to which Aristotle responds is in many ways different from ours, but the presuppositions he identifies and challenges—such as the view that courage is the greatest of the virtues, and the view that our greatest need is for power—are still important aspects of our political culture.[3] Moreover, as we have seen, Aristotle's teleology does not insist on the correctness of a single dominant goal that must be translated into an action-guiding rule; as a result, there is no essential conflict between his teleology and the liberal commitment to tolerating and even encouraging a wide variety of conceptions of the good.[4] Our own conceptions about the human good are not to be taken wholesale from any book; what then can we learn from Aristotle?

I suggest that we can learn a style of theorizing, a sense of the voice that is most appropriate for stating the problems of our so-

---

eral Reason, a finely argued treatment of the incoherence of traditional liberal theory and of the possibilities of a new liberal understanding which complements the discussion in this chapter.

[3] For an instructive comparison with Aristotle, consider Confucius' defense of the spirit of yielding and the importance of ceremony against the love of mastery he sees around him. This and several other illuminating Greek-Chinese comparisons are clearly presented in Schwartz, *World of Thought in Ancient China*, pp. 67–75.

[4] Thus, Rawls is quite mistaken in saying that Aristotle (or Plato) is committed to the view that "there is but one conception of the good *which is to be recognized by all persons*, so far as they are fully rational" (emphasis added); and in going on to claim that this makes teleological reflection incompatible with liberal democratic politics. This is a distortion typical of those who misread Aristotle as a Thomistic natural lawyer. "Justice as Fairness," pp. 248–249.

ciety theoretically without imposing universal theoretical laws about which we can (and should) have no real conviction. Such a voice follows from a complex understanding of human goods as theoretically commensurable, but not so precisely comparable as to allow conversion into commands. Aristotelian interventions are indeed based on a substantive teleological theory as well as a voice—the theoretical justification of the thoughtful life, the life that includes an important theoretical component—but the non-prophetic tones in which this theory is announced open the theory itself to question and revision. The way in which *Politics* 7 and *Nicomachean Ethics* 10 turn against earlier theoretical claims is but the clearest instance of this difference between the Aristotelian voice and that of, for example, Marx or Freud or the Bible. Platonic and Aristotelian texts are so far from demanding our complicity in their projects that they seem to obstruct easy access to their intentions. To force these texts into the prophetic mode, to transform them into programmatic philosophic teachers or prophetic legislators on the model proposed by Rousseau's "Allegorical Fragment or Fiction on Revelation," it is necessary to do the kind of critical violence involved in attributing a "theory of forms" to Plato or a natural law teaching to Aristotle.

Earlier chapters have argued the case for the general plausibility of the Aristotelian understanding of theory and practice. Now I want to argue that such a conception of practical theorizing is particularly important in the context of contemporary liberal democracy. A new understanding of the theoretical voice is important now, because theorizing governed by the norms of precision and immediate and direct applicability[5] has led us to an unsatisfactory result: the debate over liberalism has become a controversy between those who want to reduce liberal politics to an abstract market for the efficient exchange of values and those who want to replace it by a "community" of public-spirited republican citizens. This way of debating liberalism needlessly radicalizes the contemporary political alternatives and effectively excludes any theoretical statement of what is valued most in liberal politics by the great majority of its supporters. If I am correct in holding that this exclusion results from a mistaken conception of the relation of theory to practice (of what we must expect from practical theorizing), then we need to see in what way Aristotelian theorizing might

[5] Or governed by modern rule morality's mirror image, *tout comprendre, c'est tout pardonner* contextualism.

suggest a more promising and practically useful liberal problematic.

The central theoretical claim I want to advance here is that it is wrong to regard democracy either as a value-neutral decision procedure (for example, majority rule) *or* as a morally compelling ideal (for example, a participatory community of equal citizens). Democracy here is to be understood neither as morally neutral nor as morally ideal but as morally indefinite—a term covering a range of moral possibilities. In Aristotelian language, democracy is a potentiality susceptible of a variety of actualizations; it is matter rather than form. Whether democracy is a good or a bad thing is strictly beside the point.[6] That is, democracy is the name we give to a type of regime in which a particular social class or group has the ruling power, and democratic regimes of this kind can be wonderfully good, despicably evil, and much in between. The position I want to defend involves the following steps:

(1) "Liberal democracy," one which refuses to limit individual lives arbitrarily, is the name we give to a good democracy.

(2) The determination whether a limit is arbitrary is a matter of contextual judgment, rather than rule application.

(3) The question whether any given democracy is liberal or not will thus depend primarily on the character of its citizens, and not in the first instance on the laws and institutions (legislatures, markets, courts, schools, armies, churches) that regulate conduct in the democracy.

(4) Such institutions matter, however, because of the way they affect the character of citizens, and should be evaluated in that light.

(5) Such evaluation can guide action only when it is historically and temporally specific, and so can never be permanent or precise.

The major advantage gained by an Aristotelian turn is that it brings into clear focus the difference between a flourishing and a troubled democratic character, between a healthy and a troubled "people." There can be no final theoretical solution to such a ques-

---

[6] Of course, for Aristotle a regime is itself the actualization of a city. But no *polis* is simply a democracy—it is an agrarian or a commercial democracy, moderate or extreme, and so on. In general, actuality and potentiality, form and matter, are relative terms—perhaps best understood as degrees of definiteness. In cases of political choice and action, it seems reasonable to stress the indefinite character of "democracy" relative to any existing *polis*.

tion, but by excluding it liberal theory both radicalizes and obscures the real problems of liberal democracy.

Liberal Democracy as Incoherent Theory

The radicalization of the critique of liberal democracy involves claiming that such a regime—perhaps best defined as the *Weltanschauung* that tolerates indefinitely many *Weltanschauungen*[7]—is not only flawed but internally contradictory, perhaps actually nonexistent, and necessarily unstable. Since the Hegelian critique of liberalism, the charge that no polity can have as its goal the protection of individual striving has been a staple of nineteenth-and twentieth-century political criticism. Here is Hegel, in the *Philosophy of Right*: "Particularity by itself, given free rein in every direction to satisfy its needs, accidental caprices, and subjective desires, destroys itself and its substantive concept in this process of gratification."[8] In a similar way, Marx in *On the Jewish Question* argues that liberal democracy represents the illusory sociality of actually isolated individuals ("monads"); it is a regime whose essence is inseparable from its evanescence. Hegel and Marx view liberalism from the perspective of dogmatic belief in a progressive and substantial history; from that perspective, liberalism seems not only bad, but somehow false, illusory, not really there.

This sense of the insubstantiality of liberalism persists in German culture criticism even after the belief in providential history is abandoned. For Nietzsche, human life after the death of God signifies nothing less than the presence of the two most fundamental alternatives: we must either sink below the level of humanity and become *letzten Menschen* or, should this plausible nightmare yield to desperate hope, transcend ourselves and become more than human. For Max Weber, modern liberals, especially Americans, trapped in the iron cage of an ethic absurdly separated from its ground, must expect either "mechanized petrification"[9] and the increasing domination of specialists without spirit, or the triumph

[7] See Strauss, "Philosophy as Rigorous Science and Political Philosophy," p. 37. It seems to me that Strauss's attitude to liberalism is that there is a crisis not in liberalism, but in our ability to articulate and defend it. Tarcov's reading of Strauss on this point is correct: "Not modern liberalism but loss of confidence in it constitutes the crisis. . . . Strauss' purpose is not to undercut liberalism practically but to find a theoretical solution to the problem posed by its having already been undercut." "Philosophy and History," p. 9.

[8] *Philosophy of Right*, paragraph 185, p. 123.

[9] *Protestant Ethic*, p. 182.

of some new and mindless religious awakening. Twentieth-century critics, such as Heidegger and Arendt, continue to stress the theme of the rootlessness and insubstantiality of liberalism.[10] As George Kateb notes, Arendt's persistent animosity toward the European bourgeoisie is marked by the unusual (for this extensively empathic author) absence of any attempt at an empathic understanding of bourgeois life.[11] But empathy is impossible with a nonexistent subject, and the unreality of the life characteristic of liberal culture has been a standard theme in critiques of liberalism since even before Hegel, as Rousseau's famous thematic statement in *Emile* makes plain: "Whoever wants to preserve the primacy of natural sentiments in the civil order doesn't know what he wants. Always in contradiction with himself, always wavering between his inclinations and his duties, he will be neither man nor citizen; he will be good neither for himself nor for others. This will be one of the men of our days: a Frenchman, an Englishman, a Bourgeois; this will be nothing."[12] The antiliberal view of liberalism's incoherence appears to rest on an unwillingness to see—or perhaps a willing denial of—anything substantial in the historical form of life that brought modern liberalism into being. This denial of the substantial reality of bourgeois life is as pervasive among critics of liberalism as is their rejection of Enlightenment rationality as either incomplete or simply wrong.

But defenders of liberal modernity (and Enlightenment rationality) also tend to abstract from the historical circumstances of bourgeois life even as they set out to defend it. This treatment of individuals as abstract from *any* social or cultural context is characteristic of Hobbes, Locke, and their nineteenth- and twentieth-century successors. This tendency can partly be explained as an attempt to fashion a political doctrine as universal and abstract as modern mathematical physics; but in the seventeenth-century context it also makes sense to suppose that Hobbes's and Locke's

[10] MacIntyre varies the Heideggerian theme a bit by arguing that liberalism is in fact a tradition (one founded on and subservient to the bourgeois market), but a profoundly dishonest one that disguises its traditional status from itself. *Whose Justice?* chap. 17. But liberalism is central to modernity, and the fate toward which modernity is moving is "rootless cosmopolitanism" (p. 388).

[11] Kateb, *Hannah Arendt*," pp. 66–68.

[12] Rousseau, *Emile*, Bk. 1; in Rousseau, *Oeuvres Complètes*, vol. 4, pp. 249–250. On the history of the term "bourgeoisie," see Furbank, *Unholy Pleasure*, chap. 2. Furbank's point is that the term by now is an all-purpose slur disguised (from its users) as a neutral category, and is thus an important linguistic barrier to accurate social perception. For a perverse transvaluation, see Rorty's cheerful endorsement of "Postmodernist Bourgeois Liberalism" in his article of that title.

refusal to recognize the importance of family and tradition stems not from scientistic innocence, but from the opinion that family status and traditional institutions operated primarily to block the attempt to overcome ancient and arbitrary privileges of wealth and rank by an appeal to the liberty of fundamentally equal human beings. As Joyce Appleby says, "what shocked contemporaries about Hobbes was his insistence that men were naturally equal."[13] The abstract quality of Hobbesian and Lockean political thought looks very different if we see it not as mechanistic atomism run wild, but as a reasonable estimate of the sources of restraints against individual liberty in their time.[14] As with the exaggerated modern assault on inquiry-blocking teleology, we should consider whether this abstraction from context and culture is an essential feature of liberal theory or an artifact of a long-resolved historical controversy.

The Hobbesian and Lockean justifications of liberal democratic politics are open to the charge that they attempt to bring together fundamentally incompatible terms. Democracy is understood by Hobbes and Locke simply as popular sovereignty, or rule by a majority of naturally equal individuals, without any further consideration of the ways of life or virtues that might distinguish democrats from other people. Democracy, then, is simply popular rule. But how does the adjective "liberal" qualify that rule? For Hobbes and Locke, the answer is clear: liberal democratic rule must be both popular and directed toward the protection of individual rights or liberties. But given this understanding of the key terms, liberal theorists are confronted with a puzzle concerning reason and motive: why should a majority consider the protection of private rights to be the chief political goal? And even if this is theoretically reasonable, what can motivate a popular majority to place

---

[13] Appleby, *Capitalism*, p. 20. Appleby illustrates this by quoting a conservative critic of Hobbes, William Lucy, whose caricature has a good deal in common with twentieth-century civic republican and radical feminist critiques of early liberalism: "Methinks that he discourses of Men as if they were terrigene, born out of the earth, come up like Seeds, without any relation one to the other. . . . [By nature, a human is] made a poor helpless Child who confides and trusts in his Parents, and submits to them."

[14] Appleby's response to de Jouvenal's charge that social contract theories "are the views of childless men who must have forgotten their childhood" is apposite here: "The traditionalist begins with a person as a member of society born into a complex of obligations and identities, whereas the liberal analyst starts with the individual who possesses a common set of needs. Locke and Hobbes had not forgotten their childhoods. Rather they had the prescience to realize that one's childhood was becoming less important—from a political point of view—than one's autonomy as an adult." *Capitalism*, p. 36.

such a goal (or any public good) first, whenever it conflicts with other interests? In this way, the theorists of liberal democracy, from Hobbes through Rawls and Nozick, have conceived a crisis of political obligation as the central element of the problem of liberal democracy: for what reasons and impelled by what motives will any given aggregate of free individuals agree to accept a political agenda that may conflict with the preferences of many of their number?

Abstracting from specific cultures, this theme of the radical incoherence of liberal democracy flourishes in the twentieth century. Formal or positive political theorists articulate their conception of the central problem of democracy in terms of the various paradoxes of voting, devices designed to capture the absurdity of democratic political action or political choice.[15] Politics is conceived as a sort of "prisoner's dilemma" game, a form of interaction pointing to the conclusion that the most reasonable political choice, for unrelated individuals, is that of the free rider,[16] the person who attempts to secure the benefits of political cooperation without paying any of its costs, a strategy whose eventual (though not short-run) futility is illustrated by the "tragedy of the commons." As long as no limit is set on the preferences individuals may act on, there seems to be no compelling way to make a case for commitment to a political order whose goal is the protection of the interests of each individual.

The way in which the first liberal theorists sought to solve this paradox of liberal democracy was to derive a political obligation from unspecified self-interest through the imagery of the state of nature and the social contract. Hobbes attempts to demonstrate that only an extreme failure of natural reason could prevent an individual from grasping the evident rationality of yielding one's power of private judgment in cases of conflict over scarce resources. Appropriating religious language, and with palpable irony, he asserts that only "the fool hath said in his heart, there is no such thing as justice; and sometimes also with his tongue."[17] But as every reader of *Leviathan* knows, it is by no means foolish to wonder how the more extreme demands of democratic citizenship, such as military service, can be seen as a rational means to

[15] I have discussed the paradoxes of voting in "Who Knows Whether It's Rational to Vote?"

[16] See Olson, *Logic of Collective Action*.

[17] Hobbes, *Leviathan*, chap. 15.

the end of individual survival, as the best strategy for decreasing the individual's chances of avoiding violent death.

If the content of individual interest is left at this broad level of generality, it becomes clear that some more powerful motive than enlightened self-interest is required to motivate citizens to take risks and forswear crimes for the sake of the aggregate public good. Hobbes and Locke were surely aware of this problem—it is at this point that Aristotle in *Politics* 2 claims that the law's only power derives from a long-standing habit of obedience—and it is their awareness of this problem of authority that makes their work so much more interesting and useful than that of later liberal theorists. Without science, for Hobbes, there can be no adequate demonstration of the human need for politics, but by itself scientific demonstration lacks the power to persuade individuals to accept good decisions, to endow its conclusions with moral and political authority: "The sciences are small power; because not eminent. . . . For science is of that nature, as none can understand it to be, but such as in good measure have attained it."[18] In chapter 30 of *Leviathan* he speaks of the need for third parties to present the conclusions of good science to people who would not trust scientists. This group makes up the great majority of hardworking humanity, who will accept the truth only when they hear it "chiefly from divines in the pulpit, and partly from such of their neighbours or familiar acquaintance, as having the faculty of discoursing readily, and plausibly, seem wiser and better learned in cases of law and conscience, than themselves."

Hobbes was thus not so foolish as to be a blind optimist about the efficacy of either fear of punishment or political enlightenment; in his role of universal legislator he, no less than Rousseau's figure in Book 2 of the *Social Contract*, is compelled to place his teachings in the mouth of the biblical God, in the hope that the hypothetical rules of reason will be perceived as binding natural laws. Locke, too, insists on the need for a civil religion of sorts, even while (in the *Letter concerning Toleration*) denying its legitimacy. And yet these appeals to religious motive seem thin, and the god of Hobbes and Locke is little more than a great enforcer in the sky, called in at need to buttress the shaky foundation of civil authority.[19] Religion here seems a patchy remedy rather than part of a plausibly attractive way of life. I think it not unfair to say that

[18] Ibid., chap. 10.
[19] Like Rousseau's "Poul-Serrho" in *Emile*, Bk. 4. *Oeuvres Complètes*, vol. 4, pp. 634–635n.

these gestures toward divinity call attention to a perceived crisis of liberal democracy rather than propose a means of alleviating it.

Another way of overcoming the tension between liberty-as-opportunity and democratic equality is to specify more narrowly the interests served by politics in general and liberal democratic politics in particular. To do this would require a discussion of the connection between democratic politics and a particular conception of a virtuous personality or way of life. In effect, this would involve a direct challenge to the antiliberal argument that liberalism is the politics that answers the requirements of bourgeois nullities. Hobbes and Locke indeed suggest a very distinct picture of the kind of people who will and will not be inclined to decent politics. For Hobbes, those people who love ease and fear wounds will be inclined to obey a common power, but not so those "needy men and hardy" and all those "ambitious of military command," who would choose to accept the risks of internal war, since "there is no honour military but by war; nor any such hope to mend an ill game, as by causing a new shuffle."[20] Locke is even more distinct in specifying the character of those who can be good citizens, saying that "the commonwealth . . . embraces indifferently all men that are honest, peaceable, and industrious," and that the interests or needs served by civil society are "life, liberty, health, and indolency of body; and the possession of outward things, such as money, lands, houses, furniture, and the like."[21]

But Hobbes and Locke do not justify their preference for people who are anxious about indolency (freedom from pain) of body and who love ease and furniture. In this respect they fail to provide an adequate theoretical challenge to the idea of human and political virtue sustained by the Periclean tradition and its republican heirs—the idea that virility is the primary virtue and that public-spiritedness is the best motive—and to suggest a liberal alternative. In the absence of liberal theorizing about virtue, the concern with indolency of body can be dismissed as evidence of "corruption"—the republican term indicating the threat posed by mere private interests to fully committed citizenship—or radicalized into a fuzzy prefiguring of the later theoretical norm of "economic man," the perfect capitalist whose life is dominated by the continual pursuit of profit maximization.

There is indeed a conception of human virtue, of a praiseworthy human life, in the writings of Hobbes and Locke, and it is a richer

[20] *Leviathan*, chap. 11.
[21] Locke, *Letter concerning Toleration*, pp. 56–57 and p. 17.

and less theoretically narrow conception than is generally asserted by neo-Machiavellian critics of bourgeois nullities (noncitizens), or by Marxist critics searching for early evidence of the tendency to identify rationality with the quest for unlimited acquisition of capital. This conception presents as normally and healthily human a life concerned with preserving one's property based on an awareness of how difficult property is to acquire, an awareness and a concern not possible for those who have inherited wealth and status. Such a life can become stereotypically capitalist, but that is not its only potentiality. Nathan Tarcov makes this point about the Lockean attitude toward property in his discussion of Locke on the virtue of liberality: "One can say that the emphasis is neither on acquisition nor on spending but on preservation. Yet ultimately it is only an appreciation of the labor or pain required for acquisition that acts as a restraint on spending and a spur to preservation."[22] Human excellence requires attention to the difficulty of the material conditions of human life, more than the capacity to transcend those conditions.

But even if such a conception of virtue is implicit in these texts, it is clear that there is no explicit teleological argument linking this virtue to a conception of the human good, no discussion of why the commonwealth should embrace those who are honest, peaceable, and industrious, and not, for example, the pious, charitable, and merciful, or the virile and patriotic. Such arguments would defend Hobbesian and Lockean preferences, but only at the expense of violating their central methodological canon, excluding teleology from rational argument. As a result, liberal virtue is left without clear formulation or defense by the founders of modern liberal theory, and their preferences for some ways of life rather than others seem forced, externally imposed, prejudices called in to aid a faltering argument. This consideration leads us again to a sense of the incoherence of liberal democratic theory, since the defense of the liberal regime seems to call for a conception of the good life or culture, and since such a conception violates the definitions of the terms in which the problem is set: democracy as the sovereignty of *any given* people and liberty as the opportunity to secure the interest of *any given* individual.

We need to consider the possibility of a causal link between this paradox in the logic of liberal democratic theory and the striking tendency to see liberal democratic practice as similarly incoherent, to emphasize liberal anomie or narcissism, and to underscore

[22] Tarcov, *Locke's Education for Liberty*, p. 145.

215

whatever evidence there might be of a crisis of authority or legitimacy ("sovereignty recollected in tranquility," in Ernest Gellner's definition)[23] in contemporary liberal democracies, in spite of a very high degree of voluntary association membership (particularly in North America)[24] and a very high degree of political stability.[25] Given the unanimity and force with which critics of liberalism have for over two centuries urged that liberal politics has a profound emptiness (or, for Marxians, a profound schizophrenia) at its core, and given liberal theory's self-imposed incapacity to argue the case for liberal virtue, the lack of fit between the degrees of difficulty that confront liberal practice on the one hand and liberalism considered theoretically on the other is not surprising. Harvey Mansfield's conclusion is apt: "In our day liberals and liberal causes have prospered, but liberalism is in trouble."[26] Forms of social order indeed persist—in families, churches, universities, firms, unions, political organizations, and so on—but their significance may be overlooked because their foundation is understood as irrational and hence unstable.[27] Insofar as images of Periclean Athens, or Sparta, or republican Rome supply contemporary theory with a way of locating real politics historically, and given the theoretical difficulties in the way of articulating modern liberal or bourgeois virtues, it is not surprising if we understand ourselves as an unstable amalgam of conflicting interests rather than a community formed by a common sense of virtue.[28]

[23] Gellner, *Legitimation of Belief*, p. 24.

[24] Bellah et al., *Habits of the Heart*, pp. 167, 321 n. 1.

[25] Gellner, speaking of the study of legitimacy, says that "those who have the most opportunity to theorise about the matter live in societies in which the question is not immediate and urgent. . . . To put it another way, most social scientists are members of fairly prosperous and stable societies. Despite the self-advertised revival of 'basic questioning' in the 1960s, the seriousness of which it is easy to exaggerate, sovereignty or legitimacy is not very seriously in dispute in such societies" (*Legitimation of Belief*, p. 24). But for theoretical people, who are to begin with certain of the essential instability of liberal politics, legitimacy disputes *ought* to be there, and so evidence for them is more interesting and noteworthy than evidence of liberal stability and vitality.

[26] Mansfield, *Spirit of Liberalism*, p. 114. The tension between the relative abundance of social and political activity in America and the failure of the categories of American political language to express and defend that activity is the subject of Bellah et al., *Habits of the Heart*, chaps. 7 and 8.

[27] As Flacks notes, "Appeals to Americans to shake off their apparent moral indifference and critiques of moral callousness often miss the point that to be concerned about 'humanity' may be thought of as contradicting one's felt moral obligations to those whom one actually knows, loves, and must care for." "Moral Commitment, Privatism, and Activism," p. 346.

[28] Ignatieff argues powerfully for the modern lack of an authentic language in

An indication that this self-understanding might be mistaken comes from the fascinating story of Yen Fu, the late nineteenth-century Chinese translator of Spencer, Mill, and Montesquieu, among others. As portrayed by Benjamin Schwartz,[29] Yen Fu, convinced that China was poorly served by its attachment to orthodox Confucianism, set out through travel and study to discover the secret of Western wealth and power. The remarkable conclusion Yen Fu reached was that the secret of Western success was a public-spiritedness that was lacking in Confucian China. Seeing Mill and Spencer as explicating a kind of civil spirit, and not individualism, is more than a misreading of their intention. In a sense, Yen Fu may have been seeing through the theoretical self-interpretation of liberalism to grasp the presence of a liberal culture that contained and moderated capitalist enterprise. Schwartz's comments are instructive:

> One theme running through all Yen Fu's writings . . . and which probably rests on his own observations of English life is the praise of Western 'public spirit' (*kung-hsin*). . . . Again, to the Westerner who has been indoctrinated concerning the 'social virtues' of the Chinese, it may seem surprising to see the 'public spirit' of capitalist England contrasted with the narrow selfishness of Confucian China. . . . In China there are duties of individuals to individuals. There are no duties of individuals to society.[30]

What Yen Fu saw—and what Spencer, Mill, and Smith overlooked—was the way in which Christianity and the spirit of (relative) equality created a sense of membership in a national community and hence a willingness, at times, to act politically (as Englishmen living according to the laws of England) rather than according to the theorists' construction of an abstract utilitarian calculus.

Yen Fu was not a naive Anglophile, and he objected to much of what he saw in the West. Perhaps his deepest thought concerning the comparison of the two cultures is that what any good *politeia* requires is to overcome the tendency to separate interest and virtue too sharply. Here is Schwartz again, quoting Yen Fu's commentary on the *Wealth of Nations*:

---

which to articulate our needs and interests, one that does not depend on a false and nostalgic reminiscence of republican virtue. *Needs of Strangers*, pp. 139–140.

[29] Schwartz, *In Search of Wealth and Power*.

[30] Ibid., pp. 69–70.

The true cleavage here is not so much between China and the West as between the modern world and the past. The cleavage between 'righteousness' and 'interest' (*i/li*) has been most detrimental to the advance of civilization. Mencius states, 'All one needs is righteousness and humanity. Why speak of interest?' Tung Chung-shu asserts, 'Act righteously and do not scheme to advance your interests. Make manifest the Way and do not calculate advantage.' The ancient teachings of both East and West all draw a sharp line between righteousness and interest. The intention was most sublime, but the effect in terms of bringing men to the Way has been negligible in all cases.[31]

Yen Fu suggests that any successful culture must convince its members that living according to the culture's conception of virtue is in the interest of each; certain ways of life are desirable. Since the seventeenth century, most analysts of liberal culture, both supporters and critics, have presupposed a dichotomy between interest and virtue, between the private interest of the rising bourgeoisie and the citizen virtue of a fading republican order. But this presupposition may lead to a misperception of the possibilities of liberal democracy; at best it makes it difficult to speak coherently of liberal virtues, and hence to evaluate the problems and possibilities of liberalism.

In the remainder of this chapter, I recall an alternative conception of liberal democracy, one consistent with the Aristotelian assumption that virtue and interest are not distinct, but that a society's conception of virtue suggests its understanding of human interest or need. This conception is drawn from what Ralph Lerner calls "the American commercial republican as the new-model man,"[32] the psychological portrait of liberal democratic citizenship presented by, among others, Tocqueville and a number of the founders of the American republic, rather than from the more abstract and less psychologically concerned defenders and critics of liberalism. Liberal democracy is to be understood not simply as popular sovereignty plus limited government, but as rule by the kind of people who are primarily concerned with personal independence and an income adequate to achieve this comfortably, rather than victory or glory or salvation. Such a regime is at its best when members of the ruling people are marked by the character-

---

[31] Ibid., p.125.
[32] Lerner, *Thinking Revolutionary*, p. 218.

istic virtues of liberality or generosity or moderation, and at its worst when typically liberal vices, such as stinginess or wastefulness or avarice (as distinct from the civic republican's notion of the most serious vices, traits like effeminacy[33] and luxurious selfishness), predominate.

Rather than saying that in commercial liberalism private vices are somehow made to yield public benefits, I suggest we look more carefully at the peculiarly liberal understanding of vices and virtues, and avoid stressing those distinctions between public and private and between virtue and interest that are central to the discourse of civic republicanism. The practical effect of this shift in the language of evaluation is to draw attention to the ways in which existing institutions and practices support or obstruct the actualization of the liberal virtues, directly or otherwise. Instead of attending primarily to the question of the circumstances under which private individuals are justly obligated to obey the laws, we would begin with the problem of the moral consequences of contemporary institutional arrangements; "moral consequences" with regard not to some abstract universal law, but to better and worse actualizations of specifically democratic potentialities. Before turning to the substance of this contemporary problem, I want to establish a comparative point of reference by looking at the way Aristotle in his context frames the issue of democracy understood as a set of possibilities, rather than as an ideal or a matter of fact.

Aristotle and the Educability of the Dēmos

The Platonic account of moral education takes its bearings from a perception that the greatest human problem is not the ubiquity of conflicting human goods but rather what Socrates calls our common ignorance in thinking that we know when we do not. Far from being mere intellectual arrogance or presumption, this ignorance is linked with that passionate association of power and happiness which is the hidden ground of human *pleonexia*—the tyrannical dream that power is the one thing we need to be happy (as reflected in Glaucon's story of the ring of Gyges) which affects

---

[33] "Economic man as masculine conquering hero is a fantasy of nineteenth-century industrialisation (the *Communist Manifesto* is of course one classic example). His eighteenth-century predecessor was seen as on the whole a feminised, even an effeminate being, still wrestling with his own passions and hysterias and with interior and exterior forces let loose by his fantasies and appetites, and symbolised by such archetypical goddesses of disorder as Fortune, Luxury, and most recently Credit herself." Pocock, *Virtue, Commerce, and History*, p. 114.

even decent people and which ensures that humanity lives continually at risk of anxiety and disorder. All human goods—material security, group solidarity, moral virtue—derive their value from their effectiveness as sources of resistance to pleonectic confusion, and there may well be insoluble conflicts among such goods, for Plato as for Aristotle; the ever-present tension between Socrates and the city, or between the philosophic life and the *nomoi* as forms of order, are perhaps the most fundamental and permanent of such conflicts. But this difficulty, though serious, is more a consequence of attempts to solve the problem of disorder than a principal cause of the problem itself. Since order is both needed and not spontaneous, education is necessary for its establishment. Since the ignorance (or the mistaken view of the human good) reflected in the shapeless tyrannical dream is both deep and not accidental, an education equal to conquering it cannot take the form of mere preaching or admonition (which the Eleatic Stranger calls the traditional way of the fathers and the many; *Sophist* 229e4–230a3). It must be indirect and charming on the model provided by Socratic *elenchos*. But Socratic teaching can never flourish in public settings, since democratic assemblies always reinforce the mistaken view of the good that *paideia* seeks to overcome.[34]

Aristotle's assessment of the possibilities of democratic education are very different, as we shall see, from Plato's; nonetheless, his understanding of the principal obstacle to human well-being is much the same as his teacher's. The central antithesis in Aristotle's moral vocabulary is the distinction between the *spoudaioi* and the *phauloi*, between those who are serious about living virtuous lives and those who are concerned with pursuing particular pleasures in a disorderly way.[35] The *phauloi* are defined as those who aim at

[34] The Platonic opposition to democracy no more follows from an unreasoned prejudice against the poor or the lower classes than his estimate of the need for order reflects an obsessive philosopher's preference for logical consistency. Democracy is the regime next worst to tyranny because of the disorderliness it tolerates (*Republic* 6, 557a9–558c6). Moreover, in the *Statesman* (303a2–b5) democracy is ranked above oligarchy, the latter standing next to tyranny in that dialogue.

[35] As Else says (*Aristotle's Poetics*, pp. 71–78), the closest English approximation for *hoi phauloi* is not "the vicious" but the Southern American "the no-account." In general, Aristotle's terms of moral blame cause serious translation problems, and can block our access to the text in important ways. In particular, we need to avoid giving terms such as *mochthēros*, *ponēros*, *kakos*, and *phaulos* a Christian gloss by translating them as "vicious" or "wicked." One need not accept wholly Nietzsche's distinction between master and slave moralities to see that such words have nothing to do with sin and power (though others, such as *deinos* or *panourgos*, are closer); they instead call to mind wretchedness, misery, and being burdened by toils. A good example of the importance of this issue is the way in which different

no definite end, but at *pleonexia* (*NE* 9, 1167b9–12). They do not take seriously the problem of living well, but are concerned only with the acquisition of particular things: money, honor, and somatic pleasures (*NE* 9, 1168b15–23). The *spoudaios/phaulos* distinction is a traditional one, but Aristotle differs from tradition (as does Plato's Socrates; *Republic* 1, 347a10–b2) in associating *pleonexia* not only with the poor person's love of money or the common attachment to physical pleasure but with the apparently respectable love of honor as well. This has, as we shall see, important consequences for Aristotle's discussion of the relative merits of oligarchy and democracy.

In the discussion of Aristotle's diagnosis of the human problem in Chapter 2, a central element of his analysis was seen to be the claim that most people prefer to live in a disorderly way (*zēn ataktōs*; *Pol.* 6, 1319b31–32). For Aristotle, this preference reflects no corruption peculiar to the lower classes, but rather our common and biologically inherited attachment to living, an attachment which is ordinarily much stronger than any commitment to an ordered conception of how we should live our lives (*Pol.* 3, 1278b25–30). In his discussion of the economic art in Book 1 of the *Politics*, Aristotle says that some people mistakenly think that the function of the art is to increase one's property without limit, and he gives the following explanation: "The cause of this disposition (*diathesis*) is being serious (*spoudazein*) about living but not about living well. As the desire for living is unlimited, so also the desire for the things instrumental to living is unlimited" (*Pol.* 1, 1257b40–1258a2).

However natural in one sense our inclination to *pleonexia* may be,[36] the fact remains that human happiness requires not simply

---

translators render in English the important claim in the discussion of the causes of crime at *Pol.* 2, 1267b1 that *"ponēria* is insatiable among human beings." *Ponēria* is rendered as follows: Lord: "wickedness," Irwin: "viciousness," Sinclair: "depravity," Jowett: "avarice," Rackham: "baseness," Barker: "naughtiness." The first three suggest satanism or mental illness; "avarice" is too limited; "baseness" is close but hopelessly archaic; and "naughtiness," while etymologically accurate, coming as it does from "having naught" and implying a falling short rather than a going too far, in modern English suggests harmless schoolboy high jinks as the paradigm of nonvirtuous conduct. I do not know that there is a good single solution to the translation problem, but somehow the notion of misery or wretchedness needs to be included in our reading of Aristotle's (and Plato's) terms for bad character. Otherwise, we can make no sense of how difficult Plato seems to think it is, for example, for Socrates to persuade others that tyrants are *phauloi*, though he would have no trouble in gaining agreement that they were *deinoi*.

[36] For a good discussion of Aristotle's use of *pleonexia*, see Williams, "Justice as a Virtue."

the absence of arbitrary restraints but also a life lived according to a reasonable order of the sort which may be provided by the *nomoi* of our city or culture. The laws may not be the last word in *paideia*, but they will have done their job adequately insofar as they cause us to choose not "to have more (*pleonektein*) either of money or of honor or of both" (*Pol.* 2, 1266b37–38). Since such an education may run counter to our powerful attachment to our own survival, it presents an extremely difficult problem of persuasion or political education. In discussing a plan for a weighted voting arrangement in Book 6 of the *Politics*, Aristotle remarks that while it is surely difficult to see where distributive justice lies in working out franchise schemes (given the irreducible—even if commensurable—conflicts possible between the necessary and the constitutive conditions of political life), "still it is easier to hit upon this than to have it accepted by those who have the power to get more (*pleonektein*)" (*Pol.* 6, 1318b1–4). Still, this is what political education and the laws must aim to do, as Aristotle says in criticism of Phaleas' suggestion that the tendency to injustice can be cured by equalizing property: "the starting point (*archē*) in such things, then, rather than levelling property, is to render those people by nature decent (*epieikeis*) such as not to desire to have more (*pleonektein*) and the *phauloi* incapable of doing so" (*Pol.* 2, 1267b5–8).

To this point, Plato and Aristotle are in general agreement: the greatest injustices are caused by disorderly tyrannical dreams, which are manifested primarily in the love of money and the love of honor (*Pol.* 2, 1271a16–18)[37] and in the mistaken belief that an orderly life such as is lived within a genuine *politeia* (one whose goal is education in virtue) is slavery rather than salvation (*Pol.* 5, 1310a34–36). But whereas Plato holds that the many as such are not open to the sort of persuasion at which good laws aim, Aristotle takes a very different view. This difference begins to appear in the theoretical intervention in *Politics* 3 concerning the *aporia* about whether the best *polis* should be ruled by the few people who are best or by the multitude (*to plēthos*; 1281a12).[38]

[37] Aristotle calls these injustices voluntary, while Plato calls them involuntary, but this is a terminological quarrel: for Aristotle, "voluntary" means "originating with the agent"; for Plato, it means "with the full understanding of the agent." Thus there is no contradiction between the claim that injustice always originates with the agent and the claim that injustice never originates in the full understanding of the agent.

[38] I am taking *plēthos* and *dēmos* as equivalent terms, as does Newman in *Politics of Aristotle*, vol. 4, p. 517. The same equivalence in Plato can be seen in Alcibiades' speech in the *Symposium*.

As we saw in Chapter 3, while it would appear obvious that the best should rule, Aristotle sets out several arguments that deny this. His initial claim is that while each individual member of the many (*hoi polloi*) may not be a serious man (*spoudaios anēr*), the many "when coming together admit of being better than those who are best, not individually, but as a whole (*hōs sumpantas*)." The argument for this is a series of analogical metaphors. First, it is said that just as a dinner paid for out of everyone's pocket will be better than any one person can provide, so the combined virtue and wisdom of *to plēthos* may add up to a greater whole than the good qualities of the best; thus, Aristotle says, the many are better judges of music and poetry than any one individual. But this analogy is hardly conclusive since, as Aristotle quickly points out, it could as well be used to make a case for the superior judgment of a large number of beasts. His conclusion is typically poised: while it has not been shown that *every plēthos* is superior to the few best, it is still possible that *some* given *plēthos* may be superior. Our concern with this possibility is immediately reinforced by noting that not allowing *to plēthos* to share in the regime is a frightening thing (*phoberon*), since a city full of poor and disenfranchised people is a city full of enemies. Since a *polis* has several functions, and must take into account the security as well as the character of its citizens, a city in which the many are somehow "mixed" with the better may be capable of the best judgments; this is supported by another metaphor which relates that impure (*mē kathara*) food mixed with pure is more nourishing than a small amount of pure food alone. The discussion concludes (1283b33–35) with the tentative assertion that nothing stands against the possibility that the many may sometimes be better than the few, "not as individuals, but as a whole [or 'in a crowd,' *hōs athroous*]." We are left to wonder about the circumstances in which a *dēmos* is such that it can be made more *katharos*, and about the agency through which this *katharsis* occurs.

The best political judgments are those free from personal or party bias, that look to the good of the *polis* as a whole; political mistakes (injustices) are the result of *pleonexia* or passion generally, but more specifically of the manly passions: as we are humans rather than gods, "spiritedness (*thumos*) distorts the rule of even the best" (*Pol.* 3, 1287a31–32). The cure for this deficiency is the rule of law, since even though there may surely be bad laws, law as such is a sort of reason without desire (*aneu orexeōs nous ho nomos estin*; 1287a32). Law is thus an important source of the rationalizing order (*hē gar taxis nomos;* 1287a18) that is the greatest human need. For Aristotle, the *dēmos* may be more open to this kind of structure than, say, the rich or the well-born. In language which is directly antithetical to the Platonic position stated in the *Gorgias,* Aristotle takes the position that many times a crowd (*ochlos!*) judges better than an individual; the explanation for this is no longer the simple summing-of-individual-degrees-of-virtue proposed in 1281b, but rather the claim that the many are often less corruptible than the few (*to plēthos tōn oligōn adiaphthorōteron*), since the people as a whole are less likely to be overcome by anger (*orgē*) or by some response to angry feelings—such as spiritedness—and so to make the usual political mistakes (*Pol.* 3, 1286a31–35). The potentially superior reasonableness of the *dēmos* is stated in another way in *Politics* 4; after remarking that many of those who wish to establish an aristocracy (rule of the truly best) make an important mistake by giving too much power to the wealthy, Aristotle explains why this is an error by saying that "the graspings (*pleonexiai*) of the wealthy subvert the regime (*politeia*) more than those of the *dēmos*" (1297a11–13). The basis for Aristotle's explanation is not a romantic idealization of the virtues of every *dēmos,* but the predictive proposition that the wealthy will tend to be motivated by the love of honor and the *dēmos* by the love of gain (*kerdos*), and that the greatest crimes, the greatest *pleonexia,* are consequences of an unlimited love of honor and preferential regard (*Pol.* 2, 1267a12–16). The form of *pleonexia* which troubles the *dēmos* is easier to check than that which drives the wealthy, so under certain circumstances a democracy can be a regime in which a substantial degree of political virtue is realized.

These circumstances are primarily economic, having to do with both the amount and the kind of wealth the citizens possess. Democracies can be the most measured or reasonable (*metriōtatē*) of those regimes that do not aim explicitly at virtue because in the best democracies the laws, rather than the citizens, are permitted to rule (*Pol.* 4, 1289b4–5, 1292a7–11), thus reducing the occasions for pleonectic vice. These democracies are those in which the dominant element is composed of farmers or herdsmen of middling wealth (*Pol.* 4, 1292b25–27; *Pol.* 6, 1318b8–11); such people have substance enough to live as long as they work but not much leisure, and so will be inclined to rule according to laws (1292b27–29), and thus will be open to the sort of *logos* the laws approximate, given the impartiality of the *nomoi* and their braking effect on *pleonexia* (*Pol.* 4, 1295b5–34).[39] A good democracy is thus one in which a certain opinion about the best life prevails among the citizens, an opinion which gives highest marks to industrious and law-abiding people. The easiest way of securing this opinion is not by direct instruction but by economic regulations that favor farming, limit the amount of property which may be held, reduce poverty, and separate political office from financial reward (*Pol.* 6, 1318a27–b5). This opinion that orders the life of the best *dēmos* or *plēthos* does not ensure but at least leaves open the possibility that the political leadership will be composed of decent people (*epieikeis*), so avoiding the Platonic charge that every democracy is necessarily *phaulos* (1319a4–32).

If Aristotle's conception of the best agrarian democracy is not a Jeffersonian pastoral, neither is it a Machiavellian republic (Aristotle would never say, as Machiavelli does in the *Discourses*, that in the best republic the state should be rich and the citizens poor). Nor does he hold that in the best democracy each citizen is wholly occupied with private affairs; people of middling wealth neither flee from nor are eager for rule (*Pol.* 4, 1295b12–13), and a *polis* in which the citizens are strangers to one another is a fitting place for a tyranny rather than a democracy (*Pol.* 5, 1313b16–18). The best democracies are informed by a particular civic opinion, an opinion which is conservative (rather than acquisitive or ambitious) toward familial prosperity and strongly committed to the maintenance of the rule of law as an instrument of this conservation. Such an opinion can be indirectly strengthened by economic regulations, sumptuary laws, and the like, but the best way of securing good public opinion is directly through a system of *paideia* which is supportive of the regime, a strategy which is now "neglected by all" (*Pol.* 5, 1310a12–14). For Aristotle, such an education involves more than the acquisition of skills; it is a process by which decent characters may be formed by learning to love and hate the right sorts of things (*Pol.* 8, 1340a14–18). The most important task of democratic education would be to secure the public against what Aristotle regards as the greatest threat to democratic opinion and virtue: the extravagant teaching of demagogues concerning the meaning of freedom (*Pol.* 5, 1304b).

The substance of this demagogic teaching is that the status of a free person consists not in ruling and being ruled in turn, but in

---

[39] Overly wealthy people are inclined to *hubris* and major crime, overly poor people to smaller villainy (1295b9–10), and the former inclination is much more difficult to subdue than the latter (1267a9–16).

living as one likes (*to zēn hōs bouletai tis*; *Pol.* 5, 1310a25–28; *Pol.* 6, 1317b10–12). Such a belief is held in some way by all democrats, and is powerfully supported by the mistaken inference that since slaves live not as they please, free people must live exactly in the opposite manner. Its danger is that it obscures the distinction between the reasonable order flowing from the *politeia* and the unreasonable constraints of slavery, and as a result leads its adherents to suspect that citizenship and slavery are indistinguishable, opening the way for the triumph of a democratic version of Plato's tyrannical dream and greatest ignorance, the view that power and mastery are the true sources of happiness. Unlike Plato, Aristotle believes that a form of public *paideia* which opposes the spread of this dream is possible, though generally neglected and quite difficult. But the discussion of *paideia* in the unfinished eighth book of the *Politics* does not address this question directly, since it is concerned primarily with the education of the young and with music education in a relatively narrow sense.[40]

Whatever specific Greek institutions and practices Aristotle might have thought best suited to democratic moral education, the general outline of his approach to the problem of democracy is clear. The worth of any given democracy will depend on the moral character of that democracy, and so political actors in democracies must be seriously concerned with the possibilities for moral education that exist in their particular places. What can we say, then, about the particular problems and possibilities of liberal democracy?

America: Liberal Democracy as Historical Reality

The starting point for this analysis is to treat liberal democracy as a historically specific phenomenon reflecting the aspirations of certain people, rather than as a theoretical possibility. That aspiration can be seen in Rainborough's defense of popular sovereignty in seventeenth-century England on the grounds that "the poorest he that is in England hath a life to live, as the greatest he," so that wealth and birth are arbitrary factors compared to the human need to live a life—not merely to survive, but to organize one's existence in a reasonable way.[41] For Tocqueville, the emergence of demo-

[40] Cf. Lord, *Education and Culture.*

[41] Rainborough's argument against property qualifications for electing representatives turns on the claim that rational beings (which all men are) must have a measure of control over the laws they obey. Equality is the key here, but always as

cratic politics, the rule of the many dominated by a passion for equality, is intelligible only by reference to that regime that democracy rejects and supersedes, the old regime of the hereditary aristocracy in which a few families rule and in which the dominant motive is honor, rather than the need to live a life. Like Tocqueville, Aristotle characterizes the major alternative to democracy as the rule by the wealthy (oligarchy), by those who are so secure in their wealth and power that their major concern is the acquisition of honor—their "lives," in Rainborough's sense, are already made for them. Democracy, for Aristotle, is only accidentally the rule of the many; essentially, it is the rule of the "poor"—poverty understood here not as a condition of destitution, but as the situation of people who have to earn their livelihood by work of some kind and who will, therefore, be most concerned with acquiring the wealth they lack, rather than honor or military glory. Aristotle's preference for democracy over oligarchy derives from his predictive hypothesis that the poor who love wealth present greater possibilities for education in virtue than do the wealthy who love honor.

Aristotle's democracy differs from the modern in several ways, size being the most obvious. Perhaps the principal difference concerns the mode of acquiring wealth: agricultural in Aristotle's democracies, commercial and (later) industrial in modern ones. We must, however, be careful not to overstate the differences in such a way as to dichotomize virtuous small-state farmers and self-interested large-state traders. Notice, for example, that the existing *polis* most highly praised by Aristotle (*Pol.* 2, 1272b38–41) is neither Sparta nor any other small Greek *polis* based on agriculture, but the very large, non-Greek, commercial city of Carthage.[42] Just as Aristotle must not be seen as an enemy of commerce—or as holding that a commercial life necessarily excludes all virtue—so it must be seen that a preference for a farming life is perfectly compatible with the greatest enthusiasm about commercial, rather than subsistence, farming. This indeed seems to have been Thomas Jefferson's position; Jefferson's preference for a farming

---

the equality of rational beings. From "Debates on the Putney Project, 1647," in Mason, *Free Government in the Making*, pp. 8–22.

[42] We have very little information about the Carthaginian regime other than what Aristotle provides. For discussion, see Newman, *Politics of Aristotle*, vol. 2, pp. 401–408. At any rate, the praise of Carthage, along with the discussion of the need for political people to be concerned with commercial matters in *Pol.* 1, provides strong evidence that it is a mistake to associate Aristotle with what Finley calls "the landowning ideology of the ancient upper classes." *Ancient Economy*, p. 122.

rather than a manufacturing society did not reflect any opposition to using property to make money for the sake of securing a comfortable existence,[43] although Jefferson did indeed warn against an excessive or exclusive concern with money as the dangerous liberal vice.[44]

Although Aristotle was aware of the importance of commerce and the issue of exchange value, the Greek world had no experience comparable to the development of independent commercial markets that began to spread through Europe in the late Middle Ages. These markets, by the seventeenth century, had begun to establish a new form of human relationship, one not tied to political or religious traditions, an institution that enabled individuals to establish themselves by means of clever enterprise. What was novel here was not only the increase in productivity that the markets encouraged, but the opportunity they offered poor individuals to rise and prosper. The possibilities opened by the markets increased the importance of money, and thus Tocqueville is in full agreement with Aristotle concerning the preeminent democratic passion: "Men living in democratic times have many passions, but most of these culminate in or derive from the love of wealth. That is not because their souls are smaller but because the importance of money really is greater then."[45] Tocqueville is surely critical of the quality of some democratic lives, in a manner that at times seems to anticipate Nietzsche and Weber: the unceasing quest for wealth can produce much pointless agitation and, in the observer, boredom. Yet while this outcome can result from an unmixed enthusiasm for profit, Tocqueville does not see such a life as the inevitable product of an irrational or weak regime. The love of wealth as such is an appropriate and perhaps inevitable response to the conditions of life in a world in which birth or rank provides no security, in which lives must be lived, for better or worse, without the guarantee supplied by family ties. We must bear in mind not only the philistine Babbittry of the typical Americans according

---

[43] Appleby argues strongly against assimilating Jefferson to the model of neo-Machiavellian republicanism. See her "Political Philosophy of Thomas Jefferson," pp. 304–305, and Capitalism," chap. 4, as well as Lerner, "Commerce and Character," p. 19 n. 46.

[44] Jefferson, Notes on the State of Virginia, Query 17, Selected Writings, p. 50.

[45] Tocqueville, De la démocratie en Amérique, vol. 2, pt. 3, chap. 17, p. 236. Translations from Tocqueville in this and the following chapter are my modifications of the George Lawrence translation of Democracy in America. Hereafter in this and the next chapter, citations to this work will appear in the text and will refer to the page numbers in the Doubleday edition.

to Weber's *Protestant Ethic*, but the thoughtful voices of those like Elizabeth Cady Stanton who recognize without embarrassment "the pleasure that pecuniary independence must ever give"[46] in a world without guaranteed places.

Any serious attempt to understand the possibilities of democratic politics must begin by assuming the persistence of this motive and considering the ways it might be (or already is) shaped, moderated, and directed in particular places, rather than dreaming of its extirpation. Democracy, for Tocqueville, is the name of a relatively definite potentiality susceptible of a variety of actualizations, some compatible with liberty and some resembling a new industrial despotism (pp. 555–558). The work of political theorizing or social science is to identify those *mores* and laws—both economic and other—that affect the way democracy is actualized in different times and places, and thus to identify central political issues, in the Aristotelian manner, rather than to establish a science of universal rules or natural laws in the manner of the early modern liberal theorists.

For Tocqueville, then, the love of wealth and the attachment to commercial market interactions can have a variety of outcomes, depending on the context of other affections and institutions in which the market operates. A person who cares only for wealth will be different from one who also cares for friends, family, religion, or country. But the predominant attitude of early modern political theorizing toward this motive was less nuanced. Both defenders and detractors of the commercial spirit tended to the view that a fundamental choice must be made between the life of commerce and private gain and the life of public-spirited virtue, between, in Pocock's terms, the paradigm of commerce which excluded virtue and the paradigm of virtue which disdained commerce. The association of the neo-Machiavellian party of virtue with publicity and virility is clear; as Albert O. Hirschman argues in *The Passions and the Interests*, the early political (noneconomic) defense of capitalist or commercial enterprise was that it *always* encouraged—in spite of itself, that is, independent of the intentions of its avatars—a form of life that produced not virtue but peace and widespread social welfare.[47] This theoretical praise of commercial activity and of the love of wealth was frequently accompanied by a not well-hidden contempt for those whose en-

---

[46] From Stanton's speech to the House Judiciary Committee in 1892; in Schneir, *Feminism*, p. 159.

[47] Hirschman, *Passions and the Interests*.

ergies were directed toward gain rather than glory, notably in the case of Adam Smith's use of the invisible hand metaphor.[48] Theorists, with connections other than the market and concerns other than gain, could hardly avoid a contemptuous tone in making the theoretical claim about the inevitably beneficial consequences of the despicable and unchecked love of wealth.[49] If the greatest public benefits flow from the springs of unregulated avarice, a concern with moral education would seem to be utterly irrational in a commercial society. As long as the needs of the poor (broadly defined) are the measure of good government, the only public policy required is that which liberates and encourages the private pursuit of wealth. The virtues of commercial people, the bourgeoisie, thus became by the eighteenth century either not worth mentioning (to liberalism's friends) or a central part of the attack on liberalism by those republican friends of patriotic virtue who looked back to an earlier heroic time.

The founders of the American republic inherited and participated in this debate in a variety of ways. Interpretations of the thoughts of the founders have shifted over the past twenty-five years, from the view associated with Louis Hartz[50] that a Lockean commercial liberalism unconcerned with virtue was the common ground of political discourse, to the view held by Arendt (in *On Revolution*) and Pocock that "a political culture took shape in the eighteenth-century colonies which possessed all the characteristics of neo-Harringtonian civic humanism."[51] But it seems evident that much of the political discourse of late eighteenth- and early nineteenth-century America cannot handily be fit into either the paradigm of commerce or the paradigm of virtue (in Pocock's terms). Pocock recognizes that "the confrontation between virtue and commerce was not absolute" in America in the 1780s, but explains

---

[48] See Cropsey, "Invisible Hand," pp. 82–83.

[49] Pope's "Epistle to Burlington" gives a lovely sample of this. The poem attacks the crude lack of taste of the new men of wealth, but ends its judgment by abandoning moral discourse entirely in recognition of the gains the rich man's vice yields to the poor:

> Yet hence the Poor are cloath'd, the Hungry fed;
> Health to himself, and to his Infants bread
> The Lab'rer bears: What his hard Heart denies,
> His charitable Vanity supplies.
>
> (II. 169–172, p. 153)

[50] Hartz, *Liberal Tradition in America*.

[51] Pocock, *Machiavellian Moment*, pp. 506–507.

this by saying that this gap between theoretical categories and political discourse "furnishes reason to believe that the founders of Federalism were not fully aware of the extent to which their thinking involved an abandonment of the paradigm of virtue."[52] This explanation excludes the possibility that a central strand of this discourse was aiming not at abstract commerce or abstract civic virtue, but at another kind of regime altogether, one that supported both the importance of commercial exchange and a conception of virtue substantially different from the ideal of the republican citizen soldier.

It seems quite clear, for example, that many of the most enthusiastic supporters of commercial development utterly rejected the unseen hand hypothesis that private vices make public virtues. As Herbert Storing says, "The Federalists did not, it should be emphasized, rely on some unseen hand to produce public good out of individual selfishness."[53] Hamilton, in arguing the case for a strong national government in *Federalist* 6, rejects the thesis that "the spirit of commerce has a tendency to soften the manners of men," and asks, "Has commerce hitherto done anything more than change the objects of war? Is not the love of wealth as domineering and enterprising a passion as that of power or glory?"[54] The Federalist solution to the problem of the consequences of the unchecked love of wealth is to establish a complex political system, expressed in the Constitution, by which interest may be made to counter interest or to correspond with duty. The political system can thus moderate the importance of habits and outcomes that belong to the system of market exchange. Such a political system, when combined with the "multiplicity of interests" that characterize an extended commercial republic, will be sufficient to ensure that American democracy will be liberal in effect; that is, that "the rights of individuals, or of the minority, will be in little danger from interested combinations of the majority" (*Federalist* 51, p. 324). Given the adequacy of this political solution, it would be unnecessary to attempt to provide support for the educational project of "giving to every citizen the same opinions, the same passions, and the same interests" (*Federalist* 10, p. 78). The hand that channels the pursuit of private wealth by making potentially vicious avarice play by the rules of the polity as well as by those of the commercial market will by no means be unseen, but it will be suf-

[52] Ibid., p. 525.
[53] Storing, *What the Anti-Federalists Were For*, p. 73.
[54] *Federalist Papers*, p. 57.

ficient to obviate the need for any direct moral education to check the pursuit of wealth and nudge it toward liberality.

Disagreement as to this last point—the need for public moral education—rather than any more fundamental quarrel about the appropriate ends of government, formed the central controversy between the Federalists and their opponents. Arguing against the Constitution, the Federal Farmer sees a tacit conspiracy between the wealthy and the Shayites against "the men of middling property, men not in debt on the one hand . . . content with republican governments, and not aiming at immense fortunes, offices, and power." The republican government such people defended was not a polity of freely active and patriotic citizens but, in the Federal Farmer's evocative phrase, a "free and mild government": "Liberty, in its genuine sense, is security to enjoy the effects of our honest industry and labours, in a free and mild government, and personal security from all illegal restraints."[55]

For most Anti-Federalists, however, individual rights could be adequately protected only in small republics and only when citizens shared certain fundamental opinions and characteristic virtues. The means by which these opinions and virtues were to be secured was not the subject of extensive discussion, but seems to have rested principally on avoiding extremes of wealth and poverty and on maintaining the power of shared Protestant religious beliefs as obstacles to avarice and not, as Arendt sometimes implies, on a revival of Roman patriotism.[56] But there undoubtedly were profound differences within Protestantism, differences between evangelical Calvinists[57] and theological liberals, all equally committed to the new republic but strongly at odds over doctrine and style, and over the degree to which religion should influence political life. Concern for these differences, rather than a narrow commercial spirit, may have been the principal motive in the decision not to provide for the public support of a religious system. As Storing says, "the Constitution and its defenders deliberately

[55] Federal Farmer, "Observations," p. 62 and pp. 69–70.

[56] Storing, *What the Anti-Federalists Were For*, pp. 15–23. Sometimes the two views seem to have been, against probability, amalgamated, as in Samuel Adams's wish that America might be a Christian Sparta. Bellah, *Broken Covenant*, p. 31. Bellah's book makes an excellent case for the importance of religious movements and motives in both the Revolutionary period and during the "second founding" of the Civil War. See also Wood, *Creation of the American Republic*, pp. 426–429, and especially Diggins, *Lost Soul of American Politics*.

[57] For a discussion of the importance of radical evangelical sects in the formation of independent America, see Marini, *Radical Sects*.

turned away from religion as the foundation of civil institutions,"[58] but this by no means indicates that they opted for politically regulated avarice over fully committed republican citizenship. There was general agreement about the virtues required of American citizens—industry, thrift, sobriety (rather than virility)[59]—but disagreement over whether direct religious instruction was the best means to moral education.[60]

A new understanding of virtue was emerging during the late eighteenth and early nineteenth centuries, one particularly appropriate for a commercial people, an understanding that cannot be designated either capitalist or republican in the Periclean sense. According to this understanding, virtue did not mean heroically overcoming one's interests for the sake of God or country, but pursuing one's need to amass exchange value in a reasonable and orderly way, a way of life that valued public service without despising the pursuit of financial security and that encouraged scientific inquiry as well as national prosperity. There is no single authoritative text containing this vision, but the attempt to overcome the constraints of the commerce–civic virtue choice figures perhaps most clearly in the writings of Franklin and Jefferson.[61] Franklin's witty discussion of his "bold and arduous project of arriving at moral perfection" in the *Autobiography* describes his plan for mastering the virtues—after he decides that religion has little to teach beyond those doctrines common to "all the religions we had in our country": "the existence of the Deity; that he made the world and govern'd it by his Providence; that the most acceptable service of God was the doing good to man; that our souls are immortal; and that all crime will be punished, and virtue rewarded, either here or hereafter." With this thoroughly civil—and undemanding—religion as background, Franklin goes on to list thirteen virtues: temperance, silence, order, resolution, frugality ("make no expense but to do good to others or yourself; i.e., waste nothing"), industry, sincerity, justice ("wrong none by doing injuries, or omitting

[58] *What the Anti-Federalists Were For*, p. 23.

[59] Appleby suggests that the meaning of "virtue" (along with the meaning of "liberty") was shifting during the eighteenth century away from disinterested civic virtue, so that "by the end of the century virtue more often referred to a private quality, a man's capacity to look out for himself and his dependents—almost the opposite of classical virtue." *Capitalism*, pp. 14–15.

[60] Jefferson's argument against teaching religion in the public schools includes recognition of the need to provide some alternate form of moral education. *Notes on the State of Virginia*, Query 17, *Selected Writings*, p. 44.

[61] This notion of virtue is the focus of Lerner's discussion of "commercial republicanism" in "Commerce and Character" and of Appleby's *Capitalism*.

the benefits that are your duty"), moderation, cleanliness, tranquillity, chastity, and humility. Courage is notably lacking from this list, as is piety; liberality or generosity is not present, but something like those virtues is implied in the definition of frugality and in the charmingly imaginative account of chastity: "Rarely use venery but for health or offspring, never to dullness, weakness, or the injury of your own or another's reputation."[62]

Franklin's list does not seem to warrant MacIntyre's conclusion that his is a strictly utilitarian catalogue of virtues directed toward the external good of "happiness understood as success, prosperity in Philadelphia and ultimately in heaven,"[63] nor is Franklin justly seen as the proto-capitalist Philistine of D. H. Lawrence's diatribe.[64] Franklin, like Jefferson, was concerned with the virtues of ordinary citizens; this democratic commitment informs his contributions to the Constitutional Convention, where he strongly opposed property qualifications for voting and holding public office.[65] Perhaps the best way of characterizing the nature of the goal that underlies this conception of virtue is, as Appleby suggests, to see it as the hope of achieving a comfortable life, something as different from becoming wealthy as it is from achieving glory.[66] The novelty of such a life is that it is neither "public" nor "private," but rather one in which economic success supports and encourages political activity, both aiming at an independent life rather than at an unlimited acquisition of power. Jefferson states this goal in a letter to John Adams:

> Here every one may have land to labor for himself if he chuses; or preferring the exercise of any other industry, may

[62] Franklin, *Autobiography*, pp. 87–104.

[63] *After Virtue*, p. 173. For a more fair assessment of Franklin's supposed utilitarianism, see Bellah et al., *Habits of the Heart*, pp. 32–33; the authors there contend that Franklin combines strands of selfish utilitarianism and public spirit. I would rather say that his sketch of the virtuous character is something new, not merely a combination of incompatibles. For an excellent, nuanced reading of the *Autobiography*, see Lerner, *Thinking Revolutionary*, chap. 1.

[64] D. H. Lawrence, *Studies in Classic American Literature*, pp. 19–30.

[65] Madison's notes record this response to a proposed property qualification for members of Congress: "Doctor Franklin expressed his dislike of everything that tended to debase the spirit of the common people. If honesty was often the companion of wealth, and if poverty was exposed to peculiar temptation, it was not less true that the possession of property increased the desire of more property. Some of the greatest rogues he was ever acquainted with, were the richest rogues." Solberg, *Federal Convention*, p. 277.

[66] *Capitalism*, p. 90. The fundamentally antidemocratic character of the civic republican conception of virtue is clearly presented by Arendt at the conclusion of *On Revolution*, pp. 281–284.

exact for it such compensation as not only to afford a comfortable subsistence, but wherewith to provide for a cessation
from labor in old age. Every one, by his property, or by his
satisfactory situation, is interested in the support of law and
order. And such men may safely and advantageously reserve
to themselves a wholesome controul over their public affairs,
and a degree of freedom, which in the hands of the Canaille
of the cities of Europe, would be instantly perverted to the
demolition and destruction of every thing public and private.[67]

This is, in effect, an attempt to sketch the character of the liberal
culture, the culture needed for the success of a liberal democratic
polity. It involves, in the eighteenth-century context, an important
rethinking of the positive virtues of middling levels of wealth, and
emphasizes a concern with comfort as a support for the development of human rationality. This culture is prefigured in Locke's
discussion of civil interests, and portrayed in some of the novels
of Jane Austen, especially *Mansfield Park*.[68]

This conception of a kind of liberal virtue to match a concern
with comfort—the appropriately human *way* to be concerned with
comfort—is, I think, central to Tocqueville's discussion of democracy in America: "If one tries to think what passion is most natural
to men both stimulated and hemmed in by the obscurity of their
birth and the mediocrity of their fortune, nothing seems to suit
them better than the taste for comfort. The passion for physical
comfort is essentially a middle-class affair . . . [but it soon spreads
up and down throughout society so that now] love of comfort has
become the dominant national taste" (pp. 531–532).

Before looking at Tocqueville, I want to turn briefly to Aristotle's
discussion of moral virtue in order to fix the possibility of thinking
about virtue in a way that does *not* turn primarily on a tension
between interest and morality or on a distinction between private

[67] Jefferson, "Letter to John Adams," October 28, 1813. *Selected Writings*, pp. 78–
79.
[68] The narrative of *Mansfield Park* concerns the attempt to achieve a form of comfort that is equally economic and psychological. The author magically restores all
the decent characters to "tolerable comfort" at the end of the novel (the beginning
of chap. 48), but not before showing how difficult such a goal is to achieve and the
demands it makes, particularly on the virtues of kindness and liberality. For an
excellent discussion of the importance of kindness and other "hidden virtues" in
Austen's *Emma*, see White, *When Words Lose Their Meaning*, chap. 7. For a persuasive argument that the novels of Iris Murdoch aim at a liberal reconception of the
virtues, see Levenson, "Liberals in Love."

and public realms. This may seem strange, since so many authors have associated Aristotle's name with the tradition of Periclean politics and republican virtue. As we saw in Chapter 4, however, there is excellent reason to believe that the Periclean Aristotle is as distant from the Aristotelian texts as is the Thomistic Aristotle. Considering Aristotle on moral virtue and friendship will confirm this, and indicate how attention to Aristotle's style of practical theory can help us think about liberal culture and liberal politics.

SIX

RECONCEIVING LIBERAL DEMOCRACY, PART II: LIBERAL VIRTUES AND THE PUBLIC LIFE

Aristotle on the Virtues

Civic humanists and classical liberals agree that education in virtue means a training in overcoming private interest for the sake of some public good or duty. If this is so, then democratic moral education must be radically transformative, if it is to exist at all. For republicans and Kantians, true virtue is defined by its opposition to interest, or at any rate to private interest. For classical or Millian liberals, virtue is strictly a private matter rather than a public concern.[1] For the classical republican, moral education is a good thing, and it means learning how to overcome your private interest for the sake of higher duty. For the Lockean, public moral education is necessarily a bad thing if it means imposing values on individuals, rather than allowing mature adults freedom of choice. This agreement about the meaning of virtue is masked by the controversy between the two camps over whether moral education is a good thing, and so obscures an entirely different way of understanding moral education, one which sees virtue or excellence as self-interest properly understood—without assuming that "self-interest" is always satisfied by increasing one's private powers or resources.

While the theoretical language of moral education used in this way may seem exotic, I think that it fits our historical and contemporary practice much better than do either the language of ancient civic virtue or that of some mythical community of abstract individuals. In practice, the American liberal conception of the virtues

---

[1] There is a welcome tendency among some modern liberal theorists to reject the idea that democracy requires moral neutrality or relativism. See, for example, Gutmann, *Democratic Education*, chap. 1.

has been much less narrow than the republican vision of the committed citizen and yet more substantial and definite than the neutrality about the good insisted on by classical liberal theorists. The Aristotelian conception of virtues as those habitual dispositions of character that contribute to the happiness and success of the person who has them fits the historical liberal democratic sense of a good person better than the two modern theories, which define virtues either by impossibly objective principles or hopelessly subjective preferences. Thus in spite of the fact that Aristotle himself was neither a liberal nor a democrat, the Aristotelian way of talking about virtue can provide a connection between modern democratic theorizing and an important aspect of modern democratic experience.

The Aristotelian conceptions of *aretē* and *kakia*, virtue or excellence and wretchedness, must not be understood as if *aretē* required the painful and unworldly overcoming of passion or private interest for the sake of some principle or publicly defined good. Aristotle has a distinction that corresponds to this later notion of virtue, and that is the distinction between *enkrateia* and *akrasia*, moral strength and moral weakness. At the beginning of Book 7 of the *Nicomachean Ethics*, Aristotle distinguishes between these two pairs, and says that human virtues or excellences (*aretai*) belong only to human beings, not to beasts or gods. Human virtue is thus not a transcendence of humanity but is the name given to those personality traits or settled states of character that contribute to human happiness. Virtue must not be understood as separate from the goal of happiness, but as constituting *eudaimonia*, at least so long as bad luck does not intervene between a virtuous potentiality and a happy outcome. As J. O. Urmson says, "for Aristotle, having to make oneself behave properly, however admirable the deed, betrays a defect of character. Excellence of character is not the triumph of grace over the old Adam. . . . [it is] how Adam would have acted when *eudaimōn* before the fall."[2] Human happiness, for Aristotle, does not, of course, mean being pleased with oneself; it means living in a thoughtful way.

Aristotle's human virtue has little in common with the civic re-

___

[2] Urmson, "Aristotle's Doctrine of the Mean," p. 160. Urmson's essay is a lucid exposition and defense of the plausibility of Aristotle's conception of virtue, as well as a guide to the differences between the Aristotelian and Christian conceptions. Aristotle provides a list of the components of *eudaimonia* in *Rhet.* 1, 1360b19–24. They are: good birth, many friends, good friends, wealth, good children, many children, a good old age, beauty, health, strength, stature, power, fitness for contests, good repute, honor, virtue, and good luck.

publican view, which he would place with moral strength and Spartan courage as approximations of virtue rather than the real thing. What then *is* virtue for Aristotle? First of all, it is adverbial—a way or manner of living, rather than a particular sort of action or even a particular will (recall the significance of the adverbial formulations of virtue and wretchedness in the *Politics*: *eu zēn* [living well], *zēn ataktōs* [living in a disorderly way], and so on). Since "living" itself is a general term for a number of specific activities, so virtue will be a general term that collects the appropriate ways of acting in response to feelings and actions that we encounter in our lives, the name for the manner in which a person of practical wisdom or seriousness would act. Perhaps the best way to get a sense of the nature of Aristotelian virtues is to present them, as Aristotle suggests (*NE* 2, 1107a32–33), in a diagram. The table given here lists virtuous and wretched states of character (*hexeis*), metaphorically expressed as the mean and extreme (excess and deficiency) possibilities for reacting to some emotion or situation calling for action-choice.

An examination of the list brings several interesting features of the Aristotelian approach to light. First, there is no suggestion that the list of virtues is exhaustive, or that an exhaustive list could ever be compiled.[3] Yet the truth concerning the virtues is contained more in lists like this than in any general formulation, Aristotle's own included: "Not only must this universal alone be stated, but it must be fitted to the properties of each particular [virtue]. For in discourses (*logoi*) concerning actions, the universals are more common [belong to more cases] but the [statements] about parts are truer; for actions are particular and the discourse must accord with them" (*NE* 2, 1107a28–33). The important discussions of virtue have to do with particular virtues and vices, not with the statement of the universal rule,[4] even though no exhaustive account of the particular virtues is possible. Theorizing about virtue can inform practical thinking about actions but cannot replace it.

[3] A slightly different list appears in *EE* 2, 1220b–1221a. That list treats shame as a virtue, and includes justice, practical wisdom, hardiness (*karteria*—associated in the *NE* with *enkrateia* rather than virtue), and dignity. The *EE* list omits the nameless virtues of moderate ambition and wittiness.

[4] This is the ground for the difference between Aristotelian and rule morality discussed in chap. 3. Even true knowledge of universals about action—for example, knowing that rationality is the human good—does not provide sufficient information to make it possible to arrive deductively at action-choices in particular circumstances. Thus, theoretical rankings of the virtues are possible, but action-governing rules—on the order of natural laws—are not.

OCCASIONS FOR VIRTUE/VICE (Pathos/Praxis)	STATES OF CHARACTER (Hexeis)		
	Excess	Mean	Deficiency
Fear/Confidence	Boldness (no name)	Virility	Cowardice
Pleasure/Pain (not all; mostly pleasures of touch—food, drink, sex)	Self-indulgence	Moderation	Feelinglessness (no name)
Money matters (small-scale)	Wastefulness	Liberality (eleutheria)	Illiberality, Stinginess
Money matters (large-scale—such as liturgies)	Vulgarity	Magnificence (megaloprepeia)	Cheapness (mikroprepeia)
Honor/Dishonor (large-scale)	Vanity	Greatness of Soul	Smallness of Soul
Honor/Dishonor (small-scale)	Ambition	(no name)	Lack of Ambition
Anger (no real names)	Short temper	Gentleness	Apathy
Speeches, Actions concerning Truth	Boastfulness	Truthfulness	Irony
Speeches, Actions concerning Play (paidia)	Buffoonery	Wittiness	Rusticity
Speeches/Actions concerning Daily Life (suzēn)	Obsequiousness	Friendliness (philia, but without affection)	Grouchiness
Pleasure/Pain concerning the Fortune of Others	Envy	Righteous Indignation (nemesis)	Spite
Feelings about Others' Opinions	Shyness	Shame (not a virtue, but like one)	Shamelessness

Second, there is no essential connection made between virtue and the political life, and no emphasis laid on the very common Greek distinction between the private and the public life.[5] The discussion of justice, in Book 5 of the *Nicomachen Ethics*, is indeed about political virtue, and justice is there said, in one of its several senses, to be the complete virtue concerning our conduct toward

[5] This distinction is much more vital to Pericles and to characters like Plato's Callicles than to either Plato or Aristotle. The absence of concern with the private/public distinction in the list of the virtues is simply one more indication of the Greek philosophic critique of one of the leading features of Greek political culture.

others (*NE* 5, 1129b31–33); but this is only because *nomoi* aim, as all the virtues do, at the human good, not because political activity is especially ennobling. Moreover, Aristotle's pointing to certain virtues and vices for which there are no readily available Greek names suggests some clear criticisms of Periclean morality: there is no name for excessive virility, no good vocabulary for articulating the virtue of gentleness, and no name for the virtue of everyday honor. These gaps in the language are not surprising for a people not inclined to think of gentleness as a virtue, or of the possibility that there might be an excess of virility, or that small honor was worth thinking about at all. Finally, one might notice the specific character of the Aristotelian virtues. If we bear in mind the derogation of virility discussed in Chapter 4, and if we note that people of middling means are not likely ever to encounter occasions involving large-scale issues of money or honor, the Aristotelian virtues (in the *NE* list) are moderation, liberality, moderate ambition, truthfulness, wittiness, affability (friendliness without affection), and righteous indignation. This list seems to fit the sense of human happiness that informs Benjamin Franklin and Fanny Price much better than it would the standard roster of the heroes of neo-Machiavellian republicanism.

Beyond the metaphor of the mean, which analogizes virtuous activity to activities that require choice through perception rather than rule-application in matters where no rule is available—such as the medical art, or craftsmanship in general (*technitai*; *NE* 2, 1106b13)[6]—Aristotle has, intentionally, little to say about those attributes universally shared by human virtues. He does say that they all can be seen as ways in which the person of practical wisdom, the *phronimos*, would thoughtfully respond to the occasion— the act to be done or the passion experienced—in question (*NE* 2, 1106b36–1107a2). The only measure for deciding whether an action is good or not is our sense of how a *spoudaios*, a serious person, would perform it (*NE* 3, 1113a25–33). Just what a *spoudaios* is cannot be precisely stated, but must always be the concern of our theorizing about actions. Perhaps one generalization that can be ventured is that a *phronimos* or *spoudaios* is someone who takes the

---

[6] The importance of being able to make correct choices in situations where no rules apply is the theme of several of the stories in the Taoist text called the *Chuang Tzu*. The story of Duke Huan and the wheelwright—who knows that the right stroke for making wheels is neither too slow nor too fast, but also knows that this mean cannot be put into words and transmitted—seems especially Aristotelian. See Waley, *Three Ways of Thought in Ancient China*, pp. 15–16.

present act or feeling neither more nor less seriously than it deserves to be taken with regard to its place in a thoughtful human
life.

Politics, Friendship, and the Virtues

Justice and the political life clearly have important parts to play in
human life for Aristotle, but they by no means deserve the preeminent role that civic humanists suggest. The virtue of justice is
discussed at greater length than any other virtue in the *Nicomachean Ethics*, but this is due as much to the word's ambiguity and
its wide range of meanings in the political culture of Aristotle's
Greece as to his theoretical assessment of its human significance.
The bulk of the consideration of justice in *Nicomachean Ethics* 5 is
devoted to two arenas of activity that are not, for Aristotle, of major importance to the central concern of politics: the activity of settling conflicting rights-claims, deprecated in Book 3 of the *Politics*
as the sort proposed by the sophist Lukophron, and not the real
business of politics, which concerns the problem of living well;
and economic activity, the concern with just prices in the exchange
of material goods. The tone of the discussion in *Nicomachean Ethics*
5 is mathematical and precise; questions on this level can be settled
with lawlike precision. These discussions are followed by a consideration of decency (or "equity," *to epieikes*), that explicitly connects
justice with law or *nomos*, and says that the decent person is in a
sense just, yet is better than the just person because not bound to
think and act according to a system of general rules (1137a31–
1138a2).

Much less space in the *Nicomachean Ethics* is devoted to justice
than to *philia* (addressed in Books 8 and 9), an activity that seems
in some ways to replace or duplicate both moral virtue as such and
justice in particular—like virtue and politics, the best sort of
friendship aims at the good or happiness of the friends. But as we
have seen, it is emphatically not the case that the best friendships
are political (*EE* 7, 1242a), or that *philia* for Aristotle is essentially a
political relationship. His argument is that politics becomes better
insofar as it becomes (within limits, since it is impossible to be genuinely friendly with more than a few people)[7] more like a friendship, and not vice versa (*NE* 8, 1155a22–28; *NE* 9, 1167a26–30).
Someone who had *only* political relationships (for example, a

[7] "Those who have many friends and treat them all as intimates seem to be
friends to no one, except in a political way" (*NE* 9, 1171a15–17).

Rousseauian citizen defined by the general will) would be incapable of the best friendships, those that aim at the excellence of the friends. Perhaps the clearest statement of the relationship between the political virtue of justice and friendship comes at the beginning of the discussion of *philia* in *Nicomachean Ethics* 8: "Friends don't need justice, but just people need friendship; and justice seems especially to be an aspect of friendship" (*NE* 8, 1155a26–28). Perhaps we could say that politics is to friendship as commerce is to politics; this is a bit too schematic, though, since the term friendship can refer to political and commercial relationships as well as to the best kind. Still, Aristotle's position seems to be that while we all need political life—at its best, ruling and being ruled relative to just *nomoi*—fully human happiness requires that we regard politics as less crucial (in one sense) to our well-being than our relationships with close friends. It is at this point, I think, that the agreement between Aristotle and modern liberal politics (although not modern liberal theory, which has nothing to say about friendship) becomes strongest: anyone who takes politics too seriously will, like those who take commerce too seriously, overlook the central importance for human moral development of relationships that are neither political nor commercial (although they may be familial).[8]

Philia, like the virtues (justice included), is to be understood teleologically as a relationship through which human beings flourish. Its difference from moral virtue can be seen by noting that the virtue relative to *suzēn*, ordinary social interaction (*NE* 4, 1126b11–12), is said to be a nameless virtue (I have called it affability) that resembles *philia*. The excess of this virtue is exemplified by someone gushingly friendly to everybody, while the deficiency is found in a quarrelsome grouch. The virtuous person will deal in a friendly manner with others—sometimes agreeing, sometimes opposing— but unlike a friendship, this virtue is "without emotion (*pathos*) and affection (*stergein*)" (*NE* 4, 1126b22–23); it is not that the affable person is cold, but rather that friendships depend on a certain close and affectionate feeling that simply cannot be shared with the world at large.

Real *philia*, then, is both intimate and critical; friends are interested in one another's goodness, and so will not be simply accepting of one another. What friendship gives us is the opportunity to

[8] The best discussion of justice and friendship in Aristotle is Cropsey, "Justice and Friendship."

become more human, not through altruistic concern, but through our being able to see and examine what we are, affectionately and critically, through talking with our friends, since essentially "a friend is another self" (*NE* 9, 1166a31–32), and since "a good person (*spoudaios*) will perceive the friend's being together with one's own, and for this friends must live together (*suzēn*) sharing especially *logoi* and thought (*dianoia*); for this is what *suzēn* would seem to be when said of human beings, and not pasturing in the same place as it is for grazing animals" (*NE* 9, 1170b10–14). Nor is the best human relationship the political one, although politics, raising children, trading, and feeding can all be done in humanly better or worse ways. All of these relationships need to be maintained rather than reduced to a single *koinōnia*. Again, this would seem to be the point of clearest convergence of Aristotle's classical liberalism and modern liberal democratic politics. What is called for now is a modern theory that sustains and justifies this sort of politics, and constitutes its claim to superiority over the modern theoretical alternatives of the preeminence of either political or economic relationships. What is required, in other words, is some way of evaluating economic and political institutions at least partially in terms of the extent to which they make genuine friendships possible, something that, in Aristotelian terms, would seem—given the possibilities of democratic politics discussed in Chapter 5—to be more likely in a liberal democracy than in Sparta or republican Rome.

The quality of any democracy will depend on the attitude democrats take to the pursuit of wealth, income, and security, a pursuit that is a necessary feature of democratic lives. This attitude in turn is primarily determined by the nature of the customs and traditions that inform democratic life in particular places. Unlike modern theorists, the Aristotelian social scientist interested in democracy will not abstract from these particulars by attempting to formulate a universal decision procedure that makes obligation rational or reconciles interest and duty. Rather, the task of this science or theory is twofold: to articulate forms of life that exhibit the best and worst possibilities inherent in a particular context and to examine the laws and customs of the place with an eye to determining how they do or do not moderate the pursuit of wealth intrinsic to all democracies. The best example of this kind of social science is Tocqueville's *Democracy in America*.

Tocqueville: An Aristotelian Approach
to American Democracy

Democracy in America is concerned with the formation rather than the summation of preferences, and its focus is not abstractly universal but specific to American democracy and European aristocracy.[9] It is in this way less democratic than more familiar social science, at least insofar as Tocqueville is correct in saying that "democratic men love general ideas because they save them the trouble of studying particular cases" (p. 440). My characterization of Tocqueville as Aristotelian may appear to conflict with Tocqueville's claim for the novelty of his work, which he introduces by saying that a "new political science is necessary for a world wholly new" (p. 12). But Tocqueville's new political science is not, like Hobbes's or Machiavelli's, based on a confident rejection of the teleological method of ancient philosophy or political philosophy. The novelty Tocqueville claims is not for his method, but for the object of his study: the problem of modern democracy, a regime in which rule is by the poor, who passionately love money and equality of status (pp. 50, 252, 504), and one in which connections among individuals over space and time are continually at risk (p. 507).

The greatest danger here is that the democratic character will become marked by what Tocqueville calls, using a new word to describe a new phenomenon, "individualism," "a considered and peaceable sentiment that disposes each citizen to isolate himself from the mass of his fellows and withdraw into the circle of family and friends, in such a way that after having created a little society for his own use he willingly abandons society at large to its own devices" (p. 506). If such an opinion becomes predominant, the regime will become stagnant (p. 645), and degenerate either into anarchy or, more probably, into servitude (p. 667). It is, I think, important to note that Tocqueville's diagnosis of the efficient cause

---

[9] For an excellent discussion of the importance of this distinction, and an attempt to remedy the lack of attention to preference formation (or moral education) in contemporary liberal theory and empirical social science, see Elkin, *City and Regime*. Other illuminating investigations of this important point are to be found in Bluhm, "Liberalism," and McPherson, "Want Formation." For a valuable discussion of the perplexing question of the rhetoric of *Democracy in America*, see Bruce James Smith, *Politics and Remembrance*, pp. 181–200. According to Smith, "as aristocratic pedagogy, the *Democracy* moves deftly back and forth between persuasion and commiseration, sharing the aristocrat's distaste for democratic things while softening his pride" (p. 191).

of individualism is *not* the same as the civic republican's complaint about the corruption of political life due to commerce and luxury: "individualism is based on misguided judgment rather than depraved feeling. It is due more to inadequate understanding than to perversity of the heart" (p. 506). Better theorizing—not the transformation of mere human beings into republican citizens—is needed to show democrats why they need to be concerned with the interests of society at large.

The dangers posed by individualistic drift are not grounds for despairing of the possibilities of democracy. The democratic character may tend toward a dissipating individualism, but democrats are at the same time more compassionate and more gentle than their aristocratic predecessors who, like Aristotle's oligarchs, love honor more than wealth and so are prone to inhumanity and war (pp. 564–565). In the new world of the commercial democracy, "Mores are gentle and laws humane. Though heroic devotions and any other very high, very brilliant, and very pure virtues are few, habits are orderly, violence rare, cruelty almost unknown. Human life becomes longer and property more secure. Life is not very glamorous, but very easy and very peaceable" (p. 703). Though democracy aims at this comfort-as-happiness as a goal, it does not always achieve it, since it also contains contrary tendencies in the directions of individualism and despotism. These contrary potentialities set the task for Tocqueville's practical theorizing. The problem "is no longer to preserve the particular advantages that inequality of conditions procures for men, but to secure the new goods that equality can offer them. We should not try to make ourselves like our fathers but should strive to attain the sort of greatness and happiness that is proper to us" (p. 705). Tocqueville's intention, then, is not to find a way to reconcile interest and duty in the abstract, nor to discover a rule for public choice to which all rational beings must accede, but to identify those attitudes and practices that have the greatest bearing on the particular possibilities that define democratic life.

Tocqueville's solution to the problem of democracy is deceptively simple: "I maintain that there is only one effective remedy against the evils that equality can produce, and that is political liberty" (p. 513). Political liberty is the key, but the meaning of the term is, for us at any rate, difficult to ascertain because it does not correspond to the way the term is used by either liberal theory or republicanism. It is immediately apparent that Tocqueville does not mean the opportunity to pursue one's own good in one's own way, in J. S. Mill's terms; limitless independence is frightening (p. 440), and the aim of democracy should be to regulate and legitimize power, not to destroy it (p. 601). But if Tocqueville's understanding of freedom is not that of early modern liberalism, it is equally clear that his conception of freedom is not republican citizenship on the model of Machiavelli or Rousseau. He is as little attracted to the idealized images of republican life in Periclean Athens and republican Rome as are the authors of the *Federalist*, and for similar reasons: the code of honor that shapes the civic culture of republican citizens, a code that exalts courage above all the other virtues, is inseparable from a taste for turbulence and war (pp. 620–627). To embrace such an ideal is to neglect the distinctive moral possibilities of a poor person's democracy in which "everybody works, and work opens all doors" (p. 623).

The moral resources of a society implicitly committed to the value of work are nowhere better illustrated than in the speeches of Abraham Lincoln relating to American slavery. Lincoln's opposition to slavery did not stem from a conviction of racial equality. He was and knew himself to be what Frederick Douglass called him in Douglass's brilliant memorial oration, "pre-eminently the white man's President, entirely devoted to the welfare of white men." And yet, as Douglass goes on to say, "though Mr. Lincoln shared the prejudices of his white fellow-countrymen against the negro, it is hardly necessary to say that in his heart of hearts he loathed and hated slavery."[10] The source of this hatred lay not simply in expansive humanity, and not at all in measured theoretical judgment, but in Lincoln's devotion to work and consequent antagonism to leisurely exploitation. Douglass puts it this way: "Born and reared among the lowly, a stranger to wealth and luxury . . . he was a man of work. A son of toil himself, he was linked in brotherly sympathy with the sons of toil in every part of the Republic."[11] Lincoln's commitment to republican principles was focused specifically on the moral significance of work and economic self-sufficiency. Speaking of the black woman in the Springfield speech, Lincoln says this: "In some respects she certainly is not my equal; but in her natural right to eat bread she earns with

---

[10] Douglass, "Oration in Memory of Abraham Lincoln," pp. 245, 248.

[11] Ibid., pp. 249–250. Douglass shared Lincoln's sense of work as the activity that confers identity; this can be seen especially in his argument against taking pride in one's color rather than in one's achievements: "The only excuse for pride in individuals or races is in the fact of their own achievements." "Nation's Problem," p. 316.

her own hands without asking leave of anyone else, she is my equal, and the equal of all others."[12] There is no question here of adherence to an abstract principle; rather, there is the expression of a moral possibility located in a life shaped by abiding concern with work and with money.

Such moral possibilities pertain to a way of life that embodies certain genuine virtues, but ones very different from those of committed or instinctive patriotism: "Commerce is the natural enemy of all violent passions. It loves moderation, delights in compromise, and is most careful to avoid anger. . . . Commerce makes men independent of one another and gives them a high idea of their individual worth; it leads them to want to manage their own affairs and teaches them how to succeed therein. Hence it makes them inclined to liberty but disinclined to revolution" (p. 637). The life of acquisitive enterprise is, of course, not by itself sufficient to produce those virtues that justify and define it—any more than internal conflict, without its context of political and religious institutions, suffices to produce Roman freedom on Machiavelli's reading. Unchecked and untempered, the acquisitive instinct can, in Tocqueville's view, lead to the despotism of an atomized mass society. But possibility is not necessity. The importance and distinctiveness of Tocqueville's analysis lie in his characterization of the spirit of acquisitive enterprise, the spirit that is the driving force of the new democratic majority, as neither a deformity (as it is for Rousseau, Marx, Weber, and Nietzsche) nor a panacea (in the manner of the early defenders of capitalism on political grounds), but rather as a *potentiality*. Democracy understood in this way must be informed and educated in the light of its own best possibilities, not, as the imagery of the crisis of modernity would lead us to believe, utterly transformed. Thus I think it is misleading to see Tocqueville as struggling toward a radical vision of civic republicanism, but held back by his commitment to the categories of liberal thought.[13] Perhaps it would be better to say that Tocqueville manages to avoid the literary attractions of republican radicalism (such as rhetorical vividness and force) in presenting a thoroughly liberal critical understanding of the *problem* (and not the "crisis")

---

[12] Lincoln, "Speech in Springfield, Illinois," p. 535. And in the Second Inaugural Address he speaks of the strangeness that "any men should dare to ask a just God's assistance in wringing their bread from the sweat of other men's faces." "Second Inaugural Address," p. 311.

[13] For an interesting view somewhat to the contrary, see Sullivan, *Reconstructing Public Philosophy*, p. 216. Another defense of Tocqueville as a republican thinker of a special kind is Bruce James Smith, *Politics and Remembrance*, pp. 155–250.

of liberal democracy. The poor—in his sense—whose competitive desires rule democracy need to be educated in a manner appropriate to their own genius, not transformed into citizens: "It is therefore essential to march forward and hasten to make the people see that individual interest is linked to that of country, for disinterested love of country has fled beyond recall" (p. 236).

The education in liberty has nothing to do with direct teaching or manipulation by theorists who stand outside the democratic polity. It consists, rather, in identifying (very much in the manner of *Pol.* 4–6) those factors that have in fact given American democracy a liberal or generous direction. The principles and limits of this education—one that aims at institutionalizing a certain kind of political interaction—are clearly stated in the context of a discussion of self-interest properly understood: "No power on earth can prevent increasing equality from turning men's minds to look for the useful or disposing each citizen to get wrapped up in himself. One must therefore expect that individual interest will more than ever become the chief if not the only motive behind all actions. But we have yet to see how each man will interpret his individual interest" (p. 527). Tocqueville's intention is not to legislate, or even to show the need for fundamental legislation, but instead "to show, by the American example, that laws and above all mores can allow a democratic people to remain free" (p. 315). The whole of the inquiry is an attempt to explain the reasons for the liberal quality of American democracy, by distinguishing the sources and supports of liberality from those aspects of American life that threaten it.

Some of those sources are economic in the narrow sense, such as the absence of any large class of propertyless and destitute persons (p. 238), the fact that "wealth circulates there with incredible rapidity" (p. 54), and the expenditure (contrary, he says, to official proclamations of economy in government) of "enormous sums" on "maintenance of the needy and free education" (p. 214 n. 11). One of the great threats to American liberty is posed by the possible increase of economic inequality as society becomes more industrial (pp. 556–557)—since increasing the gap between wealthy and poor and reducing the numbers of those in a middle position is a development that threatens the possibility of liberality and tends to give rise, for Tocqueville as for Aristotle (*Pol.* 4, 1295b), to a polity composed only of masters and slaves. The character of economic life is therefore a significant item on the political agenda whose aim is the encouragement of a liberal interpretation of private interest among democrats. But it is by no means the only, and perhaps not even the most, important one.

Perhaps Tocqveville's most famous idea is that active participation in local political associations is the "free school" through which the democratic personality becomes inclined toward liberality and civic friendship (p. 522). Speaking of universal suffrage, he says that it "is certainly not the elected magistrate who makes the American democracy prosper, but the fact that the magistrates are elected" (p. 512). Just as the economic system must be evaluated in terms of its effect on moral development, so the most important (though generally overlooked) feature or function of any method of summing preferences is the effect such a method has on the *formation* of preferences. But Tocqueville's stress on the need for political participation and on the critical importance of decentralized political life is not aimed at training republican citizens, but at encouraging a partial commitment to the nation through stronger attachment to polities that have nothing to do with war and glory or the need to overcome individual interest:

> In a little country such as Connecticut, for example, where the opening of a canal or the cutting of a road is the main political business, where there is no army to pay or war to finance . . . nothing could be more appropriate to the nature of things than a republic. . . . Public spirit in the Union is, in a sense, only a summing up of provincial patriotism. Every citizen of the United States may be said to transfer the concern inspired in him by his little republic into his love of the common motherland. In defending the Union, he is defending the increasing prosperity of his district, the right to direct its affairs, and the hope of pressing through plans for improvements there which should enrich himself—all things which, in the normal run, touch men more than the general interests of the country and national glory. (P. 162)[14]

The virtuous habits of mind and heart to be acquired through political activity are clearly and specifically liberal: "The free institutions of the United States . . . provide a thousand continual reminders to every citizen that he lives in society. . . . Having no

[14] Elkin argues that the problems of political economy in a commercial republic must not be narrowly understood as concerned only with encouraging business growth: "Promoting a commercial republic—and thus attending to the commercial public interest—requires that inducing business performance be seen in the larger context of securing republican government." *City and Regime*, p. 144.

particular reason to hate others, since he is neither their slave nor their master, the American heart easily inclines toward benevolence" (p. 512). Note here both the echo of Aristotle and Tocqueville's sense that the limits of the American polity were such that it could never successfully integrate exslaves into the body of citizens.

In spite of his recognition of the importance of local politics, Tocqueville does not incline to the Arendtian view that increasing the importance of local control will be sufficient for a republican education in virtue.[15] Administrative centralization is a powerfully dangerous democratic tendency (pp. 88, 96), but at the same time it is (not accidentally) the case that "the federal government is more just and moderate in its proceedings than those of the states" since—because of the Constitution—legislative power is less likely to rule unchecked there (p. 155). Participatory politics is not an inevitably desirable means of regulating liberal individualism; it can work in that way, but only insofar as such political activity is shaped or bound by certain attitudes that do not always accompany political debate, but which happen to do so—at least some of the time—in the American case.[16]

The Institutional Sources of American Political Character

The institutional practices and standards connected with the common law are, for Tocqueville, indispensable forces shaping politi-

---

[15] In *On Revolution*, pp. 252–259, Arendt cites Jefferson's enthusiasm for breaking up the counties into small wards as evidence of the view that genuine happiness was to be found only in political life. In order to reinforce her republican conception of political life as an end in itself, she says that "on one point, however, Jefferson remained curiously silent, and that is what the specific functions of the elementary republics should be" (p. 258). But Jefferson's ward plan had a very specific object; the wards were initially to be free school districts, so as to permit worthy individuals to rise without inherited wealth and status. Moreover, Jefferson was quite specific about the functions of public management best suited to ward governments: "My proposition had for a further object [beyond public schooling] to impart to these wards those portions of self-government for which they are best qualified . . . the care of their poor, their roads, police, elections, the nomination of jurors, administration of justice in small cases, elementary exercises of militia. . . ." ("Letter to John Adams, October 28, 1813," in *Selected Writings*, p. 78). Jefferson's intention here, like Franklin's and Tocqueville's (but unlike Arendt's), is to harmonize economic and political relationships—in order to reach the goals of liberal democratic politics—rather than to separate them.

[16] Hochschild's *New American Dilemma* is a Tocquevillean study of school desegregation policy which explores the tension between liberal goals and local control in a particularly crucial case.

cal life and attitudes in America. That there is "hardly a political question in the United States which does not sooner or later turn into a judicial one" is, for Tocqueville, decidedly a good thing (p. 270), since it enforces a disciplined search for authoritative standards and so serves as a counterforce to both liberalism and the "ill-considered passions of democracy" (p. 264). The common law perspective is introduced into the language of everyday political life through the institution of jury trials, a practice whose importance can hardly be overestimated: "Juries, especially civil juries, instill some of the habits of the judicial mind into every citizen, and just those habits are the very best way of preparing people to be free" (p. 274). If local participation is a school for freedom it is so only for people whose minds have been shaped and prepared by something like the discipline of judicial reflection: "I do not know whether a jury is useful to the litigants, but I am sure it is very good for those who have to decide the case. I regard it as one of the most effective means of popular education at society's disposal" (p. 275).

Tocqueville's emphasis on the importance of the common law background of American politics helps place his understanding of liberty. The language of the common law (or of the federal Constitution), the language which constitutes the "habits of the judicial mind," is necessary for a liberal democracy because "it spreads respect for the courts' decisions and for the idea of right throughout all classes. With those two elements gone, love of independence is merely a destructive passion" (p. 274). What Tocqueville calls for here sets his understanding apart from both the fierce commitment to the conventions of the city demanded by republicans and the ruthless critique of all conventions, the common law especially included, insisted on by Hobbes, Locke, and liberal theory generally.[17] Throughout his consideration of the American regime, Tocqueville is looking for institutions and practices that provide a certain kind of unobtrusive authority or structure. His metaphoric account of the function of authority is particularly tell-

[17] See Appleby on the differences among three senses of liberty in the eighteenth century: liberal liberty (opportunity), republican self-determination, and the legal title to property or the privilege of doing something without fear of arrest or punishment. *Capitalism*, pp. 16–22. Bellah comments on the striking lack of express recognition given to the traditionally English roots of American politics: "In many respects the unprecedented degree of self-government existing in the colonies almost from the beginning was due to specifically English political and constitutional developments. . . . And yet there is remarkably little to show of English influence in the new republic at the level of myth and symbol." *Broken Covenant*, p. 21.

ing: "just as every people, to express its thoughts, must have some grammar shaping its language, so all societies, in order to exist, must submit to some authority without which they would relapse into anarchy" (p. 72). The problem is to identify the grammar of liberal democratic authority, and Tocqueville believes that the common law has a crucial role to play in that structure.[18]

Tocqueville examines a number of other customary patterns of interaction—including the structure of the American family and the relations between the sexes—with an eye to the way these *nomoi* affect moral development.[19] This teleological mode of analysis tends to work against the force of the public/private distinction by calling attention to the ways in which the character of "public" life is decisively affected by habits developed in "private" settings. His account of the political significance of American religion (which should "be considered as the first of their political institutions") has much the same bearing as his discussion of common law institutions and practices (p. 292). Political liberty requires some structure of religious authority, though not necessarily an established church: "For my part, I doubt whether man can support complete religious independence and entire political liberty at the same time" (p. 444). While Tocqueville is of course not arguing for a theocracy, he maintains that liberal politics must exist alongside a flourishing religious culture. The work of religious institutions in a liberal democracy is not the sort of enforcement function envisaged by Locke—a device for frightening or enticing democrats into keeping their promises: "I have known zealous Christians who constantly forgot themselves to labor more ardently for the happiness of all, and I have heard them claim that they did this only for the sake of rewards in the next world. But I cannot get it out of

---

[18] Contemporary analyses of the place of legal practices and languages in contemporary politics carry Tocqueville's inquiry forward into the present. The traditional language of the common law is under strong attack on two fronts: from the law-and-economics approach, which argues that common law argumentation is too crude and imprecise and should be replaced with a theoretical model of behavior treating public wealth maximization or economic efficiency as the single rationalizing good; and from the critical legal studies movement, which reads traditional discourse as a crude cover for oppression. The law-and-economics position is usually conservative, though not always. Ackerman's *Reconstructing American Law* is an interesting liberal defense of a more economic jurisprudence in the name of the values of precision and method, tempered by a marginal worry about losing the civilizing effect of legal discourse in a world of economic technocrats.

[19] Tocqueville's discussion of American gender relations and family structure is interesting and controversial, and provides a fruitful starting point for discussions of their contemporary significance in a liberal polity. See Goldstein, "Europe Looks at American Women," and Winthrop, "Tocqueville's American Women."

my head that they were deceiving themselves. I respect them too much to believe them" (p. 529).

The function religion can perform in democracies is much less apparent and much more like the implicit work of the common law vocabulary: it can educate, unobtrusively and without compulsion, those who love comfort and worry about wealth in the habits of even-tempered benevolence and liberality, which are the measure of the best democratic lives. Religion does this by contesting the empire of the spirit of individual independence (p. 449), but not all religions can perform this task in the appropriately democratic and liberal manner. So much at least is clear from the way Tocqueville's teleological account leads to unfavorable evaluative judgments about a wide variety of religions, including Islam (and by implication Judaism), pantheism (or transcendental Unitarianism), and fundamentalist evangelical Protestantism (pp. 445, 451–452, 534–535). Like every other institution, religion in America is discussed from the perspective of the extent to which it can develop of those liberal attitudes and ways of life that actualize the peculiarly democratic virtues and forestall the peculiarly democratic vices.

The issue of the function of religion in the American regime poses a number of difficult questions, and must not be reduced to a simple matter of principle. Tocqueville makes it clear that religion is central to moral education, but also shows how religion can operate against the goals of the regime, and moreover calls attention to the ways in which other relationships—economic, legal, educational, familial—can serve this same function: religion is not the unique moral educator. For liberals like Franklin and Jefferson, the dangers of religious sectarianism outweighed potential gains and led them to seek alternative forms of public moral education. Jefferson, in his sketch of a plan for public education in the *Notes on the State of Virginia* (Query 14), says that schools should avoid teaching children the Bible "at an age when their judgments are not sufficiently matured for religious enquiries." Instead,

> their memories may here be stored with the most useful facts from Grecian, Roman, European and American history. The first elements of morality too may be instilled into their minds; such as, when further developed as their judgments advance in strength, may teach them how to work out their own greatest happiness, by shewing them that it does not depend upon the condition of life in which chance has placed them, but is

always the result of a good conscience, good health, occupation, and freedom in all just pursuits.[20]

But will secular public education be powerful enough to sustain a
commitment to the virtues of liberal democracy, especially when
large issues and difficult sacrifices are in view? It is no accident
that the most persuasive patriotic music expresses providential
themes, from William Billings's great "Chester" ("Let tyrants
shake their iron rods / Let slavery clank her galling chains / We
fear them not, we trust in God / New England's God forever
reigns") to "The Battle Hymn of the Republic" (not to mention
"Solidarity Forever"). Is it possible to act well in such matters—
putting aside for once the legitimate and generally humanizing
concern with comfort and security—without some deep assurance
that one's action has some historical significance? As free-thinking
a man as Jefferson needs religious language to articulate the practical meaning of American slavery: "Indeed I tremble for my country when I reflect that God is just: that his justice cannot sleep
forever."[21] But is it possible to share this language without bringing about the intolerance that destroys liberalism? This looks very
much like the kind of *aporia* that Aristotle's theoretical interventions bring to light while at the same time insisting on the wrong-
headedness of seeking universally valid theoretical solutions.[22]

A similar debate surrounds American higher education, a topic
Tocqueville could safely ignore, since in his America "primary education is within the reach of all; higher education is hardly available to anybody" (p. 55). Higher education, especially in so-called
research universities, is flourishing. These institutions provide a
home for theory of all kinds in the American polity, and represent
the triumph of the view that the function of the university is to
produce and disseminate new knowledge. Max Weber spoke for
this ideal of inquiry as *Wissenschaft* in "Science as a Vocation":

[20] *Selected Writings*, p. 44.
[21] *Notes on the State of Virginia*, Query 17, *Selected Writings*, p. 51. A superb discussion of the problem of American political religion, bringing together Jefferson's
remarks in the *Notes* with Lincoln's Lyceum speech, is presented by Jaffa, *Crisis of
the House Divided*, pp. 236–245.
[22] Thoughtful discussions of the issue of religion and politics at this level are presented by Galston, "Liberalism and Public Morality," and by Werpehowski, "Political Liberalism and Christian Ethics." Bellah et al. use the distinction between
"church" and "sect" to help distinguish among the ways different religious practices support and undermine American civic life. *Habits of the Heart*, chap. 9. The
relationship of classical and American liberalism is provocatively stated by Berns,
"Speculations on Liberal and Illiberal Politics."

"Science today is a 'vocation' organized in special disciplines in the service of self-clarification and knowledge of interrelated fact."[23] But for Weber science, which of course includes the "historical and cultural sciences"—in other words, the humanities, as well as the natural sciences—is not the way to good politics, as it was for Hobbes. The larger project of the specialized Weberian scientists or scholars is that of disenchanting the world; theory cannot help us with the question of how we ought to live, since it deals only with facts and not "values." This is surely not Hobbes's position, but it is equally distant from the Aristotelian conception of the way theorizing can inform practical wisdom.

Outside the large universities, liberal education of the sort that goes on in the descendants of the colonial American colleges is less easy to defend in terms of democratic aspirations.[24] Liberal education in these colleges (and their simulacra within the large universities) has a different and more deeply political end in view: to educate citizens in the habit of reflective responses to complex problems. This is neither to teach facts nor to implant moral dogmas. As Eva Brann says, the point of such education is neither the discovery and dissemination of knowledge nor the identification of a specially gifted elite, nor yet the imposition of a set of special moral "values" or beliefs; rather, "it is an intention—much more dependent for its realization on desire than on talent, and therefore potentially universal—to be thoroughly aware of what one does and says and thinks."[25] This ideal of self-awareness bears a superficial resemblance to the Weberian goal of clarity, but the difference is crucial. For Weber, science allows us to understand as "interrelated facts" the consequences and antecedent conditions of our desires. The aim of liberal education is not so exclusively cognitive; what is sought here is the development of the habit of reflecting about one's desires, of wanting to be able to infuse our desires with critical thought, the desire to live according to what Aristotle calls *prohairesis*.

This goal can be realized in different ways, though it must be done indirectly; the most widely practiced is a program of active reading and response to difficult texts, works that defy reduction

[23] Weber, "Science as a Vocation," p. 152.

[24] A superb discussion of this problem and the ways it can be met is Brann's *Paradoxes*. Brann is especially good at showing that the tension between classical literary education and scientific training is present from the early days of the republic (pp. 79–102). See also Hawkins, "Liberal Education and American Society."

[25] Brann, *Paradoxes*, p. 106.

to simple categories and help develop an ability and a taste for the work of clarifying ambiguous situations. The books that can best serve liberal education are those that demand a clear response where no certainty is possible and so in this way provide practical training for deliberation. This education is primarily literary because words, rather than numbers and other similarly unequivocal signs, are the humanly appropriate access to the world.[26] But this is not to say that liberal education excludes science or theory; only that science is considered here in a different manner from that in which students learn to become masters of the specialized sciences. Not surprisingly, Aristotle was quite aware of this difference, and expresses it as follows at the beginning of *Parts of Animals* (639a):

> In every theory and inquiry, whether humbler or more noble, there seem to be two ways in which the subject can be grasped; one is finely called scientific knowledge, the other is a sort of educated judgment, since the power to judge accurately what is finely said by a speaker and what is not is the way of the educated person. For such we think the wholly educated person to be, and being thoroughly educated means having the power to do this. . . . So clearly in the case of natural history it is necessary to begin with some such concepts (*horoi*) by reference to which one can test the manner of an exposition, apart from knowing whether what is said is true or false.

Aristotle then goes on to discuss the concepts of substance, matter, and cause; a modern counterpart might include the concepts of energy, mass, and theory.[27] But whatever the particulars, liberal education both literary and scientific can at its best develop a resistance to the simplifying responses of those specialized perspectives—whether religious sects or political ideologies or technocratic routines—which tempt us all to hand over our capacity for *phronēsis* and deliberation, to give up the uncertainty of liberal democracy for some plausible despotism powered either by special-

[26] Murdoch puts the primacy of literary studies in practical education as follows: "But the most essential and fundamental aspect of culture is the study of literature, since this is an education in how to picture and understand human situations." *Sovereignty of Good*, p. 34.

[27] For a modern proposal for increasing scientific literacy that accords with Aristotle's sense of what the well-educated person needs, see Arons, "Achieving Wider Scientific Literacy."

ized technocratic professionalism or by a pious yearning for traditional—and thoughtless—community.

In considering religion, or law, or higher education, what matters is not whether a particular school or church or legal approach is the one best way to develop these habits of thoughtful reflection, but that we ask such questions in discussing these practices. Tocqueville's analyses of American institutions all seem to suggest something like the following as a central evaluative criterion: mores and institutions are democratically valuable insofar as they develop habits of mind or dispositions (*hexeis*, in Aristotle's Greek) that incline people toward rule without tyranny and obedience without slavishness. A similar focus informs his discussion of what he calls the doctrine of self-interest properly understood. This doctrine sounds like the Hobbesian-Lockean notion of enlightened self-interest, but unlike these classical liberal theorists Tocqueville considers the doctrine not as a theoretical truth, but as a more or less ennobling myth. The belief that it pays to be generous or beneficent "cannot make a man virtuous, but its discipline shapes a lot of orderly, temperate, moderate, careful, and self-controlled citizens. If it does not lead the will directly to virtue, it establishes habits which unconsciously turn it that way" (p. 527). We must note the way Tocqueville's understanding of the term "virtue" here follows civic humanist usage in applying the term exclusively to public-spiritedness and withholding it from other habitual characteristics such as moderation and orderliness. Nonetheless, his experience of the liberal character rises above the limits of his republican vocabulary and suggests to him that good citizenship can appear in guises other than the mask of the Roman patriot. As with Christianity understood as a system of divine rewards and punishments, self-interest properly understood allows people to misunderstand their own virtuous habits for the sake of sustaining those habits more comfortably:

> It gives them [the Americans] pleasure to point out how an enlightened self-love continually leads them to help one another and disposes them freely to give part of their time and wealth for the good of the state. I think that in this they often do themselves less than justice, for sometimes in the United States, as elsewhere, one sees people carried away by the disinterested, spontaneous impulses natural to man. But the Americans are hardly prepared to admit that they do give way

to emotions of this sort. They prefer to give the credit to their philosophy rather than to themselves. (P. 526)

This analysis reinforces a sense of the profound subtlety and tact that teleological theorizing about liberal democracy requires, since the most important agents of democratic education seem from the theoretical perspective to function in ways different from, and generally and perhaps necessarily concealed by, their official practical justification. Self-interest properly understood is an example of this, as is carrot-and-stick Christianity. But the same is true of a wide variety of other institutions and their justifications: welfare spending is not a mode of economic efficiency; universal suffrage is not a way of electing the best people; jury trials are not a means for reaching the best verdicts. The value of these institutions is not limited to their immediate or direct functions, and they must not be evaluated solely in terms of their success in achieving them. Theorizing serves liberal democracy by making the foundations of political authority accessible to reflection and critique, but it must do so without suggesting for a minute that universal linguistic theory, as it were, can replace the local rules of grammar as a framework for practical speech.

Tocqueville's ambivalence about democratic institutions is nowhere more apparent than in his treatment of what Aristotle would call *philia*. The democratic challenge to arbitrary authority brings with it, in addition to the threat of individualism, a certain strengthening of family ties: "Democracy loosens social ties, but it tightens natural ones. At the same time as it separates citizens, it brings kindred closer together" (p. 589), although in much smaller families than in aristocratic Europe. This development looks threatening to Tocqueville, since the absence of conventional hierarchy and status in a democracy encourages the formation of "small private circles . . . little private societies held together by similar conditions, habits, and mores. . . . Each [American] freely recognizes every other citizen as equal, but he only accepts a very small number as his friends or guests" (p. 604). This poses the important democratic danger that citizens will care too little about the nation to resist the emergence of tyranny. Yet at the same time the phenomenon Tocqueville notices calls to mind the possibility that friendships based on what Aristotle would call virtue or character might help take the place of the inherited and customary relationships that organized society under the old regime. Tocqueville's republican (and aristocratic) tendency to associate virtue

259

only with activities that are distinctly public and his loathing for what he sees as the pettiness of bourgeois life cause him seriously to underestimate the extent to which the activities of the domestic sphere could expand into politics in strongly liberalizing ways, particularly in the case of the abolition and women's movements, the latter just beginning in the 1840s.[28]

Appreciation of Tocqueville's insight into the problems and possibilities of American politics must be accompanied by a recognition of the way our present political order differs from the one he saw. We are an immensely larger and more diverse polity; the population of Tocqueville's America was closer to that of the Greek *poleis* than to our own. It can no longer be said that we have no great wars to fear (pp. 169–170), and there is no longer a land beyond the frontier to be developed. Economic development has also changed the prospects of democracy in ways that are impossible to characterize simply: the growth and decline of manufactures, the rise of large firms and of organized labor, the increased mobility of capital across national borders, and the development of a powerful national state all give rise to questions that Tocqueville could not consider. Given these changes, mechanical application of Tocquevillian conclusions about institutional reform are always out of place. But what remains is the fact that we are still a democratic people, individuals who must or at any rate do work to secure physical comfort and a place in the world, and that the moral poles that define our activity are those that measure the space between the virtues of liberality and deliberative competence and the vices of mindless individualism and majority (whether national or local) tyranny. Tocqueville's articulation of the problems and possibilities of democratic life can inform our political judgments by emphasizing the need to attend to the sources of indirect and unobtrusive education in deliberation and liberality in order to achieve a genuinely liberal democracy.

Adopting this theoretical approach to liberal democracy establishes an alternative to "crisis" theories which lead us to understand ourselves in the misleading light of a contrast between some Nietzschean or Marxian nightmare of a radically privatized present and a dream of a republican community of virtuous citizens. Such a contrast is as dangerous as it is distorting, because the virtues of

[28] For a thorough discussion of the extent to which Tocqueville shared the nineteenth-century prejudice against the bourgeoisie, see Boesche, *Strange Liberalism of Alexis de Tocqueville*, especially chap. 4. For a discussion of European confusion concerning American women, see Goldstein, "Europe Looks at American Women."

public-spirited citizens are not the appropriate virtues for liberal democracy; as George Kateb says in a similar context, "We have left the world of constitutional democracy behind when we affirm community."[29] In addition to blocking theoretical concern with liberal virtues and vices, the "crisis" formulation concentrates attention on political movements that are sporadic, episodic, and generally directed against the national government rather than those which aim at asserting the rights of those previously excluded from full citizenship. As a result, our very idea of politics takes on the color and characteristics of war and thus tends to subvert Tocqueville's hopes for the salutary operation of the myth of self-interest properly understood. Following Tocqueville's lead, we might attend more carefully to the relationships among different kinds of social interaction,[30] and to the way the character of the language in which political proposals are stated and argued affects the formation of democratic preferences toward and away from liberal disposition. For Tocqueville, the jurist's habits of mind were crucial to sustaining liberty; what about the those of economist or the psychoanalyst?[31] Charles Anderson's account of the logic of liberal theorizing presents clearly the Tocqueville-Aristotle conception of the possible contributions of theory to practical reason: "What is required is an appreciation both of the distinctiveness of the particular community of practice, its objectives, traditions, and normative structure, and a critical sense for the ways in which lib-

[29] Kateb, "On the 'Legitimation Crisis,' " p. 719. For a strong defense of American constitutionalism against the communitarian critique, see Hirsch, "Threnody of Liberalism."

[30] It is especially hard to counter the view that the economic system is self-contained and that profitability is the most important criterion governing economic policy choices. There are a number of interesting arguments against the autonomy of economic theorizing, from a variety of points on the political spectrum—this is not a left vs. right issue. For three good discussions, see Nisbet, *Quest for Community*, especially pp. 236–241, Lindblom, *Politics and Markets*, and Bowles and Gintis, *Democracy and Capitalism*.

[31] An extended discussion of the problem of the contemporary grammar of political talk is found in Bellah et al., *Habits of the Heart*, where it is argued that "between them, the manager and the therapist largely define the outlines of twentieth-century American culture" (p. 47). The authors argue that the decay of biblical and traditional republican language, and the corresponding growth of economic and psychoanalytic ways of thinking and speaking, are political dangers of the greatest significance. Something like this point, though without attachment to communitarian values, is also made by Berns: "Where can liberal rationalism turn to find allies of sufficient strength to ensure its survival? The best allies for liberal rationalism, I suggest, are traditional patriotism and the revealed religions." "Speculations on Liberal and Illiberal Politics," p. 241 n. 13. In both cases, it seems to me that too little is said about the importance of traditional legal culture and institutions, and about the possible conflicts of religion and liberal virtues.

eral precepts and ideals may suggest improvements in its performance, improvements that serve to bring the particular enterprise into greater conformity with the underlying ideals of the liberal regime."[32] One need only add to this account that theorizing liberal democracy also requires a consideration of the presuppositions about the human good underlying the liberal regime itself, as well as of the presuppositions of communities of practice (economic, religious, educational), within that regime. But it is precisely here—in being reasonably suspicious of the ideals and precepts of unexamined authorities—that the liberal project and the Aristotelian and Tocquevillian tradition of evaluative explanation have their strongest point of agreement.

Aristotle and Modern Liberalism

Aristotelian theory is often cited as an alternative to Enlightenment science, especially by those whose attack on the Enlightenment is the ground for a critique of liberalism. Aristotle is in a way at odds with Enlightenment thought; the exclusion of teleology from science, the preeminence of precision and quantifiability as scientific norms, and the belief that applied theory can replace practical wisdom are at odds with Aristotle's way of theorizing. But I think the agreement between Aristotle and the Enlightenment—or modern science—is much deeper than any disagreement; this is the agreement that the function of science is to make plain the nature of the things that are, an agreement that presupposes in turn the belief that there is a nature (or natures) to be made plain. Similarly, Aristotle's disagreements with modern liberalism are real enough. But they are less important than the agreement that devotion to the political life must be considered not as the consummately humanizing passion but as the basis for an interaction that is both liberating and dangerous, and that political authority is justified only insofar as it serves the interests of citizens; that the political life is not an end in itself, and that an aptitude for tactful theorizing about particular customs and forms of discourse, rather than principled commitment, is our deepest political need. That both modern science and modern liberal politics rejected an Aristotelianism that had become synonymous with a very un-Aristotelian reverence for authority is not a reason for concluding that reading Aristotle now is anachronistic. My goal

---

[32] Charles W. Anderson, "Pragmatic Liberalism," p. 208.

here has been to show that such a reading of Aristotle, and of Plato, is one of the best ways we have of improving the quality of theoretical discourse about contemporary political life.

Philosophy for Plato and Aristotle is not system-building, nor a matter of developing tricky proofs to support clear and precise conclusions. What makes these writers philosophers is a commitment to the life of inquiry or reason and an opposition to dogmatic or reductive systems of explanation. This is not to say that they are relativists or contextualists: the commitment to a life of *logos* must presuppose objectivity, a sense of a world that is there to be explained and sometimes evaluated, preserved, or changed. The motive for inquiring into the character of this world—the deep human need such theorizing tries to satisfy—is not the drive for precise and unquestionable foundations, but rather a sense of the inadequacy of our received opinions and of our interest in the power of self-criticism. But there are many ways of explaining the world that can serve these ends; often this can be done by a metaphor better than by syllogistic deduction, and it is on the quality of his metaphors that Aristotle's stature as a philosopher, like Plato's, rests: the self-doctoring doctor, the Athens-Thebes road, the regrouping army, the eye-as-animal, the blind wrestler, the unresponsive plant. Aristotle himself distinguishes good from bad theorizing not in terms of an epistemological or logical or even metaphysical criterion, but in terms of a particular way of life:

> sophistic and dialectic are concerned with the same genus [beings] as philosophy, but philosophy and dialectic differ, on the one hand, in the manner of their potential (*tōi tropōi tēs dunameōs*), but philosophy and sophistic on the other hand differ in terms of the way of life deliberately chosen (*tou biou tēi prohairesei*); and dialectic is tentative concerning the things philosophy knows, but sophistic gives the appearance of knowing although it does not know. (*Metaphysics* Gamma, 1004b23–26)

Dialectic investigates beings through the opinions of others and is tentative, philosophy is more direct and certain—but they are the same way of life, organized around the same goal, that of making plain the structure of things. Good theory requires a taste both for listening to others and for independent inquiry; good theory about human actions requires in addition a clear sense of the subordinate character of political theory as a mode of thought that can greatly improve the quality of particular political choices but can never supply the precise and universal solutions immature political actors crave.

This Aristotelian understanding of the function of political philosophy is not only compatible with the contemporary liberal regime; it is in fact needed to sharpen our sense of what liberalism is for, and the ways of life this regime aims at supporting. In *Federalist* 51, Madison expressed a central liberal dogma in saying that "if men were angels no government would be necessary." But what conclusions about the positive function of political authority can be drawn from this maxim? Not, I would argue, the claim that humans are despicable little creatures—Rousseau's bourgeois nullities or Machiavelli's *uomini tristi* or Nietzsche's *letzten Menschen*—who can be saved only by radical transformation into citizens or overmen or species-beings. Nor, on the other hand, does our lack of perfection require a government limited to resolving conflicts among humans, either for the sake of maximizing public wealth or promoting toleration (even perhaps celebration, in the manner of chapter 3 of Mill's *On Liberty*) of difference and individuality as such. Liberalism cannot be collapsed into either the republican or the libertarian (whether capitalist or romantic) extreme. Instead, on the conception I have argued for here, liberal political authority aims at actively promoting different ways of life and at encouraging and regulating, though not resolving, conflicts among them— at channeling conflict and disagreement into institutionalized debate. The central truth of liberalism is that human lives are always made in an intermediate space, somewhere between beatitude and hellishness, between knowledge and ignorance, and that this condition requires the establishment of places where we can safely and vigorously examine our lives together, not in some imaginary time or space but as we live them. Liberal politics establishes such opportunities not for the sake of reaching some ultimate and perfect truth (which does not exist concerning the human things), nor for the sake of achieving any separate communal goal or public interest. The deepest justification for genuinely liberal toleration is the belief that encouraging those conflicts which inspire deliberation is the best way for each distinct human individual to understand his or her needs and capacities, the better to live a life that is deliberately chosen rather than arbitrarily or willfully determined. To clarify this kind of liberalism, a sympathetic consideration of the practical philosophy of Plato and Aristotle seems—at the present stage of our political self-awareness—a more necessary enterprise than further elaboration of the programs of Locke or Mill, Marx or Nietzsche.

REFERENCES

References to Aristotle and Plato are to the page and line numbers in the Oxford Classical Text editions.

Ackerman, Bruce A. *Reconstructing American Law.* Cambridge, Mass.: Harvard University Press, 1984.

Ambler, Wayne. "Aristotle on Acquisition." *Canadian Journal of Political Science* 17 (1984): 487–502.

———. "Aristotle on the City." *Review of Politics* 47 (1985): 163–185.

———. "Aristotle on Nature and Politics: The Case of Slavery." *Political Theory* 15 (1987): 390–410.

Anderson, Charles W. "Pragmatic Liberalism: Uniting Theory and Practice." In *Liberals on Liberalism*, ed. Alfonso J. Damico, 201–219. Totowa, N.J.: Rowman & Littlefield, 1986.

Anderson, Warren D. *Ethos and Education in Greek Music.* Cambridge, Mass.: Harvard University Press, 1966.

Anscombe, G.E.M. "Modern Moral Philosophy." In *The Collected Philosophical Papers of G.E.M. Anscombe*, vol. 3, 26–42. Minneapolis: University of Minnesota Press, 1981.

Appleby, Joyce. "What Is Still American in the Political Philosophy of Thomas Jefferson?" *William and Mary Quarterly*, 3d ser., no. 39 (1982): 287–309.

———. *Capitalism and a New Social Order: The Republican Vision of the 1790s.* New York: New York University Press, 1984.

Archie, Joseph Patrick. "Callicles' Redoubtable Critique of the Polus Argument in Plato's 'Gorgias.'" *Hermes* 112 (1984): 167–176.

Arendt, Hannah. *The Human Condition.* Chicago: University of Chicago Press, 1958.

———. *On Revolution.* New York: Viking Press, 1963.

———. "The Crisis in Culture: Its Social and Its Political Significance." In *Between Past and Future*, 197–226. New York: Penguin Books, 1968.

———. "On Humanity in Dark Times: Thoughts about Lessing." In *Men in Dark Times*, 3–31. New York: Harcourt, Brace & World, 1968.

Arendt, Hannah. "Tradition and the Modern Age." In *Between Past and Future*, 17–40.

———. "What Is Authority?" In *Between Past and Future*, 91–142.

———. "What Is Freedom?" In *Between Past and Future*, 143–171.

Arnhart, Larry. *Aristotle on Practical Reasoning*. DeKalb, Ill.: Northern Illinois University Press, 1981.

Arons, A. B. "Achieving Wider Scientific Literacy." *Daedalus* 112 (1983): 91–122.

Arthur, Marilyn B. "Review Essay: Classics." *Signs* 2 (1976): 382–403.

Austen, Jane. *Mansfield Park*. In *The Complete Novels of Jane Austen*. [1814.] New York: Random House, n.d.

Austin, M. M., and P. Vidal-Naquet. *Economic and Social History of Ancient Greece: An Introduction*. Berkeley and Los Angeles: University of California Press, 1980.

Balme, D. W. "Aristotle's Biology Was Not Essentialist." *Archiv für Geschichte der Philosophie* 62 (1980): 1–12.

Barber, Sotirios A. *On What the Constitution Means*. Baltimore: Johns Hopkins University Press, 1984.

Barker, Ernest, trans. *The Politics of Aristotle*. London: Oxford University Press, 1958.

Barnes, Jonathan. "Aristotle and the Methods of Ethics." *Revue Internationale de Philosophie* 34 (1980): 490–511.

Beiner, Ronald. *Political Judgment*. Chicago: University of Chicago Press, 1983.

Bellah, Robert N. *The Broken Covenant: American Civil Religion in Time of Trial*. New York: Seabury Press, 1975.

———. "The Ethical Aims of Social Inquiry." In *Social Science as Moral Inquiry*, ed. Norma Haan, Robert N. Bellah, Paul Rabinow, and William M. Sullivan, 360–381. New York: Columbia University Press, 1983.

Bellah, Robert N., Richard Marsden, William M. Sullivan, Ann Swidler, and Steven M. Tipton. *Habits of the Heart: Individualism and Commitment in American Life*. Berkeley and Los Angeles: University of California Press, 1985.

Benardete, Seth. *The Being of the Beautiful*. 3 vols. Chicago: University of Chicago Press, 1984.

Berger, Harry, Jr. "Levels of Discourse in Plato's Dialogues." In *Literature and the Question of Philosophy*, ed. Anthony J. Cascardi, 77–100. Baltimore: Johns Hopkins University Press, 1987.

Berns, Laurence. "Speculations on Liberal and Illiberal Politics." *The Review of Politics* 40 (1978): 231–254.

———. "Spiritedness in Ethics and Politics: A Study in Aristotelian Psychology." *Interpretation* 12 (1984): 334–348.

Bernstein, Richard J. *Philosophical Profiles*. Philadelphia: University of Pennsylvania Press, 1986.

Bluhm, William T. "Liberalism as the Aggregation of Individual Preferences: Problems of Coherence and Rationality in Social Choice." In *The Crisis of Liberal Democracy: A Straussian Perspective*, ed. Kenneth L. Deutsch and Walter Soffer, 269–296. Albany: State University of New York Press, 1987.

Boesche, Roger. *The Strange Liberalism of Alexis de Tocqueville*. Ithaca: Cornell University Press, 1987.

Boorse, Christopher. "Wright on Functions." *Philosophical Review* 85 (1976): 70–86.

———. "Health as a Theoretical Concept." *Philosophy of Science* 44 (1977): 542–573.

Bowles, Samuel, and Herbert Gintis. *Democracy and Capitalism: Property, Community, and the Contradictions of Modern Social Thought*. New York: Basic Books, 1986.

Brann, Eva T. H. *Paradoxes of Education in a Republic*. Chicago: University of Chicago Press, 1979.

Broughton, John M. "Women's Rationality and Men's Virtues: A Critique of Gender Dualism in Gilligan's Theory of Moral Development." *Social Research* 50 (1983): 597–642.

Burnet, John, ed. *The Ethics of Aristotle*. London: Methuen & Company, 1900.

Carter, L. B. *The Quiet Athenian*. Oxford: Clarendon Press, 1986.

Caton, Hiram. "Domesticating Nature: Thoughts on the Ethology of Modern Politics." In *Sociobiology and Human Politics*, ed. Elliot White, 99–133. Lexington, Mass.: D. C. Heath & Company, 1981.

Charles, David. *Aristotle's Philosophy of Action*. Ithaca: Cornell University Press, 1984.

Clark, Stephen R. L. *Aristotle's Man*. Oxford: Clarendon Press, 1975.

———. "Aristotle's Woman." *History of Political Thought* 3 (1982): 177–191.

———. *The Nature of the Beast*. London: Oxford University Press, 1982.

Cohen, Bernard. *The Birth of a New Physics*. New York: W. W. Norton & Company, 1985.

Cooper, John M. *Reason and the Human Good in Aristotle*. Cambridge, Mass.: Harvard University Press, 1975.

———. "Aristotle on Friendship." In *Essays on Aristotle's Ethics*, ed. Amélie Oksenberg Rorty, 301–340. Berkeley and Los Angeles: University of California Press, 1980.

Cropsey, Joseph. "Hobbes and the Transition to Modernity." In *Political Philosophy*, 291–314.

———. "The Invisible Hand: Moral and Political Considerations." In *Political Philosophy*, 76–89.

———. "Justice and Friendship in the *Nicomachean Ethics*." In *Political Philosophy*, 252–273.

———. *Political Philosophy and the Issues of Politics*. Chicago: University of Chicago Press, 1977.

Delbrück, Max. "How Aristotle Discovered DNA." In *Physics and Our World*, ed. Kerson Huang, 123–130. New York: American Institute of Physics, 1976.

Descartes, René. *Discours de la Méthode*. Paris: Garnier, 1966.

Diamond, Cora. "Losing Your Concepts." *Ethics* 98 (1988): 255–277.

Diels, Hermann, and W. Kranz, eds. *Die Fragmente der Vorsokratiker*. 6th ed. Berlin: Weidmann, 1961.

Dietz, Mary. "Citizenship with a Feminist Face: The Problem with Maternal Thinking." *Political Theory* 13 (1985): 19–37.

Diggins, John P. *The Lost Soul of American Politics*. Chicago: University of Chicago Press, 1986.

Dostal, Robert J. "The World Never Lost: The Hermeneutics of Trust." *Philosophy and Phenomenological Research* 47 (1987): 413–434.

Douglass, Frederick. "Oration in Memory of Abraham Lincoln." April 14, 1876. In *The Political Thought of American Statesmen*, ed. Morton J. Frisch and Richard G. Stevens, 242–251. Itasca, Ill.: F. E. Peacock Publishers, 1973.

———. "The Nation's Problem." April 16, 1889. In *Negro Social and Political Thought, 1850–1920*, ed. Howard Brotz, 311–328. New York: Basic Books, 1966.

Dworkin, Ronald. *Taking Rights Seriously*. Cambridge, Mass.: Harvard University Press, 1978.

———. *Law's Empire*. Cambridge, Mass.: Harvard University Press, Belknap Press, 1986.

Eldredge, Niles. *Time Frames: The Rethinking of Darwinian Evolution and the Theory of Punctuated Equilibrium*. New York: Simon & Schuster, 1985.

Eliot, T. S. "Tradition and the Individual Talent." In *T. S. Eliot: Selected Essays*, 3–11. New York: Harcourt, Brace & Company, 1950.

Elkin, Stephen L. *City and Regime in the American Republic*. Chicago: University of Chicago Press, 1987.

Else, Gerald F. *Aristotle's Poetics: The Argument*. Cambridge, Mass.: Harvard University Press, 1957.

Elshtain, Jean Bethke. *Public Man, Private Woman*. Princeton: Princeton University Press, 1981.

Euben, J. Peter. "Justice and the *Oresteia*." *American Political Science Review* 72 (1982): 22–33.

——, ed. *Greek Tragedy and Political Theory*. Berkeley and Los Angeles: University of California Press, 1986.

Federal Farmer. "Observations Leading to a Fair Examination of the System of Government Proposed by the Late Convention." In *The Anti-Federalist*. An abridgment by Murray Dry of *The Complete Anti-Federalist*, ed. Herbert J. Storing, 23–101. Chicago: University of Chicago Press, 1985.

Finley, M. I. *The Ancient Economy*. Berkeley and Los Angeles: University of California Press, 1973.

Flacks, Richard. "Moral Commitment, Privatism, and Activism." In *Social Science as Moral Inquiry*, ed. Norma Haan, Robert N. Bellah, Paul Rabinow, and William M. Sullivan, 343–359. New York: Columbia University Press, 1983.

Flanagan, Owen J., Jr. "Virtue, Sex, and Gender: Some Philosophical Reflections on the Moral Psychology Debate." *Ethics* 92 (1982): 499–512, and 529–532.

Flanagan, Owen J., Jr., and Jonathan E. Adler. "Impartiality and Particularity." *Social Research* 50 (1983): 576–596.

Flanagan, Owen J., Jr., and Kathryn Jackson. "Justice, Care, and Gender: The Kohlberg-Gilligan Debate Revisited." *Ethics* 97 (1987): 622–637.

Flaumenhaft, Mera J. "The Undercover Hero: Odysseus from Dark to Daylight." *Interpretation* 10 (1982): 9–41.

Flemming, Arthur. "Reviving the Virtues." *Ethics* 80 (1980): 587–595.

Forster, E. M. *Howards End*. [1921.] New York: Random House, n.d.

Frankena, William K. "MacIntyre and Modern Morality." *Ethics* 93 (1983): 579–587.

Franklin, Benjamin. *Autobiography and Other Writings*. New York: Random House, 1944.

Furbank, P. N. *Unholy Pleasure; or, The Idea of Social Class*. Oxford: Oxford University Press, 1985.

Gadamer, Hans-Georg. *Truth and Method*. New York: Continuum Publishing Corp. 1975.

———. "On the Scope and Method of Hermeneutical Reflection." Trans. G. B. Hess and R. E. Palmer. In *Philosophical Hermeneutics*, 18–43.

———. *Philosophical Hermeneutics*. Trans. and ed. David E. Linge. Berkeley and Los Angeles: University of California Press, 1976.

———. "The Problem of Historical Consciousness." In *Interpretive Social Science: A Reader*, ed. Paul Rabinow and William M. Sullivan, 103–162. Berkeley and Los Angeles: University of California Press, 1979.

———. *The Idea of the Good in Platonic-Aristotelian Philosophy*. Trans. P. Christopher Smith. New Haven: Yale University Press, 1986.

Galston, William. "Defending Liberalism." *American Political Science Review* 76 (1982): 621–629.

———. "Liberalism and Public Morality." In *Liberals on Liberalism*, ed. Alfonso J. Damico, 129–147. Totowa, N.J.: Rowman & Littlefield, 1986.

Geertz, Clifford. *The Interpretation of Cultures*. New York: Basic Books, 1973.

———. "Deep Play: Notes on the Balinese Cockfight." In *Interpretive Social Science: A Reader*, ed. Paul Rabinow and William M. Sullivan, 181–224. Berkeley and Los Angeles: University of California Press, 1979.

———. "From the Native's Point of View: On the Nature of Anthropological Understanding." In *Interpretive Social Science: A Reader*, 225–242.

———. *Local Knowledge*. New York: Basic Books, 1983.

———. "Anti Anti-Relativism." *American Anthropologist* 86 (1984): 263–278.

Gellner, Ernest. *Legitimation of Belief*. London: Cambridge University Press, 1974.

Gilligan, Carol. *In a Different Voice: Psychological Theory and Women's Development*. Cambridge, Mass.: Harvard University Press, 1982.

Goerner, E. A. "On Thomistic Natural Law: The Bad Man's View of Thomistic Natural Right." *Political Theory* 7 (1979): 101–122.

———— "Thomistic Natural Right: The Good Man's View of Thomistic Natural Law." *Political Theory* 11 (1983): 393–418.

Goldstein, Leslie Friedman. "Europe Looks at American Women, 1820–1840." *Social Research* 354 (1987): 519–542.

Gotthelf, Allan. "Aristotle's Conception of Final Causality." *Review of Metaphysics* 30 (1976): 226–254.

————. Review of *Aristotle's De Motu Animalium* by Martha Nussbaum. *Journal of Philosophy* 77 (1980): 365–378.

Gould, Stephen Jay. *The Panda's Thumb.* New York: W. W. Norton & Company, 1980.

Granger, Herbert. "The Scala Naturae and the Continuity of Kinds." *Phronesis* 30 (1985): 181–200.

Grimshaw, Jean. *Philosophy and Feminist Thinking.* Minneapolis: University of Minnesota Press, 1986.

Gutmann, Amy. *Democratic Education.* Princeton: Princeton University Press, 1987.

Haan, Norma. "Hypothetical and Actual Moral Reasoning in a Situation of Civil Disobedience." *Journal of Personality and Social Psychology* 32 (1975): 255–270.

————. "Two Moralities in Action Contexts: Relationships to Thought, Ego Regulation, and Development." *Journal of Personality and Social Psychology* 36 (1978): 286–305.

Habermas, Jürgen. *Knowledge and Human Interests.* Trans. Jeremy J. Shapiro. Boston: Beacon Press, 1971.

————. "Hannah Arendt's Communications Concept of Power." *Social Research* 44 (1977): 3–24.

————. *Communication and the Evolution of Society.* Trans. Thomas McCarthy. Boston: Beacon Press, 1979.

————. "Moral Development and Ego Identity." In *Communication and the Evolution of Society,* 69–94.

Hamilton, Alexander, James Madison, and John Jay. *The Federalist Papers.* [1788.] New York: New American Library, 1961.

Hart, H.L.A. "Positivism and the Separation of Law and Morals." In *The Philosophy of Law,* ed. Ronald Dworkin, 17–37. London: Oxford University Press, 1977.

Hartz, Louis B. *The Liberal Tradition in America.* New York: Harcourt, Brace & World, 1955.

Hatch, Elvin. *Culture and Morality: The Relativity of Values in Anthropology.* New York: Columbia University Press, 1983.

Hawkins, Hugh. "Liberal Education and American Society: A History of Creative Tension." *Change* 15 (October 1983): 34–37.

Hegel, G.W.F. *Hegel's Philosophy of Right*. [1821.] Trans. T. M. Knox. Oxford: Oxford University Press, 1967.

———. *The Phenomenology of Mind*. Trans. J. B. Baillie. New York: Harper & Row, 1967.

Hirsch, H. N. "The Threnody of Liberalism: Constitutional Liberty and the Renewal of Community." *Political Theory* 14 (1986): 423–449.

Hirschman, Albert O. *The Passions and the Interests: Political Arguments for Capitalism before Its Triumph*. Princeton: Princeton University Press, 1977.

Hobbes, Thomas. *Leviathan; or, The Matter, Forme, and Power of a Commonwealth Ecclesiasticall and Civil*. [1651.] Ed. Michael Oakeshott. Oxford: Basil Blackwell, n.d.

Hochschild, Jennifer L. *The New American Dilemma: Liberal Democracy and School Desegregation*. New Haven: Yale University Press, 1984.

Hume, David. *A Treatise of Human Nature*. [1739.] Ed. L. A. Selby-Bigge. Oxford: Clarendon Press, 1888.

———. *An Enquiry concerning Human Understanding*. [1748.] Ed. Eric Steinberg. Indianapolis: Hackett Publishing Company, 1977.

Ignatieff, Michael. *The Needs of Strangers*. New York: Viking Penguin, 1985.

Irwin, Terence, trans. *Aristotle: Nicomachean Ethics*. Indianapolis: Hackett Publishing Company, 1985.

Jaeger, Werner. "Aristotle's Use of Medicine as Model of Method in His Ethics." *Journal of Hellenic Studies* 77 (1957): 54–61.

Jaffa, Harry V. *Thomism and Aristotelianism*. Chicago: University of Chicago Press, 1952.

———. *Crisis of the House Divided*. Garden City, N.Y.: Doubleday & Company, 1959.

Jefferson, Thomas. *Thomas Jefferson: Selected Writings*. Ed. Harvey C. Mansfield, Jr. Arlington Heights, Ill.: AHM Publishing Corp., 1979.

Jonas, Hans. "The Philosophical Aspects of Darwinism." In *The Phenomenon of Life: Toward a Philosophical Biology*, 38–63. New York: Dell, 1966.

Jowett, Benjamin, and Thomas Twining, trans. *Aristotle's Politics and Poetics*. New York: Viking Press, 1957.

Joyce, James. *Letters of James Joyce*. 2 vols., ed. Richard Ellmann. London: Faber and Faber, 1966.

Kahn, Charles H. *The Art and Thought of Heraclitus*. Cambridge: Cambridge University Press, 1979.

Kateb, George. "On the 'Legitimation Crisis.' " *Social Research* 46 (1979): 695–727.

———. "The Moral Distinctiveness of Representative Democracy." *Ethics* 91 (1981): 357–374.

———. "Looking for Mr. Good Life." *American Scholar* 51 (1982): 432–436.

———. "Democratic Individuality and the Claims of Politics." *Political Theory* 12 (1984): 331–360.

———. *Hannah Arendt: Politics, Conscience, Evil*. Totowa, N.J.: Rowman & Allanheld, 1984.

Keller, Evelyn Fox. *Reflections on Gender and Science*. New Haven: Yale University Press, 1985.

Kennington, Richard. "Strauss's *Natural Right and History*." *Review of Metaphysics* 35 (1981): 57–86.

Klein, Jacob. *A Commentary on Plato's Meno*. Chapel Hill: University of North Carolina Press, 1965.

Kohlberg, Lawrence. "From Is to Ought: How to Commit the Naturalistic Fallacy and Get Away With It." In *Cognitive Development and Epistemology*, ed. Theodore Mischel, 151–235. New York: Academic Press, 1971.

———. "The Claim to Moral Adequacy of a Highest Stage of Moral Judgment." *Journal of Philosophy* 70 (1973): 630–646.

———. "A Reply to Owen Flanagan and Some Comments on the Puka-Goodpaster Exchange." *Ethics* 92 (1982): 513–528.

Kosman, L. A. "Understanding, Explanation, and Insight in Aristotle's *Posterior Analytics*." In *Exegesis and Argument: Studies in Greek Philosophy Presented to Gregory Vlastos*, ed. E. N. Lee, A.P.D. Mourelatos, and R. M. Rorty. *Phronesis*, supp. vol. 1 (1973): 374–392.

Kuhn, Thomas S. *The Structure of Scientific Revolutions*. 2d ed. Chicago: University of Chicago Press, 1970.

Lawrence, D. H. *Studies in Classic American Literature*. [1923.] Garden City, N.Y.: Doubleday & Company, 1951.

Lawrence, George, trans. *Tocqueville's Democracy in America*. New York: Doubleday & Company, 1969.

Lennox, James G. "Aristotle on Genera, Species, and 'the More and the Less.' " *Journal of the History of Biology* 13 (1980): 321–344.

———. "Aristotle and the Functions of Reproduction." Unpublished essay.

Lerner, Ralph. "Commerce and Character: The Anglo-American as New-Model Man." *William and Mary Quarterly*, 3d ser., 36 (1979): 3–26.

———. *The Thinking Revolutionary*. Ithaca: Cornell University Press, 1987.

Levenson, Michael. "Liberals in Love." *New Republic*, vol. 198, no. 23 (June 6, 1988): 40–44.

Lincoln, Abraham. "Speech in Springfield, Illinois." June 26, 1857. In *Free Government in the Making*, 3d ed., ed. Alpheus Thomas Mason, 533–537. New York: Oxford University Press, 1965.

———. "Second Inaugural Address." In *American Political Thought*, rev. ed., ed. Kenneth M. Dolbeare, 310–311. Chatham, N.J.: Chatham House Publishers, 1984.

Lindblom, Charles E. *Politics and Markets*. New York: Basic Books, 1977.

Lloyd, G.E.R. *Aristotle: The Growth and Structure of His Thought*. London: Cambridge University Press, 1968.

———. "The Role of Medical and Biological Analogies in Aristotle's Ethics." *Phronesis* 13 (1968): 68–83.

———. *Science, Folklore, and Ideology*. London: Cambridge University Press, 1983.

Locke, John. *A Letter concerning Toleration*. [1689.] Indianapolis: Bobbs-Merrill, 1955.

Lord, Carnes. "Politics and Philosophy in Aristotle's *Politics*." *Hermes* 106 (1978): 336–357.

———. *Education and Culture in the Political Thought of Aristotle*: Ithaca: Cornell University Press, 1982.

———, trans. *Aristotle, The Politics*. Chicago: University of Chicago Press, 1984.

Lucas, D. W. *Aristotle, Poetics: Introduction, Commentary, and Appendixes*. Oxford: Clarendon Press, 1968.

McDowell, John. "Virtue and Reason." *Monist* 62 (1979): 331–350.

MacIntyre, Alasdair. *After Virtue: A Study in Moral Theory*. Notre Dame: Notre Dame University Press, 1981.

———. *Whose Justice? Which Rationality?* Notre Dame: Notre Dame University Press, 1988.

McPherson, Michael S. "Want Formation, Morality, and Some Interpretive Aspects of Economic Inquiry." In *Social Science as Moral Inquiry*, ed. Norma Haan, Robert N. Bellah, Paul Rabinow, and William M. Sullivan, 96–124. New York: Columbia University Press, 1983.

McShea, Robert J. "Human Nature Theory and Political Philosophy." *American Journal of Political Science* 22 (1978): 656–679.

Mahowald, Mary Briody, ed. *Philosophy of Woman*. 2d ed. Indianapolis: Hackett Publishing Company, 1983.

Mansfield, Harvey C., Jr. *The Spirit of Liberalism*. Cambridge, Mass.: Harvard University Press, 1978.

Mara, Gerald. "Liberal Politics and Moral Excellence in Spinoza's Political Philosophy." *Journal of the History of Philosophy* 20 (1982): 129–150.

———. "The Role of Philosophy in Aristotle's Political Science." *Polity* 19 (1987): 375–401.

Marini, Stephen A. *Radical Sects of Revolutionary New England*. Cambridge, Mass.: Harvard University Press, 1982.

Marx, Karl. *The Marx-Engels Reader*. 2d ed., ed. Robert Tucker. New York: W. W. Norton & Company, 1978.

Mason, Alpheus Thomas, ed. *Free Government in the Making*. 3d ed. New York: Oxford University Press, 1965.

Masters, Roger D. "Politics as a Biological Phenomenon." *Social Science Information* 14 (1975): 7–63.

———. "The Value—and Limits—of Sociobiology: Toward a Revival of Natural Right." In *Sociobiology and Human Politics*, ed. Elliot White, 135–165. Lexington, Mass.: Lexington Books, 1981.

———. "The Biological Nature of the State." *World Politics* 35 (1983): 161–193.

Mayr, Ernst. *The Growth of Biological Thought: Diversity, Evolution, and Inheritance*. Cambridge, Mass.: Harvard University Press, Belknap Press, 1982.

Midgley, Mary. *Beast and Man: The Roots of Human Nature*. Ithaca: Cornell University Press, 1978.

———. "The Absence of a Gap between Facts and Values." *Proceedings of the Aristotelian Society*, supp. vol. 54 (1980): 207–223.

Mill, John Stuart. *Utilitarianism*. Ed. George Sher. Indianapolis: Hackett Publishing Company, 1979.

Mulhern, J. J. "Mia Monon Pantachou kata Physin hē Aretē." *Phronesis* 17 (1972): 260–268.

Murdoch, Iris. *The Sovereignty of Good*. New York: Schocken Books, 1971.

Newman, W. L. *The Politics of Aristotle*. 4 vols. Oxford: Clarendon Press, 1887.

Nichols, Mary P. "The Good Life, Slavery, and Acquisition: Aristotle's Introduction to Politics." *Interpretation* 11 (1983): 171–183.

———. "Women in Western Political Thought." *Political Science Reviewer* 13 (1983): 241–260.

Nietzsche, Friedrich. *Beyond Good and Evil*. Trans. Walter Kaufmann. New York: Random House, 1966.

———. *Thus Spoke Zarathustra*. Trans. Walter Kaufmann. New York: Viking, 1966.

Nisbet, Robert A. *The Quest for Community*. London: Oxford University Press, 1969.

Nussbaum, Martha Craven. *Aristotle's De Motu Animalium: Text with Translation, Commentary, and Interpretive Essays*. Princeton: Princeton University Press, 1978.

———. "Shame, Separateness, and Political Unity: Aristotle's Criticism of Plato." In *Essays on Aristotle's Ethics*, ed. Amélie Oksenberg Rorty, 395–435. Berkeley and Los Angeles: University of California Press, 1980.

———. "Flawed Crystals: Henry James's *The Golden Bowl* and Literature as Moral Philosophy." *New Literary History* 15 (1983): 25–50.

———. *The Fragility of Goodness: Luck and Ethics in Greek Tragedy and Philosophy*. Cambridge: Cambridge University Press, 1986.

———. " 'Finely Aware and Richly Responsible': Literature and the Moral Imagination." In *Literature and the Question of Philosophy*, ed. Anthony J. Cascardi, 169–191. Baltimore: Johns Hopkins University Press, 1987.

Nye, Andrea. "Woman Clothed with the Sun." *Signs* 12 (1987): 664–686.

Okin, Susan Moller. *Women in Western Political Thought*. Princeton: Princeton University Press, 1979.

O'Laughlin, Mary Ann. "Responsibility and Moral Maturity in the Control of Fertility—or, A Woman's Place Is in the Wrong." *Social Research* 50 (1983): 556–575.

Olson, Mancur. *The Logic of Collective Action*. Cambridge, Mass.: Harvard University Press, 1965.

Ostwald, Martin, trans. *Aristotle: Nicomachean Ethics*. Indianapolis: Bobbs-Merrill, 1962.

———. *Nomos and the Beginnings of the Athenian Democracy*. Oxford: Clarendon Press, 1969.

Owen, G.E.L. "Tithenai Ta Phainomena." In *Aristotle: A Collection of Critical Essays*, ed. J.M.E. Moravcsik, 167–190. Notre Dame: Notre Dame University Press, 1968.

Pangle, Thomas. "Socrates on the Problem of Political Science Education." *Political Theory* 13 (1985): 112–137.

Pitkin, Hanna Fenichel. "Justice: On Relating Private and Public." *Political Theory* 9 (1982): 327–352.

Pocock, J.G.A. *The Machiavellian Moment: Florentine Political Thought and the Atlantic Republican Tradition*. Princeton: Princeton University Press, 1975.

———. *Virtue, Commerce, and History*. Cambridge: Cambridge University Press, 1985.

Pomeroy, Sarah B. *Goddesses, Whores, Wives, and Slaves: Women in Classical Antiquity*. New York: Schocken Books, 1975.

Pope, Alexander. "Epistle to Burlington." In *Alexander Pope, Epistles to Several Persons (Moral Essays)*, ed. F. W. Bateson, 134–156. London: Methuen & Company, 1951.

Prufer, Thomas. "A Reading of Hume's *A Treatise of Human Nature*." *Review of Metaphysics* 30 (1976): 115–119.

Putnam, Hilary. *Reason, Truth, and History*. Cambridge: Cambridge University Press, 1981.

———. "Taking Rules Seriously—A Response to Martha Nussbaum." *New Literary History* 15 (1983): 193–200.

Rackham, H. M. *Aristotle: Politics*. Cambridge, Mass.: Harvard University Press, 1959.

Rawls, John. *A Theory of Justice*. Cambridge, Mass.: Harvard University Press, Belknap Press, 1971.

———. "Justice as Fairness: Political Not Metaphysical." *Philosophy and Public Affairs* 14 (1985): 223–251.

Rorty, Richard. *Philosophy and the Mirror of Nature*. Princeton: Princeton University Press, 1979.

———. "Pragmatism, Relativism, Irrationalism." In *Consequences of Pragmatism: Essays (1972–1980)*, 160–175. Minneapolis: University of Minnesota Press, 1982.

———. "Postmodernist Bourgeois Liberalism." *Journal of Philosophy* 80 (1983): 583–589.

———. "On Ethnocentrism: A Reply to Clifford Geertz." *Michigan Quarterly Review* 25 (1986): 525–534.

Rousseau, Jean-Jacques. *Discourse on the Origin of Inequality*. Trans. Judith R. Masters and Roger D. Masters. New York: St. Martin's Press, 1964.

———. *Oeuvres Complètes*. 4 vols., ed. Bernard Gagnebin and Marcel Raymond. Paris: Gallimard, 1969.

Ruddick, Sara. "Maternal Thinking." *Feminist Studies* 6 (1980): 342–367.

Runciman, W. G. *The Methodology of Social Theory*. Cambridge: Cambridge University Press, 1983.

Ruse, Michael. *The Philosophy of Biology*. London: Hutchinson & Company, 1973.

Sadurski, Wojciech. "To Each According to His (Genuine?) Needs." *Political Theory* 11 (1983): 419–431.

Salkever, Stephen G. "Virtue, Obligation, and Politics." *American Political Science Review* 68 (1974): 78–92.

———. "Freedom, Participation, and Happiness." *Political Theory* 5 (1977): 78–92.

———. "Rousseau and the Concept of Happiness." *Polity* 11 (1978): 27–45.

———. " 'Cool Reflexion' and the Criticism of Values: Is, Ought, and Objectivity in Hume's Social Science." *American Political Science Review* 74 (1980): 70–77.

———. "Who Knows Whether It's Rational to Vote?" *Ethics* 90 (1980): 203–217.

———. "Beyond Interpretation: Human Agency and the Slovenly Wilderness." In *Social Science as Moral Inquiry*, ed. Norma Haan, Robert N. Bellah, Paul Rabinow, and William M. Sullivan, 195–217. New York: Columbia University Press, 1983.

Saxonhouse, Arlene W. "The Philosopher and the Female in the Political Thought of Plato." *Political Theory* 4 (1976): 195–212.

———. "Men, Women, War, and Politics: Family and Polis in Aristophanes and Euripides." *Political Theory* 8 (1980): 65–81.

———. "Family, Polity, and Unity: Aristotle on Socrates' Community of Wives." *Polity* 15 (1982): 202–219.

———. *Women in the History of Political Thought*. New York: Praeger, 1985.

Schneir, Miriam, ed. *Feminism: The Essential Historical Writings*. New York: Random House, 1972.

Schwartz, Benjamin I. *In Search of Wealth and Power: Yen Fu and the West*. Cambridge, Mass.: Harvard University Press, Belknap Press, 1964.

———. *The World of Thought in Ancient China*. Cambridge, Mass.: Harvard University Press, Belknap Press, 1985.

Sennett, Richard. *Authority*. New York: Random House, 1980.

Shapiro, Ian. *The Evolution of Rights in Liberal Theory*. Cambridge: Cambridge University Press, 1986.

Shaw, Michael. "The Female Intruder: Women in Fifth-Century Drama." *Classical Philology* 70 (1975): 255–266.

Sherman, Nancy. "Character, Planning, and Choice in Aristotle." *Review of Metaphysics* 39 (1985): 83–106.

———. "Aristotle on Friendship and the Shared Life." *Philosophy and Phenomenological Research* 47 (1987): 589–613.

Sinclair, T. A., trans. *Aristotle: The Politics*. Rev. and re-presented by Trevor J. Saunders. New York: Penguin Books, 1981.

Smith, Bruce James. *Politics and Remembrance*. Princeton: Princeton University Press, 1985.

Smith, Rogers. *Liberalism and American Constitutional Law*. Cambridge, Mass.: Harvard University Press, 1985.

Smith, Steven B. "Goodness, Nobility, and Virtue in Aristotle's Political Science." *Polity* 19 (1986): 5–26.

Solberg, Winton U., ed. *The Federal Convention and the Formation of the Union*. Indianapolis: Bobbs-Merrill, 1958.

Sorabji, Richard. *Necessity, Cause, and Blame: Perspectives on Aristotle's Theory*. Ithaca: Cornell University Press, 1980.

Spinoza, Benedict de. *Ethics*. Trans. R.H.M. Elwes. New York: Dover Publications, 1955.

Spragens, Thomas A., Jr. *The Irony of Liberal Reason*. Chicago: University of Chicago Press, 1981.

———. "Reconstructing Liberal Theory: Reason and Liberal Culture." In *Liberals on Liberalism*, ed. Alfonso J. Damico, 34–53. Totowa, N.J.: Rowman & Littlefield, 1986.

Stanton, Elizabeth Cady. "Solitude of Self." In *Feminism: The Essential Historical Writings*, ed. Miriam Schneir, 157–159. New York: Random House, 1972.

Storing, Herbert J. *What the Anti-Federalists Were For*. Chicago: University of Chicago Press, 1981.

Stout, Jeffrey. *The Flight from Authority*. Notre Dame: Notre Dame University Press, 1981.

Strauss, Leo. *Natural Right and History*. Chicago: University of Chicago Press, 1953.

———. "What Is Political Philosophy?" In *What Is Political Philosophy? and Other Studies*, 9–55. Glencoe: Free Press, 1959.

———. "Philosophy as Rigorous Science and Political Philosophy." In *Studies in Platonic Political Philosophy*, 29–37.

———. *Studies in Platonic Political Philosophy*. Chicago: University of Chicago Press, 1983.

Sullivan, William M. *Reconstructing Public Philosophy*. Berkeley and Los Angeles: University of California Press, 1982.

Tarcov, Nathan. "Philosophy and History: Tradition and Interpretation in the Work of Leo Strauss." *Polity* 16 (1983): 5–29.

———. *Locke's Education for Liberty*. Chicago: University of Chicago Press, 1984.

Taylor, Charles. "Language and Human Nature." In *Philosophical Papers*, 2 vols. Vol. 1, 215–247. Cambridge: Cambridge University Press, 1985.

Tocqueville, Alexis de. *De la démocratie en Amérique*. In *Oeuvres Complètes*, vol. 2, ed. J. P. Mayer. Paris: Gallimard, 1951.

Tronto, Joan C. "Beyond Gender Difference to a Theory of Care." *Signs* 12 (1987): 644–663.

Urmson, J. O. "Aristotle's Doctrine of the Mean." In *Essays on Aristotle's Ethics*, ed. Amélie Oksenberg Rorty, 157–170. Berkeley and Los Angeles: University of California Press, 1980.

Vernant, Jean-Pierre. *The Origins of Greek Thought*. Ithaca: Cornell University Press, 1982.

Vlastos, Gregory. "Reasons and Causes in the *Phaedo*." In *Plato: A Collection of Critical Essays*. Vol. 1: *Metaphysics and Epistemology*, ed. G. Vlastos, 132–166. Garden City, N.Y.: Doubleday & Company, 1971.

Waley, Arthur. *Three Ways of Thought in Ancient China*. Stanford: Stanford University Press, 1982.

Walzer, Michael. "Philosophy and Democracy." *Political Theory* 9 (1981): 379–399.

Waterlow, Sarah. *Nature, Change, and Agency in Aristotle's Physics*. Oxford: Clarendon Press, 1982.

Weber, Max. *The Protestant Ethic and the Spirit of Capitalism*. Trans. Talcott Parsons. New York: Charles Scribner's Sons, 1958.

———. "Science as a Vocation." In *From Max Weber: Essays in Sociology*, trans. H. H. Gerth and C. Wright Mills, 129–156. New York: Oxford University Press, 1958.

Werpehowski, William. "Political Liberalism and Christian Ethics: A Review Discussion." *The Thomist* 48 (1984): 81–115.

White, James Boyd. *When Words Lose Their Meaning*. Chicago: University of Chicago Press, 1984.

Wieland, Wolfgang. "Plato and the Idea of the Good: On the Function of the Idea of the Good." Trans. David Mallon. *Contemporary German Philosophy* 4 (1985): 104–125.

Wilkes, K. V. *Physicalism*. Atlantic Highlands, N.J.: Humanities Press, 1978.

Williams, Bernard. "Justice as a Virtue." In *Essays on Aristotle's*

Ethics, ed. Amélie Oksenberg Rorty, 189–199. Berkeley and Los Angeles: University of California Press, 1980.

———. "Persons, Character, and Morality." In *Moral Luck: Philosophical Papers 1973–1980*, 1–19. Cambridge: Cambridge University Press, 1981.

———. *Ethics and the Limits of Philosophy*. Cambridge, Mass.: Harvard University Press, 1985.

Winthrop, Delba. "Tocqueville's American Women and the True Conception of Democratic Progress." *Political Theory* 14 (1986): 239–261.

Wollheim, Richard. *The Thread of Life*. Cambridge, Mass.: Harvard University Press, 1984.

Wood, Gordon S. *The Creation of the American Republic, 1776–1787*. Chapel Hill: University of North Carolina Press, 1969.

Zeitlin, Froma I. "The Dynamics of Misogyny: Myth and Mythmaking in the *Oresteia*." *Arethusa* 11 (1978): 149–181.

———. "Thebes: Theater of Self and Society in Athenian Drama." In *Nothing to Do with Dionysos*, ed. John J. Winkler and Froma I. Zeitlin. Princeton: Princeton University Press, 1989.

Zuckert, Catherine H. "Aristotle on the Limits and Satisfactions of Political Life." *Interpretation* 11 (1983): 185–206.

———. "On the Theory of Political Economy: Is Liberalism Really Dead?" In *Political Economy in Western Democracies*, ed. Norman J. Vig and Steven E. Schier, 19–45. New York: Holmes & Meier, 1985.

INDEX

Jaeger, Werner, 92n, 173
Jaffa, Harry, 109n, 136n, 153n, 255n
Jefferson, Thomas, 225, 227–228, 233–
  234, 235n, 251n, 254, 255n
Jonas, Hans, 62n

Kahn, Charles, 15n, 54n
kakon (bad), 220n
Kateb, George, 137n, 174n, 210, 261
Kant, Immanuel, 4, 48n, 61n, 67n, 73n,
  106, 108, 110, 113–114, 120, 124,
  126n, 127n, 128, 153, 159–160, 167,
  237
Keller, Evelyn Fox, 201n
Kennington, Richard, 34n, 50n
Klein, Jacob, 151n
Kohlberg, Lawrence, 123–129, 137, 159
Kosman, Aryeh, 44n, 46, 74n
Kuhn, Thomas, 22, 55n, 61

law. See *nomos*
Lennox, James, 51n, 183n
Lerner, Ralph, 218, 233n, 234n
liberalism, 5, 7, 156–157, 205, 207, 247;
  liberal democracy, 8, 208–219; liberal
  education, 3–5, 103, 255–258; liberal
  individualism, 73, 113–114, 169, 186,
  245–247
Lincoln, Abraham, 123, 247–248, 255n
Lindblom, Charles, 261n
Lloyd, G.E.R., 71n, 92n, 169n, 181n,
  182
logos (speech, rationality), 15, 96, 105–
  106; attribute that defines humanity,
  69; relationship to political life, 74–79
Locke, John, 24, 72, 166, 205, 210–211,
  213–215, 235, 237, 252–253, 264
Lord, Carnes, 5n, 69n, 79n, 80n, 188n,
  194n, 198n, 202n, 221n, 226n

McDowell, John, 109n, 111, 138, 142n
MacIntyre, Alasdair, 6, 25, 31–33, 37–
  39, 73n, 107–109, 111, 115n, 117,
  118n, 137n, 156n, 169, 210n, 234
Machiavelli, Niccolò, 109–110, 174, 198,
  200, 202, 225, 245, 247–248
Madison, James, 88, 234n, 264
Mansfield, Harvey, 216
Mara, Gerald, 25n, 148n, 200n
Marx, Karl, 5, 114, 116n, 153n, 155,
  157, 166, 173–174, 194n, 205n, 207,
  209, 248, 260, 264
Masters, Roger, 37n, 51n
Mayr, Ernst, 20n, 22n, 23, 47n, 51n,
  66n, 182n
mean, the: as characterization of practi-

cal wisdom, 116–117, 139–140, 241;
  as metaphor for the human good,
  78–79
medicine: analogous to politics, 92, 94,
  98–99; disanalogies, 86–87
Mencius, 218
metaphor, 98–99, 103, 117, 152, 223,
  263
Midgley, Mary, 24, 28, 41, 52n, 185n
Mill, J. S., 4, 107, 110, 112, 114, 128,
  151, 217, 237, 247, 264
misology, 36
moral education: and the American
  founding, 230–235; in a democracy,
  219–226, 260; family as site of, 194–
  195; human need for, 81–82, 103; indirect, 248–251; philosophy and,
  202–203; as preference formation,
  245n; relationship to other needs,
  86–91; and republican virtue, 237–238
Murdoch, Iris, 9, 107, 109, 111, 117n,
  118n, 120–121, 123n, 129n, 166, 235n
music, 79n, 89, 187

natural law: Aristotelian agent morality
  and, 90–91, 109, 136–142, 239n; eternal, 160; modern moral philosophy
  and, 153, 213; Thomistic, 174, 206n
nature: Aristotelian versus early modern conceptions, 80; Aristotle's use
  of, 4–5; early modern view of, 21;
  Heraclitean conception, 15; and social science, 115
Newman, W. L., 79n, 222n, 227n
Nichols, Mary, 144n, 183n, 186n
Nietzsche, Friedrich, 6, 24–25, 27–28,
  32, 34n, 55, 62n, 108n, 109–110,
  118n, 155, 166–168, 200, 202, 209,
  220n, 248, 260, 264
Nisbet, Robert, 261n
nomos, 16, 59, 75–77, 87–91, 121, 136,
  144–145, 155, 224–225
Nussbaum, Martha, 15n, 42n, 44n,
  47n, 49n, 66n, 72n, 73n, 76n, 129n,
  130n, 136n, 142n, 144n, 151n, 153n,
  160n, 166n, 169n, 171n, 179n, 194n
Nye, Andrea, 167n

Okin, Susan Moller, 169n, 179
O'Laughlin, Mary Ann, 126n
Ostwald, Martin, 5n, 110n, 155n
Owen, G.E.L., 14n

Pangle, Thomas, 177n
Parmenides, 17n, 18n, 19n, 23n, 28, 42